THE BEIJING CONSENSUS?

Is there a distinctive Chinese Model for law and economic development? In *The Beijing Consensus?*, scholars turn their collective attention to answering this basic but seemingly underexplored question as China rises higher in its global standing. Advancing debates on alternative development programs, with a particular focus on social and political contexts, this book demonstrates that, essentially, no model exists. Engaging in comparative studies, the contributors create a new set of benchmarks to evaluate the conventional wisdom that the Beijing Consensus challenges and that of the Beijing Consensus itself. Has China demonstrated that the best model is in fact no model at all? Overall, this title equips the reader with an understanding of the conclusions derived from China's experience in its legal and economic development in recent decades.

WEITSENG CHEN is an Assistant Professor at the National University of Singapore Faculty of Law, where he is also Deputy Director of the Center for Asian Legal Studies. He received his JSD from Yale Law School and was a Fulbright scholar and Hewlett Fellow of the Center on Democracy, Development, and the Rule of Law (CDDRL) at Stanford University.

Donald Clarke, The George Washington University Law School
"The relationship between law and development is a question that just will not go away. This volume assembles a top-notch group of scholars to examine what China's experience can tell us. While much of the previous work on this field has been done by economists, the contributors here are intimately familiar with the details of China's legal system and offer new and stimulating insights in this terrific collection of essays."

Tom Ginsburg, The University of Chicago Law School
"In this volume, a set of first-rate scholars turns their collective attention to dissecting a slogan and helps us to understand what we can – and cannot – conclude from China's experience of tremendous economic growth in recent decades. By presenting the real lessons of the Chinese developmental model, the book marks an important step forward for the law and development field."

John Haley, Washington University School of Law
"This collection of essays on law and development in China is an especially timely contribution. China has recently emerged as the world's largest national economy in terms of its gross national product, although as the world's most populous nation, China ranks behind all of Europe, most of Latin America, and much of East Asia in terms of per capita income. The contributors include ten leading specialists of Chinese and comparative law from universities in Canada, China, Singapore, and the United States as well as two scholars from Brazil who add an especially cogent comparative perspective. They collectively question the applicability of the 'Washington Consensus' on the critical legal reforms necessary for sustained economic growth but differ in their varied perspectives on a 'Chinese Model' or a 'Beijing Consensus.' Provocative and insightful, *The Beijing Consensus? How China Has Changed Western Ideas of Law and Economic Development* is a must-read for those concerned with law reform and economic development."

John Ohnesorge, The University of Wisconsin Law School
"The 'Beijing Consensus' has been a co-production of Left critics of the market-oriented Washington Consensus, Beijing's insecure authoritarian leadership, and pundits eager for a sound bite to capture China's complex political economy. The contributions to this volume do an excellent job of breaking down the 'Beijing Consensus' into concrete policy realms and helping us decide if there really is any 'there' there."

Susan Rose-Ackerman, Yale Law School
"This excellent collection of essays shows that no clear 'Beijing Consensus' exists. Instead, the Chinese experience provides something even more interesting; its challenge to the 'Washington Consensus' invites reformers everywhere to engage in dialogue about the strengths and weaknesses of Chinese policies both for the future economic and political development of China itself and for reformers in other emerging economies."

Michael Trebilcock, Faculty of Law, The University of Toronto
"In public policy discussions of alternative development strategies, it has become common to contrast the Beijing Consensus with the Washington Consensus, often without stipulating with much precision what exactly the key elements in the purported Beijing Consensus are. In this book, a distinguished international group of law and development scholars decomposes the idea of a Beijing Consensus by examining in detail the evolution of a number of areas of law in China, including tax law, property law, corporate law, securities law, and anticorruption law, with a view to addressing three key questions: how distinctive is the development trajectory of China's legal system in these areas as compared to other legal systems? What accounts for China's deviation from conventional models in these areas? If there is a distinctive general Chinese Model of development, or law and development, is this model replicable in other developing countries? In many important respects, the contributions to this book importantly advance debates about alternative development paradigms beyond unhelpful clichés or overgeneralizations through much more pragmatic evaluations of the relationship between law and development in particular social and political contexts."

THE BEIJING CONSENSUS?

How China Has Changed Western Ideas of Law and Economic Development

Edited by

WEITSENG CHEN

CAMBRIDGE
UNIVERSITY PRESS

CAMBRIDGE
UNIVERSITY PRESS

University Printing House, Cambridge CB2 8BS, United Kingdom

One Liberty Plaza, 20th Floor, New York, NY 10006, USA

477 Williamstown Road, Port Melbourne, VIC 3207, Australia

314-321, 3rd Floor, Plot 3, Splendor Forum, Jasola District Centre, New Delhi - 110025, India

79 Anson Road, #06-04/06, Singapore 079906

Cambridge University Press is part of the University of Cambridge.

It furthers the University's mission by disseminating knowledge in the pursuit of education, learning and research at the highest international levels of excellence.

www.cambridge.org
Information on this title: www.cambridge.org/9781316503034
10.1017/9781316481370

First published 2017
First paperback edition 2018

A catalogue record for this publication is available from the British Library

ISBN 978-1-107-13843-8 Hardback
ISBN 978-1-316-50303-4 Paperback

CONTENTS

FIGURES

CONTRIBUTORS

WEITSENG CHEN is Assistant Professor and Deputy Director of the Center for Asian Legal Studies at the National University of Singapore Faculty of Law.

WEI CUI is Associate Professor of Law at the University of British Columbia.

MICHAEL W. DOWDLE is Associate Professor of Law at the National University of Singapore Faculty of Law.

HUALING FU is Professor of Law and Associate Dean of the Faculty of Law, the University of Hong Kong.

JEDIDIAH KRONCKE is Professor of Law at Fundação Getulio Vargas São Paulo School of Law, Brazil.

JI LI is Associate Professor of Law at Rutgers University.

BENJAMIN L. LIEBMAN is the Robert L. Lieff Professor of Law and Director of the Center for Chinese Legal Studies at Columbia University.

CURTIS J. MILHAUPT is the Parker Professor of Comparative Corporate Law and Fuyo Professor of Japanese Law at Columbia University.

MARIANA MOTA PRADO is Associate Professor and Associate Dean (Graduate Program) at the Faculty of Law, the University of Toronto.

TAN CHENG-HAN is Professor of Law and Chairman of the Centre for Law and Business at the National University of Singapore Faculty of Law.

YINGMAO TANG is Associate Professor of Law at Peking University.

FRANK K. UPHAM is the Wilf Family Professor of Property Law at the New York University School of Law.

ACKNOWLEDGMENTS

This book represents the product of a concerted effort to examine China's law and economic development in a comparative law context. Most contributors are not the typical "China law scholars" but experts from different areas of law. Each was asked to scrutinize the extremely broad topic (the Beijing Consensus) from narrowly defined fields of law in which he or she specializes. I appreciate their willingness to take the challenge to complete this pioneering project. This project also demonstrates the value of comparative law research in China's legal development. We need to continue to create new sets of benchmarks by comparing China with other developing and developed countries sharing similar developmental trajectories. The contributors to this book have drawn rich implications from such comparisons (with Hong Kong, Japan, South Korea, Taiwan, Singapore, and Brazil).

I thank Tomoo Marukawa (Tokyo University) and Jinhua Cheng (East China University of Political Science and Law), guest commenters at our conference in 2015. The project would not have been possible without the financial support of National University of Singapore (R-241-000-122-112) and the NUS Center for Asian Legal Studies or without excellent assistance from the NUS community: Leong Lijie, Ng Jia Min, Jisheng Liu, Damian Wong, Kenneth Chan, Nadene Law, Ramandeep Kaur, Shafkat Fahmid, and Clarence Tan. Last, but not least, I would like to dedicate this book to my grandmother Hsieh Bao-Jun (1923–2016), who was a true witness to contemporary Chinese history.

Weitseng Chen, Singapore

Introduction

Debating the Consensuses

WEITSENG CHEN

China's rapid growth gave birth to the notion of "Beijing Consensus" to conceptualize China's seemingly unorthodox approach to development. The Beijing Consensus has generated much discussion in academia and public forums for some time and was advanced by many as a worthy rival to the neoliberal "Washington Consensus." Despite the overwhelming interest in this notion, scant legal literature exists on how the Beijing Consensus affects the relationship between law and economic development – and even less literature provides a comprehensive review of its constituent components. Yet, it is the right time for legal scholars to investigate the debate about the two Consensuses and, more importantly, for China to reflect on the understanding of her own success. Summer 2015 witnessed the largest stock market collapse since China began reforming its economy in 1979. The market lost one-third of its value in just two weeks and triggered global panic. I recalled that a colleague once confident of China's economic prospects, then deeply frustrated, said, "The Chinese model is gone!" The contributors of this book go further, in fact a lot further, by contemplating whether the Chinese Model was ever born in the first place.

The vacuum of literature was the impetus for this book, a project that aims not only to provide a theoretical account of the Beijing Consensus but, more importantly, also to discuss the Beijing Consensus in respect of specific areas of law. This book does not focus on public law such as human rights, democracy, and constitutionalism – subject matter which has already received much treatment by modern China law studies scholars. Instead, this book focuses on areas of law that have received less attention, but yet, by general consensus, are vital for economic development. Areas such as tax, property, and corporate law are key areas of concern for orthodox law and development theory, including the Washington Consensus. As such, we think these areas deserve their due treatment as the fundamental concern of any law and development scholar interested in the Beijing Consensus is to know what are the institutional configurations of the various subsectors of China's legal system that have contributed to one of the greatest economic transitions in human history. Briefly, we ask, what exactly does the Beijing Consensus (if it truly exists) look like in the context of property, tax, corporate law, and other specific areas of law?

The book is organized in three parts. Part I contains three chapters and provides various accounts of the "Chinese Model" from a comparative perspective. To begin, **Michael W. Dowdle** and **Mariana Mota Prado** examine three models of development that claim to be derived from China's experience: Joshua Ramo's "Beijing Consensus," Randall Peerenboom's "East Asian Model," and Dani Rodrik's "New Development Economics." They conduct an intense debate about each of these models and focus on what China's development might have to tell us about the processes and strategies of law and development more generally. **Jedidiah Kroncke** further deconstructs the Beijing Consensus from a Brazilian perspective, another developing country with unique experiences of its own. The increasing Sino-Brazilian discourse provides an excellent context for investigating how China's developmental experience is interpreted outside of China, and Brazil serves as a direct example of whether other developing countries are benefiting from the supposed Chinese Model, specifically in the context of labor law. **Tan Cheng-Han** concludes Part I and deconstructs the Beijing Consensus in reverse from the perspective of a developed country that also saw rapid economic growth through state capitalism – Singapore. Tan notes that while China has been looking anew for developmental inspiration from Singapore, China does not seem to have understood the overarching structure of Singapore's state capitalism very well. Nevertheless, Singapore may still offer China several crucial lessons.

Part II furthers this discussion by examining the Beijing Consensus in the context of specific areas of law. These areas were specially chosen because they are the building blocks of the rival Washington Consensus. Part II begins with **Wei Cui**'s discussion of the rule of law in the context of China's once applauded decentralized model, or "Federalism, Chinese-style." Cui's discussion focuses on how this model has impacted the quality of legislation, law enforcement, and the overall governance through legal institutions in China. **Frank K. Upham** examines Chinese property law and reflects on the applicability of conventional property theories, which are based on private ownership and the role of property institutions, in the Chinese context. **Weitseng Chen** then scrutinizes China's strategic policy to internationalize renminbi (RMB) and examines whether this potential game changer in the global financial world as well as China's domestic banking system exemplifies any component of the Beijing Consensus. **Ji Li** examines whether a coherent model can be drawn from China's tax reforms, which commentators generally view as a success. **Yingmao Tang** then turns to securities regulation. He examines the developmental trajectory of China's capital markets and demonstrates how various obstacles and the solution to these obstacles, rather than a specific regulatory ideology, have shaped the regulatory model and market practices to date.

While Part II delivers a generally skeptical view about the existence of the Beijing Consensus, Part III explores whether any alternative theory or approach is capable of capturing China's experiences and focuses particularly on China's pragmatic approach toward capacity building. **Benjamin L. Liebman** examines the capacity building of China's judiciary and concludes, "China's own experience suggests that the best model for legal reform may be no model at all." **Hualing Fu** looks at the recent historical development of China's anticorruption campaigns, in particular examining the bifurcation of the anticorruption enforcement system, which consists on one hand of party disciplinary measures and on the other of legal mechanisms. The choice between the two reflects how law enforcement can be molded by capacity considerations. Finally, **Curtis J. Milhaupt** proposes that "corporate capitalism" (as adapted by the party-state) can be used as a framework to conceptualize China's state-directed economy – the major source of financing for China's capacity-building projects.

When examining the Beijing Consensus as a general model, ensuring that discussions are not excessively contextualized is a major challenge, as it may fragment the theoretical dialogue this book aims to initiate. To address this concern, all contributors have agreed to a common analytical framework, although some leeway may be required to best fit how each contributor addresses his or her topic: (1) Given that the Beijing Consensus was derived from China, how distinctive is the developmental trajectory of China's legal system as compared to other legal systems? (2) What accounts for China's deviation from conventional models and is such deviation explainable by existing literature? (3) How are we to better conceptualize China's experiences? Through the lens of the Beijing

Consensus, or is there any other alternative? Can China's experiences be theorized as a specific Chinese Model, and if such a model exists, is this model replicable in other developing countries?

Here, I attempt to provide readers a general response to the three questions by selecting and combining parts of each contributor's work, albeit risking an oversimplification or an incomplete representation of their work.

I Given That the Beijing Consensus Was Derived from China, How Distinctive Is the Developmental Trajectory of China's Legal System as Compared to Other Legal Systems?

Michael Dowdle and Mariana Prado start by pointing out that the factors behind China's economic success are not unprecedented. They argue that the Beijing Consensus, initially coined by Joshua Ramo, would probably be more accurately described as the "Taipei Consensus," and the term "Beijing Consensus" was able to generate global interest because it was marketed as the anti–Washington Consensus. Nonetheless, China's gradual and experimental approach toward her growth provides good lessons for the developing world. In this sense, the Beijing Consensus probably serves as a model in a procedural rather than a substantive sense. That said, whether one can construct a developmental model based merely on gradualism and experimentalism remains debatable in that both theories concern the means rather than the ends (i.e., a set of substantive policy guidelines). As Dowdle argues, experimentalism should not obscure normative issues, which are currently the most pressing for developing countries.

Resonating with Dowdle and Prado, Jedidiah Kroncke proposes the idea that the Beijing Consensus is an "anti-model" through the developmental experiences of Brazil, one of the strongest and most recent rhetorical repudiators of the Washington Consensus. Brazil demonstrates a general rejection of the very notion of the coordinated global advocacy of a universal set of policy prescriptions. Still, the Brazilian experience does little to solidify the workability of the Beijing Consensus because both left- and right-wing politicians use such anti-model narratives to their own favor, and this adds little value to substantive policy contemplation. Furthermore, labor law, as a core aspect of any model of political economy, is routinely neglected when emulation of China is advanced. Nonetheless, while the examination of the Beijing Consensus on prescriptive terms may fail owing to its anti-model nature, it has the potential to enrich development debates when it provokes thought beyond ideological contrasts and steers debates into concrete studies of individual policies similar to the efforts demonstrated in this book. In fact, this parallels the advances made in understanding Western economic history that have emerged out of critiques of the Washington Consensus. After all, the Beijing Consensus as "an anti-model can liberate nations from old global dogmas but then leave them to become mired anew in their own insular partisan ideologies. It could inhibit experimentation as much as it may liberate domestic policies debates from errant external influence."

Moving the examination of the Beijing Consensus into specific areas of law, a generally skeptical view about the distinctiveness of a Chinese Model was expressed by contributors as well. With respect to property rights, for instance, Frank Upham suggests that the developmental trajectory of the property rights regime in China is in line with many other developing countries. When the property regimes in such countries, as in China, were initiated, informal institutions and political commitment mattered more for economic growth than formal, well-defined property rights. Also, it seems highly unlikely that China would have grown faster if property rights were enforced. Nonetheless, China's experiences do point out some loopholes of orthodox property theory, which emphasizes the importance of fully defined property rights and independent courts. In other words, economic development is not conditioned upon well-defined property rights and the courts' willingness to enforce these rights;[1] to the contrary, such enforcement may harm economic take-off. Therefore, Chinese growth undermines, as Upham suggests, the conventional wisdom that dictates attention to creating or reforming legal systems of developing nations according to the templates derived from Western models.

China's experiences may not be unique, but unlike its much smaller predecessors, China is too big to be ignored. This brings us to another oft-mentioned feature of China's model – size, which has not been carefully examined by existing literature. Does a country's size matter to law and development and, if so, to what extent, and how? Weitseng Chen examines how this distinctive characteristic – an extraordinarily large-scale market – plays out for China in its quest to internationalize the RMB

[1] Upham also points out that Harold Demsetz and Douglass North defined "institutions" to include both formal and informal rules and organizations. Unfortunately, this broad definition of "institution" has not survived the transition from theory to practice. It is in this narrower sense of "institution" that China's experience presents a challenge.

and whether it unveils any meaningful dimension of the Beijing Consensus. Interestingly, Chen's scrutiny demonstrates that the substance of the RMB internationalization scheme is almost identical to the orthodox policies prescribed by the Washington Consensus. In terms of implementation, while China's large size does provide immense advantages, it also poses similarly great challenges to the internationalization scheme, as any overhaul of China's fragmented and heterogeneous banking and financial systems must be on a wide scale. Such an overhaul, however, would be hindered by coordination difficulties, high monitoring costs, and interlocked systemic risk. Nevertheless, the size of a country does not support any form of Beijing Consensus because it affects the ability to implement statewide currency policies in other countries too, as demonstrated by Chen's case studies of Taiwan and Singapore. In other words, the size of a developing country is not integral to any averred Chinese Model; size has been shown to force China as well as other countries down a path of dependence.

II What Accounts for China's Deviation from Conventional Models, and Is Such Deviation Explainable by Existing Literature?

Chen's claim that China has led itself down a path of dependence leads us to the second question: can China's deviance from Western development theories be explained by existing literature? Wei Cui answers this question squarely, attributing China's deviance to its decentralized governance regime, which, in turn, affected China's legal system. China practices legislative centralization and administrative decentralization, where legislation is promulgated by central bodies but its implementation is left to local bodies. This awkward mix, however, has negatively affected the quality of promulgated legislation. The central bodies lack information feedback from local bodies and, therefore, pass legislation without a full understanding of how a specific law will be practiced. At the same time, local bodies, which are cut off from the legislative process, implement and enforce these laws with their own purposive interpretations. This mismatch explains to a large extent the irregularities observed within China's legal system. Thus, the larger the hierarchical gap between the legislative process and the enforcement of legislation, the worse the consequences will be upon the legal system of that country.[2]

[2] Yet, according to Cui, reforms to reduce the gap have principally been neglected or faced opposition in China.

With respect to securities regulation in China, which in many ways contradicts the principles advocated by Western regulatory models, Yingmao Tang suggests that the China Securities Regulatory Commission's (CSRC) dual role of administrator and regulator, and its non-market-oriented, paternalist mind-set, gave rise to the current configurations seen within China's securities markets and capital market practices. Unlike its US counterpart, the SEC, the CSRC does not play the role of a mere regulator; it also bears extra obligations to carry out economic policies as an administrative body, guides Chinese firms as an incubator, and stabilizes the capital markets and financial system as if it were a central bank. As such, the policies prescribed by the Washington Consensus are unlikely to fit China's reality anytime soon, albeit some current measures adopted and proposed reforms that are in line with those advocated by Western models, such as a disclosure-based regulatory regime.

In the area of tax administration, Ji Li provides a historical account of how Chinese officials implemented tax policies, demonstrating the central government's strategic attitude in the face of opposition and potential political backlash. Interestingly, however, what this incremental strategy represents is a set of tax policies very similar to the conventional paradigm proposed under the Washington Consensus. Li's analysis reveals the highly path-dependent process by which China developed a high level of technocratic competency within its tax bureaucracy, a partial side effect of intra-administrative competition that is often lacking in other countries.

Hualing Fu points to China's pragmatism by virtue of the ways in which China carries out its high-profile anticorruption campaigns. In the face of weak judicial mechanisms plagued by insufficient personnel and lack of independence from local politics, the central government has had to resort to party disciplinary mechanisms, which lack transparency and feature controversial extra-legal or extra-extra legal measures. However, this may be transitional. Despite episodic drawbacks, Fu notes that the overall trend of the development of China's legal system seems clear – "the sphere of law had been expanding, reaching out to and occupying more fields; and formal rules are occupying more commanding heights in governance in relation to extralegal rules and practices."

In short, while contributors posit that China's legal experiences do not fully support the Beijing Consensus's elevation as a rival developmental model to conventional paradigms, they demonstrate the importance of China's pragmatism in policy implementation. The trajectory of law and policy evolution in China is not esoterically peculiar but is readily explainable.

III How Are We to Better Conceptualize China's Experiences? By the Beijing Consensus, or Is There Any Other Alternative? Can China's Experiences Be Theorized as the Chinese Model, and If Such a Model Exists, Is This Model Replicable in Other Developing Countries?

How are we then to reconceptualize the Chinese experience without resorting to the notion of the Beijing Consensus? Curtis Milhaupt's examination of China's corporate capitalism shows that this is a matter of national capacity building. Like all other successful economies, he argues, the corporate form has proven to be extraordinarily useful in providing the Chinese party-state with a scalable, adaptable, and relatively anonymous vehicle for economic activity as well as with a template for structuring the state sector and for scaling it to globally important proportions. Similar to other species of corporate capitalism, the basic corporate attributes in China are affected by and adapted to local conditions. While Japanese corporate organizational structure overwhelmingly places the interests of employees over those of shareholders, Chinese managers extend the Leninist approach to state organizations.[3] In other words, corporate capitalism can be shareholder-centric, board-centric, employee-centric, state-centric, or, in the case of China, party-centric. On one hand, the CCP replaces conventional risk sharing and monitoring functions with party-state monitoring; on the other, the party system provides high-powered incentives to managers, for whom success in business often brings success in other realms of state management.

Is this Party-State Inc., as a strategy of capacity building, efficient in economic terms? Although the objective of his essay is not to debate the model's efficiency, welfare effects, or sustainability, Milhaupt nonetheless suggests that the distinctive features of China's approach are not beneficial to corporate performance; yet there are also good reasons to think Party-State Inc. is an enduring rather than transitional phenomenon. His observation resonates with a prevailing view shared by commentators of different disciplines – the process of China's capacity building is fast and powerful but also wasteful and takes place at the expense of the development of other social and economic sectors.

Benjamin Liebman and Hualing Fu also evaluate China's judicial developments from the lens of capacity building instead of any distinctive

[3] In this regard, Milhaupt suggests that China's large SOEs could be understood better as Party-linked companies than through the conventional lens of state-owned versus privately owned dichotomy.

model. Liebman suggests that Chinese courts are not converging toward the American model but rather have evolved in many ways that resemble courts in other authoritarian systems. Nevertheless, aspects of China's system appear unique, including the strong influence of populism on the Chinese legal system. The best indicator of courts' capacity and the roles courts play in China come through examination of everyday cases – not from examination of the ability of courts to restrain other party-state actors. Fu also suggests that the CCP has to rely on extra-legal party mechanisms for curbing rampant corruption as legal mechanisms still lack the capacity to forcefully deal with corruption, which has reached a level where the party's legitimacy has been seriously threatened. In the future, how these bifurcated systems converge serves as an indicator of the capacity of the Chinese judiciary.

Furthermore, several contributors emphasize the role of the state in national capacity building. Ji Li argues that, although the Washington Consensus almost mirrors Chinese tax policies, the implementation of Washington Consensus–like policies still is given a Chinese touch because their implementation is highly dependent on certain structural factors rather unique to China. In the context of tax reforms, the central government appeared to be able to mitigate disputes and trade short-term interests, favored by vested power-holders, for long-term redistribution of the country's revenue. Weitseng Chen also contends that China's internationalization of the RMB is a set of liberalization experiments designed and led by the state. Similarly, Frank Upham suggests that an ambiguous property regime allows the state to aggregate and reallocate property rights, which is necessary and vital for China's growth at the initial stage. Resonating with this view, Curtis Milhaupt contends that the weak institutional environments in developing economies often render autonomy from governmental authority – usually associated with private property ownership – illusory; instead, governments retain fairly extensive control over all firms, whether state or privately owned. All in all, China demonstrates a gradualist, state-led implementation process that was left out by, and probably contradicted, the Washington Consensus, which had suggested that market forces rather than the state play a leading role in the implementation of its prescribed policies.

Regardless of the skepticism about the Beijing Consensus, our discussions eventually lead to another interesting question: is China's model replicable in other developing countries? Some contributors address this question by asking whether it is worth replicating in the first place. Michael Dowdle casts doubts on this possibility by arguing that what China has done has mainly been to remove some of the more catastrophic policies implemented during its prereform years. As a result, what remains missing in China today is a highly sophisticated regulatory system to support a sustainable modern economy that requires efficient monitoring, crisis management, and wealth redistribution. Together with Dowdle, Jedidiah Kroncke questions the way in which China's "success" is measured, suggesting that the measurement of "success" should not be focused on GDP growth only but on more comprehensive benchmarks such as the Human Development Index. In the area of tax reform, Ji Li argues that China has not achieved comparatively exceptional levels of performance; empirical studies suggest that China's efforts in tax policy and implementation are merely passable.

Others respond to the question of replicability in a more direct way. Curtis Milhaupt suggests that China's model is neither completely distinctive nor deserving of the label of "model," despite the useful lessons it contains. Ji Li also points out that replicating China's model of tax reform requires at least a central government with relatively low discount rate and a tax agency of adequate bureaucratic capacity, neither of which may be available in many developing countries. As Benjamin Liebman further concludes, "the question is not whether China has created a model that may be relevant for other developing legal systems; the central question is whether the Chinese model can work in China."[4]

In fact, for informed observers, it should not be too difficult to sense the anxiety of the Chinese leaders as to how the Chinese Model can continue to work for China. As such, recent cohorts of Chinese leaders and policy makers have been looking to Singapore for inspiration. As Weitseng Chen points out, some of the recent changes that China made to its regulatory regime for the purposes of RMB internationalization were inspired by Singapore. Singapore has demonstrated that state-owned enterprises can be extremely efficient, that regular elections can be carried out, that governance can be world-class, and that the government receives high approval ratings, all despite being an authoritarian state for decades. Responding to China's search for an alternative developmental paradigm in the likes of Singapore, Tan Cheng-Han offers a historical

[4] Liebman suggests, however, that China's judicial developments have the greatest potential to contribute to current discourse on authoritarian judicial systems since literature has long noted such possibility of significant development of courts in authoritarian systems. Thus far, however, China and elsewhere have overlooked this perspective in favor of the ideas laid down by US-led jurisprudence.

account of the institutional settings and political economy underlying the Singapore Model.

According to Tan, what makes the Singapore Model workable and successful is something that remains missing in China – genuinely competitive elections and normative commitment to the rule of law and democracy, albeit an illiberal vision of democracy. In Tan's words, "there is nothing to stop the Singapore government from interfering [with Temasek and other state-owned enterprises] if it wishes to do so. However, there exists a strong convention build up over many years against such interference." Such convention, notably, comes from the electoral democracy that makes the ruling party determined to render its firms independent of political influence for the sake of corporate performance. In this regard, Tan's assertion is consistent with another point raised by some contributors, that is, that economy and politics are always intertwined, and therefore any developmental success cannot be reduced to mere economic policies.

Additionally, echoing Weitseng Chen, Tan posits that size matters and that Singapore's small city-state scale also accounts for the success of her highly centralized, state-led development model. Singapore's model therefore may not be fully replicable in China. Eventually, this comparison resonates with the fundamental debate on law and development scholarship between Mariana Prado and Michael Dowdle in the beginning of this book. That is, methodologically, whether one can construct a development model based on comparative empiricism and to what extent institutions matter or development is more about the alchemy of several vital but noninstitutional factors such as size, resources, and overall political economy. As Prado suggests, a model based on experimentalism in procedural terms probably makes more sense.[5]

There is no doubt that China is at the crossroads, as evidenced by the contrasts between rampant corruption and fierce anticorruption campaigns, worrying economic slowdown and aggressive acquisitions of assets around the world by Chinese firms, and the stock market turmoil at home and the ambitious internationalization of the RMB overseas. The objective of this book is not to forecast China's future; rather, it is about

[5] Prado and Dowdle disagree on this proposition of experimentalism as a model. The issue lies in whether one can separate the discussion of the ends from the means when contemplating a model for development. Dowdle argues that this separation is not feasible, whereas Prado posits the opposite and therefore suggests that a thin concept of experimentalism is desirable, with the ends being defined elsewhere through a process that does not need to be an experimental one.

understanding China's past and present from a comparative perspective. Through the dialogue between micro- and macroanalyses, law and other disciplines, and studies of Chinese law and the law of other countries, the contribution of this book depends on whether we can prevent what an old Chinese saying describes – "the blind man feels the elephant" – and assumes that a part is the whole. Regardless of whether the Beijing Consensus exists, we believe a better understanding of law and economic development can emerge out of a debate about the Consensus.

PART I

Deconstructing the Beijing Consensus

1

Dialogus de Beijing Consensus

MICHAEL W. DOWDLE AND MARIANA MOTA PRADO

I Prologue

Beijing Consensus was a term initially coined by Joshua Cooper Ramo in 2004, as a superior, and distinctly Asian, developmental model.[1] Ramo's claim of a "Beijing Consensus" triggered much academic interest and resistance in the West, as some questioned whether the developmental policies Ramo's model prescribed accurately described China's path to economic development. In 2007, Randall Peerenboom, in a book titled *China Modernizes: Threat to the West or Model for the Rest?*, advanced what he termed an "East Asian Model," which prioritizes economic reforms over liberal political reforms and is characterized by a distinctively gradualist approach to development.[2] A couple years later, Dani Rodrik advanced a similar model – "New Development Economics." Similar to the East Asian Model, it emphasizes pragmatism and experimentation and considers China's post-Mao development as its principal exemplar.[3]

In this chapter, Pessimo (Dowdle) and Optimo (Prado) debate the merits and pitfalls of each of these instantiations of the idea of a consensus. We conclude – somewhat surprisingly – that it is in the discussion they generate, rather than in their substantive prescriptions, that the real value of these models lies.

II On Joshua Ramo's Original Idea of a "Beijing Consensus"

Joshua Ramo introduced the term *Beijing Consensus* as a particular developmental strategy that was superior to the then still popular, but

[1] Joshua Cooper Ramo, *The Beijing Consensus* (London: Foreign Policy Centre, 2004).

[2] Randall P. Peerenboom, *China Modernizes: Threat to the West or Model for the Rest?* (Oxford: Oxford University Press, 2007).

[3] Dani Rodrik, "The New Development Economics: We Shall Experiment, but How Shall We Learn?," in *What Works in Development? Thinking Big and Thinking Small*, Jessica Cohen and William Easterly (eds.) (Washington, DC: Brookings Institution Press, 2009), 24–47.

increasingly discredited, "Washington Consensus." According to Ramo, the Beijing Consensus consists of "three theorems about how to organize the place of a developing country in the world."[4] We examine each theorem in turn.

A On Ramo's First Theorem

"The first theorem repositions the value of innovation. Rather than the 'old-physics' argument that developing countries must start development with trailing-edge technology (copper wires), it insists that on [*sic*] the necessity of bleeding-edge innovation (fiber optic) to create change that moves faster than the problems change creates. In physics terms, it is about using innovation to reduce the friction losses of reform."[5]

Pessimo on Development as "Bleeding-Edge" Innovation

To me, this is just a buzzword salad. What does it mean to "create change that moves faster than the problems change creates"? What problems do copper wires cause that immediate transition to fiber optics outruns?

Beyond this, studies suggest that it is almost impossible to sustain competitiveness in "bleeding-edge" (or, more conventionally, "leading-edge") innovation anywhere but in the most advanced of industrial and postindustrial economies.[6] Such innovation requires what Michael Storper has termed "agglomeration effects," a synergistic spill-over of knowledge that results when a critical density of highly skilled and educated workers live and work in close proximity with each other.[7] This requires large amounts of local wealth and very high standards of living to attract and maintain this kind of labor force.[8] Moreover, since agglomeration gives the possessing region an absolute rather than simply a comparative advantage in the relevant areas of production, this means that some other regions cannot succeed by simply "competing" with rival existing centers of agglomeration (absolute advantage means that competition is impossible).[9]

[4] Ramo, *Beijing Consensus*, 11–12. [5] Ibid.

[6] Giovanni Arrighi, Beverly J. Silver, and Benjamin D. Brewer, "Industrial Convergence, Globalization, and the Persistence of the North-South Divide," *Studies in Comparative International Development* 38 (2003): 3.

[7] Michael Storper, *The Regional World: Territorial Development in a Global Economy* (New York: Guilford Press, 1997), 9–14.

[8] Alan J. Scott, *Regions and the World Economy: The Coming Shape of Global Production, Competition, and Political Order* (Oxford: Oxford University Press, 1998), 131.

[9] Storper, *Regional World*, 107.

A good example of this is found in China's efforts to set up industrial parks. These were modeled after the Asian industrial parks that stimulated high-tech design competitiveness in Taiwan and South Korea. In Taiwan and South Korea, the high-tech industrial park environment brought together a wide diversity of synergistic industries, academics, and professionals to stimulate agglomeration. In China, the same strategy simply ended up providing a one-stop forum in which elite foreign firms could source and monitor suppliers. There was neither agglomeration nor moving up the value chain. Similar results occurred when other developing countries, such as Malaysia and Thailand, tried to emulate this model.[10]

Even today, some ten years after Ramo's claim, China does not produce anything that is of "bleeding-edge" innovative design.[11] China's economic success remains firmly planted in low-cost production of design-standard products. Its principal innovations may have come in the form of discovering ways of sweating labor (see, e.g., the *hukou* system).[12] This is because innovation in bleeding-edge technologies is a product of development, not a path to development. Nothing in China's experience suggests otherwise.

Optimo's Response

Pessimo argues that a series of preexisting economic factors associated with advanced economic development are prerequisites for effective innovation and the use of bleeding-edge technologies. I do not subscribe to Pessimo's deterministic tone for two reasons.

First, taken to its extreme, Pessimo's claim seems to suggest that a country's ability to move up the value chain (which is how Pessimo is characterizing Ramo's reference to the use of the term *bleeding-edge technology*) must be driven purely by exogenous factors. However, countries can use institutional reform to promote this kind of development.

[10] Frederic C. Deyo, "Addressing the Development Deficit of Competition Policy: The Role of Economic Networks," in *Asian Capitalism and the Regulation of Competition: Towards a Regulatory Geography of Global Competition Law*, Michael W. Dowdle, John Gillespie, and Imelda Maher (eds.) (Cambridge: Cambridge University Press, 2013), 283.

[11] Zhouying Jin, "Globalization, Technological Competitiveness and the 'Catch-up' Challenge for Developing Countries: Some Lessons of Experience," *International Journal of Technology Management and Sustainable Development* 4 (2005): 35–36.

[12] International Confederation of Free Trade Unions, *Whose Miracle? How China's Workers Are Paying the Price for Its Economic Boom* (Brussels: International Confederation of Free Trade Unions, 2005).

Peter Evans's analysis of how Taiwan and South Korea emerged as high-developed countries in the 1970s and 1980s shows the role that institutions can play in this process.[13] Evans posits that the key lies in a country's ability to promote and exploit what he termed "embedded autonomy." The state's capacity to produce innovation requires a combination of the "autonomy" prescribed by the Weberian bureaucratic model, while also requiring the cooperation of private actors that can only be obtained if the state is "embedded" in society. Under embedded autonomy, the state has an important role to play in promoting innovation. In other words, innovation is not determined simply by economic–geographic factors nor by the spontaneous initiatives of economically rational actors. Instead, it can be triggered by domestic institutional design. To be sure, this "embedded autonomy" is a "contradictory balance" that is hard to find. Moreover, Evans acknowledges that there is more than one way for a state to be embedded in society, as the contrasting examples of Taiwan and South Korea show.

Second, Pessimo implies that to benefit a particular locale, the bleeding-edge technology must have been invented there. This ignores the fact that developing countries can make important developmental use of bleeding-edge technologies that have been invented elsewhere.

Indeed, Ramo seems concerned with the kind of technology developing countries should use to "start development." Such technologies can be imported from elsewhere. For instance, mobile banking in African nations has revolutionized financial transactions on the continent, allowing money transfers between cell phones without the intermediation of a financial institution.[14] This innovation builds on a bleeding-edge technology (mobile telephony) created in developed countries to bring change to another industry in the developing world – banking.

Pessimo's argument seems to assume that there is a linear process in which bleeding-edge innovation promotes development. However, cell phones show that a bleeding-edge innovation that was created in one place for one purpose (communication) has been significantly embraced in other places for other purposes (banking), helping to promote development elsewhere.

[13] Peter Evans, *Embedded Autonomy: States and Industrial Transformation* (Princeton, NJ: Princeton University Press, 1995).

[14] "Mobile Money in Africa – Press 1 for Modernity: One Business Where the Poorest Continent Is Miles Ahead," *The Economist*, April 28, 2012, www.economist.com/node/21553510.

Pessimo's Clarification

Optimo's response to my pessimism regarding Ramo's particular articulation of the Beijing Consensus deserves some clarification of my position and perhaps of the terms of our dialogue. These include (1) the nature of "development" and (2) the nature of my developmental "determinism."

My relatively deterministic stance toward the possibilities of institutionally fed development applies only to one particular conceptualization of development: the one that equates "development" with increased relative geographical (national) capacity to produce and capture material wealth (e.g., with moving from what the World Bank calls a "low-income" to a "medium-income" country or from a low- or medium-income country to a "high-income" country). But of course, there are other ways of conceptualizing "development" – such as Sen's development as freedom,[15] or improvements in general quality of life, or simply development as alleviation of the brutality of material poverty (my preference).[16] When conceptualized in these terms, I am much less a determinist – probably no more so than most people.

Along these lines, I would hypothesize that the particular example of technology-driven development that Optimo cites – mobile banking in Africa – certainly contributes to "development" in the sense of improved "freedom" or improved quality of life or reductions in the more brutal aspects of material impoverishment, but they do not necessarily lead to a country's increased capacity to generate and retain greater material wealth relative to the rest of the world.[17]

Second, I am not a determinist with regard to a country's level of development per se. Certainly countries can and do "develop" in the sense of increasing their capacity to generate and retain material wealth relative to the rest of the world; Taiwan and South Korea are clear examples of this. My determinism lies more limitedly in our capacities to promote development through strategic (re)design of institutions of governance (including the legal institutions that are the subject of law and development). Hence I find Evans's explanation as to what caused Taiwan and South Korea to effectively "develop" unpersuasive; rather, the economic

[15] Amartya Sen, *Development as Freedom* (Oxford: Oxford University Press, 1999).

[16] See Abhijit V. Banerjee and Esther Duflo, *Poor Economics: Barefoot Hedge-fund Managers, DIY Doctors and the Surprising Truth about Life on Less than $1 a Day* (New York: Penguin Books, 2011).

[17] Simplice A. Asongu, "How Has Mobile Phone Penetration Stimulated Financial Development in Africa?," *Journal of African Business* 14 (2013): 7.

development of both Taiwan and South Korea can be fully explained simply by their close geographical and cultural proximity to Japan, together with perhaps the even closer cultural proximity to the United States that emerged during and owing to the Cold War.[18] As suggested by a recent study by AnnaLee Saxenian and Charles Sabel, Taiwan's and South Korea's embedded autonomy could be seen as simply being an organic outgrowth of this proximity.[19]

Optimo on the Relationship between Different Notions of Development

Pessimo suggests that the example of innovation that I provided may improve "quality of life" or reduce "the more brutal aspects of material impoverishment, but they do not necessarily lead to a country's increased capacity to generate and retain greater material wealth relative to the rest of the world." However, in my opinion, it is very hard to separate these two concepts. A certain policy can make the lives of people in Latin America, Asia, and Africa much easier, while simultaneously bringing increased efficiency, improving job opportunities, and contributing to economic growth.[20] In sum, other dimensions of development can still be connected with economic growth.

B On Ramo's Second Theorem

"The second Beijing Consensus theorem is that since chaos is impossible to control from the top you need a whole set of new tools. It looks beyond measures like per capita GDP and focuses instead on quality of life, the only way to manage the massive contradictions of Chinese development. This second theorem demands a development model where sustainability and equality become first considerations, not luxuries. Because Chinese society is an unstable stew of hope, ambition, fear, misinformation, and politics only this kind of chaos-theory can provide meaningful organization. China's new approach to development stresses chaos management."[21]

[18] Anis Chowdhury and Iyanatul Islam, *The Newly Industrialising Economies of East Asia* (London: Routledge, 1993), 35–41.

[19] AnnaLee Saxenian and Charles Sabel, "Roepke Lecture in Economic Geography Venture Capital in the 'Periphery': The New Argonauts, Global Search, and Local Institution Building," *Economic Geography* 84 (2008): 379.

[20] See also Sen, *Development as Freedom*, 111–45.

[21] Ramo, *Beijing Consensus*, 12.

Pessimo on the Role of Sustainability and Equality in Development

The problem here is that sustainability and equality both require highly sophisticated regulatory systems whose costs are such that they generally cannot be supported by anything less than an advanced industrial economy. These systems involve not simply advanced technologies for regulating and responding to environmental degradation without interrupting the productive activity of the polluting industry (which China does not have[22]) but highly evolved banking systems, auditing systems, and socially pervasive accounting practices that can effectively collect and redistribute wealth through an efficient taxation system (which China also does not have). (See, e.g., Chen, Chapter 6, and Li, Chapter 7, for discussions of China's efforts to create modern financial institutions and a tax system modeled on orthodox Western institutions.)[23] Contrary to Ramo's claim, China's development has in fact resulted in an infamously massive increase in social inequality (as measured by GINI) and staggering levels of environmental degradation.[24] Nor is China unique in this regard: the technologies and quality of labor needed to support effective wealth redistribution and sustainable development are simply too expensive for lesser-developed countries to develop, attract, and maintain.[25]

There is also no evidence of any meaningful "crisis management" coming out of the central level in China. In fact, many attribute China's pronounced political suppression of civil society (including educational institutions and the study of sociology) precisely to political insecurity resulting from a lack of crisis management regulatory technologies.[26] Like

22 Yamei Sun, Yonglong Lu, Tieyu Wang, Hua Ma, and Guizhen He, "Pattern of Patent-Based Environmental Technology Innovation in China," *Technological Forecasting and Social Change* 75 (2008): 1032; Kate E. Swanson and Richard G. Kuhn, "Environmental Policy Implementation in Rural China: A Case Study of Yuhang, Zhejiang," *Environmental Management* 27 (2001): 481–91.

23 Raphael W. Lam and Philippe Wingender, *China: How Can Revenue Reforms Contribute to Inclusive and Sustainable Growth?* (Washington, DC: International Monetary Fund, 2015), 3–12.

24 Shi Li, Hiroshi Sato, and Terry Sicular, eds., *Rising Inequality in China: Challenges to a Harmonious Society* (Cambridge: Cambridge University Press, 2013); Jonathan Kaiman, "China's Toxic Air Pollution Resembles Nuclear Winter, Say Scientists," *The Guardian*, February 25, 2014.

25 Partha Dasgupta and Karl-Göran Mäler, "Wealth as a Criterion for Sustainable Development," *World Economics: A Journal of Current Economic and Policy* 2 (2001): 19.

26 Jianrong Yu, "Rigid Stability: An Explanatory Framework for China's Social Situation," *Contemporary Chinese Thought* 46 (2014): 72.

redistribution and environmental sustainability, crisis management is an expensive technology to maintain, due to both monitoring costs and the fact that personnel in this area are expensive to train and keep.[27]

Optimo's Response

I disagree with Pessimo for three reasons.

First, Ramo's second theorem is best read as an aspirational statement: it invites developing countries to focus on other goals rather than focus exclusively on economic growth. Thus, whether China has actually achieved the developmental objectives stated by the model does not strike me as particularly relevant. Ultimately, what we are looking for is whether the model holds some internal coherence. This is grounded on some form of credible knowledge (theoretical or empirical) and can be a source of positive inspiration to developing countries. Ramo's second theorem does this.

Second, it is not clear if Ramo was concerned with environmental sustainability. Ramo may be referring to policy sustainability, i.e., the capacity to maintain in place policy decisions. Similarly, Pessimo seems to assume that Ramo is using the word "equality" to refer to income or wealth equality. However, Ramo could be referring to policies that do not *intentionally* produce significant winners and losers out of reforms. This is entirely speculative on my part, but the dual-track reforms implemented during the Chinese transition from a centralized economy to a market system seem to perfectly exemplify the concerns with sustainability (of the policy decision) and equality (in the distribution of the gains produced during the transitional period).[28]

Third, Pessimo seems to focus on the idea of managing chaos, while ignoring Ramo's invitation to adopt a plurality of objectives. Ramo's proposal reflects a healthy and refreshing shift in development thinking, especially if contrasted with the economically centered discourse of the Washington Consensus. And if I am interpreting it correctly, this part

[27] Arjen Boin and Allan McConnell, "Preparing for Critical Infrastructure Breakdowns: The Limits of Crisis Management and the Need for Resilience," *Journal of Contingencies and Crisis Management* 15 (2007): 52–53.

[28] Yingyi Qian, "How Reform Worked in China," in *In Search of Prosperity*, Dani Rodrik (ed.) (Princeton, NJ: Princeton University Press, 2003). See also Lawrence J. Lau, Yingyi Qian, and Gérard Roland, "Pareto-Improving Economic Reforms through Dual-Track Liberalization," *Economics Letters* 55 (1997): 285.

of Ramo's second theorem seems quite consistent with Pessimo's urging that development needs to focus on "quality of life" instead of GDP.

Finally, a question for Pessimo: China seems to be a great example of a country in which millions of people have been lifted out of poverty and have had their lives improved in the last decades. Isn't this enough to show that they have some sort of promising strategy in place?

Pessimo's Clarification and Response to Optimo

Optimo is correct to note that the mere fact that mainland China has not actually conformed to the Beijing Consensus does not by itself refute the power of that so-called consensus as a developmental model (although it would probably be more accurately termed if we called it the "Taipei Consensus"). However, I would assert that the fact that China's experiences have not conformed to the claims advanced by that model is nevertheless still significant, in that it suggests that we actually have no hard evidence that the "Consensus" actually works as a developmental model, even in China.

Consistent with Optimo's observation, by "sustainability" I read Ramo as meaning policy sustainability. Simply put, I would argue that developing countries do not have the wealth necessary to sustain the kinds of regulatory technologies that Ramo advances in the second theorem. This makes the Beijing Consensus unsustainable as a developmental model.

And while I do indeed agree with Ramo's focus on quality of life rather than simply on GDP, I do not believe that that by itself a model makes. As I will elaborate, a model is a guide to action, not an abstract goal. Such guide to action is absent in the second theorem. At best, chaos management, crisis management, and sociology simply address some of the problems of development, but are ancillary to the ultimate project of development. Ramo's second theorem is like Gertrude Stein's Oakland – there is no "there" there.[29]

Finally, in response to Optimo's query to me, yes, China has lifted millions of people out of poverty. However, that by itself does not necessarily make it a "great example." One could argue that China's developmental strategy, at least to date, has consisted simply of a gradualist removal of a set of failed command-and-control and isolationists policies that had drastically suppressed China's wealth generation for decades – policies

[29] Gertrude Stein, *Everybody's Autobiography* (New York: Random House, 1937), 289.

that we have already long known to be dysfunctional.[30] The real lesson of China's growth might ultimately be trivial – command economies do not work and it is good to have your economy open to international trade. There may be a good lesson in all this insofar as North Korea is concerned, but it is not really of much relevance to the rest of the developing world.

C *On Ramo's Third Theorem*

"[T]he Beijing Consensus contains a theory of self-determination, one that stresses using leverage to move big, hegemonic powers that may be tempted to tread on your toes. This new security doctrine is important enough that I treat it later in a separate chapter."[31]

Pessimo on Law, Development, and Self-Determination

While there is some truth to this third theorem, this is a condition that clearly lies outside the reach of any domestic development "model." China's autonomy may purely and simply be a function of its size.[32] It is not a meaningful "model" for other developing countries.

Another problem with this particular theorem is that Ramo seems to argue that the principal threats to economic autonomy are other states and international organizations ("hegemonic powers"). In fact, the much bigger problem is domination by international markets. Asian countries in particular have had some success insulating their economies from international currency markets, and perhaps from the more invidious aspect of international investment arbitration regimes.[33] However, they are still supremely subject to private market threats to relocate production, harassing litigation and lobbying, and intellectual domination of the World Trade Organization and other international financial institutions and organizations – all of which is a much greater threat to economic autonomy and development than "hegemonic powers."[34]

[30] Gregory C. Chow, "Economic Reform and Growth in China," *Annals of Economics and Finance* 5 (2004): 128–29.

[31] Ramo, *The Beijing Consensus*, 121. [32] Peerenboom, *China Modernizes*, 22.

[33] Eric Helleiner and Troy Lundblad, "States, Markets, and Sovereign Wealth Funds," *German Policy Studies* 4 (2008): 59; M. Sornarajah, *Resistance and Change in the International Law on Foreign Investment* (Cambridge: Cambridge University Press, 2015).

[34] See, e.g., Nita Rudra, *Globalization and the Race to the Bottom in Developing Countries: Who Really Gets Hurt?* (Cambridge: Cambridge University Press, 2008); Peter Drahos and John Braithwaite, *Information Feudalism: Who Owns the Knowledge Economy?* (London:

Optimo's Response

Pessimo here appears to suggest that self-determination would be restricted to "domestic financial autonomy." But Ramo may be referring to self-determination in policymaking.

If self-determination refers to a country's ability to determine its domestic policies independently from the influence of other nations, then it is clear that size is not a precondition for such self-determination. Despite their smaller size, Japan, South Korea, and Taiwan are largely able to escape policy domination by the so-called hegemonic powers (e.g., the United States, the World Bank, the WTO) as evinced, for example, in their ability to resist efforts by those international forces to impose the Washington Consensus as *the* developmental policy applicable to all countries.[35]

Along these lines, Pessimo also criticizes Ramo's third theorem for failing to provide any meaningful guidance for action. I disagree. At its heart, the third theorem seems to call for a disregard for the World Bank and the IMF. This guides action by telling countries what not to do (see also Kroncke, Chapter 2).

Pessimo's Clarification

Optimo and I are not in much disagreement regarding Ramo's third theorem. My own understanding is that Ramo is referring to domestic autonomy with regards to policymaking, and I suspect even more particularly with regards to monetary policy. Indeed, Beijing's refusal to float the RMB is probably the most well known and oft-referred to example of Beijing's autonomy from global (American) economic orthodoxy.

Optimo is also probably right in suggesting that I placed too much weight on national and/or national-economic size in setting out a country's capacity to achieve policy self-determination. However, I do think that is the case with regards to China. Contrary to Rodrik's suggestion, Japan and South Korea are not good counterexamples. In both cases, their success in developing nonstandard regulatory responses to global

Earthscan, 2002); Sornarajah, *Resistance and Change in the International Law on Foreign Investment.*

35 See Dani Rodrik, "Goodbye Washington Consensus, Hello Washington Confusion?," *Journal of Economic Literature* 44 (2006): 985; Robert Wade, "Japan, the World Bank, and the Art of Paradigm Maintenance: The East Asian Miracle in Political Perspective," *New Left Review* (1996): 3.

economic competition derived, not from innovative institutional arrangements, but from Washington's unwillingness to risk their possible political disapproval – an unwillingness that resulted from these countries' unique front-line status during the Cold War.[36]

III On Randall Peerenboom's "East Asian Model"

Another developmental model that has been drawn from China's experience is what Randall Peerenboom termed the "East Asian Model."[37] The East Asian Model is characterized by a gradualist approach to development, in contrast to the big-bang approach that was used in the economic transition in the states of the former Soviet Union and Eastern Bloc, and by a developmental sequencing that focuses first on economic reforms and only later on political liberalization.

A On Gradualism and Sequencing

Pessimo on Gradualism

The East Asian Model does not actually provide guidance for promoting development in today's world. China's gradualist approach is an approach to economic transition, not to economic development. It is an approach to transitioning from a command economy to a market economy. But there are very few countries left in the world that still sport a command economy. For countries that already have a market economy, the notion of gradualism makes very little sense: what does "gradualism" look like in the context of today's India or today's Brazil? What exactly should these countries be "gradual" about in pursuing their economic development?

Perhaps the idea is that they should be gradualist about pursuing political reforms. This brings us to the second part of the East Asian Model, the idea that for most lesser-developed countries, the processes of economic development invariably involves significant and potentially destabilizing social disruption, and it is easier for more authoritarian regimes to weather such disruption than for more liberal, democratic regimes.[38] Whether or

[36] Chowdhury and Islam, *The Newly Industrialising Economies of East Asia*, 38–41.
[37] Peerenboom, *China Modernizes*, 26–81.
[38] Samuel P. Huntington, *Political Order in Changing Societies* (New Haven, CT: Yale University Press, 2006).

not this is actually the case (Pessimo is skeptical) is an open question,[39] but even if it is, these particular kinds of issues and concerns simply lie outside the reach of developmental projects.

Peerenboom could be making one of two claims here. He could be arguing that lesser-developed countries should not pursue political reforms simply because they will not work. But if this is the claim, then what he is describing is not really a "model" – it is simply a purported factual claim that may or may not be relevant to the developmental agent. There may be good reasons why a developmental agent may push for particular political reforms even with the knowledge that these reforms will probably not take root. And even if there is no good reason, it does not really matter: if the world is not changed by the attempt or lack thereof, then there is in fact no harm in trying even if it does not in fact work.

Alternatively, Peerenboom may be arguing that pursuing such reforms hurt the cause of development, perhaps by strengthening the ability of various social interests to obstruct necessary structural reforms – like land redistribution – that go against their personal interests.[40] However, it is not clear what kinds of donor-driven reform projects Peerenboom is thinking about here. I suspect that, at the end of the day, regime liberalization and democratization arise more or less spontaneously out of political and social evolutions that operate outside the reach of strategic developmental planning. If this is the case, then to the extent that sequencing offers any developmental guidance at all, it is to counsel international developmental agents to affirmatively try to *prevent* political liberalization. I do not think this is what Peerenboom actually means. But regardless, such an argument is not supported by the developmental experience of East and Southeast Asia. It is true that many of these countries experienced industrial take-off before they transited into more archetypical liberal democratic regimes, but there are no examples I can find of a country in which a prior or ongoing political liberalization worked to halt or thwart economic take-off.

Optimo's Response

While Pessimo is absolutely right in distinguishing a program of economic or political transition from a program to promote development, both can

[39] See Adam Przeworski, Michael E. Alvarez, Jose Antonio Cheibub, and Fernando Limongi, *Democracy and Development: Political Institutions and Well-Being in the World, 1950–1990* (Cambridge: Cambridge University Press, 2000).

[40] See also Huntington, *Political Order in Changing Societies*, 384–93.

be conceived as programs that try to promote institutional change. Thus, while the end goal may not be the same, the strategies and tools of one process could potentially be useful to the other. For instance, the dual-track strategy to allow state-owned corporations in China to gradually transition from a command economy to a market system is sometimes used to reform career plans in inefficient bureaucracies in an attempt to promote good governance and increase economic growth.[41]

Pessimo may challenge the idea that functional institutions are conducive to economic growth (and therefore institutional reform would be the central goal of a development program). Even so, Pessimo still would have good reason to subscribe to gradualism as a model for development: gradual implementation of policy change seems to be widely accepted in certain policy circles.[42] Perhaps the most famous and one of the earliest pieces supporting this idea is "The Science of Muddling Through" by Charles Lindblom.[43] Thus, even if one is not trying to promote development through institutional transition, but instead advocating for policy changes, gradualism should still serve as a guiding principle. In this context, perhaps the East Asian Model is the best example of such principle being applied in large scale.

Pessimo's Demurral: On the Science of Muddling Through

Optimo defends the East Asian Model's advocacy of gradualism as simply an expression of the tried-and-true developmental formula that Charles Lindblom famously termed "the science of muddling through." However, I see the East Asian Model's notion of gradualism differently. As advanced by the East Asian Model, gradualism is offered as an alternative to the rapid, big-bang approach that "Western" advisors (most famously Jeffrey Sachs) pushed on the former Soviet bloc nations in the 1990s.[44] In this sense, it is clearly referring to a strategy for capitalist transformation – for

[41] For strategies of bureaucratic reform, see Michael J. Trebilcock and Mariana Mota Prado, *Advanced Introduction to Law and Development* (Cheltenham, UK: Edward Elgar, 2014). For the dual track strategy, see Qian, "How Reform Worked in China," and Lau, "Pareto-improving Economic Reforms," 285.

[42] See, e.g., Michael J. Trebilcock, *Dealing with Losers: The Political Economy of Policy Transitions* (New York: Oxford University Press, 2014); Matt Andrews, *The Limits of Institutional Reform in Development: Changing Rules for Realistic Solutions* (Cambridge: Cambridge University Press, 2013).

[43] Charles E. Lindblom, "The Science of 'Muddling Through,'" *Public Administration Review* 19 (1959): 79.

[44] See Joseph E. Stiglitz, *Globalization and Its Discontents* (New York: W. W. Norton, 2002).

transiting from a command economy to a liberal market economy.[45] As I note, there are very few developing countries left in the world that still operate a command economy, and for this reason gradualism as originally envisioned seems a moot point insofar as a universalizable developmental model is concerned.

Along these lines, I would argue that "the science of muddling through" is a different kettle of fish. To say that we are "muddling through" is not to say that we are being gradualist; it is not to say that we need to avoid moving "too fast" in promoting development. Again, it simply makes no sense to say that Brazil or Thailand or Romania needs to adopt a gradualist approach to development – "gradualist" in what sense? What does "gradualism" look like in the context of these countries? I would argue that it does not look like anything – to say that Brazil should adopt a "gradualist" approach to development is like saying that Optimo should adopt a "gradualist" approach to proving me wrong: the word "gradualist" simply does not have meaning when used in such a context.

As per Lindbolm, I believe that "muddling through" has always been our approach to the development of national economies that are already capitalist. But it actually offers very little in the way of a developmental model. What distinguishes good muddling from not so good muddling? It cannot simply be the presence of failure, because frequent failure is the distinguishing feature of muddling. How does one model "muddling through"? To "muddle" is simply to muddle – is Brazil not "developing" because it is not muddling? Or is it just not muddling the right way?

This brings us to our last variant of the Beijing Consensus, Dani Rodrik's "New Development Economics" and its experimental approach to development. It is to this we now turn to.

IV On Dani Rodrik's "New Development Economics"

More recently, several scholars began advancing another kind of development model derived from China's experience. One of these is Dani Rodrik's "New Development Economics,"[46] which – inspired by Sebastian Heilmann's "Policy Experimentation in China's Economic Rise"[47] – calls

45 See also Shang-Jin Wei, "Gradualism versus Big Bang: Speed and Sustainability of Reforms," *Canadian Journal of Economics* 30 (1997): 1234.

46 See Rodrik, "The New Development Economics."

47 Sebastian Heilmann, "Policy Experimentation in China's Economic Rise," *Studies in Comparative International Development* 43 (2008): 1.

for "an approach that is explicitly experimental, and which is carried out using the tools of diagnostics and evaluation . . . The proof of the pudding is in the eating: if something works, it is worth doing."[48] Does such experimentalism hold meaningful promise as a "model" for promoting "development" more generally?

A *Pessimo on Experimentalism*

To begin, I want to clarify what I see as the attributes of a "model." A "model" is by its definition a universal template – a developmental model is a template for development that can be effectively applied independently from context (unless some prerequisite context is specified in the model itself, which is not the case with "new experimental economics"). Also, to the extent that "law and development" models seem ultimately to be devoted to promoting development assistance, that model needs to provide direction for how such assistance should be constructed. A developmental "model" that provides no significant guidance to action is not really a model.

Following this, I would argue that Rodrik's model is not really a model, in that it does not really provide any meaningful guidance for action. This is because ultimately it provides no universal or generalizable template for developmental assistance – at least in the area of law and development.

This is for a number of reasons. First, an experimental approach only really works when the developmental ends are agreed upon. New Development Economics is a process by which we can identify different means that better serve some given ends. However, for many aspects of law and development, the means are the ends. With regards to China, for example, the issues are generally not "how best to promote rule of law" – you promote rule of law by promoting the institutions associated with rule of law. There's no real need to "experiment" given that the means and ends are the same. The real developmental issue is whether these "rule of law" institutions should receive priority over other possibly competing goals – like "modernization" or "economic growth." These are ultimately normative questions; experimentalism offers no aid in their resolution.

For example, both the Chinese and international developmental organizations may agree that China needs to develop stronger "judicial independence." But judicial independence is a social construct. It can mean very different things – both in terms of institutional structure and its

[48] Rodrik, "The New Development Economics," 25.

contribution to the legal system – to different people. One study suggests that donors are more likely to conceptualize judicial independence as a means for promoting procedural justice, whereas the Chinese are more likely to conceptualize judicial independence as a means of promoting substantive justice or factual accuracy in decision making.[49] Many attribute China's problems with achieving the kind of "rule of law" that Western donors are seeking to advance to its failure to produce something akin to a Western vision of judicial independence.[50] However, if this is the case, this is a disagreement over the ends, not over the means. Experimentalism cannot address this problem.

In fact, many "law and development" issues in China appear to be precisely of this sort. There is much disagreement between China's political leadership and the law and developmental community as to what goals law and development should be striving to promote. This observation is true not only for "thick" notions of law and development, as defined by Randall Peerenboom, i.e., notions that see developmental as necessarily including promoting human and political rights, and various (liberal) conceptualizations of "justice."[51] It also applies to more economically oriented developmental projects. China and "the West" often have very different understandings as to the role that market capitalism should play in society. China's understanding is much more akin to what is sometimes termed "economic nationalism," while "the West's" understanding is much more naturalist and cosmopolitan.[52] For this reason, even economic legal reforms projects – such as reforms to competition regulation[53] – are ultimately thwarted by disagreement over ends, not by ignorance with regards to means. Here, too, experimentalism does not seem to offer any real help.

Another limitation to experimentalism is that it does not seem particularly well-suited for addressing issues of *national* legal (or economic)

[49] See generally Mavis Chng and Michael W. Dowdle, "The Chinese Debate about the Adjudication Committee: Implications for What 'Judicial Independence' Means in the Context of China," *Chinese Journal of Comparative Law* 2 (2014): 233.

[50] See, e.g., Keith E. Henderson, "Halfway Home and a Long Way to Go: China's Rule of Law Evolution and the Global Road to Judicial Independence, Judicial Impartiality, and Judicial Integrity," in *Judicial Independence in China: Lessons for Global Rule of Law Promotion*, Randall Peerenboom (ed.) (Cambridge: Cambridge University Press, 2010), 23.

[51] See Randall P. Peerenboom, *China's Long March towards Rule of Law* (Cambridge: Cambridge University Press, 2002), 55–125.

[52] Shaun Breslin, "The 'China Model' and the Global Crisis: From Friedrich List to a Chinese Mode of Governance?," *International Affairs* 87 (2011): 1323.

[53] See, e.g., Michael W. Dowdle, "On the Public-Law Character of Competition Law: A Lesson From Asian Capitalism," *Fordham International Law Journal* 38 (2015): 303–86.

development. As described by Rodrik, experimentalism is a very contextualized developmental process (e.g., Kroncke, Chapter 2, for a discussion of experimentalism in Brazilian context). Its strength lies in its ability to avoid one-size-fits-all approaches to development. A national legal system, by contrast, is by its very nature a one-size-fits-all arrangement. Here, a developmental model that focuses on discovering and responding to minute nuances of local context is of little utility. At most, experimentalism would counsel the developmental agent to promote decentralization, *local* experimentation, and perhaps data-gathering. However, what would this accomplish insofar as a national regulatory system is concerned? Any local success or local failure could well hinge on contexts that are unique to the locale. As such, local successes or failures arrived at à la experimentalism are unlikely to be able to serve as positive or negative models for elsewhere, even after they have been "evaluated" by central entities.[54] This was well evinced, for example, in China's recent "new socialist countryside" initiative, which did generate local successes through experimentation, but also found that these successes were unique to the locale, and did not provide many usable insights for other locales.[55]

In sum, decentralization and experimentalism might promote local legal development, but not *national* legal development. This is problematic from the perspective of law and development, because it is precisely in promoting the development of *national* legal systems that international law and development facilitators enjoy any comparative intellectual advantage over domestic processes. The principal value-added provided by international legal developmental aid lies in its greater familiarity with more global experiences with law and development. The more localized and locally contextualized the problems are, the less a developmental facilitator who is located internationally is able to bring to the table in the form of usable knowledge. Here, "legal development" becomes reduced primarily to simply being a source of funds for local projects developed by local actors. And even here there is a problem, because the donor's lack of contextualized knowledge makes her or him ill-equipped for identifying promising recipients and projects.[56]

Is simply being a content-less source of funds sufficient to constitute a developmental model? This is an open question. But even if it is, whether

[54] Cohen and Easterly, *What Works in Development?*

[55] Anna L. Ahlers and Gunter Schubert, "'Building a New Socialist Countryside' – Only a Political Slogan?," *Journal of Current Chinese Affairs* 38 (2009): 55.

[56] See, e.g., Pasuk Phongpaichit and Chris Baker, *Thailand's Crisis* (Singapore: Singapore Institute of Southeast Asian Studies, 2000), 35–82.

it is a *feasible* model is another issue. Such a model would be particularly costly to implement. Development of local legal institutions costs about the same as development of national legal institutions. Yet they benefit far fewer people. Costs would be even further increased by the experimental nature of the development project, because it would involve funders paying for a lot of failures in addition to the occasional localized success. Given its extremely high cost-to-benefits ratio, it seems very unlikely that many funders would embrace such a model.

B Optimo's Response

Pessimo offers two challenges to the idea that experimentalism could potentially serve as a model for development. His first argument is that experimentalism does not address the normative questions of development. Its utility is therefore limited to situations in which the ends are already defined, which is often not the major problem confronted by developing countries.

However, can a distinction really be drawn between the means and the ends, as suggested by Pessimo? Any attempt to define the goals of legal development, i.e., to define the goals a society ultimately aims to achieve with its legal system, is itself highly dependent on the political, cultural, and social context. Thus, abandoning the idea that there could or should be a model to define the ends of development may actually be the beginning of a much more promising conversation than what the development field has experienced thus far. Indeed, I would argue that experimentalism seems to have abandoned the intention to define ends, and has focused instead on means. This is not only a differentiating feature of this model over the Washington Consensus model, but it may actually be considered a significant upgrade, as development models go. It is a model that is aware of its limitations and which operates within realistic boundaries.

This is not to say that the search for a way to define and determine the ends of development is futile and should be abandoned. To the contrary, the entire development enterprise operates under the assumption that there is some search for a common goal of some sort, lest the concept of development becomes so diluted as to encompass "anybody's notion of utopia."[57] However, even if it is the case (i.e., even if the model that helps to search for the ends is not and should not be the same as the one

[57] H. W. Arndt, *Economic Development: The History of an Idea* (Chicago: University of Chicago Press, 1989), 165.

that helps to deal with the means), experimentalism may still provide a meaningful model for development. In other words, a model does not need to address end goals.

To sustain this claim, I would like to distinguish between form and substance. While the substance of experimentalism could be argued to be context dependent, this does not apply to the form of experimentation. It is this formal or procedural dimension – i.e., how experiments can be conducted – that would allow us to generate generalizable knowledge from them. The beauty of experimentalism is that it gives us a common conceptual template so that we may arrive at different solutions *through the same process.* Thereby lessons can then be compared to identify and separate the generalizable from the context dependent.

A recent essay by Kevin Davis and Mariana Prado suggests that experimentalism and other recent theories represent a move away from substantive commonalities toward meta-principles.[58] Since context-dependency prevents a productive conversation about shared lessons and transplanted solutions, the conversation may be more productive if the focus shifts from the *substance* of development policies to its *form.* This move echoes the idea of meta-principles as with an increased focus on procedural and formal aspects of reforms in law and development theories, rather than their content. Therefore, there is still a role for what Pessimo refers to as the internationally located "development facilitator."

Pessimo's second point is the incompatibility between the development of the national legal system and the focus of experimentalism. According to Pessimo, the former intrinsically involves a top-down process that is antithetical to the central tenets of experimentalism, which intrinsically focus on decentralization. I disagree. Experimentation is not necessarily tied to decentralization. Indeed, with regards to China, Chenggang Xu from the University of Hong Kong argues that decentralization and experimentation are different features. Experimentation does not require decentralization, and vice-versa.[59]

Moreover, decentralization does not necessarily mean that national reforms cannot follow local reforms. While both decentralization and experimentation have been present in China, their combination created a

[58] Kevin E. Davis and Mariana Mota Prado, "Law, Regulation, and Development," in *International Development: Ideas, Experience, and Prospects*, Bruce Currie-Alder et al. (eds.) (Oxford: Oxford University Press, 2014), 204.

[59] Chenggang Xu, "The Fundamental Institutions of China's Reforms and Development," *Journal of Economic Literature* 49 (2011): 1076.

particular type of decentralization. This, in turn, catalyzed national legal reforms.[60] One such experiment involved land reform in the late 1970s, which was initially done at the local level. According to Xu, these local experimentations were ultimately "endorsed by the central government and implemented by all levels of government nationwide." While such experimentation was more prominent at the earlier stages of reform, it was significantly reduced as higher levels of economic growth had been achieved. Nevertheless, the fact that such experimentation occurred and changed China's national law and policy suggests that this could be part of the Beijing Consensus.

C *Pessimo's Clarification*

I think the problem of identifying ends is much more critical in the context of experimentalism than it is in the context of best practices (e.g., the Washington Consensus), because of the former's critical reliance on ex post evaluation. If we can't agree on the ends, then we really can't do that evaluation, and experimentalism becomes reduced to simple decentralization.

Optimo appears to acknowledge the special difficulties that such normative questions pose for experimentalism, but suggests that that model can still survive. In this, I question whether Optimo underestimates how domineering normative issues are in the context of law and development (as contrasted with, for example, developmental economics). Law is a strongly normative phenomenon, and at the end of the day, we simply cannot separate its normative from its procedural demands: even the simplest procedural requirements, such as the one that subjects dispute to argument rather than to force, betrays a normative preference.[61] Almost all of the law and development projects that I am aware of have ultimately been informed by strongly normative understandings and commitments (including those devoted to economic development as well). I would therefore at least hypothesize that experimentalism's distinct difficulty with the normative may be significantly more problematic in the context of law and development than it is in other areas of development.

In responding to my skepticism regarding the suitability of experimentalism to national-level law and development projects, Optimo suggests

[60] Ibid.

[61] See, e.g., Lawrence Lessig, "The Regulation of Social Meaning," *University of Chicago Law Review* 62 (1995): 968–72.

that "the beauty of experimentalism is that it gives us a common conceptual template so that we may arrive at different solutions *through the same process.* Thereby lessons can then be compared to identify and separate the generalizable from the context dependent." I assume this is related to Optimo's subsequent discussion of meta-principles. I am not completely clear how these might work, but I do not see anything occurring in or coming out of China that fits this particular description – certainly they have not been identified in the experimentalist literature referencing China. Of course, this is ultimately an empirical question, and therefore beyond the terms of our dialogue (which is primarily conceptual).

But then, Optimo does raise this empirical issue when discussing the work of Chenggang Xu, who – like many – identify Chinese experimentalism with numerous, spontaneous local rural land reform initiatives that took place in the 1970s. This is a commonly heard trope – but there are a number of problems with it. First, this was not really experimentalism, it was reversion. China had a regime of private, agrarian land use rights in the 1950s, and these so-called experiments simply reintroduced that regime.[62] It did not really develop anything new, which seems to be the raison d'être of experimentalism as a developmental *model.* Deng had simply revived the free-market structure China had enjoyed in the early 1950s.

Relatedly, one could also argue that these reforms were primarily an expression of gradualism rather than experimentalism. There was never any question that Deng was going to bring to China the free-market structure it had enjoyed in the early 1950s and that is found in the vast majority of today's national economies. Again, this is not a question of experimentalism – there was already much experience with these reforms, there really wasn't that much variation from locale to locale, and they were known commodities. In fact, spiritually, these local experiments had much more in common with the Washington Consensus than they did with experimentalism. Moreover, China's gradualism was ultimately dictated by political concerns rather than pure technical developmental concerns,[63] and for this reason too, it would not seem to represent a developmental model.

[62] See David Goodman, *Deng Xiaoping and the Chinese Revolution: A Political Biography* (London: Routledge, 2002), 92–94, 123–24.

[63] Chow, "Economic Reform and Growth in China," 140.

D Optimo on the Ends and Means of Experimentalism

In the last post, Pessimo provided some illuminating comments about what is often portrayed as an example of experimentalism: land reform in China. Pessimo challenges the widespread idea that there was much experimentation in this process. Nevertheless, perhaps more significantly, Pessimo also raises an important question about whether experimentalism can serve as a model for development. Pessimo argues that experimentalism cannot bracket the normative issues, which are currently the most pressing issues in the field. In the words of Pessimo: "Law is a strongly normative phenomenon. Ultimately, its normative form cannot be separated from its procedural form."

As a clarification, I am not diminishing the importance of addressing normative issues. The sheer fact that I am proposing experimentalism as a model for development has already a normative undertone. The issue is whether we can separate the discussion of the ends from the means when contemplating a model for development. Pessimo seems to suggest that this separation is not feasible (and perhaps not desirable). In contrast, I suggest the opposite.

As an illustration, the discussion about the Rule of Law (ROL) in development circles has provided us with a myriad of definitions of ROL. Some authors have usefully distinguished between thick and thin definitions of ROL.[64] Thin definitions are primarily procedural, e.g., if rules are applied impartially and equally to all parties involved, one could claim that there is ROL, regardless of the content of these rules. The criticism to thin definitions is that abusive and dictatorial regimes can easily meet these criteria. To address this criticism, thick definitions incorporate not only procedural features, but also substantive ones. Thick definitions are then criticized for searching for something akin to a universal concept of justice, and reducing the possibility of context-dependent solutions.[65]

While Pessimo seems to be asking for a thick concept of experimentalism – i.e., a type of experimentalism that would help us define the means and ends, or procedure and substance – I am proposing that we can use a thin one, i.e., a procedural form of experimentalism. Thus, the ends of the

[64] See Peerenboom, *China's Long March towards Rule of Law*, 66–67. See also Michael Trebilcock and Ronald Daniels, *Rule of Law Reform and Development: Charting the Fragile Path of Progress* (Cheltenham, UK: Edward Elgar, 2008), 23–25.

[65] Ibid.

experiment would be defined elsewhere and this process does not need to be an experimental one. In sum, with this thin concept of experimentalism, once the ends have been defined, an experimental process should be used to try to achieve these ends.

If one adopts the thin concept of experimentalism that I am proposing here as a model for development, it is possible to address two criticisms raised by Pessimo.

First, in the context of the Chinese reform, Pessimo says that the fact that the reforms were not new is antithetical to the raison d'être of experimentalism. According to the definition I proposed, the substance of the reforms does not need to be new. What is required is a process of experimentation, i.e., the idea that reforms will be reverted and revised, if they do not work.

Second, Pessimo claims that the fact that the end of the reform was predetermined (i.e., there would be free market in China) defeats that purpose of experimentation. As I have argued here, this is only a problem if one subscribes to a thick concept of experimentation. According to the thin concept of experimentation, however, the ends can be defined according to other processes, including political processes. Experimentation comes only as the procedure according to which one will find the means to achieve these ends.

IV Conclusions: From Beijing Consensus to Beijing Dialogue

A *Optimo: Replacing the Search for Consensus with Open Dialogue*

Pessimo and I may have numerous disagreements about the strategies to enhance efficiency and generate economic growth, but we also have many points of agreement, contrary to what we assumed when we started this exercise. Indeed, if we move beyond economic concepts of development (such as the GDP per capita, as used by the World Bank), Pessimo's determinism seems to fade away and we are on common ground. While this is not of much utility here, as the Beijing Consensus seems to be primarily focused on economic growth, this may be a topic to be fruitfully explored in a future dialogue.

The discussion about Ramo's three theorems helped us to define the terms of our debate. On the substance of the debate, we agreed that a Beijing Consensus does not need to show that China has done things right or has already succeeded. Therefore, a discussion about the Consensus should not be based on empirical disputes about what has happened in China. The question that we need to focus on is whether the proposals inspired by China can serve as a model for other countries.

The discussion about Ramo also helped us refine and agree on what we mean by a "model for development." We are both looking for sustainable and feasible guidance for action, with internal coherence, and grounded on some form of credible knowledge (theoretical or empirical). The only difference is that I may be more open to accept negative guidance ("do not follow the Washington Consensus").

On the East Asian Model proposed by Randall Peerenboom, the terms of the debate as stated earlier did not reveal much of a consensus. We debated and disagreed about the meaning of the term "gradualism" and whether the gradualism implemented by Asian countries could serve as a model for the rest of the world. I am more optimistic about seeing at least the semblance of a model in the ideas of sequencing and gradualism than Pessimo is. This is partially because I am conceiving of these two ideas as meta-principles. Pessimo, by contrast, associates gradualism more limitedly with transition from planned to market economies. I am wondering if – acknowledging that – we can still transport the strategy to other contexts. Thus, the reason of my optimism is largely connected with the idea of meta-principles.

Regarding the East Asian Model, there was one point of agreement that did not come across explicitly in our exchange. Pessimo indicated that he did not disagree with the normative argument presented by Amartya Sen, but he was worried that neither Sen nor the supposed East Asian Model offered strategies on how to promote political liberalization. Indeed, Pessimo indicated that without a concrete strategy, there was very little utility in such a normative statement. This is certainly a point in which we agree on.

Our principal disagreement revolved around experimentalism, which seems to be also the most elaborated and cited version of the idea of Beijing Consensus. Pessimo has challenged the possibility of using experimentation as a model because it does not help us define what the ends of development are. This is in line with Pessimo's earlier claim (regarding the East Asian Model) that muddling through is not a model, as we do not have a system to define the ends and therefore to assess successes.

I disagree. I have proposed that a thin conception of experimentation could bracket the question about end goals while providing guidance for action. Perhaps Cass Sunstein's "incomplete theorized agreements" illustrates my "thin" conception of experimentation.[66] Actors do not need to agree on the ends in order to collaborate on the implementation of means, as long as these means are conducive to the different ends pursued by these actors. This seems to be perfectly feasible in the development field. As I stated at the beginning of the debate, development goals are not as antithetical to each other as some have portrayed. Indeed, promoting economic growth, enhancing capabilities, or eliminating abject poverty are often intertwined processes. In fact, sometimes they are so entangled that it is not only hard to separate them analytically or empirically, but also unproductive to do so.

In sum, in the process of mapping points of disagreement, we have surprisingly found much common ground. Indeed, if I were to extract any lessons from this discussion, it might be that if one aims for Dialogue, you may find Consensus (but it does not work the other way around). Thus, for those in search for a model, dialogue may be a far more productive strategy in the development field than the ones adopted so far.

B Pessimo: "Whither Beijing Consensus" – It Is Not Necessarily Where You Might Think

The Beijing Consensus, including its various derivatives, is not a model, it is a narrative. Moreover, as a narrative, it is for the most part not particularly about China, nor is it particularly about development. Rather, it is – paradoxically – a story that is primarily about the United States, and about America's place in human evolutionary history.[67] But this is not necessarily a bad thing.

It is highly questionable whether China actually presents us with a show-case example of "development." As noted above, as least some portion of China's development has been a product of an earlier economic insanity that needlessly devastated China's productive capacity for over two decades. Beyond this, taking the costs of environmental degradation into account suggests that China's economic growth is significantly less than commonly calculated.[68] Related to this, China significantly

[66] Cass R. Sunstein, "Incompletely Theorized Agreements," *Harvard Law Review* 108 (1995): 1733.

[67] Cf. Michael W. Dowdle, "Whither Asia? Whiter Capitalism? Whither Global Competition Law?," in Asian *Capitalism and the Regulation of Competition*, Dowdle, Gillespie, and Maher (eds.), 313–19.

[68] Beina Xu, "CFR Backgrounders: China's Environmental Crisis," *Council for Foreign Relations*, April 25, 2014, www.cfr.org/china/chinas-environmental-crisis/p12608.

underperforms its income class in terms of inequality-adjusted Human Development Index (iHDI), environmental sustainability, and subjective well-being, suggesting that even if China is "growing" economically, it may not be growing into a country in which most people would actually want to live.[69] All of these give very good reasons to question whether China's particular pathway to economic "growth" is really something other countries ought to replicate.

However, as noted above, the Beijing Consensus was never really about China in the first place. The term is clearly a play on the "Washington Consensus," a developmental model that became popularized with the apparent success of the American intervention in the Mexican Peso crisis of 1994.[70] Here, the term "Beijing" – like the term "Asian" – is simply a representation of "the other." The Beijing Consensus had nothing really to do with Beijing. It is really just a pithy way of calling it the "anti-Washington" consensus (see also Kroncke, Chapter 2).

All in all, our stories about China's "development" – both positive and negative – are ultimately not stories that are really about China. They remain, for the present at least, stories about what China has to tell us about being, for lack of a better term, "Western."

And this is not at all a bad thing. As Baruch Spinoza so cogently identified, knowing the world and knowing oneself are symbiotic endeavors.[71] The more we can learn about who we really are, as distinguished from who we like to think we are, the more we are likely to truly understand and appreciate our place in the world, and through that, the world as it actually is. Seen in this light, endeavors to identify (and contest) a Beijing Consensus, even though they are really about America, are indeed nevertheless very much worth the effort.

So yes, on this last – and probably most important point – Pessimo and Optimo are in total agreement. Regardless of whether there is or is not anything that can meaningfully be called a "Beijing Consensus," there still remains the very real possibility of a Beijing Dialogue: a dialogue that may or may not result in consensus, but which could very well result in something even better – what Edward O. Wilson calls "consilience," i.e.,

69 John Williamson, "What Washington Means by Policy Reform," in *Latin American Adjustment: How Much Has It Happened?*, John Williamson (ed.) (Washington, DC: Institute of International Economics, 1990), 5–20.

70 Paul Krugman, "Dutch Tulips and Emerging Markets: Another Bubble Bursts," *Foreign Affairs* 74 (1995): 28.

71 Benedictus De Spinoza, *Ethics*, Edwin Curley (ed.) (New York: Penguin Books, 1996).

new forms of knowledge that arise when different experiences, narratives, and disciplines collide with one another.[72]

Wait . . . did Pessimo just end on a note of optimism?

[72] Edward O. Wilson, *Consilience: The Unity of Knowledge* (New York: Alfred A. Knopf, 1998). See also Michael W. Dowdle, "Public Accountability: Conceptual, Historical, and Epistemic Mappings," in *Public Accountability: Designs, Dilemmas and Experiences*, Michael W. Dowdle (ed.) (Cambridge: Cambridge University Press, 2006), 1–26.

2

Imagining China

Brazil, Labor, and the Limits of an Anti-model

JEDIDIAH KRONCKE[1]

I The Beijing Consensus as Anti-model

The idea of a consensus in development discourse is ever alluring. Much like discussions of universal "best practices," asserting the existence of a consensus offers up the possibility that the most fundamental, if oft-elided, challenge of development has been transcended – that of politics. Especially in the postcolonial era, the universal language of empirical social science has, at its best, expanded the possibility of cross-cultural knowledge exchange while, at its worst, fallen prey to merely cloaking cultural chauvinism or geopolitical self-interest. In this way, the rise of the Washington Consensus was itself as much the construction of a particular vein of development economics as it was an outgrowth of the 1990s post-Soviet euphoria that gave rise to the claim that the United States had achieved a demonstrable and well-understood economic track record. A track record that could be universalized into a model that was powerful enough to transcend global socio-cultural diversity, much akin to Francis Fukuyama's proclaimed end of history.

In similar stead, the relative decline of the influence of the Washington Consensus reflects as much concerns about the empirical validation of its underlying policy prescriptions as it does the end of the 1990s optimistic imagining of a unipolar liberal world order. Understanding the rise of the idea of the Beijing Consensus thus begs the question of what would generate interest in a new "consensus" in a very different, multi-polar, geopolitical context. Such search for an alternative was presaged by

[1] I am deeply indebted in this piece to the work of my research assistant, Marcela Mattiuzzo. The majority of Portuguese translations are originally hers, some of which I have modified. Many thanks are also due to the participants in the NUS Workshop on the Beijing Consensus for their comments and insightful criticisms.

the focus in the 1980s on Japan as the source of a new "alternative" model of development, spurred then by the Japanese economic and international discord following stagflation and energy crises in the West during the late 1970s.

This chapter will argue that the contemporary geopolitical context and backlash against the Washington Consensus has given rise to the use and invocation of the Beijing Consensus as an *anti-model.* As an anti-model, the Beijing Consensus discourse is only partly a reaction against the underlying policy content of the Washington Consensus. More fully, it is also a general rejection of the very notion of the coordinated global advocacy of a universal set of policy prescriptions. This observation is not in itself completely novel. Now popular deconstructions of the Beijing Consensus have shown that attempts to present it as a concrete model of development are either empirically shallow or presume factors unreplicable elsewhere – and thus not of the same species of consensus as the Washington Consensus. However, such deconstructions do not capture completely how the Beijing Consensus operates in practice within international policy discourse – and thus these critiques are unlikely to lessen its current popularity. Following this interpretation, the chapter will explore the interpretation of the Chinese developmental experience in one of the strongest recent rhetorical repudiators of the Washington Consensus, Brazil.

In doing so, the chapter will carry out its own deconstructive process by highlighting the uneasy or invisibilized place of labor regulation in debates about a Chinese model of development – even as such regulation is central to Chinese economic and political development. Rather than arguing that the Beijing Consensus is merely a celebration of the demise of the Washington Consensus, the chapter will argue that the operation of the Beijing Consensus as an anti-model is not simply misguided or feckless but has its own inherent liabilities. While the specific content of the Washington Consensus may, to varying degrees, be normatively undesirable or historically inaccurate, it did stimulate an intellectual counterreaction that emphasized a greater understanding of Western, specifically American, economic development. The fallout from the Washington Consensus also elevated empiricism as a central tool for interrogating/challenging extant development ideologies.

The discourse on the Beijing Consensus has similarly invited greater specific study of China's own economic development, but its operation as an anti-model has made such a lower priority even among many of its critics, who themselves are more often concerned with attacking the idea of China as an exemplar on ideological or geopolitical terms. This aempiricism is to be contrasted with the previously cited explosion of studies concerning Japanese development and governance in the 1980s which spurred a generation of specific legal and economic studies that not only revealed much about the strengths and limits of Japan as a model, but also inaugurated the global growth of comparative corporate law as field, alongside calls for innovation in labor regulation.[2]

As a result, much like the earlier debate on "Asian Values," the popularity of the Beijing Consensus in Brazil and elsewhere carries with it the possibility of a retreat to a renewed domestic parochialism, and with it a more insular development discourse, rather than a more honest engagement with the international development experience of China. In some ways, this is the policy autonomy that critics of the Washington Consensus have lobbied for. The invocation of China in Brazil performs much of this anti-model function, shielding domestic debates in Brazil from the influence of international development discourse. Yet, the underspecified nature of the Beijing Consensus has consequences not only for Sino-Brazilian interactions but also for Brazil's use of international development experiences for stimulating its own domestic reform discourse.

II The Consensus of Nonconsensus

Much has been made of the early twenty-first century as a shift away from the bipolar and unipolar geopolitics of the mid- to late twentieth century. Many of the once vaunted economic and political trends tied to liberalism and democratization have stagnated or faced significant criticism. Nevertheless, knowing what is not happening is far from knowing what is. In framing development itself, even the common evaluative resort to GDP growth has come under scrutiny. This has complicated debates about economic policy in developed and developing countries alike. The retreat from larger development narratives such as the Washington Consensus reflects some recognition that less faith exists for universal development prescriptions, or at the least that there is a wider diversity of possible development narratives from which nations can draw on. This lack of a shared development narrative is what Dani Rodrik refers

[2] Donald Clarke, "'Nothing but Wind'? The Past and Future of Comparative Corporate Governance," *American Journal of Comparative Law* 59 (2011): 75; Marcia Cavens, "Japanese Labor Regulation and the Legal Implications of Their Possible Uses in the United States," *Northwestern Journal of International Law & Business* 5 (1983): 585.

to in his now oft-cited article "Goodbye Washington Consensus, Hello Washington Confusion."[3]

In this context, the idea of the Beijing Consensus has drawn attention because it is derived not only from a non-Western developing country, China, but also because it offers itself up more as a development sensibility than a set of definite policy prescriptions. While John Williamson was able to outline the ten specific policy objectives that came to be associated with the Washington Consensus, no one has been able to articulate the Beijing Consensus in similar terms. Jolted by the Global Financial Crisis in 2008, the appeal of turning to China for development wisdom reflects how the morass of empirical lessons and failures of past development policies has not deadened the hope that somewhere holds out answers that can sideline the intransigent contest of domestic politics.

Tellingly, the original articulation of the Beijing Consensus as such by Joshua Ramo operated at a relatively high level of abstraction. Whatever specific content Ramo advanced about China as an "innovative" economy has been recurrently critiqued,[4] but this has not lessened the circulation of the Beijing Consensus as discourse meme. This circulation does validate in part Ramo's commentary on the Consensus which emphasizes indigenization "where integration of global ideas is first rigorously gut-checked against the demands of local suitability."[5] Subsequent attempts to distill "lessons" from China's development experience frequently return to this quality of empiricism and localization.

Routinely included in the Consensus's more aesthetic qualities is an emphasis on how the state can play a role in leading or coordinating economic development, what McNally calls "refurbished state capitalism."[6] This rejection of the pro-privatization content of the Washington Consensus is an idea that Chinese academics have not been shy about promoting, not the least of which is former World Bank Vice President Justin Yifu Lin.[7] Yet, this is not the corporatist form of state developmentalism of

[3] Dani Rodrik, "Goodbye Washington Consensus, Hello Washington Confusion?," *Journal of Economic Literature* 44 (2006): 973.

[4] Dirlik calls Ramo's model the "Silicon Valley Model of Development," with a misplaced characterization of China's economy as one driven by innovation. Arif Dirlik, *Global Modernity: Modernity in the Age of Global Capitalism* (New York, NY: Paradigm, 2007), 171.

[5] Joshua C. Ramo, *Beijing Consensus* (London: The Foreign Policy Center, 2004), 34.

[6] Christopher McNally, "The Challenge of Refurbished State Capitalism: Implications for the Global Political Economic Order," *Der Moderne Staat* 6 (2013): Art. 3.

[7] Yifu Lin, *The Quest for Prosperity: How Developing Economies Can Take Off* (Princeton, NJ: Princeton University Press, 2012).

earlier eras, but one that promotes private-public coordination through a form of policy experimentalism.[8] All of these qualities define themselves negatively in reference to the Washington Consensus or in reference to the power of prescriptive models writ large. Herein, one tension emerges in the anti-model operation of the Beijing Consensus – it is still sourced from the idea that some universal knowledge has been discovered about development while trying to shift all of its weight to a form of procedurally oriented contextual pragmatism.

The recalcitrant popularity of the Beijing Consensus because of, not in spite of, its anti-model qualities is why attempts to interpret or articulate it in parallel terms to the Washington Consensus have failed. Scott Kennedy has written of the "Myth of the Beijing Consensus,"[9] and even Randal Peerenboom, long a defender of China's development path to date – at least its uncritical judgment by outside commentators – has found the concept of the Beijing Consensus as such wanting.[10] Like every contributor to this book, most academic China experts have rejected the idea that China itself follows a singular, coherent development model,[11] as well as whether its recent development experience should be so easily characterized as a success.[12] Moreover, the very operation of the Beijing Consensus as an anti-model framed as a form of policy pragmatism cannot easily answer normative questions such as whether the CCP's one-child policy reflects a victory of rational planning or a damnable trampling of individual rights.[13]

Even those who are able to distill more general principles from China's recent developmental path,[14] are just as likely to claim that such

[8] Xin Li, Kjeld Erik Brodsgaard, and Michael Jacobsen, "Redefining Beijing Consensus: Ten Economic Principles," Discussion Paper 29 (Asia Research Centre, Copenhagen Business School, 2009), http://openarchive.cbs.dk/bitstream/handle/10398/7830/CDP%202009–029.pdf?sequence=1.

[9] Scott Kennedy, "The Myth of the Beijing Consensus," *Journal of Contemporary China* 19 (2010): 461.

[10] Randall Peerenboom, "China and the Middle-Income Trap: Toward a Post Washington, Post Beijing Consensus," *The Pacific Review* 27 (2014): 651.

[11] Chris Colley, "China's Reforms at 30 and the 'Beijing Consensus,'" *Pambuzuka* 417 (2009): 1. www.pambazuka.net/en/category.php/africa_china/53757.

[12] Dirklif, *Global Modernity*, 9.

[13] Reza Hasmath, "White Cat, Black Cat or Good Cat: The Beijing Consensus as an Alternative Philosophy for Policy Deliberation?," Working Paper 14–02 (Barnett Papers in Social Research, 2014), 7, www.spi.ox.ac.uk/fileadmin/documents/PDF/Barnett_Paper_14-02.pdf.

[14] Dickson has articulated the common principles now invoked: the promotion of "national champions," a focus on developing increased domestic consumption, allocation of public

principles do not represent a model that could serve as a direct reference for other developing countries without China's specific demographic and institutional contexts.[15]

The studies included in this volume are a testament to the gaps in knowledge about China's development in the legal arena. Frank Upham emphasizes the highly contextual nature of the interaction between informal and formal regulation in Chinese property rights, often including illegal and unconstitutional practices (Upham, Chapter 5). In different terms, Yingmao Tang urges us to consider the argument that many legal parallels between China and other countries are not true analogies, but forms of homologous convergence, such as in securities share registration (Tang, Chapter 8). Fu Hualing's study of the Central Committee for Disciplinary Inspection in the anticorruption context and Wei Cui's study of the Chinese lawmaking and administration show how ecologically embedded are key facets of China's legal development (Fu, Chapter 10; Cui, Chapter 4). Further still, Ji Li's attempt to extrapolate lessons from China's often touted tax administration leads him to focus on Beijing Consensus–like practices such as pluralistic comparative learning and internal meritocratic promotion, but he acknowledges that the emergence of these very qualities in China were the result of path-dependent contests within the Chinese state rather than a consciously pursued state policy (Li, Chapter 7).

What remains then is more a discourse on the aesthetics of development discourse than a substantive model. This quality establishes the basic objection advanced by Michael Dowdle in his debate with Mariana Prado, which argues that the Beijing Consensus gives no concrete guidance to actual policy decisions (Dowdle and Prado, Chapter 1). Perhaps the very best example of this ambiguity is that, as Weitseng Chen discusses in Chapter 6, some aspects of China's development in fact continue to follow the prescriptions of the Washington Consensus. Such recognition also informs Curtis Milhaupt's proposal of the more actionable frame of "corporate capitalism" to describe the ways in which China does and does not mesh with global legal experience (Milhaupt, Chapter 11).

By contrast, the one area in which the Beijing Consensus has garnered the most coherent and concrete discussion is not in the realm of

capital towards infrastructure projects, and improving the quality of local governance. Bruce Dickson, "Updating the China Model," *The Washington Quarterly* 34 (2011): 39.

15 Barry Naughton, "China's Distinctive System: Can It Be a Model for Others?," *Journal of Contemporary China* 19 (2010): 437.

domestic Chinese development *per se*, but in Chinese foreign policy. Though still largely defined through its opposition to Western foreign investment practices, China's lack of an overarching normative justification for its foreign investments, such as encouraging democratization or other forms of social development, reflects the Beijing Consensus's putative emphasis on self-determination and sovereignty. While rigorous empirical comparisons are still nascent, whatever China's foreign policies are, they operate outside of, or at least not in coordination with, the policy leveraging practices of international financial institutions such as the World Bank and the International Monetary Fund that were so central to propagating the Washington Consensus.[16] This is why Beeson and Li argue that China in not achieving a "hegemonic transition" that would have it displace the current role of the United States in international affairs.[17] Instead, China acts as a beacon for those who want to achieve independence from the influence of international financial institutions, if not simply the power of US financial sanctions.

Perhaps no better flashpoint of this foreign policy differentiation has been China's engagement with Africa, which has sparked a new flood of academic and popular commentary both laudatory[18] and critical[19] of its deviation from Western practices. Yet, even here studies of China's comparative track record in Africa have been clouded by ideological posturing, only recently yielding to closer empirical study of its actual contours and consequences.[20] Perhaps in this context the assertion of a Beijing Consensus will also lead to concomitant re-interrogation of the foreign policies of Western nations, which in practice are less unlike China than ideological representations would presume.[21] Furthermore, such analysis may expose how China's foreign policy better represents many

[16] Zhimin Chen, "Soft Balancing and Reciprocal Engagement," in *China's Reforms and International Political Economy*, David Zweig and Zhimin Chen (eds.) (Abingdon, UK: Routledge, 2007), 53.

[17] Mark Beeson and Fujian Li, "What Consensus? Geopolitics and Policy Paradigms in China and the United States," *International Affairs* 91 (2015): 93.

[18] Deborah Brautigam, *The Dragon's Gift* (New York: Oxford University Press, 2009).

[19] Stephan Halper, *The Beijing Consensus: How China's Authoritarian Model Will Dominate the Twenty-First Century* (New York: Basic Books, 2010).

[20] Drew Thompson, "China's Soft Power in Africa: From the Beijing Consensus to Health Diplomacy," *China Brief* 5 (2005); Tim Webster, "China's Human Rights Footprint in Africa," *Columbia Journal of Transnational Law* 51 (2013): 626.

[21] "An examination of data on Chinese and US overseas aid shows that both go to approximately the same mix of free and unfree regimes." John Givens, "The Beijing Consensus Is Neither," *St. Antony's International Review* 6 (2011): 10.

ideological positions on economic development advocated in domestic Western political discourse.[22] This parallelism reflects, in part, the fact that Chinese state capitalism is hardly antagonistic to the logic of the current international system, as it is as much, if not more, co-dependent on market capitalism in the United States and elsewhere than it is in competition.

Nonetheless, while the CCP is itself unclear about its global role, it is much more comfortable in asserting regional leadership. Here the more nebulous attributes of the Beijing Consensus also fit this ambivalence nicely. Such ambivalence dogs attempts to define what exactly will be the difference between multilateral institutions such at the BRICS bank and the World Bank. China has already shown that it sees the Asian Infrastructure Investment Bank as a vehicle to leverage its regional influence, not as an attempt to globally symbolize a new form of lending politics.

While the foreign policy context may implicate development ideas by virtue of China's asserted political agnosticism, it does reveal that while the examination of the Beijing Consensus on prescriptive terms may fail because of its anti-model nature, it can enrich development debates when it provokes moves beyond ideological contrasts and into concrete studies of individual policies. Thus, every recurrent declaration of the Beijing Consensus' failure as an emulative model can help foster a better understanding of China's actual development experience. Much of the novel empirical work in this volume exhibits the best promise of this provocation, deepening or understanding of what actually the Chinese legal developmental experience is.[23]

In many ways, these newly stimulated investigations parallel the advances made in understanding Western, especially American, economic history that have emerged out of critiques of the Washington Consensus, such as Ha-Joon Chang's *Kicking Away the Ladder* or renewed interest in historian William Novak's work on the myth of the "weak" American developmental state.[24] While such work has done less to improve the frequency with which more partisan constructions of Western economic

[22] Spalding argues, in the context of the FCPA, that "China is more accurately understood as substantially laissez-faire." He concludes that US foreign policy represents a form of Progressivism at odds with its pro-growth arguments popular in development forums. Andrew Spalding, "The Irony of International Business Law: US Progressivism and China's New Laissez-Faire," *UCLA Law Review* 59 (2011): 354, 361.

[23] For a parallel attempt in the economic realm, see Philip Hsu, Yu-Shan Wu, and Suisheng Zhao (eds.), *In Search of China's Development Model: Beyond the Beijing Consensus* (New York: Routledge, 2011).

[24] Ha-Joon Chang, *Kicking Away the Ladder* (London: Anthem Press, 2003); William Novak, "The Myth of the 'Weak' American State," *American History Review* 113 (2008): 752.

development are still (too often) authoritatively referenced, there is evidence that the anti-model operation of the Beijing Consensus may not preclude stimulating similar improvements in collective understandings of China's recent development, even within China – to the extent that such debates can escape the same form of developmental jingoism still alive in the United States.

III New Experimentalism or Old Parochialism?

Ultimately, normative evaluation of the Beijing Consensus is still very much an open question. Its anti-model elements may result in a beneficial growth in global policy experimentation that its proponents often predict.[25] Here, we can return again to Ramo's own declaration that China provides "hope" for those countries that have failed to reach their own development goals by following the Washington Consensus.[26]

Yet, while there are encouraging signs of greater specific study of China's development experience, there is still a danger inherent in the anti-model aspects of the Beijing Consensus. This danger is that instead of provoking better understanding of the strengths and limitations of China's own development, countries will only invoke China's experience at a high level of abstraction in defensive reaction to the Washington Consensus. This necessitates defending China's development experience solely on the terms of its strength, relative GDP growth, rather than using the many alternative rubrics, such as the Human Development Index, under which its success is less clear.[27]

Such defensive reaction may act as a shield against the pressures of the Washington Consensus. Yet, this defensiveness may never then translate into the policy experimentation, and instead ultimately exacerbate the ever-present gravity of domestic parochialism. Example *par excellence*, the decline of the Washington Consensus has not led to greater policy experimentation in US domestic discourse, but has only intensified the traditional rehashing of ideological visions of US history as the basis of policy debates.

If one desires a more dialogic international discourse on development that can enrich and inform domestic policy debates, then the dominance of an anti-model has severe limitations. An anti-model can

[25] Hasmath, "White Cat, Black Cat or Good Cat," 14. [26] Ramo, *Beijing Consensus*, 60.

[27] "Given the theoretical and policy stakes involved, it is surprising that the debates and discussions on how well China has actually performed have occurred at a very high level of aggregation and have focused on a very narrow set of economic data (mainly GDP)." Yasheng Huang, "Rethinking the Beijing Consensus," *Asia Policy* 11 (2011): 1, 5.

liberate nations from old global dogmas while leaving them to become mired anew in their own insular partisan ideologies. Though this parochialism may legitimately resonate better on some level with democratic norms, it could inhibit experimentation as much as it may liberate domestic policies debates from errant external influence.

IV The Chinese Experience Reconstructed in Brazil

The global popularity of the BRICS acronym – representing Brazil, Russia, India, China, and South Africa – also reflects much of the growing appreciation of, or desire to reinforce, the multipolar world order of the post–Washington Consensus era. These countries' representation of the majority of the world's population, coupled with their recent history of proactive state intervention in economic development, has made the invocation of the BRICS a shorthand for many of the developmental sensibilities associated with the Beijing Consensus. But akin to the Beijing Consensus itself, such popularity has given rise to more questions than answers as to what the BRICS in fact represents. What specific qualities or principles justify their grouping besides simply not being the United States or Europe?

Within the BRICS countries, the grouping of Brazil and China acutely highlights this disjuncture. Both countries conjure up the same implicit consequential import because of the relative size of their populations and, in recent years, shared periods of significant economic growth. However, in policy terms, the two countries have pursued widely divergent approaches in regards to political and social development. Brazil's modern democracy was inaugurated the same year as China's infamous Tiananmen Massacre. Brazil had also followed a much more circumscribed policy of economic internationalization than China, focusing more on building a low-intensity welfare state than a low-wage export manufacturing economy.

Yet, for all their differences, assertions about the rise of the Beijing Consensus often refer to Brazil as an example of its influence. Starting with Ramo himself, statements of former Brazilian President Lula da Silva about China are often cited as evidence of Brazil's turn away from US or European leadership, specifically as an affirmation of developmental autonomy.[28] In addition, in Brazil today, the invocation of China as a

[28] Even Dirlik, critical of the Beijing Consensus itself, cites without critical comment that "the Brazilian leader Lula da Silva expressed his admiration for the PRC and its ability to

development success, if not through the specific language of the Beijing Consensus, has increased in volume and frequency, alongside growing calls for Sino-Brazilian cooperation and reciprocal economic investment in public and private sectors. Furthermore, much of Brazil's recent economic growth, and recent stagnation, is tied to its growing dependence on commodity exports to fuel the Chinese economy.

The increasing intensity of Sino-Brazilian discourse thus offers up the possibility of investigating how China's developmental experience is interpreted outside China as a more direct test of whether China is, in fact, acting as a model for other countries. It is possible to evaluate the Beijing Consensus discourse through its debate in the US or in China.[29] However, beyond examining whether China's experience justifies its portrayal as a coherent model, looking at its impact in a third-party nation provides a less hypothetical lens through which to judge the impact of the Beijing Consensus as an anti-model. Has the idea of a Beijing Consensus opened up new spaces for Brazil's own policy experimentation or has it simply signaled a retrenchment of domestic parochialism?

A The Left–Right Divide in Divining China's Lessons

The twists and turns of Brazilian life in the twentieth century did much to consume the attention of domestic policy makers. Though impacted by its own postcolonial history and transnational influences, the geographic and demographic scale of Brazilian politics as it oscillated between democratic and dictatorial regimes left the country comparatively insulated from the forces of globalization that rendered many developing countries susceptible to the policy pressures of the Washington Consensus. Even so, after Brazil's democratic transition in 1989, the macroeconomic policies of its early administrations were focused on battling historic inflation and included waves of privatization not completely at odds with some of the specific policy content of the Washington Consensus. The election of former union leader Lula da Silva in 2002 did not result in a full repudiation of these more conservative economic polices, but in

pursue an integrated development, and to globalize without giving up its autonomy and sovereignty." Dirlik, *Global Modernity*, 157.

[29] E.g., Wei Pan, "Dangdai zhonghua tizhi – zhongguo moshi de jingji, zhengzhi, shehui jiexi" [The Contemporary Chinese System – An Analysis of the Economic, Political and Social of the China Model], in *Zhongguo moshi: jiedu renmin gongheguo de 60 nian* [The China Model: Interpreting Sixty Years of the People's Republic], Wei Pan (ed.) (Beijing: Zhejiang renmin chubanshe, 2009).

a substantial focus on partially reallocating Brazil's growing economic prosperity toward improving aspects of Brazil's social development and combating economic inequality.

In this light, Lula's approving citation of China mentioned earlier is understandable as his turn to social development represented a rejection of the principles of austerity and state nonintervention associated with the Washington Consensus. At the same time, Lula's rhetorical assertions about China were never concretely associated with any reform agenda that could be even loosely tied to China's developmental experience, or greater Brazilian public investments in the study of China. Here, Lula defensively appropriated the discourse on China in exactly the anti-model fashion, legitimating his move away from his domestic political competition to create space for Brazilian policy independence. Lula's diplomatic gestures toward China more genuinely reflected the shared foreign policy norms of the Beijing Consensus of self-determination and sovereignty, again still without embracing any specific aspect of Chinese foreign policy.

If we turn away from defensive rhetorical invocations to specific studies of China's development in Brazil, there is much less to substantiate the idea that the Beijing Consensus has stimulated any specific Brazilian arguments for Chinese policy emulation. The general idea that China represents a development success has been interpreted through the lens of Brazilian politics, especially in recent years as the Brazilian economic downturn has led many to question how Brazil can reinvigorate its recent developmental success. Nevertheless, the defensive anti-model operation of the Beijing Consensus has been unable to supply Brazil with anything more than a way to partially rebuff orthodox neoliberal prescriptions.

The first dynamic to highlight in Brazilian interpretations of Chinese development is a still evident generational gap, whereby younger generations are more open to thinking positively about China than the generation that came of age during Brazil's democratic transition. In popular discourse, there exists the same sort of antiauthoritarian discourse found in many new democracies, asserting that China is an inappropriate model for Brazilian renewal because of its political structure. Representative of this view is Clóvis Rossi, one of the longest running columnists for Brazil's most widely circulated newspaper, *Folha de São Paulo*. In a recent piece, "A China Pode Ser Um Modelo" (Can China Serve as a Model?), Rossi emphasizes that Brazil's establishment of social democracy precludes learning from China, and he expresses concern that its hard-won democratization would be threatened by implicitly validating

China's development experience.[30] Rossi explicitly cites political repression in China as a reason to deflect consideration of emulating China, and in his other writings he questions the relevance of the BRICS designation along similar lines.[31]

Rossi also exemplifies the traditional political cleavage in Brazilian views of China, as many left-wing writers focus on the authoritarian nature of China, and substantively criticize its lack of social rights, especially in regards to labor and the environment. Some go beyond criticism to argue that Brazil's development is by comparison superior to that of China. Representative of this view is historian João Fábio Bertonha, who in 2008, during the height of the Brazilian economic boom under Lula, wrote a series of articles evaluating whether other countries offered up a better model than that currently pursued by Brazil.[32] In his article "Modelos para o Brasil: China?," Bertonha wrote that because of Brazil's own successes, "the 'Chinese model' in Brazil, would actually be a step back."[33]

More economically liberal elements in Brazilian politics react differently to the use of China as an exemplar. They fear its validation of state capitalism as indirectly justifying Lula's social democratic policies, which they see as built solely on the neoliberal reforms of the 1990s and propped up by the decade's unusual commodities supercycle. Yet, even as China has come to represent the revival of state intervention in economic development, the recent Brazilian economic downturn has also reconfigured

[30] "For my part, I prefer Brazil, notwithstanding its many flaws. If one takes the 1989 Elections in Brazil, same year of the Tiananmen Square massacre, as the event that consolidated re-democratization, whereas China maintained itself in a dictatorship able to lead its citizens to 'total submission,' as Shen Tong puts it, in here [Brazil] we live in the longest yet recorded period of public liberties enforcement." Clóvis Rossi, "A China Pode Ser um Modelo?," *Folha de São Paulo*, June 5, 2014.

[31] "[BRICS] is not about a group of countries that coordinates its actions by following the same path, but instead a group of countries with different stories, institutions, policies, and economies." Clóvis Rossi, "Emergentes Para Sempre," *Folha de São Paulo*, December 22, 2013.

[32] Like many left-leaning activists of the older generation, Bertonha ultimately concludes that the best model for Brazil is Brazil. João Fábio Bertonha, "Modelos Para o Brasil. Final," *Revista Espaco Academico* 86 (2008).

[33] Ibid. Bertaonha noted that "Brazil is in a stage, in terms of modernity, far from the Chinese. Our population is mostly urban and its education and income levels are slightly better, which reflects our higher aspirations and expectations. We have labor and environmental laws that, although certainly far from perfect or fully enforced, are better than their Chinese counterparts. Lastly, we live in a democracy (imperfect as it may be, but a democracy nonetheless), which prevents the State from controlling society to the level necessary to promote changes as intense and fast [as in China]. The 'Chinese model,' in Brazil, would actually be a step back."

this liberal argument. Especially among younger liberals, China is often cast in a much less negative light. In fact, the idea that China represents a continued developmental success has led to arguments that China shows how the recent expansion of social rights in Brazil is in fact itself a causal factor in Brazilian economic decline. Representative of this view is Samuel Pessoa, an economist at the Instituto Brasileiro de Economia of FGV-Rio. Pessoa compares China's globally high savings rate to Brazil's globally low savings rate as explained by the growth of Brazil's welfare state, which has in return retarded long-term economic growth.[34] Such arguments do not make an argument against Brazilian democracy per se, but bypasses the issue of politics by using China to critique the same Brazilian developments that Rossi and Bertonha champion.[35] Here China is invoked closer to the ideal of a developmental model forwarded by Dowdle in Chapter 1 – a developmental success that putatively resolves contentious domestic debates.

There also appears to be a similar generational shift on the Brazilian left, where, while China's authoritarian policies do not go unnoted, the idea of China's developmental success has been interpreted not as a call for fewer social rights, but for greater levels of social investment. This discourse focuses on the international studies that highlight China's high investments in education,[36] infrastructure,[37] and state-led research and development.[38] Even at the outset of the Lula administration, many in Brazil were highlighting that state-led development required more than

[34] "When comparing Brazil to China, there seems to be strong indications that the Brazilian welfare social network, implemented during the past 16 years, and the labor market institutions – right to strikes, freedom for trade unions, etc. – can explain a significant part of the gap between Brazil's (15 to 19 percent GDP) and China's (45 to 55 percent GDP) domestic savings." Samuel Pessoa, "Modelo de Desenvolvimento Brasileiro," *Poupanca* 63 (2009).

[35] There is still some nostalgia for the authoritarian developmental policy of the pre-1989 military dictatorship in Brazil, recently on display in the recent re-election of Lula's success Dilma Rousseff. (Ricardo Chapola, "Protesto Contra Dilma Fecha Parte da Avenida Paulista," *Estado Conteudo*, November 1, 2014, http://exame.abril.com.br/brasil/noticias/protesto-contra-dilma-fecha-parte-da-av-paulista.)

[36] Martin Carnoy, "Higher Education and Economic Development: India, China and the 21st Century," Working Paper No. 297 (Stanford Center for International Development, 2006), http://scid.stanford.edu/publications/higher-education-and-economic-development-india-china-and-21st-century.

[37] Pravakar Sahoo, Ranjan Kumar Dash, and Geethanjali Nataraj, "Infrastructure Development and Economic Growth in China," IDE Discussion Paper No. 261 (Institute of Developing Economics, 2010), www.ide.go.jp/English/Publish/Download/Dp/pdf/261.pdf.

[38] Wim Naudé, Adam Szirmai and Alejandro Lavopa, "Industrialization Lessons from BRICS: A Comparative Analysis," Discussion Paper No. 7543 (Institute for the Study of Labor, 2013), http://repec.iza.org/dp7543.pdf.

just state ownership or industrial favoritism, but the coordination of public and private investments.[39]

These shifts toward openness in invoking the Chinese experience have found common ground across the Brazilian political spectrum in the broadly shared interpretation that the Chinese state represents an advanced form of bureaucratic efficiency. Luiz Carlos Mendonça, notable as the former President of the Brazilian Development Bank (BNDES), recently invoked China as a developing country, which, unlike Brazil, continued to build on its past successes because its administrative class was proactive while Brazilian administration was mired in politics.[40] Evandro Menezes de Carvalho, a professor at FGV-Rio who is currently engaged in a variety of academic exchanges with China, has also promoted China as an exemplar of organized policy experimentation within a long-term state-led development plan, a version of the Beijing Consensus model that he advances as nevertheless accommodating and enhancing democratic norms.[41]

B Anti-modeling and Comparative Analysis?

At first glance, these recent shifts in Brazilian citation of the Chinese experience seem to validate the idea that the Beijing Consensus can spur the

[39] Guilherme José Korte, a Brazilian journalist then living in China, and Sérgio Miranda-da-Cruz, Agri-business Development Director for the United Nations Industrial Development Organization, argued that "in China, despite different characteristics in each case, there is preliminary evidence that knowledge, generated and absorbed in research centers and in some universities has been incorporated into production." Guilherme José Korte and Sérgio Miranda-da-Cruz, "O Desafio do Desenvolvimento Sustentável e a Experiência Chinesa," *Con Jur*, February 3, 2003.

[40] "What has called the attention of some of the most respected analysts is the fact that a new generation of administrators has demonstrated courage in changing China's orientation, even when success has already been reached. This is uncommon among political administrators, who most of the time are slaved to past success and cannot move forward." Luiz Carlos Mendonça, "De Gastos, Ratos e Mercados," *Folha de São Paulo*, March 7, 2014.

[41] "In the debate regarding public administration, China might be able to give us some ideas: we could be more open to institutional experimentation before implementing definitive measures, which would reduce the risk of wasting resources and also minimize law's inefficiency; we could also have more significant participation from research centers in planning governmental action, which would grant more legitimacy to the process; lastly, we could establish an effective compromise with the people's future through long-term action plans protected from political interference. But that would not be enough. The manifestations in June 2013 were an important warning and are still present today. Administrative efficiency's growth must happen within a democratic process, so that one dimension supports the other." Evandro Menezes de Carvalho, "Lições do Modelo Chinês," *Folha de São Paulo*, April 26, 2014.

type of pragmatic experimentalism that many of its proponents value. On some level, moving beyond reactive rejection of any analysis of China's developmental experience because of its authoritarian political structure is an advancement in this regard, as a great deal of comparative development work today has sought to transcend this genre of reflexive dismissal.[42] Moreover, these Brazilian invocations of China are not driven by Chinese pressure, or submission to the policy preference of China-influenced international institutions.

However, if one presses forward into this apparently more open discourse, discovering instances of rigorous Brazilian comparative evaluation of specific Chinese legal and administrative practices is as lacking as the anti-model claim would predict. If pragmatism is key to the development sensibility embodied in the Beijing Consensus, then such analysis would be necessary to see how China's experiential lessons could be indigenized in Brazil, or what contextual barriers might need to be overcome for their translation. Beyond Brazil's democratic political context, there are many institutional differences in how Brazil's legal and administrative practices diverge from China's vast and ever-changing regulatory landscape.

Yet, the most common form of comparative analysis practiced in Brazil regarding China is of the broad macroeconomic species cited earlier, focusing almost exclusively on GDP growth. Such comparative work can provide some points of general illumination, but displays little systemic understanding of how China's development operates in practice, and can easily make the type of correlation/causation slippages routinely criticized in past and current examinations of the Washington Consensus. Similarly, within international relations scholarship, the still vibrant Brazilian postcolonial aversion to global hegemons often is preoccupied with applying the postcolonial frame to Sino-Brazilian relations rather than identifying its specific character in Brazil or elsewhere.[43]

Moreover, the lessons presumed to extend from the Chinese example to Brazil are hardly novel internationally, or even in Brazil. Arguments from the Brazilian right that high levels of social rights can retard economic growth or from the Brazilian left for greater social investment have formed

[42] Most notably in new studies of legal reform and performance under authoritarian regimes. For example, see Tom Ginsburg and Tamir Moustafa, *Rule by Law: The Politics of Courts in Authoritarian Regimes* (New York: Cambridge University Press, 2008).

[43] Javier Vadell, Leonardo Ramos, and Pedro Neves, "The International Implications of the Chinese Model of Development in the Global South," *Revista Brasileira de Politica Internacional* [Brazilian Review of International Politics] 57 (2014): 91.

the very grist of Brazilian political debates over the past two decades. Thus, self-interested citations of China on both sides of these debates reveal less new understanding of China than strategic rhetoric around preexisting political preferences, which remains the ever-present pitfall of shallow comparative analysis classically highlighted by Otto Kahn-Freund.[44]

This Brazilian dynamic thus only replicates the same type of developmental generalities that proponents of the Beijing Consensus often resort to in their definitional contortions. It does not require a focus on the Chinese experience, for example, to claim that Brazil should "learn" that it is a better long-term economic strategy to promote value-added manufacturing rather than resource extraction, or that scientific research investments have high long-term social returns.[45] Such generalities have bled over into research on "lessons" from BRICS studies,[46] where Brazil is urged to be more like China by promoting the international competitiveness of its industries, the calling card of Marcos Troyjo, international policy entrepreneur and head of Columbia University's BricLab.[47] Or that Brazil simply needs to make its economy friendlier to private investment, which China is often interpreted as having done.[48]

Perhaps to some extent such arguments are true, but they certainly do not require any specific examination of China's development experience to propound. One can easily critique the mix of economic protectionism and domestic oligopoly promoted by the Dilma administration, even in the context of Sino-Brazilian relations, without reference to China's

[44] Otto Kahn-Freund, "On Uses and Misuses of Comparative Law," *Modern Law Review* 37 (1974): 1.

[45] Raul Gouvea and Manuel Montoya, "Brazil & China: Partners or Competitors?," *Asian Journal of Latin American Studies* 26 (2013): 1, 7; Luciana Acioly, Eduardo Costa Pinto, and Marcos Antonio Macedo Cintra, "As Relações Bilaterais Brasil-China: A Ascensão da China no Sistema Mundia e os Desafíos Para o Brasil," *Comunicados do IPEA* 85 (2000): 3–17.

[46] Carl Dahlman, "Innovation Strategies of Three of the BRICS: Brazil, India and China-What Can We Learn from Three Different Approaches" (Paper presented at the conference for the Sanjaya Lall Program for Technology and Management for Development, University of Oxford, Oxford, May 29–30, 2008).

[47] Troyjo has consistently written on this topic over the past decade, but a summary of his view can be seen in a recent editorial: Marcus Troyjo, "Brasil, Chines de Menos" [Brazil, Too Little (of) China], *Instituto Millenium*, November 15, 2014, http://imil.org.br/artigos/brasil-chins-de-menos/.

[48] Journalist commentator Bill Emmott goes through all of the motions of noting Brazil and China's differences but summarily ends with this generalized pro-private investment claims. Bill Emmott, "Can Brazil Emulate China?," *Exame*, October 2007, www.billemmott.com/article.php?id=116.

pro-export industrial track record.[49] Furthermore, such exhortations all provide little concrete illumination of actual Chinese practices or show how such truisms are to be specifically achieved in Brazil.

This generality and lack of specific comparative analysis can be partially explained by understandable path-dependent deficiencies in Sino-Brazilian understanding. Brazil possesses few traditional cultural resources or historical connections to facilitate its understanding of China, and this deficiency runs in both directions of the Sino-Brazilian relationship.[50] The barrier of Brazil's status as a global minority-language nation is exacerbated by the debatable merit of Brazilian academia's traditional resistance to professional internationalization.[51] Furthermore, in contrast to China, Brazil lacks the same sort of globally dispersed diaspora seeking to inform domestic development that China drew on after its post-1978 international reopening.[52] There are new Sino-Brazilian exchanges and academic joint ventures that seek to remedy this lack of understanding,[53] but, as with the Beijing Consensus more broadly, most of the energy of such exchanges are in the foreign policy or international arena, such as the newly announced "BRICS bank."

This gap in understanding is at best only a partial explanation of a lack of Brazilian engagement with the specifics of Chinese development. Brazil has shown itself open to policy experimentation based on foreign experience, such as the bifurcation of its national stock exchange to allow space for international corporate governance standards, and regional experience, such as the influence of Colombia's policing practices in recent urban pacification reforms.[54] Here we can clearly see the downside of the operation of the Beijing Consensus as an anti-model, as while China

[49] Gouvea and Montoya, "Brazil & China: Partners or Competitors?," 9. It is also of note that the Dilma administration initially resisted promoting Sino-Brazilian trade than did the Lula administration.

[50] Ruichen Zheng, "A Percepcao Academica Chinesa Sobre o Brasil e a Relacao Bilateral" (M.A. thesis, University of Sao Paulo, 2014).

[51] "With the exception of Brazil, which has managed to hold on to an internal rating system that includes publications in its own Portuguese-language journals, scholars in all these countries face pressures toward professionalization, making them accountable to international peers rather than domestic publics." Michael Burawoy, "The Global Turn: Lessons from Southern Labor Scholars and Their Labor Movements," *Work and Occupations* 36 (2009): 87, 91.

[52] Colley, "China's Reforms at 30 and the 'Beijing Consensus.'"

[53] Notably, the Brazilian Institute of Economics of Getulio Vargas Foundation (IBRE-FGV) and the Institute of Latin American Studies of the Chinese Academy of Social Sciences.

[54] Graham Willis and Mariana Prado, "Process and Pattern in Institutional Reforms," *World Development* 64 (2014): 232; Henry Hansmann, Ronald J. Gilson, and Mariana Pargendler, "Regulatory Dualism as a Development Strategy," *Stanford Law Review* 63 (2011): 475.

is routinely discussed and invoked, the amorphous nature of the Beijing Consensus has done little to stimulate actual policy experimentation or comparative learning in Brazil, and is used solely to reinforce the terms of extant parochial debates.

The fluid and often contradictory ways in which the "lessons" of China's asserted developmental sensibilities of "pragmatism" or "experimentation" are invoked in Brazil are evidence that without robust comparative understanding, there is no indigenization of international experience. There is only a rehashing of well-worn truisms without novel insight into how they can be achieved in particular local conditions.

V Eliding Labor Rights in China's Developmental Trajectory

Perhaps the most glaring example of the anti-model quality of the Beijing Consensus is the invisibility of labor regulation in discussions of China's development "success." Typical discussions of Chinese development generally characterize China, and sometimes Chinese "culture," as valuing economic growth over the values of liberal democracy.[55] Such comparisons speak more often to ideology than they do to concrete practices, but it is certainly true that the Chinese Communist Party (CCP) has prioritized maintaining China's recent levels of economic growth at the expense of other indices of social development. Most centrally, it has prioritized maintaining its monopoly over Chinese politics. In this context, there is a common conflation between the CCP's neglect of social rights with a lack of labor rights, or a presumed "Chinese" satisfaction or revealed preference for an export model based on low-wage labor.

However, many of these traditional characterizations are neither true nor do they elucidate how central labor regulation is to whatever "model" of development China may represent today or in recent Chinese history.[56] Like many of the studies cited above that are pessimistic about deriving a generalizable model from China's development, the nature of Chinese labor regulation has shifted enormously over the past three decades while China has been subject to rampant and increasing labor protest.[57] Moreover, the CCP's consistent repression of labor unrest reflects not

[55] Mark Leonard, *What Does China Think?* (New York, NY: Public Affairs, 2008).

[56] See generally Jackie Sheehan, *Chinese Workers: A New History* (New York: Routledge, 1998).

[57] Mary Gallagher, Song Jing, and Huong Trieu, "Bottom-Up Enforcement: Legal Mobilization as Law Enforcement in the PRC" (Paper presented at the Annual Meeting of the American Political Science Association, September 2–5, 2010); Feng Chen, "Privatization and Its Discontents in Chinese Factories," *China Quarterly* 185 (2006): 42–43.

simply a judgment about optimal wage levels or a desire to attract foreign direct investment, but also a judgment that labor organization, especially private unionization, represents a preeminent challenge to its political authority.[58] Thus, actual studies of labor relations in China recurrently remind us that any developmental experience cannot be reduced to economic policies, but will always be grounded in political models composed of a variety of allocative decisions among social stakeholders, or at least those empowered to influence such decisions.[59]

This is not stated to revive the notion that China's development is inapt for study by democratic regimes, but to argue that any attempt to construct a developmental model would best begin by understanding the intertwining of economics and politics through labor law, of which China is a prime example. Furthermore, the CCP's political motivations for repressing workplace rights have not been uniform, as it has sought to privilege nonassociative employment rights and forms of corporatist bargaining through its public union structure, the All China Federation of Trade Unions (ACFTU). As such, there are many comparative parallels in the contemporary developmental experiences of Western and non-Western countries alike.[60] Yet, even this strategic decision by the CCP is itself hard to qualify as part of an emulatable Chinese Model, as the continued rise of labor protest in China is now cited with increasing frequency as undermining the CCP's political legitimacy and its claims to developmental success.

Initially, such a characterization would appear to support the claims by those like Rossi who see Brazil's emphasis on labor rights as a rejoinder to recent assertions that Brazil should learn from China. In fact, outside of Brazil itself, Brazil's system of mandatory sectoral unionization and formally strong employment protections are sometimes cited as an alternative to a Chinese labor model,[61] or as lessons for China on the importance of social rights.[62] Such a view can even be found cited from within China itself.[63]

58 See generally Ching Kwan Lee, *Against the Law* (Los Angeles: University of California Press, 2007).
59 Yongnian Zheng, "China: An Emerging Power, Is Exploring Its Own Development Model," *China Economist* 1 (2010): 71.
60 Jedidiah Kroncke, "Property Rights, Labor Rights and Democratization," *NYU Journal of International Law and Politics* 46 (2013): 115.
61 Musab Younis, "BRICS: Let's Talk about Labour," *Open Democracy*, May 14, 2013, www.opendemocracy.net/musab-younis/brics-let%E2%80%99s-talk-about-labour.
62 Geoff Dyer, "Brazil's Lessons for China," *Financial Times*, March 3, 2008.
63 Chen Weihua, "Labor Rights Make a World of Difference," *China Daily*, July 6, 2012. http://usa.chinadaily.com.cn/opinion/2012–07/06/content_15554198.htm.

There is also mounting experiential evidence that dissonance in the Brazilian and Chinese models of labor regulation has in fact stymied Sino-Brazilian economic interaction. For while both Brazilian and Chinese leaders have recognized the importance of the Sino-Brazilian trade, there has been great difficulty, especially for Brazil, in moving beyond its traditional commodity-export structure to promote more diverse cross-national investment in either economy. Less than one percent of FDI in China comes from Brazil,[64] but in recent years China has become one of the leading providers of FDI in Brazil. However, this flow of Chinese FDI has focused primarily on facilitating Chinese state-owned enterprises' access to Brazilian natural resources, rather than developing domestic Brazilian manufacturing or innovation.[65]

Attempts to further expand Chinese investments in Brazil outside of resource extraction have run into a number of problems specifically because of Chinese expectations that Brazilian unions would replicate the same disciplining and facilitative function as that performed by Chinese state-run unions.[66] Such conflicts, coupled with the recent downturn in the Brazilian economy, have led to the cancellation or suspension of a wide range of Chinese investments in Brazil.[67] Reciprocally, Brazilian executives working for Chinese firms have exhibited a markedly higher turnover rate than that of any other national demographic.[68]

These summary descriptions are far from a coherent explication of the role of China labor practices in Beijing Consensus discourse, or its comparative analysis with Brazil labor regulation. Simply put, the very absence of such explication points to the empirical superficiality of the Beijing Consensus as a "model," in large part because labor regulation is unavoidably political. The contested trade-offs and clash of values inherent in debates over labor render them anathema to the politics-transcending aspiration of development models, even as the inclusion of labor would be structurally necessary for any truly schematic understanding of China's, or any other country's, political economy. Yet, the Beijing Consensus

64 China-Brazil Business Council, *Brazilian Companies in China* (Rio de Janerio: CBBC, 2013), 11.

65 China-Brazil Business Council, *Chinese Investments in Brazil* (Rio de Janerio: CBBC, 2013), 5, 8.

66 Qingqing Miao, "An Urge to Protect Is Not Enough: China's Labor Contract Law," *Tsinghua China Law Review* 2 (2009): 179.

67 Brian Winter and Caroline Stauffer, "China Has Soured on Brazil," *Business Insider*, November 1, 2013.

68 Bradley Brooks, "Cultural Clash Complicates China's Brazil Push," *Associated Press*, May 28, 2011.

as an anti-model can elide such and continue to fall back on more abstract aesthetic regarding developmental sensibilities.

VI Learning from the Limits of China and Brazil's Successes

The difficulties in expanding Sino-Brazilian investment are not solely rooted in different regimes of labor regulation. However, the challenges generated by attempts to navigate these differences clearly show that while democratic and authoritarian regimes can become quite deeply economically intertwined, such intertwining requires a level of logistical coordination, and mutual understanding that is well beyond their current levels in Sino-Brazilian affairs. Thus, while rhetorical assertions that Brazil should learn from China, or even vice-versa, continue to be popular, they also reflect the inherent weakness of the current anti-model function of the Beijing Consensus.

Sino-Brazilian trade is certainly important to both countries, but such importance has been limited by a shared lack of workable comparative knowledge. For Brazil specifically, while multilateral international cooperation with China may still be a possibility, whatever consonance exists as a mutual desire to insulate Brazil's development agenda from the West seems to have only amplified parochialism and hardened pre-existing partisan debates. This stands in stark contrast to the flowering of policy experimentalism such insulation could hypothetically allow, especially one based on the Chinese version of policy pragmatism. Whatever value there may be in the developmental sensibilities putatively ensconced in the Beijing Consensus, its anti-model quality seems in its Brazilian instantiation to be all shield and no sword. In fact, it is a shield that darkens debate rather than frees it in order to flourish.

Forwarding this conclusion does not mean that the Chinese developmental experience is irrelevant to Brazil, even in the realm of labor. What it does mean is that such translating such relevance into actual policy experimentation is inhibited by the Beijing Consensus frame as such, a consensus. For example, while labor regulation in China and Brazil are technically quite distinct, there are many similarities in the challenges faced by union structures in managing workers' discontent. While Brazil's formally private union system does actively and routinely embrace collective striking so anathema to the CCP's ACFTU, both systems have functionally resorted to forms of corporatist wage bargaining that have largely circumvented direct worker participation in union decision making or promoted any form of competition in worker representation.[69] Just as the ACFTU has been challenged to contain labor protest in China, workers' discontent with their union representation in Brazil has led to unauthorized strikes, a fact strikingly on global display during Brazil's recent hosting of the World Cup.[70] Such tensions represent common pathways by which state developmental priorities can bypass formal differences in labor law implementation, and drive the subordination of long-term worker interests to the short-term institutional interests of union leadership who have deep corporatist ties to existing political arrangements.[71]

Moreover, outside of union organization, China and Brazil both face common challenges in labor regulation that transcend their formal structural differences, including the prevalence of informal and subcontracted work,[72] the victimization of migrant labor,[73] and the continued role of forced labor in both countries.[74] In all of these instances, the centrality of labor inspectors for the enforcement of Brazilian labor laws may, over time, have much to learn from the ongoing Chinese embrace of new governance modes of employer supervision that proactively seek to

[69] Ana Gomes and Mariana Prado, "Flawed Freedom of Association in Brazil: How Unions Can Become an Obstacle to Meaningful Reforms in the Labor Law System," *Comparative Labor and Policy Journal* 32 (2011): 843, 869; Marco Santana and Ruy Braga, "Brazil: The Swinging Pendulum Between Labor Sociology and Labor Movement," *Work and Occupations* 36 (2009): 96. For parallel critiques in China, see Mingwei Liu, "Union Organizing in China: Still a Monolithic Labor Movement?," *Industrial and Labor Relations Review* 64 (2011): 35.

[70] Claudia Costa, "Brazilian Workers Buck Union Officials to Strike," *Labor Notes*, June 23, 2014, http://labornotes.org/2014/06/brazilian-workers-buck-union-officials-strike.

[71] Simon Deakin, Colin Fenwick, and Prabirjit Sarkar, "Labor Law and Inclusive Development," Working Paper No. 447 (Centre for Business Research, University of Cambridge, 2013): 9, www.cbr.cam.ac.uk/fileadmin/user_upload/centre-for-business-research/downloads/working-papers/wp447.pdf; María Cook, "Labor Reform and Dual Transitions in Brazil and the Southern Cone," *Latin American Policy and Society* 44 (2002): 2; Anil Verma and Ana Gomes, "Labor Market Flexibility and Trajectories of Development," *Indian Journal of Industrial Relations* 60 (2014): 51.

[72] Chris Tilly et al., "Informal Worker Organizing as a Strategy for Improving Subcontracted Work in the Textile and Apparel Industries of Brazil, South Africa, India and China," *UCLA Institute for Research on Labor and Employment* (2013): 120.

[73] Aaron Halegua, "Getting Paid: Processing the Labor Disputes of China's Migrant Workers," *Berkeley Journal of International Law* 26 (2008): 254; Patricia Mallen, "Migrant Workers from Haiti Building 2014 World Cup Stadiums in Brazil Denounce Inhumane Conditions," *International Business Times*, February 4, 2014.

[74] Elise Labott, "Forced Labor Fuels Development," *CNN.com*, June 4, 2008, http://edition.cnn.com/2008/US/06/04/human.trafficking/.

address popular dissatisfaction that is now re-emerging in Brazil, and vice-versa.[75]

It is most certain that, as critical scholarship on development has long shown, there is unlikely to be any unidirectional quality to the flow of knowledge from genuinely comparative analysis of the Chinese and Brazilian developmental experiences. The desire to overlook China's developmental failures and cast China as a "success" ripe for extrapolation into a model is as shallow as recent pessimism about Brazil's development as justifying sidelining its own comparative successes in poverty alleviation. Herein, the anti-model quality of the Beijing Consensus may be more damaging for promoting comparative developmental learning than the Washington Consensus ever was, as it trades specific comparison for caricatures of China's development experience. At the end of the day, this inhibits constructive Brazilian learning from China and also displaces any systematic study of the wider range of developmental experiences in East Asia and beyond.

Improving Sino-Brazilian understanding will thus require more than the same rehashing of established developmental truisms or uncritical appropriations along existing political divisions. Instead what is needed is the careful building up of smaller-scale comparative analyses that take the different historical trajectories and starting points of Chinese and Brazilian development seriously.[76] While such studies are currently rare, they are not unknown, and range from more familiar development topics, such as compulsory licensing,[77] to the less familiar, such as landscape restoration projects.[78] Putting aside the notion of a Beijing Consensus, or even the BRICS designation, may also allow for the integration of these

[75] Christina Chen, "The Politics of Labor Protection in Authoritarian Systems: Evidence from Labor Law and Enforcement in Post-Reform China" (PhD diss., UC San Diego, 2011).

[76] For example, one comparative study of poverty reduction notes the often overlooked point that China's post-1978 economic reforms started from quite low inequality after systemic social revolution, whereas Brazil started in 1989 with high relative inequality after decades, if not centuries, without systemic social revolution. Martin Ravallion, "A Comparative Perspective on Poverty Reduction in Brazil, China and India," Working Paper No. 5080 (World Bank Policy Research, 2009), www-wds.worldbank.org/servlet/WDSContentServer/WDSP/IB/2009/11/30/000158349_20091130085835/Rendered/PDF/WPS5080.pdf.

[77] Robert Ahdieh et al., "The Existing Legal Infrastructure of BRICs: Where Have We Been and Where Are We Going?," *Northwestern Journal of Technology and Intellectual Property* 5 (2007): 503.

[78] Kathleen Buckingham et al., "Building BRICS in Restoration – The China–Brazil Landscape Restoration Exchange," *WRI Blog*, December 9, 2014, www.wri.org/blog/2014/12/building-brics-restoration%E2%80%94-china-brazil-landscape-restoration-exchange.

geopolitically significant developmental experiences within the already robust historically comparative framework employed by the varieties of capitalism literature.[79]

While China and Brazil are certainly globally important economies, there is no reason that they should ultimately find comparative lessons in each other's development than, as Mariana Prado argues in the introduction by way of Peter Evans, either would from Taiwan, Estonia, or Mexico. Such openness coupled with an appreciation for focused and empirically rigorous comparative studies – free from the distraction of any presumed consensus – is far more likely to lead to the desired interplay of experimentation and pragmatism than is the current retreat to parochialism that the inchoate Beijing Consensus has inspired.

Even experimentalism itself as a development aesthetic has its limits.[80] These limits are important to consider as development scholars, including Mariana Prado in Chapter 1, argue that a principled proceduralism is an advancement over the type of prescriptive model represented by the Washington Consensus. Therefore, while the Beijing Consensus's anti-model functions may inhibit the type of contextual comparative developmental analysis hoped for in this chapter, this is less a failure if, for example, Brazil is left to "muddle" its way through domestic experiments, carried out using scientifically rigorous policy experimentalism. While proving that the shield of the Beijing Consensus has led to a marked uptick in such experimentalism in Brazil is an empirical point worthy of specific study, it is hard to see an explosion in innovative experimentalism outside of what Prado herself has studied.[81]

Yet, if China is any guide to the possibilities of experimentalism, it must be remembered that, for all its international variations, such experimentalism is still at the margins of large political choices about the structure of the Chinese economy. "Modeling" thus is itself inevitable when any modern economy has to integrate various social and economic sectors into a cohesive whole. Labor regulation again helps remind us that no amount of pragmatic tinkering can change the basic logic of a system that invariably implicates the interests of multiple stakeholders. Purely episodic experimentalism would, taken to its extreme, lead to a form

[79] M. Ulric Killion, "Post-Global Financial Crisis: The Measure of the 'Beijing Consensus' as a Variety of Capitalisms," *Social Science Research Network*, doi:10.2139/ssrn.1701868.

[80] For a contrast, see Li, Chapter 7.

[81] Mariana Prado and Ana Chasin, "How Innovative Was the Poupatempo Experience in Brazil? Institutional Bypass as a New Form of Institutional Change," *Brazilian Political Science Review* 5 (2011): 11.

of piecemeal institutional thicketing more prone to conflicts than synergies within a development regime. The alternative is not re-embracing a universally prescriptive model, but acknowledging that national system design is never wholly a scientific exercise, but a political one. For better or worse, the centrality of CCP dominance in China is but one such species of political choice which will always subordinate experimentalism. The current crisis of faith in governance in Brazil similarly reflects the fact that no amount of technocracy in development can solve intractably political conflicts.

Thus, this chapter returns to the relative promise of comparativism over experimentalism as the unfulfilled promise of the Beijing Consensus. Comparativism, done well, invites both scientific analysis while reminding one of the political context of law. However false or damaging the Washington Consensus may have been, if we are otherwise simply left to expend our energies muddling through narrow experiments with no developmental vision in mind, then our prospects as development scholars are quite dim. The shield of the Beijing Consensus would only leave us to scramble and reformulate our agendas with every inevitable turn of national politics. Hopefully, there is more to aspire for in China, Brazil, the United States, and in every other country facing the lack of sure answers to what continue to be pressing issues across the spectrum of development challenges.

3

The Beijing Consensus and Possible Lessons from the "Singapore Model"?

TAN CHENG-HAN*

I Introduction

China's model of development, often referred to as the 'Beijing Consensus,' involves a high degree of control for the state. Such control goes beyond economic planning and includes state-owned enterprises (SOEs) that are active participants in many sectors of the economy from manufacturing to services. The Beijing Consensus is often contrasted with the Washington Consensus which involved a set of ten policies that the US government and Washington-based international financial institutions – the World Bank and International Monetary Fund (IMF) – believed were necessary elements that developing countries should adopt to increase economic growth. The Washington Consensus, at its essence, placed emphasis on the importance of macroeconomic stability and the liberalization of the economy including reducing the role of the state. As the originator of the term, John Williamson, put it, the policies "may be summarized as prudent macroeconomic policies, outward orientation, and free-market capitalism."[1] It reflected a "neoliberal" set of economic reform policies as the term "neoliberalism" – which is used in a number of ways – is most commonly understood today. Scholars using the term in this manner typically characterize three sets of polices as being neoliberal: those that liberalize the economy by eliminating price controls, deregulating capital markets, and lowering trade barriers; those that reduce the role of the state in the economy, most notably via privatization of SOEs; and those that contribute to fiscal austerity and macroeconomic stabilization,

* The author is grateful to the symposium participants for the questions and comments put to him, as well as Weitseng Chen for his comments on an earlier draft of this chapter.

[1] John Williamson, "What Washington Means by Policy Reform," in *Latin American Adjustment: How Much Has Happened?* John Williamson (ed.) (Washington, DC: Peterson Institute for International Economics, 1990).

including tight control of money supply, elimination of budget deficits, and curtailment of government subsidies.[2]

However, even before the Beijing Consensus was coined as a term, the universality of the Washington Consensus, which was largely formulated in the context of economic problems in Latin America, was doubted. Part of the reason for this was that the recipe it prescribed led to economic chaos in some ex-Communist countries such as Russia. Another major reason was that it did not fit the development experience of some East Asian economies including Singapore. Although Singapore is not a communist or socialist country, at an early stage of her postindependence history Singapore embraced state capitalism and actively promoted the incorporation of companies – often referred to as government-linked companies or "GLCs" – to engage in various sectors of the economy. This was part of a two-pronged approach to achieve industrialization[3] and GLCs continue to play an important role in Singapore's economy. According to a study that used 2008 – 2013 market capitalization data, GLCs accounted for an average of 37 percent of the stock market value of S$500 billion on the Singapore Exchange.[4]

More importantly, Singapore's use of GLCs is generally considered a success. Capital markets appear to value GLCs more highly than non-GLCs.[5] Interestingly, GLCs on the whole managed their expenses better than non-GLC companies. This lower expense-to-sales ratio among GLCs indicated that GLCs were more profitable because they ran leaner operations,[6] differentiating themselves from the generally inefficient nationalized firms run by governments. It is therefore not surprising that suggestions have been made that Singapore's GLCs may provide a good model for reforming China's SOE model.[7] In fact, it was reported

[2] Taylor Boas and Jordan Gans-Morse, "Neoliberalism: From New Liberal Philosophy to Anti-Liberal Slogan," *Studies in Comparative International Development* 44 (2009): 137.

[3] The other was to encourage multinational corporations to establish manufacturing facilities in Singapore.

[4] Isabel Sim, Steen Thomsen, and Gerard Yeong, "The State as Shareholder: The Case of Singapore," Centre for Governance, Institutions & Organisations NUS Business School (2014): 22, http://bschool.nus.edu/Portals/0/docs/FinalReport_SOE_1July2014.pdf.

[5] Carlos D. Ramirez and Tan Ling-Hui, "Singapore, Inc. versus the Private Sector: Are Government-Linked Companies Different?," Working Paper 03/156 (IMF, 2003), www.imf.org/external/pubs/ft/wp/2003/wp03156.pdf; James S. Ang and David K. Ding, "Government Ownership and the Performance of Government-Linked Companies: The Case of Singapore," *Journal of Multinational Financial Management* 16 (2006): 85–86.

[6] Ang and Ding, "Case of Singapore," 80.

[7] For example, Li-Wen Lin and Curtis Milhaupt, "We are the (National) Champions: Understanding the Mechanisms of State Capitalism in China," *Stanford Law Review* 65

recently that the Chinese government is initiating a reform of China's SOEs, and insiders expect that by the year 2020 about 30 SOEs will follow the model of Temasek Holdings (the state investment and holding company that holds the shares owned by the Singapore government in GLCs) to manage capital rather than manage assets.[8] This is yet another instance where China has attempted to draw lessons from Singapore as best exemplified by the statement made by the former paramount leader of China, Deng Xiaoping, in 1992 to "learn from Singapore" during his famous tour of the southern provinces.

This chapter seeks to explore what lessons the Singapore experience might hold that could be relevant to China's development, particularly in China's reform of her SOEs. The rest of the chapter is divided into four parts followed by a conclusion. In the next part, it will briefly discuss the Washington Consensus and why it was not an attractive model for China. In Part III, the chapter explores the elements that supposedly constitute the Beijing Consensus and why they are either nonexistent or not unique. Furthermore, there are aspects of the Beijing Consensus that can be explained by path dependency. Part IV discusses Singapore's economic development particularly in the context of her social and political circumstances at the time of self-government and eventually full independence, and Part V suggests what aspects of the Singapore experience could be relevant to China.

II The Washington Consensus

It is not within the scope of this chapter to discuss the Washington Consensus in detail which is covered more fully in some of the other chapters in this volume, but it may perhaps be remarked that the Consensus reflects the constant process of rebalancing that takes place in complex societies. It was a reaction to the economic statism that dominated development

(2013): 754–55; "Reforming China's State-Owned Firms: From SOE to GLC – China's Rulers Look to Singapore for Tips on Portfolio Management," *The Economist*, November 23, 2013, www.economist.com/news/finance-and-economics/21590562-chinas-rulers-look-singapore-tips-portfolio-management-soe-glc; Ronald Gilson and Curtis Milhaupt, "Sovereign Wealth Funds and Corporate Governance: A Minimalist Response to the New Mercantilism," *Stanford Law Review* 60 (2008): 1345; Lay-Hong Tan and Jiangyu Wang, "Modelling an Effective Corporate Governance System for China's Listed State-Owned Enterprises," *Journal of Corporate Law Studies* 7 (2007): 143.

[8] "30 Chinese SOEs to Follow Temasek Model by 2020," *Want China Times*, 2014, www.wantchinatimes.com/news-subclass-cnt.aspx?id=20140530000094&cid=1201.

economics in many developing countries for much of the postwar, post-colonial period and developed initially as a reaction to the Latin American debt crisis in the early 1980s and appropriately so at the time.[9] While many of its policies are relatively uncontroversial – Williamson has said that for the most part "they are motherhood and apple pie" – the overall concept has proved controversial.[10]

Some of the reasons for this include the term itself which seemed to signify an American hegemony imposed reluctantly on countries that made their conditions worse.[11] Contrast is sometimes made of the Indonesian and Malaysian experiences during the 1997–1998 Asian Financial Crisis where Malaysia (which did not accept the IMF's advice) appeared to weather the crisis better than Indonesia (which did).[12] A criticism is that the policies of the Washington Consensus have been elevated to the level of dogma by institutions such as the IMF,[13] thereby constraining pragmatic solutions that may better fit the particular circumstances.[14] On this view the policies of the IMF during the Asian Financial Crisis made things worse than they should have been. By tying aid to an increase in interest rates and austerity measures, the cash flow of firms was depressed and their fixed-payment obligations increased, tipping more and more into insolvency thereby accelerating the outflows and reducing the inflows.[15]

The phrase has also been associated – wrongly in Williamson's view – with another version of neoliberalism that included supply side economics and a minimal state that reduced expenditure in social areas such

[9] Williamson, "What Washington Means by Policy Reform"; John Williamson, "Beijing Consensus versus Washington Consensus?," Peterson Institute for International Economics, 2010, www.piie.com/publications/interviews/pp20101102williamson.pdf.

[10] John Williamson, "Did the Washington Consensus Fail?," Peterson Institute for International Economics, 2002, www.iie.com/publications/papers/paper.cfm?ResearchID=488.

[11] Ibid. Williamson acknowledged that the phrase "Washington Consensus" is a damaged brand name.

[12] For Malaysia, see Ethan Kaplan and Dani Rodrik, "Did The Malaysian Capital Controls Work?," Institute of Advanced Study, School of Social Science, 2001, www.sss.ias.edu/files/pdfs/Rodrik/Research/did-Malaysian-capital-controls-work.PDF. For an assessment that the IMF did not offer the best advice to Indonesia, see Stephen Grenville, "The IMF and the Indonesian Crisis," Background Paper 04/3 (IMF, 2004), www.ieo-imf.org/ieo/files/completedevaluations/BP043.pdf.

[13] Chalmers Johnson, "Economic Crisis in East Asia: The Clash of Capitalisms," *Cambridge Journal of Economics* 22 (1998): 659.

[14] It is widely acknowledged that the capital controls Malaysia imposed during the Asian Financial Crisis, contrary to the standard IMF advice, were effective.

[15] Robert Wade, "From 'Miracle' to 'Cronyism': Explaining the Great Asian Slump," *Cambridge Journal of Economics* 22 (1998): 700.

as education and housing.[16] Neoliberalism has also been blamed for an overreliance on market forces that led to the Global Financial Crisis of 2008 and the response to it has hardly been consistent with aspects of the Washington Consensus given the vast amounts of public money that have been used to bail out financial institutions and to allow quantitative easing. Finally as Williamson acknowledged, the outcomes have been disappointing in the countries that have tried to implement the Washington Consensus.[17] This may be linked to the earlier criticism about policy prescriptions that were based on dogma and ideology and which also therefore did not take into account the importance of other relevant factors for success such as politics, institutions, good public administration, and geography.[18] Accordingly, the Washington Consensus itself has evolved,[19] while simultaneously being challenged by other developmental models – thus the search for equilibrium ever continues – such as the so-called East Asian Model and the Beijing Consensus to which this chapter now turns.

III The Beijing Consensus

The phrase "Beijing Consensus" was first coined by Joshua Cooper Ramo in 2004 as an alternative to the Washington Consensus for nations that were trying to see how best to develop their economies. It is said to consist of three theorems involving innovation; measures that focus on quality of life where sustainability and equality become first considerations; and self-determination. None of these theorems would appear to support a new approach to development that is distinctively Chinese. This is because the first two theorems do not appear to be borne out by China's development experience and the third is something all nation states strive to achieve.[20]

[16] Williamson, "Did the Washington Consensus Fail?" [17] Ibid.

[18] Joseph Stiglitz, *Globalization and Its Discontents* (New York: W. W. Norton, 2002); Michael Ellman, "Transition Economies," in *Rethinking Development Economics*, Chang Ha-Joon (ed.) (London: Anthem Press, 2003), 182.

[19] Sarah Babb, "The Washington Consensus as Transnational Policy Paradigm: Its Origins, Trajectory and Likely Successor," *Review of International Political Economy* 20 (2013): 287.

[20] Much of China's growth thus far has been to leverage on its large surplus and cheap labor pool that is fast diminishing. While China understands the importance of moving up the value chain and innovation will therefore be important, there is little to suggest that much progress has been made on this front. The massive adverse environmental consequences of China's development, its rampant corruption, seizures of private property, and the *hukou* system that makes access to social services much more difficult for migrant workers from rural areas, are also hardly suggestive of a country that focuses on quality of life.

At best it can be said that China's size and growing international influence make it easier for China to achieve a higher degree of self-determination.

Underlying China's supposedly new development approach, Ramo speaks of pragmatism and flexibility, turning traditional ideas like privatization and free trade on their heads, all with the goal of improving society through the use of economics and governance. However, even here it is difficult to see any Chinese exceptionalism unless one only viewed human affairs through a narrow temporal lens. The policies introduced in the wake of the Global Financial Crisis were highly pragmatic and flexible, bearing little in common with neoliberal economics of whatever stripe, and leading to the United States and Britain holding significant stakes in a number of financial institutions. And while China does advocate recognition of political and cultural differences as well as differences in regional and national practices within a common global framework, with a global order founded not upon homogenizing universalisms that inevitably lead to hegemonism, but on a simultaneous recognition of commonality and difference,[21] this has not stopped China from being strongly assertive of its national interests as witnessed by its actions in the South China Sea. China's advocated approach also serves her position as the emerging rival of the United States in global affairs by providing a basis for other countries to distance themselves from American policies.

More importantly, even when the Washington Consensus might have been applied mechanistically by its adherents, it was never adopted by all countries. A particularly important group of economies did not abide by important aspects of the Washington Consensus. These were Japan, Korea, Singapore (which was the only one of these countries that relied heavily on SOEs in her economic development) and Taiwan where state intervention in the economy was significant and generally regarded as beneficial to their development. Indonesia, Malaysia and Thailand were in the next wave of Asian countries that experienced high growth and each also practiced state intervention though perhaps to a lesser degree than the earlier set of countries. These countries were in turn followed by China and Vietnam and arguably China's development path can be seen

See also Dowdle and Prado's discussion in Chapter 1, where they rightly point out that at least some portion of China's development has been the product of an earlier economic insanity that needlessly devastated China's productive capacity for over two decades. Considering how disastrous Mao Zedong's policies were for China, almost any economic reform with a modicum of sense would have improved the state of her economy.

21 Arif Dirlik, "Beijing Consensus: Beijing 'Gongshi'—Who Recognizes Whom and to What, End?," www.ids-uva.nl/wordpress/wp-content/uploads/2011/07/9_Dirlik.pdf.

as a continuum of what had first started in Asia several decades earlier in Japan. Thus to the extent that "state capitalism" and reliance on SOEs are aspects of the Beijing Consensus, this is not new phenomena and cannot be regarded as Chinese innovations in the state sector.

Furthermore, the approach of these Asian economies including China is also broadly consistent with Williamson's approach which he summarized as prudent macroeconomic policies, outward orientation, and free-market capitalism. Indeed, as the economies of Japan, Korea, Singapore, and Taiwan developed, they have increasingly converged toward Williamson's Washington Consensus. In fact, Yasheng Huang argues it is the Washington Consensus that fits better with the Chinese growth experience as Chinese experiments with reforms have resulted in financial liberalization and private entrepreneurship.[22] China (and Singapore) undoubtedly still relies significantly on SOEs but her privatization efforts have been notable and it is clear that China's reform of her SOEs including further privatization is ongoing. Again, one has to be cautious of temporal judgments taken at particular moments in time. China has not adopted the rapid privatization of the former East European Communist countries but given that such an approach has not been a great success,[23] China's more cautious and pragmatic approach cannot be faulted.[24]

The only really distinctive thing about China's development today is that it is taking place within a nondemocratic political system though this should be expected given that China is a totalitarian state. It is a natural consequence of the Communist triumph over the Nationalists in 1949. Yet democracy was not one of Williamson's original ten policies though it was undoubtedly formulated within the paradigm of a liberal democracy. However, to suggest that economic development can only effectively take place within a democratic-liberal capitalist system is to ignore history,[25] including the long history of China under imperial rulers. Furthermore, development within an illiberal democratic system is consistent with the

[22] Yasheng Huang, "Debating China's Economic Growth: The Beijing Consensus or the Washington Consensus," *Academy of Management Perspectives* 24 (2010): 31.

[23] As Ellman put it, the rapid privatization of inherited SOEs has been seen to be unimportant for economic growth in the transition economies of the former Eastern European communist countries. Ellman, "Transition Economies," 180.

[24] Indeed, China's generally cautious approach to economic development as a whole has been influenced by the mixed results of the big bang approach to economic development adopted in the former Eastern European communist countries, particularly in the Russian experience.

[25] Chang Ha-Joon, "Institutional Development in Historical Perspective," in *Rethinking Development Economics*, Chang Ha-Joon, 499.

developmental experiences of countries such as Singapore, Taiwan, and Malaysia.[26]

Accordingly, it is suggested that there is very little in the concept of a Beijing Consensus. Some Chinese themselves feel there is no such model or are critical of views about a Chinese Model.[27] Instead the contrast that its proponents seek to evoke with the Washington Consensus is testimony to the presently enduring force of the Washington Consensus,[28] and is also deeply political especially where it implies a viable alternative to Western market democracy.[29] This distinction between authoritarian state capitalism and liberal market democracy is ultimately the essence of the debate between both "consensuses."

IV The Historical Basis for Singapore's Economic Development

Given that China looks to Singapore as a source of potential lessons for its economic development, and is also interested in Singapore's political and governance systems – in fact, it has been asserted that the "Singapore Model" represents in perfection what the Chinese see as their own

26 Singapore has been referred to as an "illiberal democracy" in that it is a democracy with a government that has (soft) authoritarian tendencies. See Hussin Mutalib, "Illiberal Democracy and the Future of Opposition in Singapore," *Third World Quarterly* 21 (2000). For this reason this chapter occasionally refers to Singapore as an authoritarian state without intending to imply that Singapore does not practice a democratic form of government. See also Mark Tushnet, "Authoritarian Constitutionalism," *Cornell Law Review* 100 (2015): 391, where the author posits that while Singapore is not a liberal democracy, neither is she fully authoritarian, and Singapore appears to adhere to some version of normative constitutionalism.

27 E.g., the former World Bank Chief Economist Justin Yi Fu Lin has expressed the view that China does not follow a model but changes policy all the time. Andrew Batson, "Lin Urges Flexibility in Fighting Poverty," *Wall Street Journal*, February 29, 2008, www.wsj.com/articles/SB120422296784800317. See also Matt Ferchen, "Whose China Model Is It Anyway? The Contentious Search for Consensus," *Review of International Political Economy* 20 (2013): 407.

28 Sarah Babb suggests that despite a more heterogeneous world, it seems likely that no transnational policy paradigm will replace the Washington Consensus in the near future. Babb, "The Washington Consensus as Transnational Policy Paradigm," 291.

29 Ferchen, "Contentious Search for Consensus." As Kroncke points out in Chapter 2, the Beijing Consensus is an anti-model to the Washington Consensus and also a general rejection of the very notion of the coordinated global advocacy of a universal set of policy prescriptions. A similar point is made by Dowdle and Prado in Chapter 1 that the Beijing Consensus is not really about China but is a pithy way of representing the anti–Washington Consensus.

development path[30] – this section will now sketch the reasons that led Singapore down the path that she took, namely one where the state continues to play an important role in many areas such as savings and investment;[31] in land use as the largest landowner partly as a result of compulsory acquisition of land in the early years of independence; through government agencies that have roles in developing sectors of the Singapore economy such as trade and finance; and of course through ownership and control of GLCs. [32] It will also explain why the People's Action Party (PAP) has been politically dominant for more than 55 years. The reasons why Singapore developed in the way she did may provide some markers for China which will then be explored in the next section.

Singapore has been governed by the PAP since 1959 when Singapore was a self-governing British colony. Given this long period of PAP dominance in Singapore's political life, it may be difficult to recall that unlike many other postcolonial governments, the PAP government did not initially have strong mass support. The story begins with the publication of the Rendel Report in February 1954 which was to lead to elections the following year toward some degree of self-government. Lee Kuan Yew, who was later to become the first Prime Minister of Singapore, felt it was necessary to form an alliance with left-wing militants who were under the influence of the illegal Malayan Communist Party. While Lee Kuan Yew and his group were aware of the force and discontent of the Chinese educated masses, they realized that an alliance with such men, dangerous though it might be, offered the only path to political success. The future belonged to politicians who could command the allegiance of the Chinese educated.[33] The task was no doubt made more daunting by the fact that Lee Kuan Yew himself was English educated and could not speak Mandarin or any Chinese dialect fluently.

For their part, the left-wing Chinese extremists saw Lee Kuan Yew and his group as a convenient front to gain political power because they were

[30] Stephan Ortmann, "The 'Beijing Consensus' and the 'Singapore Model': Unmasking the Myth of an Alternative Authoritarian State-Capitalist Model," in *China's Economic Dynamics: A Beijing Consensus in the making?* Jun Li and Wang Liming (eds.) (London: Routledge, 2014), 83.

[31] Gregor Hopf, "Saving and Investment: The Economic Development of Singapore 1965–99," (PhD diss., London School of Economics and Political Science, 2004).

[32] Much of this section is drawn from Cheng-Han Tan, Dan Puchniak, and Umakanth Varottil, "State-Owned Enterprises in Singapore: Historical Insights into a Potential Model for Reform," (2015) 28 *Columbia Journal of Asian Law* 61.

[33] Constance Mary Turnbull, *A History of Modern Singapore, 1819–2005* (Singapore: NUS Press, 2009), 255.

more likely to be acceptable to the British. Thus, in its early days, the PAP was divided into two wings, the noncommunists under Lee Kuan Yew and the pro-communists under Lim Chin Siong. During the early years of the PAP, Lim Chin Siong, and his wing were the real force in the PAP, commanding the support of organized labor and the Chinese masses.[34] What prevented Lim's wing from taking control of the PAP was the arrest and detention of him and several others under the Preservation of Public Security Ordinance 1955 by the then Labour Front government.

The Labour Front government which had been instrumental in helping the Lee Kuan Yew group to retain control of the PAP was defeated in elections held in 1959 where the PAP obtained a strong majority winning 43 of 51 seats in the Legislative Assembly. In power, there was an urgent need to provide employment. While open unemployment at around 5 percent in 1957 was not exceptionally high, this did not take into account large numbers of people who could not be regarded as fully employed. Nineteen percent of Singapore households and 25 percent of individuals were found to be in poverty.[35] The rapid rise in the birth rate also foreshadowed future difficulties as it would eventually translate into significant labor force growth. Singapore's reliance on entrepôt commerce and the income from British military bases would be insufficient to meet the needs of the rapidly growing population which would also require an increase in social services.[36] In a 1955 report of a mission organized by the International Bank for Reconstruction and Development, Singapore's ability to meet public financial requirements from domestic resources was doubted unless additional taxes were levied and present balances drawn upon.[37]

To increase its popular support, the PAP government embarked on a program of social reform.[38] One priority was to construct more public housing. At the time, many were living in unhygienic slums and squatter settlements with only 9 percent living in government flats. Within three years of the establishment of the Housing and Development Board in February 1960 that was tasked with solving Singapore's housing problem, the board built 21,000 flats and by 1965 it had built 54,000 flats. Today,

[34] Ibid., 262.

[35] Greg W. Huff, *The Economic Growth of Singapore – Trade and Development in the Twentieth Century* (New York: Cambridge University Press, 1994), 291.

[36] Turnbull, *Modern Singapore*, 275–76.

[37] World Bank, *The Economic Development of Malaya* (Washington, DC: International Bank for Reconstruction, 1955), 28.

[38] Turnbull, *Modern Singapore*, 284–85.

more than 80 percent of Singaporeans live in public housing.[39] Other significant steps were measures to improve health facilities, utilities, and education.

Such ambitious social goals and the need to provide employment would be unsustainable without economic development. In the 1950s and early 1960s, a generally held view was that Singapore was not viable economically as an independent entity and had to be part of Malaya. Singapore's leaders were keen on merger for this and historical reasons. On August 31, 1963, Singapore together with Sabah and Sarawak joined the Federation of Malaya to form the new Federation of Malaysia. However, the period of merger proved to be a difficult one and on August 9, 1965, Singapore ceased to be part of Malaysia.

The separation from Malaysia was traumatic for the Singapore leadership as many within the PAP had not conceived that Singapore would have to go it alone.[40] A further potentially devastating blow was to come several years later when on January 15, 1968, the British government announced that its forces east of Suez would be withdrawn in December 1971. Given that the British military bases in Singapore provided substantial employment, not to mention the importance to the economy of the businesses that supported the military bases, this was a severe setback to the government of a new and developing country.[41]

It has been said that the beginnings of a significantly expanded and more intrusive role played by the government in the economy can be traced to the announcement of the military withdrawal.[42] Prior to this

[39] See "About Us," Housing and Development Board, www.hdb.gov.sg/cs/infoweb/about-us/history.

[40] Lee Kuan Yew, *From Third World to First – The Singapore Story: 1965–2000* (Singapore: Times Editions, 2000), 19.

[41] According to Lawrence Krause, British expenditures constituted 12.7 percent of GDP in 1967 and were responsible, directly and indirectly, for the employment of thirty-eight thousand local workers or 20 percent of the workforce. Lawrence Krause, "Government as Entrepreneur," in *Management of Success: The Moulding of Modern Singapore*, Kernial Singh Sandu and Paul Wheatley (eds.) (Singapore: Institute of Southeast Asian Studies, 1989), 438.

[42] After winning the 1968 general election, two of the policy directions laid down by the PAP government were the stimulation of economic growth through the cultivation of new activities and by taking advantage of new economic opportunities, and increased functional specialization in the institutions concerned with economic development. These policy directives led to the establishment of a number of public enterprises and also brought direct government participation into new spheres such as manufacturing, transport, trading, and banking. The government no longer confined itself to an indirect economic role. It assumed entrepreneurial responsibilities and moved into areas which had traditionally

the government confined itself mainly to more traditional activities and to indirect involvement in the economy.[43] Indeed Goh Keng Swee, the former Deputy Prime Minister and principal architect of Singapore's economic development, stated that by 1968 a change in emphasis took place in Singapore's industrial promotion policy. Industrial development acquired a fresh urgency when the British Labour Government decided to accelerate the end of the British military presence east of Suez.[44] The impending military withdrawal brought about a change in Singapore's economic path that has endured notwithstanding her development as an advanced economy today.

One difficulty with the industrialization strategy was that Singapore's largely entrepôt economy did not naturally lend itself to industrialization. The base of human capital necessary for this was insufficient, and the government may also not have been able or willing to look to the Chinese educated businessmen who had traditionally made up Singapore's entrepreneurs.[45] The capital markets were relatively under-developed and may not have been able to support large private undertakings, while the private sector at the same time could have been risk averse.[46] Multinational corporations were one substitute for this, the other being strong state involvement in certain sectors of the economy. It was the government's perceived need to support the transformation of the Singapore economy that led to the formation of GLCs. Singapore's leaders found control over key domestic markets and institutions the most effective way to respond to opportunities in the world economy to meet the main

been in the hands of the private sector. According to Ow Chin Hock, this should be contrasted with the government's approach in its State Development Plan (1961–1964), which focused on the pattern and financing of government development expenditure, which would support and complement the industrialization programme. From this plan, it could be seen that although the government envisaged a larger role for itself in economic development, it confined itself to the indirect role of providing economic infrastructure and incentives to attract foreign investment and promote industrial growth. Ow Chin Hock, "Singapore," in *The Role of Public Enterprises in National Development in Southeast Asia: Problems and Prospects*, Truong Nguyen (ed.) (Singapore: Regional Institute of Higher Education and Development, 1976), 158, 163.

43 Krause, *Moulding of Modern Singapore*, 438.

44 Goh Keng Swee, *The Practice of Economic Growth* (Singapore: Federal Publications, 1995), 9.

45 Greg W. Huff, *The Economic Growth of Singapore – Trade and Development in the Twentieth Century* (New York: Cambridge University Press, 1994), 320.

46 Lee Sheng Yi, "Public Enterprise and Economic Development in Singapore," *Malayan Economic Review* 21 (1976): 51.

planning objectives of absorbing surplus labor and promoting economic growth.[47]

To ameliorate the impact on Singapore from the withdrawal of British troops, the British government agreed to give some of its assets such as the naval dockyard at Sembawang which was handed over for a token sum of S$1.00. Sembawang Shipyard Pte Ltd was then subsequently established on June 19, 1968, to begin business as a commercial ship repairer. Other GLCs were also formed as a result of the receipt of such assets. The Singapore government did not stop at establishing GLCs from the assets handed over by the British. It saw GLCs as a means for the government to take the lead in establishing new industries, including in the services sector, where the private sector could not or would not. For example, Lee Kuan Yew explained that the Development Bank of Singapore, now simply known as DBS, helped finance entrepreneurs who needed venture capital because the established banks had no experience outside trade financing and were too conservative and reluctant to lend to would be manufacturers.[48]

The circumstances that Singapore found herself in probably explain the importance of GLCs in her economy compared to other Asian peers such as Japan, Hong Kong, South Korea, and Taiwan. Hong Kong's development was largely driven by private enterprise. While many large companies in Japan, South Korea, and Taiwan did benefit directly from state support, it did not lead to widespread government ownership of companies as in Singapore. What may have distinguished Singapore from these economies were the generosity of the British in giving Singapore land (virtually without charge) that could be used for economic or defense purposes, *and* the perceived market failure of a lack of entrepreneurs to support industrialization.[49] Both factors acting in tandem caused the state to become a significant market participant. This did not come about for ideological reasons though arguably the fact that the PAP was a socialist party meant that there was no ideological aversion to state participation.

Singapore's industrialization efforts proved successful. The economy saw a shift to manufacturing. Its share in total output grew from 16.6 percent in 1960 to 29.4 percent by 1979. In 1992, manufacturing contributed

[47] Greg W. Huff, "What Is the Singapore Model of Economic Development?," *Cambridge Journal of Economics* 19 (1995): 748, citing an interview with Goh Keng Swee.

[48] Lee, *The Singapore Story*, 77.

[49] Ibid., 85–86; Lee, *Public Enterprise and Economic Development*, 55.

27.6 percent of GDP and accounted for 27.5 percent of employment.[50] Public enterprises were, by the first half of 1974, thought to account for 14 to 16 percent of total manufacturing output.[51] The successful management of the Singapore economy is a major factor for the PAP's longevity as the ruling party in Singapore. For example, when elections were held in September 1963 the PAP gained a clear victory, winning thirty-one out of fifty-one seats. The Barisan Sosialis, which had been formed by former left-wing PAP members, managed to win thirteen, and the United People's Party won one. The PAP's victory in the following election held in 1968 was even more comprehensive. The Barisan Sosialis boycotted the election and the ruling party won every seat that was contested.

The 1963 election is a good indicator of a decisive switch in popular support to the PAP. While it is true that the Barisan Sosialis operated at a disadvantage in that election as some of its leaders were in prison, the outcome was not certain. According to a historian, the result of the 1963 polls appeared to hang in the balance and the PAP's clear victory was a surprise to both PAP and Barisan Sosialis supporters alike.[52] The PAP obtained just under 47 percent of the popular vote while the Barisan Sosialis obtained around 33 percent. The PAP's economic management and social policies accounted for its support from the populace. The PAP leadership under Lee Kuan Yew, well aware of its initially precarious position within Singapore's political arena, sought to win the support of Singaporeans through good economic management that would allow the government to improve social conditions. This economic strategy involved GLCs and gave the government considerable influence in certain segments of the economy.

V What Might the Singapore Experience Imply for China?

A Size

Singapore is a small city-state that did not have a large agricultural sector and therefore her developmental experience will not always be relevant to China. Many of Singapore's inherent issues stem from the fact that she is a small nation; many of China's, on the other hand, are exactly the opposite. While there is no reason why Chinese cities cannot aspire to become as developed as Singapore and indeed draw certain lessons from Singapore's experience, the process of development is unlikely to be entirely similar

50 Huff, *Singapore Model of Economic Development*, 739.
51 Lee, *Public Enterprise and Economic Development*, 64.
52 Turnbull, *Modern Singapore*, 286.

because the policy and allocative decisions and trade-offs that are necessary will be different between a city-state and a large polity that has a more diverse population and a wider range of competing considerations. Large rising powers also face greater coordination problems that can give rise to incoherent policymaking and inefficient policy implementation.[53] Nevertheless, to the extent that Singapore's experience is studied by China and is a model that China tries to learn from, it is necessary to understand what the key elements of this experience involve, and explore what they might imply for China.

B Importance of a Contested Democratic System

From the preceding section, it seems clear that the existence in the 1950s and 1960s of a contested democratic political environment played a significant role in fostering good political and economic governance in Singapore (including in GLCs).[54] This is not to downplay the integrity and ability of the early leaders of the PAP but to suggest that "environmental" factors must also have played a role in setting a clear path that had to be pursued. Lee Kuan Yew himself, for all his caveats about democracy, has said on a number of occasions that it was beneficial for his ministers and parliamentarians to submit to the will of the people every few years.[55] The PAP was aware of how the Labour Front government lost support in the 1959 election as a result of negative public perception brought about partly by allegations of corruption against a member of the cabinet. The PAP therefore sought to cast itself in the 1959 elections as the party that could provide honest and efficient government. Having won convincingly, it had to live up to its promises or risk being punished in subsequent polls. Ever since, the PAP has relied on its competent management of the economy and the fair distribution of its benefits to retain strong political support. Properly understood, Singapore does not necessarily stand as a good example of an authoritarian political system (whether with or without the trappings of democracy) being superior for early economic development. The PAP took radical steps to bring

[53] For a discussion about how size matters, see also Chen, Chapter 6. Nevertheless, it is interesting to note that China has over her long history retained her ability to rebuild herself after each period of decline. It may suggest that very large countries by their sheer size retain a significant ability to rejuvenate themselves.

[54] Tan et al., "State-Owned Enterprises in Singapore."

[55] For example, Lee, *The Singapore Story*, 192, wrote, "Singapore has shown that a system of clean, no-money elections helps preserve an honest government."

about economic development at a time when the electoral landscape was highly contested and its political support was relatively weak. Although it had the advantage of colonial era legislation that allowed it to imprison political opponents that were regarded as communists, the opposition Barisan Sosialis had substantial support in the early 1960s and it must be remembered that in the 1963 elections the PAP did not obtain a majority of the popular vote. Nevertheless, it had done enough in its first term in government to persuade enough Singaporeans to vote for it to become the party with the largest percentage of the valid votes cast.

The link between economic and political legitimacy in Singapore cannot be understated. Singapore has for most of her modern history been a largely immigrant society focused on commercial enterprise. The Chinese, Indians, and other races that came to Singapore did so to engage in trade or to find work. By the end of the nineteenth century Singapore had a secure place in the pattern of world trade with an increasingly sophisticated infrastructure of commercial institutions and expertise.[56] Singapore today is still essentially a commercial city and her survival is premised on her ability to be commercially relevant to the wider region around her and as an important node for Western commercial enterprises and investors. Thus while economic growth is important to all countries, it has an almost existential condition in Singapore. It is therefore not surprising that economic legitimacy is probably the most important determinant of political legitimacy in Singapore. Singapore's democratic system has therefore been a positive force in incentivizing the government to manage Singapore competently, and a safeguard against any desire to engage in rent-seeking conduct with the PAP government adopting and maintaining a zero-tolerance approach to corruption.

The positive influence that the democratic system has had on Singapore can be contrasted with China's initial experience under the CCP. Without the constraint of having to submit to the will of the people on a regular basis, much of the Mao Zedong period can be accounted a disaster for China that led to widespread disillusionment with socialist government.[57] As a result of this weakened mandate coupled with the hardship that many CCP members themselves encountered during the Mao period, the CCP sought to re-establish its political legitimacy by emulating aspects of the

[56] Turnbull, *Modern Singapore*, 105.

[57] Though there were achievements also; see John Fairbank and Merle Goldman, *China: A New History* (Cambridge, MA: Harvard University Press, 2006), 406; Lu Aiguo, *China and the Global Economy since 1840* (London: Macmillan, 2000), 108–16.

developmental experience of Japan, Korea, Singapore, Taiwan, as well as Hong Kong,[58] which has led to the astonishing growth that China experienced in the post-Mao period. Although the CCP had no need to be re-elected, it was no doubt well aware of the familiar historical political cycle in China where dynasties have given way to revolution when rulers were perceived to have lost the Mandate of Heaven by failing to govern well.[59] The post-Mao communist leadership found itself in a similar position to the PAP government in the late 1950s and early 1960s in that it saw economic development and the improvement of the people's well-being as essential to the party-state's political legitimacy.[60] Singapore is a particularly attractive model to China in this regard because Singapore is often regarded as an authoritarian state that has become rich and remained orderly without demonstrations or demands for human rights.[61] The question for China is whether its substitute – namely legitimacy management[62] – for the role that democracy has played in Singapore as a disciplining factor will be as efficient. It is suggested that the perceived need to retain political legitimacy is unlikely to be as consistently effective as the need to submit periodically to the will of the people.

58 Lin Yi-min, "Economic Institutional Change in Post-Mao China: Reflections on the Triggering, Orienting, and Sustaining Mechanisms," in *China's Developmental Miracle: Origins, Transformations, and Challenges (Asia and the Pacific)*, Alvin Y. So (ed.) (New York: Routledge, 2003), 31–32; Fairbank and Goldman, *China: A New History*, 408–9; Wang Gungwu, *Renewal: The Chinese State and the New Global History* (Hong Kong: The Chinese University Press, 2013), 108; Wang Jiangyu, "The Political Logic of Corporate Governance in China's State-owned Enterprises," *Cornell International Law Journal* 47 (2014): 638–39.

59 Wang, *The Chinese State*, 119–20. Frederick Mote is skeptical of any grand "dynastic cycle" theory, but it is a fact that whatever the complex reasons in each case, Chinese history has repeatedly seen one regime replaced by another as a result of certain recurring factors. See Frederick W. Mote, *Imperial China 900–1800* (Cambridge, MA: Harvard University Press, 2003), 776–77, 781–84; Fairbank and Goldman, *China: A New History*, 48–49.

60 Lu offers the view that while the Maoist model had represented a viable solution to the economic backwardness of the pre-1949 market economy, it eventually created new contradictions which meant that production could be inefficient even though the economy could still grow. The adoption of a new developmental strategy became more attractive from the example of the newly industrialized economies of East Asia. This view was reinforced by the popular yearning among the people for better living standards. The population was becoming more aware of the differences in living standards between China and the developed countries, particularly China's Asian neighbors, and this put pressure on policy makers to turn the economy around and to do it quickly. Lu, *China and the Global Economy*, 122–25.

61 Immanuel Hsu, *The Rise of Modern China* (New York: Oxford University Press, 2000), 948.

62 Wang, "China's State-Owned Enterprises," 637–39.

C *Corruption*

Corruption within the party-state machinery, which is widespread, appears presently to be most immediately worrying to the CCP as high levels of corruption have tended to precede the fall of dynasties.[63] This is because deep rooted corruption is a signal of regime decay that in turn expedites the decline of the regime. All this is symptomatic of a perennial issue in Chinese history. As a result of its vastness, the central authority often struggles to impose its will on the provinces or great families or the bureaucratic system or indeed all of the above. This is epitomized by the well-known aphorism that the emperor's writ becomes ever weaker with distance. Over time the central authority grows even weaker while abuses of power, including corruption at the local (and central) level, increases. This further increases discontent among the populace that eventually leads to revolution or the regime collapsing through "barbarian" incursions. While the latter is not a concern today, the CCP does worry about the consequences of any significant loss of its legitimacy.

Singapore provides an example of how an economy that is prepared to adopt a zero-tolerance approach toward corruption can significantly eliminate it. In an economy with many bureaucratic processes that require action or the exercise of discretion by civil servants, opportunities abound for petty corruption to take place. Small payments may have to be made to secure a license or permit or to register a business. Where the processes can be streamlined or eliminated, such opportunities diminish not to mention the efficiency gains to the economy. The PAP government took steps to simplify procedures and limit discretion by having clear published guidelines, even doing away with the need for permits or approvals in less important areas.[64]

The law against corruption was also progressively strengthened. An example of this can be seen in the law's approach toward public servants. Under Singapore law, a public servant or an agent of a public servant who receives any gratification shall be presumed to have received such gratification corruptly as an inducement or reward unless the contrary is proved by such public servant.[65] This is a departure from the general position in Singapore that the prosecution has to prove every element of

[63] Jonathan Spence, *The Search for Modern China* (New York: W. W. Norton, 2013), 210, 655–56, 680; for corruption in premodern china, see 16–21 (Ming Dynasty) and 164–65 (Qing Dynasty).

[64] Lee, *The Singapore Story*, 184.

[65] Prevention of Corruption Act, Cap 241, Rev Ed 1993, Section 8 (Singapore).

the offense. Thus where an allegation of corruption is not made against a public servant, the prosecution has to prove the receipt or giving of gratification and that such gratification was solicited or given "as an inducement to or reward for" doing or forbearing to do something.[66] In the case of public servants, all the prosecution needs to do is to show that the public servant received "gratification"[67] and the public servant then assumes the burden of establishing he did not receive such gratification for a corrupt purpose.

The PAP government also prosecuted senior figures despite their PAP affiliations.[68] This included Tan Kia Gan who was the PAP Minister for National Development until he lost his seat in the 1963 elections, Wee Toon Boon who was a junior minister in the Ministry of Environment, and Phey Yew Kok who was then President of the National Trades Union Congress and a PAP Member of Parliament.[69] In 1986 the then Minister for National Development Teh Cheang Wan was under investigation for corruption and decided to take his life.

The Singapore experience of reducing bureaucratic processes and civil servant discretion, strengthening the law and the anticorruption agency which was placed within the Prime Minister's Office, and strict enforcement of the law, is replicable in China. Indeed the CCP under Party Secretary Xi Jinping has embarked on an extensive anticorruption drive (see also Fu, Chapter 10). This augurs well for China though it is not yet clear the extent to which this is motivated by factional politics within the CCP.

D SOE Reforms

If the CCP wishes to address the problem of corruption, it is also imperative that further reform of China's SOEs takes place. Full privatization is unlikely to be an option given the advantages that the CCP derives from the state's control of her SOEs,[70] unless it can clearly be seen that SOEs are inherently not viable vehicles for commercial activity. Given that Singapore GLCs are a prime example of how SOEs can be efficiently managed

66 Ibid., Section 5.
67 This is defined broadly and includes any kind of property, any contract, and any service or favor. Ibid., Section 2.
68 Lee, *The Singapore Story*, 186–88.
69 Mr. Phey fled Singapore on December 31, 1979, while on bail but returned in 2015 and has been convicted.
70 Wang, "China's State-Owned Enterprises," 660–64.

and compete effectively in the marketplace,[71] no such case can be made out and accordingly there is no incentive for the party-state to give up control of key SOEs. Instead, the Singapore Model of GLC governance is likely to be attractive to China in the reform of her SOEs. Essentially, the Singapore approach is about getting able and honest people to manage her GLCs under the oversight of trusted establishment figures (some of whom are senior civil servants or former civil servants) and respected professionals at the board level.[72]

Importantly, the government makes no attempt to appoint managers or other personnel to manage the companies and normally does not interfere in the management of GLCs.[73] The government's interests in the GLCs are held and managed by Temasek Holdings Pte Ltd which was incorporated on January 1, 1974. Its sole shareholder is the Minister for Finance and the transfer of government assets to Temasek was to allow it to manage those assets on a commercial basis.[74] Temasek's board comprises a majority of independent directors.

Temasek states that it is an engaged shareholder that promotes sound corporate governance in its portfolio companies. This includes supporting the formation of high caliber, experienced, and diverse boards to guide and complement management leadership. Temasek's policy is not to direct the business operations or decisions of the companies in its portfolio and to leave this to their respective boards and management. Temasek does, however, advocate that boards be independent of management in order to provide effective oversight and supervision of management. This includes having mostly nonexecutive members on boards with the strength and experience to oversee management. Therefore, the boards of GLCs are policy boards rather than functional (managerial) ones.[75] Board members tend to be successful individuals in their own right with personal reputations to protect and do not consider financial considerations to be important when accepting appointment. Furthermore, the strong institutional and social aversion to corruption limits rent-seeking behavior,

[71] The PAP was wary of loss making nationalized companies elsewhere, and if GLCs could not compete effectively in the marketplace, they would be shut down. See Tan et al., "State-Owned Enterprises in Singapore."

[72] The managers of GLCs may not necessarily have strong links with the PAP, e.g., the CEO of DBS is Indian born and spent most of his career until 2009 with Citibank.

[73] Lee, *Public Enterprise and Economic Development*, 57.

[74] See information on Temasek: "FAQS," Temasek Holdings (Private) Limited, www.temasek.com.sg/abouttemasek/faqs.

[75] Philip Pillai, *State Enterprise in Singapore: Legal Importation and Development* (Singapore: Singapore University Press, 1983), 116.

and Temasek advocates that the Chairman and Chief Executive Officer roles be held by separate persons, independent of each other.[76]

While the Temasek model is intended to separate the government and the GLCs so as to enhance their ability to be managed on a commercial basis without undue governmental interference, and to ensure that there are checks and balances within Temasek and each GLC, there is nothing to stop the Singapore government from interfering if it wishes to do so. However, there exists a strong convention built up over many years against such interference. As GLCs were seen as important drivers of the economy, the government saw the importance of putting in place measures that would allow them to be run efficiently and has continued to honor this approach. Any reform in China must similarly be underpinned by the same political will.

E Contradictions of a Capitalist Society within a Socialist-Totalitarian State

The focus on economic development by the CCP has led to a conundrum. Although formally a socialist state, China in reality has become a highly capitalist society. This has given rise to many contradictions and problems. For one, very few Chinese truly believe in the ideology of the CCP. Not only was this the result of the Mao period but the more open environment of the post-Mao period has also allowed more voices and foreign ideas to circulate, and these have gathered pace through the pervasive use of the internet and online social media and the large number of Chinese who are now able to afford overseas travel. Chinese leaders also have to constantly balance competing interests such as economic development against environmental degradation, central versus provincial authority, urban and rural interests, and a desire for greater self-determination on the part of citizens set against the desire of the CCP to retain party-state control.

It will increasingly be difficult for these contradictions to be managed effectively by the party-state under a system that gives it a monopoly over governance. Diverse interest groups will increasingly want a more direct say in the formulation of public policy. There must be a manner in which these difficult issues are continually balanced in a way that is legitimate to a broad cross section of the Chinese public. This leads to the next issue of political liberalization.

[76] See "FAQS," Temasek.

F Political Liberalization

Perhaps the most profound lesson that Singapore might hold for China is in the area of political liberalization. This is the principal conundrum facing the CCP. The greater personal freedoms enjoyed by Chinese citizens stand in stark contrast with the lack of political freedoms. Singapore, as an authoritarian state that has allowed the PAP to retain power convincingly through relatively free and open elections, must be particularly intriguing especially when set against the more unrestrained electoral landscapes of Hong Kong, Korea, and Taiwan. Of course, what China sees as valuable in Singapore is what Western liberals criticize Singapore for.

Both perspectives do not fully capture the true picture. To Western liberals, it is the authoritarian nature of the PAP government that is the main reason for its overwhelming electoral success. While it is true that the PAP has not allowed opposition parties a level playing field, it is extremely unlikely that the outcome would have been significantly different as many Singaporeans are genuinely grateful to the PAP for giving them a better life through economic success. In addition, many of the advantages that the PAP government had in the past have been significantly eroded.[77] As for the Chinese party-state, the PAP's record provides evidence that an able authoritarian government can bring about economic development and continue to retain support. However, the outcome of the election in Singapore in 2011 should sound a cautionary note.

While on the face of it the PAP won yet another stunning victory with eighty-one out of eighty-seven parliamentary seats and 60.14 percent of the valid votes cast nationwide,[78] the 2011 results had many negatives for the PAP and arguably signals the beginning of a much more competitive political landscape last seen in the early 1960s. This was after all the PAP's worst showing since the 1963 elections and the opposition had six elected members[79] compared to the two in the previous parliament.[80] The PAP also lost two cabinet ministers including the highly respected

[77] For example, the control over mainstream media has been counterbalanced by sociopolitical websites and social media, and estate upgrading, which is linked to the PAP being able to manage the electoral ward in question, may no longer have the same appeal.

[78] See Ng E-Jay, "GE 2011 Roundup and Analysis," *Sgpolitics.net*, May 8, 2011, www.sgpolitics.net/?p=6789.

[79] All are from the Workers Party (WP).

[80] Subsequently the WP won a by-election in January 2013 when the PAP Speaker of Parliament resigned his seat.

Foreign Minister. Its share of the popular vote went down by slightly more than 6 percent but this is more significant than it seems because in the previous election in 2006 the majority of the seats was not contested (while in 2011 the PAP only obtained a walkover for one Group Representation Constituency comprising five seats) which suggests that in 2006 the opposition parties could field better candidates on average, concentrate resources, and target constituencies that were perceived as more vulnerable. Furthermore, in all the constituencies that the strongest opposition party contested, the PAP's share of the vote went below 60 percent. The relatively poor electoral performance of the PAP can be explained by widespread unhappiness over a number of matters including property prices, high cost of living, employment concerns, growing income inequality, and concerns over immigration and the resultant strain on infrastructure and the social fabric.

More significantly, the 2011 election was a manifestation of a more independent citizenry that feels less beholden to the PAP for its past achievements. It also reflects a maturing civil society with a greater proliferation of views as well as a desire for a better societal balance that does not focus overly on economic considerations. This change had been developing gradually prior to 2011 but has now come to the fore. The significance of it can be seen by the fact that even many members of the establishment think that a change in the ruling party cannot be ruled out within the next three to four election cycles.

While the CCP has cautiously experimented with elections at the village level, the Singapore experience should bring home the message that a functioning democracy is no respecter of authoritarian governments, even those that have generally governed well. The CCP may therefore see the Singapore experience as further proof that it should not go down such a path as it may lead to the party losing power.

This author would suggest a different conclusion. History has shown that profound social changes are unstoppable and will eventually sweep away the old order. It is difficult to see how the CCP can stand against the tide of representative government through free and fair elections. Increasingly, the citizenry will demand greater political freedoms and the party, bereft as it is by any moral authority or ideology, has no alternative compelling vision. It can find one if it is bold enough to seize a historic opportunity to introduce a democratic system of governance to China. While no system of governance is perfect, the factual "dynastic cycle" has meant long periods of chaos and hardship for the Chinese people. A democratic system provides a more orderly and effective way for political change to take place.[81] It also acts as a disciplining agent to those in power (Singapore being an example) and is arguably more effective at the local level than the oversight that the center can exercise. The CCP is in a position to help shape this new governance structure and avoid the danger of being swept away ignominiously eventually by the consequences of the reforms that it instituted.

Once again, Singapore provides potential insights. The PAP has responded to the 2011 elections by increasing the supply of public housing, tempering the property market, providing more health care facilities, and introducing new schemes to help the more vulnerable in society. These measures, together with the recent demise of Lee Kuan Yew on March 23, 2015, has led to some resurgence in support for the PAP. Singapore demonstrates that a strong and nimble political party emerging from an authoritarian phase to a more liberal Western one can continue to command the agenda.[82]

VI Conclusion

Like the Chinese people,[83] Singaporeans abhor major social upheaval. Although Singaporeans are a very Western-oriented Asian people (like

[81] While it is true that many Chinese believe that a strong authoritarian government is necessary for China given the chaos suffered by China when she was under less than authoritarian rule, it is suggested that this was because the absence of democracy meant there was no peaceful or timely method for a declining regime to be removed and replaced by a potentially more rigorous one. Suzanne Ogden, "Chinese Nationalism: The Precedence of Community and Identity over Individual Rights," in *China's Developmental Miracle*, Alvin Y. So (ed.), 226.

[82] Indeed, since an earlier draft of this chapter was submitted, Singapore held its General Election on September 11, 2015. In the election, the PAP improved significantly on its electoral performance, securing 69.9 percent of the valid votes cast, an almost 10 point increase from what it received in 2011. It also won back the seat it had lost in January 2013 to the WP in a by-election. The WP managed to retain its Single Member Constituency stronghold, and the Group Representation Constituency that it had won in 2011 – the latter by a whisker with 50.95 percent of the votes. The PAP's significantly improved performance can be attributed to the policy changes that it made after 2011, the demise of Lee Kuan Yew, the SG50 (Singapore's fiftieth birthday) celebrations, generous government giveaways, and (possibly unfair) accusations of improper financial governance against a WP-run Town Council, which is the organisation managing estate matters in a constituency. Part of the swing in the vote was probably also attributable to a concern after nomination day that the PAP might lose a high number of seats resulting in an unstable government. This likely caused an overreaction in favour of the PAP.

[83] Hsu, *Rise of Modern China*, 1016–17.

many young Chinese)and Singapore society is becoming increasingly liberal, Singaporeans in general like the orderliness and predictability that can be found in their country. They are happy with their "restrained democracy"[84] and do not want gridlock in governance. They support measures that are good for economic development even if there are interests that have to be sacrificed. As such, support for the PAP still remains strong but it is a more grudging, fluid support. The people want the PAP to be more connected to their needs and, as reflected in the 2011 election, will make their feelings known if they feel that it is out of touch. If anything, the long period of almost absolute political power caused complacency within the PAP prior to 2011 thereby weakening it. The more competitive political landscape (notwithstanding the outcome of the 2015 General Election) is an antidote for this which will hopefully lead to more fundamental reform within the PAP.[85] In addition, Singapore also illustrates how despite many years of experience with democracy politics in Singapore has on the whole been orderly and restrained. The history of Singapore is one of a society that has flourished because of her democratic system, not in spite of it. This is perhaps the most important insight for the CCP to discern from the Singapore experience.[86]

84 A term used by Hsu, ibid., 1017.

85 For example, the PAP is still reluctant to accept that it has to change its approach toward news and information given how connected Singapore is.

86 For an insight that some Chinese commentators have articulated, see Ortmann, "A Beijing Consensus in the Making?," 90–92.

PART II

Examining the Beijing Consensus in Context

4

The Legal Maladies of "Federalism, Chinese Style"

WEI CUI

I Introduction

According to those who claim the existence of a "Beijing Consensus," a key element of the Chinese Model of economic development is the willingness of China's authoritarian government to experiment with policy choices.[1] The literature on Chinese political economy has in turn analyzed policy experimentation chiefly in terms of the interactions between the national government and subnational political actors. For example, Yingyi Qian, Barry Weingast, and their fellow authors advanced the well-known hypothesis of "market preserving federalism," attributing China's economic growth before the early 1990s to both the (purported) ability and strong fiscal incentives on the part of subnational governments to implement pro-growth policies.[2] Zhang Jun, Zhou Li-An, and their collaborators have also developed a body of research demonstrating how the centralized personnel and appointment system within the Chinese Communist Party (CCP) and decentralized policy implementation jointly created conditions for a unique form of political "yardstick competition," and how the strong political incentives generated by such competition may have contributed to economic growth.[3] Other prominent social

[1] John Williamson, "Is the 'Beijing Consensus' Now Dominant?," *Asia Policy* 13 (2012): 1, cited in Edmund Malesky and Jonathan London, "The Political Economy of Development in China and Vietnam," *Annual Review of Political Science* 17 (2014): 395.

[2] Gabriella Montinola, Yingyi Qian, and Barry R. Weingast, "Federalism, Chinese Style: The Political Basis for Economic Success," *World Politics* 48 (2006): 50; Hehui Jin, Yingyi Qian, and Barry R. Weingast, "Regional Decentralization and Fiscal Incentives: Federalism, Chinese Style," *Journal of Public Economics* 89 (2005): 1719.

[3] See the essays collected in Jun Zhang and Li-An Zhou, *Weizengzhang erjingzheng: zhongguo zengzhangde zhengzhijingjixue* [Growth from Below: The Political Economy of China's Economic Growth] (Shanghai: Gezhi Chubanshe, 2008); Li-An Zhou, *Zhuanxing zhongde difang zhengfu: guanyuanjili yu zhili* [Local Governments in Transition: Official Incentives and Governance] (Shanghai: Gezhi Chubanshe, 2008); and Hongbin Li and Li-An Zhou, "Political Turnover and Economic Performance: The Incentive Role of Personnel Control in China," *Journal of Public Economics* 89 (2005): 1743.

scientists have offered critiques or modifications of such theories,[4] but all appear to agree that analyzing the dialectic between central control and subnational experimentation is key to the investigation of China's political economy.[5]

However, in the study of Chinese law (whether pursued inside or outside China), the theme of federalism – or "central-local relations" – has so far played entirely a background role. Central-local relations may enter generic descriptions of the Chinese political system in which the country's legal institutions are situated, but they are never the focus of theoretical, empirical, or even doctrinal legal analysis. Instead, aside from investigations of particular substantive areas of law, descriptions of the Chinese legal systems have privileged judicial institutions, the general discourse about the rule of law, and their relations to authoritarianism as themes for inquiry. Since analyzing center-local relations has been one of the vital sources of insight into Chinese authoritarianism, the insulation of legal studies from the study of "federalism, Chinese style" means that legal scholars' understanding of authoritarianism also remains generic and atheoretical.

In this chapter, I summarize and further develop arguments that I have made elsewhere, to the effect that the allocation of power and responsibilities among different tiers of government has indeed had major influences on the development of the rule of law in China. Specifically, the impact can be divided into two kinds. First, the extraordinary centralization of legislative power in China has resulted in a radical short supply of legal rules in virtually all areas of governance. Second, the extraordinary *de*centralization of the delivery of government services and policy implementation has directly reduced compliance with and enforcement of the laws, and indirectly undermined the development of legal institutions and the legal profession. Moreover, the adverse consequences of radical

[4] See Chenggang Xu, "The Fundamental Institutions of China's Reforms and Development," *Journal of Economic Literature* 49 (2011): 1076; Hongbin Cai and Daniel Treisman, "Did Government Decentralization Cause China's Economic Miracle?," *World Journal* 58 (2006): 505; Victor Shih, Christopher Adolph, and Mingxin Liu, "Getting Ahead in the Communist Party: Explaining the Advancement of Central Committee Members in China," *American Political Science Review* 106 (2012): 166–68; Victor Shih, *Factions and Finance in China: Elite Conflict and Inflation* (New York: Cambridge University Press, 2008). Shih's description of factions within the CCP crucially includes the category of "generalist" politicians, whose rotations through subnational political positions are determinative of their factional affiliations and policy outlook.

[5] For a recent survey, see Malesky and London, "The Political Economy of Development in China and Vietnam."

legislative centralization and radical administrative decentralization interact with one another: legislative centralization is especially inefficient, *conditional upon* administrative decentralization; administrative decentralization is especially pernicious, *conditional upon* legislative centralization. Overall, I argue, these twin arrangements have had a systematic negative impact on the Chinese legal system, and may have held back the development of the rule of law to a greater degree than even China's authoritarian government itself would like. Moreover, I believe that this negative impact could be of the first order: for what little we know empirically, the pervasive effect of these twin arrangements – which characterize virtually all aspects of Chinese governance – could exceed, in its magnitude, the effect of features of the few institutions that legal scholars have tended to study, such as the degree of independence of the judiciary.

The chapter proceeds as follows. Part II presents evidence that legislation is unusually centralized in China by commonly accepted standards, notwithstanding the prevalent assumption among the Chinese legal studies community that law *should be* centralized. It argues that centralization has inefficiently suppressed the supply of legal rules. Part III then shows that the performance of day-to-day government functions is unusually decentralized in China, again by commonly accepted standards, and highlights several ways in which this decentralization adversely impacts compliance and enforcement. Part IV discusses the ways in which studying legislative centralization and administrative decentralization brings to focus a wide range of empirical phenomena in Chinese law. Finally, Part V briefly discusses the theoretical significance of my proposal to connect the topics of federalism and the rule of law. Part VI concludes.

II Excessive Centralization in Lawmaking

A most fundamental feature of China's current legal and political system is a high degree of legislative centralization. The feature has two basic manifestations. First, within the central-provincial relationship, the central government possesses much greater legislative power. This is illustrated by the reservation of legislative power to the central government for several broad categories of policy in the Law on Legislation.[6] More importantly, this characterizes the disparate laws and regulations operative in a wide

[6] Legislation Law of the People's Republic of China, Article 8, effective July 1, 2000, www.cecc.gov/resources/legal-provisions/legislation-law-chinese-and-english-text.

array of policy areas.[7] Second, relatively few subprovincial governments have legislative power. Until 2015, only forty-nine quasi-provincial and prefecture-level jurisdictions could enact local statutes and regulations in comparison to the 333 prefecture-level, 2,856 county-level and 40,906 township-level jurisdictions across China.[8] According to the Law on Legislation, local statutes (*difang fagui*) and government regulations (*difang zhengfu guizhang*) are the only forms of local rules that have a formal legal effect and which apply generally.[9] Therefore, congressional bodies and executive offices in most municipal governments, and all county- and lower-level governments, do not have lawmaking power. People's congresses at most subprovincial jurisdictions are thus not "legislatures" but mere electoral and quasi-governing bodies, despite the constitution's recognition of them as "seats of state power."[10]

Surprisingly, such a core feature of Chinese legal institutions has received little analysis in either legal or social science scholarship. There remains a tendency among scholars studying Chinese law to believe that China's high degree of legislative centralization follows from China being a unitary and not a federalist country. But this belief is mistaken. Even in a unitary state with a single sovereign, legislative power can be delegated, whether constitutionally, systematically, or through specific legislation with respect to specific spheres or matters, to lower levels of governments. A unitary state simply means that such delegation may be withdrawn unilaterally by the sovereign, and not that the delegation cannot be made. Municipal, county and other local governments in other unitary states (e.g., the United Kingdom, Spain, Italy) routinely exercise delegated legislative power. Even in federalist countries, local governments similarly do not have inherent legislative power but instead exercise powers delegated to them by state or provincial sovereigns. Thus the limited range of government bodies that can make rules with binding legal effect in China has no foundation in any general legal doctrine and few analogues in international practice. Moreover, regional governments in many other unitary states enjoy greater legislative power than provincial governments in China.

7 For current arrangements of legislative centralization in tax policy making, for instance, see Wei Cui, "Fiscal Federalism in Chinese Taxation," *World Tax Journal* 3 (2011): 455.

8 These are located in twenty-seven provincial capitals, four cities that host special economic zones, and eighteen "relatively large cities" specially designated by the State Council.

9 Legislation Law of the People's Republic of China, Chapter 4.

10 The Constitution of the People's Republic of China, Article 2, effective December 4, 1982. www.npc.gov.cn/englishnpc/Constitution/node_2825.htm, Chapter 1.

There are two ways of answering the question, "How unusual is China's degree of legislative centralization?" The first is to follow the normal practice of comparative legal studies, and use the advanced legal systems of very few developed countries as the frame of reference. If comparisons are made this way, China would clearly look like an outlier. It is difficult to name any well-known legal system where the lowest two or three tiers of subnational government categorically lack lawmaking power (whether inherent or delegated), the way Chinese townships, counties, and most prefectural-level governments do. For example, the United States, Canada, Australia, and all European countries have property taxes, and most property tax rates are set by the lowest tiers of government (and the setting of property tax rates clearly is legally binding). This is a binary feature: either a lower-tier government has *some* lawmaking power, or it does not have *any*. If one looks instead to the scope of legislative discretion that subnational government in developed countries possess, it will be even clearer that substantial autonomy among subnational governments is the norm. For example, out of sixteen developed countries surveyed by Ebel and Taliercio, subnational governments in twelve countries had some legislative control over more than 50 percent of tax revenue.[11]

A second, more rigorous approach to evaluating how unusual China is in its legislative centralization is to compare representative countries from both the groups of developed and developing economies. Gadenne and Singhal recently presented data that suggests that developing countries generally are more centralized than developed countries, as measured by the proportion of subnational government budget to overall government budget (expenditure responsibility) and the proportion of subnational tax revenue to overall tax revenue (tax assignment).[12] Ebel and Taliercio, using more refined measures of fiscal autonomy than the IMF data relied on by Gadenne and Singhal, show that subnational governments in East Asian developing economies display a special lack of fiscal autonomy. In each of China, Cambodia, and Vietnam, revenue over which subnational governments have some legislative control represents less than 5

[11] Robert Ebel and Robert Taliercio, "Subnational Tax Policy and Administration in Developing Economies," *Tax Notes International* 37 (2005): 925.

[12] Lucie Gadenne and Monica Singhal, "Decentralization in Developing Economies," *Annual Review of Economics* 6 (2014): 581. They argue that this is the case even if developing countries from the twenty-first century are compared with developed countries in the late nineteenth century.

percent of subnational tax revenue.[13] These studies suggest that China might be less of an outlier when compared to other developing countries. This perspective, however, complements the one obtained from the first approach and gives even greater urgency to studying Chinese centralization. Chinese-style legislative centralization is unusual relative to the legal systems normally used as reference frames by Westerners – and by most legal scholars in China – *and* studying this unusual feature may shed some light on developing countries in general. These perspectives, however, are virtually unheard of in current literature.

My further contention is that China's extreme legislative centralization is worth studying because it has had a systematic negative impact on the rule of law. However, a quite opposite perception is prevalent in China (and not uncommon among Western scholars who study China): local governments are perceived to be more likely to run afoul of legal rules than the central government, and centralization is an instinctive response to local government behavior that deviates from the law. In short, law is often conflated with central control. However, this view is too unreflective. To put it in a somewhat tautological fashion: if local governments were to be able to make their own legal rules, they would be much less likely to violate legal rules. Deviations from the law by local governments may be the inevitable consequences of legislative centralization. In that case, it would be ironic to think that these deviations can be cured or prevented by legislative centralization.

A more substantive formulation is this. To adopt national policy in the form of national law to be applied for all of China requires gathering an enormous amount of information about social preferences and social and economic circumstances across the country and aggregating such information and preferences. This is sometimes impossible to do: there may simply be no policy that would work across the country. Moreover, in many other circumstances it is difficult to achieve (whether through authoritarian or democratic politics). Knowing the high likelihood of adopting inadequate or wrong rules, national lawmakers would naturally be hesitant to make rules. To use common Chinese bureaucratic parlance, they are more likely to wait – sometimes for decades – for circumstances of enacting legislation to become "mature" (*chengshu*). Thus giving the

[13] Such percentage is also relatively low in Thailand (10.9 percent) and Indonesia (15 percent), compared to 84 percent in Spain and 96 percent in Denmark (both of which have unitary political systems). Ebel and Taliercio, "Subnational Tax Policy and Administration in Developing Economies," 926.

central government a monopoly on lawmaking increases the likelihood that rules will turn out to be inadequate for local circumstances, or that no rule will be promulgated. Both these eventualities, however, increase the likelihood of local governments straying from centrally made law, or making policies outside all legislative frameworks, to fill the gaps left by the central government.

Like the central government, provincial governments may also suffer similar disadvantages with respect to policy issues specific to subprovincial jurisdictions. A general formulation of the problem would be as follows. The range of government entities authorized to make law has been highly restricted (as a means to exert political control). However, the information disadvantage, as well as incentive deficit, suffered by these entities results in an under-supply of adequate legal rules. Facing this problem, local governments that are outside the range of authorized lawmakers, in order to carry out their governance functions, adopt their own rules that are not supported by the legislative, interpretive, and administrative apparatus that formal legal rules command.

To support these claims, one needs to first show that legal rules are in short supply in China, and second that such short supply is significantly (though by no means exclusively) caused by legislative centralization. As to the first point, I believe that most Chinese legal professionals would agree with it at least at an anecdotal level: the shortage of legal rules in China is quite severe, particularly given both the size of the government and the level of development of the economy.[14] It is widely agreed that statutes adopted by the national legislature tend to contain merely principled statements and too few detailed rules, along with an abundance of rules that delegate further rulemaking to the executive branch. It is also generally known that the State Council leaves a vast amount of policy questions unanswered in the administrative regulations and decisions it issues, and makes generous delegations to national ministries. To assess the quantity and quality of the diverse bodies of regulations, rules, and

[14] For quite some time, and perhaps even today, a contrary claim can be heard among scholars of Chinese law, to the effect that China does not have a shortage of law: rather the law is simply not implemented. I believe this claim is merely rhetorical. Logically, the fact that law is unimplemented or not complied with does not contradict the view that there is a shortage of law for those who are willing to comply with the law. Moreover, that many legal rules are not implemented may suggest that they are poorly designed rules. In short, noncompliance with existing law is consistent with the shortage of supply of law. Practically, I find the claim a bit perverse, and reflective of the disengagement of legal scholarship from the practice of law.

policy guidance issued by national agencies requires substantial professional expertise, but I believe that most lawyers in their respective fields would agree that existing law and policy guidance contain large gaps, and such gaps tend to remain unfilled for long periods of time (often decades). The examples are innumerable.[15]

Nevertheless, how can one make such impressionistic evidence more systematic? One possibility is to systematically identify instances of rules adopted by local government agencies that could easily have general application, but to which correspond gaps in national rules. There are certainly many examples of such local rules, especially those that would promote local economic growth, tax collection, and other items central to the government agenda. Under the Company Law, for instance, whether in-kind (i.e., noncash) contributions of capital were permitted was unclear before the 2005 revision of the Company Law, and how to deal with such contributions remained vague at the national level after 2005. Against this backdrop, various local governments adopted explicit rules to facilitate the formation of businesses. Under the laws governing personal income tax, how income from investment partnerships should be treated was unclear at the national level, but various local governments adopted explicit local rules in order to encourage the growth of private equity. Various local tax bureaus also have explicit rules to distinguish taxable fringe benefits from nontaxable work supplies, an important problem in tax compliance facing many businesses. The notable features of all these cases are: (1) there has been no delegation of rulemaking authority from the central government to the local governments and administrative agencies; and (2) the local governments nonetheless adopted explicit rules to fill in obvious gaps in national rules, naturally, out of the need for regulation and administration.

Such local policy interpretations sometimes shade into problematic lawmaking – the adoption of rules that are contrary to, or at least unauthorized under, national rules. They are typically looked at askance by legal scholars.[16] But insofar as the rules adopted do not substantially involve

[15] For instance, after twenty years of the adoption of the Company Law, corporate "mergers" and "divisions" still lack basic definitions. In the area of corporate and personal income taxes, basic income tax concepts such as what constitutes individual residence in China, what is employment income, what determines ownership, etc., remain crudely defined after thirty years of income tax collection.

[16] See, e.g., Donald C. Clarke, "How Do We Know When an Enterprise Exists? Unanswerable Questions and Legal Polycentricity in China," *Columbia Journal of Asian Law* 19 (2005): 50.

local circumstances (e.g., there is nothing local about the question of whether work uniforms are taxable fringe benefits), they could be seen as meeting generic demands for legal rules that the central government has failed to supply. However, centralization means that even such local rules are in fact rarer than they should be, since local governments, supposedly acting as mere agents of the central government in the implementation of policy, have not been delegated any rulemaking authority. Their ability to meet demands for legal rules is already being strongly suppressed.

In a recent co-authored paper, I provide a more direct illustration of the failure of centralized rulemaking, by studying how Chinese provincial governments set local tax rates pursuant to nationally delegated powers.[17] In particular, we examine two episodes of tax-rate-setting for the vehicle and vessel tax (VVT) in 2007 and 2011, respectively. We exploit the fact that revenue from the VVT, like the revenue of numerous other small, local taxes, has been assigned in all provinces to subprovincial governments, who are also responsible for VVT collection. As a result, provincial rate-setting constitutes an instance of legislative centralization, even though it occurs at the subnational level: the range of decision-makers has been restricted, and information and incentives relevant to the decisions likely lie at lower levels of government. In delegating VVT rate-setting power to provinces, the national government signaled that it lacked information to set rates for different parts of the country. Legislative decentralization, therefore, ought to improve efficiency. We show, however, that provincial governments did not in fact incorporate provincial information in the choices of tax rates; instead they copied one another. Because the political motives for tax mimicry found in other jurisdictions, such as yardstick competition due to local elections, expenditure competition, or tax competition, are not present in the setting of VVT rates, it is highly plausible that provincial governments acted out of indifference as well as a lack of information. Thus the central and provincial governments collectively failed to adopt appropriate legislation. The detriments of centralization, interestingly, are observed at the provincial level.[18]

[17] Wei Cui and Zhiyuan Wang, "The Inefficiencies of Legislative Centralization: Evidence from Chinese Provincial Tax Rate Setting," *China: An International Journal* 13 (2015): 49.

[18] Cui and Wang's study directly supports the argument made by Gadenne and Singhal, that "the involvement of central governments in determining state and local taxes often limits the fiscal capacity of subnational governments... Imposing centrally determined taxes also severely undermines the potential efficiency benefit of these taxes: Taxes are less likely to reflect better local information and less likely to approximate user fees." Gadenne and Singhal, "Decentralization in Developing Economies," 594.

The kind of empirical test offered in Cui and Wang is useful for establishing the specific causal origin of the shortage of legal rules in centralization. In most countries, legal rules may be felt by the private sector to be in short supply. Law is a public good that is costly to produce, and even putting aside fundamental challenges of social choice and of politics, it may not be socially optimal to have legal rules resulting in precise determinations for each and every circumstance that transpires. In common law countries and countries with vibrant civil societies, courts, and professional associations may fill in some of the legal gaps left by legislators and administrative agencies. In other countries lacking similar mechanisms, the shortage of legal rules may be a more severe problem. Finally, countries like contemporary China have young legal systems, which imply less time to accumulate and revise legal rules. Given these general factors, it may seem difficult to claim an *additional* explanation (such as artificial restrictions on who can make law) is required to explain the shortage of law. But the study offered in Cui and Wang shows that such a claim can be substantiated.

What is even more plausible and commonsensical is that legislative centralization is problematic *in combination with* administrative decentralization. As Part II will discuss, a primary manifestation of administrative decentralization in China is the poor staffing of the central government bureaucracy. When national ministries are woefully under-staffed, how could they possibly supply enough legal rules? In addition to resource constraints, the lack of experience directly administering the law (a task relegated to local civil servants of much lower ranks) may also undermine the ability of central bureaucrats to draft appropriate legal rules. Such limitations of resource and experience may apply to provincial bureaucrats as well. Nonetheless, it is likely that China's high degree of legislative centralization is inefficient not only in combination with radical administrative decentralization, but even in the absence of such decentralization.

Ironically, one challenge for the proposal to study the consequences of Chinese legislative centralization empirically is that the inefficiencies of centralization in many areas of government activity may seem a priori to most students of federalism, such that it may not appear worthwhile to provide empirical evidence for it. However, neglecting the significance of legislative centralization in China is such an entrenched habit that perhaps only extensive documentation of centralization's negative impact can change the current discourse. Part III will discuss additional phenomena in Chinese law that may be explained by excessive legislative centralization.

III Excessive Administrative Decentralization

Although administrative decentralization in China is discussed more often than legislative centralization, several crucial refinements of the meaning of decentralization are necessary for one to evaluate its impact on the rule of law.[19] I define "administrative decentralization" as comprising two components.[20] First, there is a single bureaucratic hierarchy, and decentralization means that government functions vis-à-vis citizens are performed at the lowest levels of the hierarchy. By contrast, higher levels of the bureaucracy do not directly exercise government power with respect to citizens, but instead issue commands to bureaucratic subordinates. Second, the lower the bureaucratic rank, the more geographically dispersed are the units within that rank, and the smaller is their geographical reach. Decentralization thus implies that the scope of functions of a particular, citizen-facing government unit is usually delineated by reference to the finer geographic divisions of government.[21] What is unusual about China is first, how deep (i.e., multilayered) the bureaucratic hierarchy is, and second, how resolutely the tasks of government administration are placed at the bottom ranks of the hierarchy.

The most direct way (especially for comparative purposes) to present Chinese administrative decentralization is to consider the vertical distribution of government personnel. Information on such distribution is surprisingly scant. Yuen Yuen Ang has offered a few data points regarding the Chinese civil service as a whole, based on pre-1998 information.[22] She shows that while the net size of public employment in China in 1997 was one-third below the then global mean (3.1 percent of total population as compared to 4.7 percent), China's local (provincial level and below)

[19] See also Dowdle and Prado, Chapter 1, for a discussion of decentralization as part of the New Development Economies model.

[20] This section draws on Wei Cui, "Administrative Decentralization and Tax Compliance: A Transactional Cost Perspective," *University of Toronto Law Journal* 65 (2015): 186.

[21] These two components resemble what Professor Zhou Li-An calls "*xingzheng fabao*" (administrative outsourcing) and "*shudi guanli*" (territorial management) in his book, which argues that the pair of arrangements characterizes the environment for political yardstick competition in China. See Zhou, *Local Governments in Transition.*

[22] Yuen Yuen Ang, "Counting Cadres: A Comparative View of the Size of China's Public Employment," *The China Quarterly* 211 (2012): 676.

public employment size per capita of 2.5 percent was among the highest in the world, more than twice the global average of 1.1 percent. It follows "that China's public employment is heavily concentrated among local governments compared to other countries."[23] In fact, China's national-level and provincial-level civil service has probably become even thinner (relative to the total size of public employment) since the late 1990s, after several rounds of government downsizing. China's current Minister of Finance Lou Jiwei, for example, estimated that the central government staff comprised only 7 percent of the total civil service in 2006.[24] On the basis of this estimate, Lou states that China has the "smallest central government in the world."

China's tax bureaucracy, which employs more than 10 percent of the total population of civil servants, offers a vivid illustration. The national State Administration of Taxation deploys just over 0.1 percent of total workforce in tax administration. As can be expected, the agency undertakes very little direct administrative responsibility vis-à-vis taxpayers. According to a recent OECD study,[25] which covered 35 OECD countries and seventeen non-OECD countries/regions, in 2011 China had by far the smallest percentage of tax administration staff working at headquarters (i.e., national offices) among the fifty-two countries surveyed. Furthermore, if provincial tax bureaus are counted as a form of regional offices, China's percentage of tax administrators working at either national or regional offices is also the lowest among all countries surveyed.

Data compiled by the State Administration of Taxation (SAT) allow us to obtain an even finer-grained view of the "bottom-heaviness" of Chinese governance. In 2003, provincial-level employees accounted for only 5 percent of the staff in the State Tax Bureau system. In contrast, prefectural-level employees accounted for 16 percent, while those at the

[23] She then draws the correct conclusion "that given the complexity of policy-making in such a populous country, China's central government employment may be too small." Ibid., 691.

[24] See Jiwei Lou, "Xuanze gaigede youxiancixu" [Choosing the Optimal Sequence of Reforms], *21st Century Business Herald*, August 6, 2006. Lou's estimate of the proportion of centrally employed civil servants is much smaller than Ang's for the 1990s (20 percent; Ang, "Counting Cadres," 693). Lou has since then revised the estimate down even further for comparative purposes, to 4 percent. See Jiwei Lou, "Yangdi guanxi zaichonggou" [Restructuring Central and Local Relations Once Again], *Caijing Magazine*, April 2, 2012.

[25] OECD, *Tax Administration 2013: Comparative Information on OECD and Other Advanced and Emerging Economies* (Paris: OECD, 2013), 83.

county level or below represented an overwhelming 79.5 percent. A similar distribution can be found for the Local Tax Bureau system. If we were to visualize Chinese tax administration in a pyramidal figure, divided into five tiers (corresponding to the national, provincial, prefectural, county, and subcounty levels), the proportions of each tier from the national to the subcountry level would have the ratios of 0.1:4.9:15:40:40.

There are other measures of administrative decentralization than personnel distribution – such as the actual allocation of administrative powers – which I do not elaborate here. The type of decentralization that characterizes Chinese tax administration is in fact shared by a majority of the Chinese administrative state. In most areas of governance – be it business registration, public health and food safety, environmental protection,[26] policing, education, labor and social security, land management, and cultural and media regulation – the Chinese state is decentralized, i.e., bottom-heavy in a geographically dispersed hierarchy.

Suppose it is accepted that China's degree of administrative decentralization makes it an international outlier. What does this have to do with the rule of law? The answer is: quite a lot. To begin, consider what impact decentralization has on the county-level or lower-level civil servants as enforcers of the law. The positions they occupy resemble those of legal professionals, yet they are seriously disadvantaged as professionals. For one, their geographic jurisdiction is limited, and this gives them relatively little incentive to specialize within their fields of work. Any type of transaction or situation to which specialized law applies is less likely to occur in a small jurisdiction compared to a big one. Moreover, because they are situated at such low rungs of the bureaucratic hierarchy, the career incentives for developing professionalism are also limited – the chances of rising to higher positions are minimal. These disadvantages can be crippling, even if the civil servants begin with high levels of education.

Consider further the incentives of regulated subjects (e.g., taxpayers) vis-à-vis these low-level law enforcers. Although China's civil service, relative to international standards, is not bloated in per capita terms, assigning most civil servants to limited geographical jurisdictions does give regulated subjects readier and cheaper access to law enforcers. As a

[26] For a discussion of decentralization in environmental protection agencies, see Benjamin Van Rooij, *Regulating Land and Pollution in China: Lawmaking, Compliance, and Enforcement; Theory and Cases* (Leiden: Leiden University Press, 2006), 267–71.

result, regulated subjects will face two, potentially very different, sources of law. One is law as it is generally publicized by the government and interpreted by the legal profession. The other is whatever rules the low-level civil servant will most likely enforce. Because of the civil servants' professional disadvantages, the rules low-level civil servants are likely to enforce may frequently deviate from the law as publicized. Yet since it is the rules that are likely to be enforced that matter most of the time – in the system of administrative decentralization, higher level bureaucrats rarely interact with citizens directly – most regulated subjects may have incentives to learn these rules only. For this reason, publicized law may often fail to regulate behavior.

Add to all this the fact that legislation is extremely centralized in China: because the law enforcers are so removed from the rule-makers – even though they are most likely all employed by the same bureaucracy – communication and coordination can be very costly. It is hard for the rule-makers to know how legal rules are enforced, and it is hard for the enforcers to know why the publicized rules are adopted.

Is it possible to empirically verify the negative consequences that administrative decentralization brings as I have predicted? Such systematic verification has not yet been offered, but I have argued that in the context of tax administration these predictions fit well with two easily observable phenomena. One is the under-utilization of courts: taxpayers sue tax agencies very infrequently.[27] This would be the natural outcome if most taxpayers either do not comply with the tax law, or they comply only with the law dictated by low-level enforcement officers but not with the requirements of formally publicized law (possibly due to a lack of awareness). The other is the underdevelopment of the tax profession: there is no room for legal professionals if all that matters is the propensities for law enforcement by individual, low-level civil servants.

The potential causal connection between administrative decentralization and the failure of enforcement and compliance implies that the conditions for the rule of law may often be violated in China well before disputes arise and reach courts, such that the presence or absence of an independent judiciary may be of secondary significance for important regulatory areas. Moreover, excessive administrative decentralization may

[27] Wei Cui, "Zhongguo shuiwu xingzheng susong shizheng yanjiu" [An Empirical Study of Tax Litigation in China], *Qinghua faxue* (2015): 135.

have held back the rule of law in ways that are contrary to the preference of China's authoritarian government itself.

IV Seeing "Federalism, Chinese-Style" in Chinese Law

The anomalous combination of legislative centralization and administrative decentralization – each arguably excessive in its own, and each made worse in its impact by the other – may be labeled "federalism, Chinese style" in the realm of law. A wide range of phenomena in the Chinese legal system can be traced at least partly to this combination.

Part I has already highlighted the sparseness in content of national statutes and regulations. This feature, particularly within the more exalted categories of Chinese law, is especially remarkable given the insular nature of China's lawmaking process. Like parliamentary systems elsewhere, the Chinese executive branch gets to write the law, often with little input or public discussion. The drafters of statutes, formal regulations, and informal administrative guidance, are likely to be all the same bureaucrats. In this type of setting, where there are few veto players in the legislative process, it is common in other countries to see a great amount of detailed rules in statutes, reflecting the bureaucratic expertise of the executive branch. Yet the insular policymaking process in China does not have such effect. This phenomenon, which is of great interest to lawyers, clearly calls for an explanation.

The perspective outlined in Parts I and II provides one such explanation. To begin, the tiny size of the central government bureaucracy – the result of administrative decentralization – means that central ministries often lack staff resources for policy research and legislation. Yet at the same time, the ministries essentially monopolize lawmaking. Central ministerial employees often have little experience actually administering the law. They also lack contact with the low-level government employees who do have such experience. They are thus often poorly positioned to furnish drafting detail: they lack the channels of information both ex ante and ex post to be confident that any detailed provision drafted are appropriate. The safer approach for employees at the central ministries (and their bosses) is to make only statements of principle in statutes and formal regulations, even though few would veto more detailed proposed statutory or regulatory language.[28]

[28] For a narrative example, see Wei Cui, "Dui qiyechongzu shuiwuguize qicaoguochengde fansi" [Reflections on the Making of the Income Tax Rules for Enterprise Reorganizations],

In fact, the small pool of manpower and the lack of information on the part of central ministries explain many features of the legislative and agency rule making processes in China when viewed up close.[29] For example, the paucity of formal ministerial regulations and the overwhelmingly prevalent practice of issuing informal circulars[30] are not due to any onerous procedural requirements (such as notice and comment) imposed on formal regulation. Instead, they are arguably the result mainly of staffing constraints and an unwillingness of the central ministries to commit to legal positions. To use another example, it is a surprise for many to learn of the unfading popularity of comparative studies among legislators in China despite the size of China's population and economy as well as regional variations (there are no dearth of examples in China). Yet Chinese lawmakers are perennially interested in the laws of other countries, including even countries that are much smaller, countries that have different circumstances, and countries that do not have advanced legal systems. Yet, this interest is unlikely to be a reflection of some irrational belief in the effectiveness of legal transplants. The more plausible explanation is that this interest stems from the sheer lack of information about what is actually happening in China. This lack of information, on the part of the central government, is in no small part attributable to the combination of legislative centralization and administrative decentralization.

The central government's lack of information can also be seen in its frequent inability to commit even to rules and policies enshrined in statutes. As a number of commentators have pointed out, it is not just the lower-level governments that nonchalantly issue ultra vires rules and policies that conflict with applicable law of higher status. Central ministries also do so with alarming frequency. Nicolas Howson has asked how the Chinese Securities Regulatory Commission, with a most elite legal staff, could

in *Tax Law and Case Review: Volume 1*, Xiong Wei (ed.) (Beijing: Law Press, 2010). Income tax rules for corporate reorganizations were developed during the 1990s through informal administrative guidance, and remained virtually unchanged between 2000 and 2007. In 2007 these rules were included in the State Council's draft administrative regulation for implementing the new Enterprise Income Tax Law but were deleted at the last minute because they were perceived to be too complex by lawyers in the State Council's Legislative Affairs Office. Furthermore, none of the few SAT staff members who understood the rules happened to be available to explain them to the State Council's lawyers.

29 These processes have not been closely documented in Chinese legal studies. Some scholars in China participate in them but generally choose not to write about them while the few accounts presented by scholars outside China tend to be sparse.

30 For examples in Chinese taxation, see Wei Cui, "What Is the 'Law' in Chinese Tax Administration?," *Asia Pacific Law Review* 19 (2011): 75.

issue informal circulars on insider trading that flatly contradict the Securities Law.[31] Yet such instances of ultra vires rule making can be found in China wherever one looks,[32] and they are especially notable for the following reasons. First, the notion that statutes and regulations tend to reflect the preferences of lawmakers in the parliament or State Council while agency guidance tends to reflect the distinct preferences of a different group of bureaucrats is incorrect. As noted above, the distinction between legislation and rulemaking in China is weak. Ultra vires rule making often reflects not the actions of errant agents but changes of mind of principals. Second, such changes of mind often occur not as a result of any change in the circumstances surrounding policy. Nor are most of the ultra vires rules promulgated by subordinate ideologically or politically compelling. Their rationales are miscellaneous and banal. The suggestion here is that their banality may also have a banal explanation. After having monopolized lawmaking, the central government constantly struggles to deliver legal rules.

In terms of phenomena observed in respect of the enforcement end of the legal system, although the analysis summarized in Part II implies many predictions, one of the most critical is that the legal profession tends to be excluded from ordinary law enforcement in many regulatory areas. As a result, legal professionals tend not to observe how law enforcement activities are carried out, and their impressions of law enforcement are likely to be patchy. This does not mean that relevant phenomena cannot be identified or lack legal significance. One example is as follows. It has been observed in some policy areas that Chinese regulatory agencies impose low sanctions on noncompliant subjects. The fines levied on violators of environmental laws seem systematically lie at the lower end of the permitted range even though this arguably makes for ineffective enforcement.[33] This is probably true in the tax area as well. Decentralization can offer an explanation for this clearly important aspect of China's legal system. Where regulated subjects have frequent contact with regulators, including consulting the latter on the consequences of their actions, it is easier for

[31] Nicolas Howson, "Enforcement without Foundation? Insider Trading and China's Administrative Law Crisis," *American Journal of Comparative Law* 60 (2012): 955. See also Tang, Chapter 8.

[32] See, e.g., Cui, "What Is the 'Law' in Chinese Tax Administration?"

[33] Van Rooij, *Regulating Land and Pollution*, 288–89; Benjamin Van Rooij, "The People's Regulation, Citizens and Implementation of Law in China," *Columbia Journal of Asian Law* 25 (2012): 10–12.

violators to argue that they have had the explicit or tacit approval of regulators. Such frequent contact may be what makes it difficult to impose high fines.

V Implications for Two Existing Literatures

The account given in this chapter of "federalism, Chinese style" from the perspective of the law has substantial implications for the literature on Chinese political economy. It has been the norm in that literature to portray explanations of Chinese economic growth, in terms of central-local relations, as either repudiations or innovative supplementations of orthodox institutional economics. The logic of the political economists' arguments typically goes: China does not have an independent judiciary or legal regimes for securing property rights or guaranteeing the enforcement of contracts; then, why did China's economy grow so rapidly for such a long period of time? Chinese-style federalist arrangements (as theorized in different ways) are then offered as substitutes for the missing legal institutions.

The account given in this chapter suggests that some features that are indeed unique about Chinese intergovernmental relations in fact *undermine* the operation of legal institutions. If we posit that a relatively clear set of legal rules for governments and private actors to follow is conducive to economic growth, then, Chinese-style legislative centralization is antigrowth. If government actors deem it desirable that the policies they have chosen be reasonably and reliably implemented through compliance with legal rules, then, Chinese-style administrative decentralization prevents this from happening. Thus, it seems that Chinese-style federalism not only operates *in the absence of legal institutions* but also *inhibits the potential contribution of legal institutions.* China does not just happen to have the intergovernmental relations it has, plus the absence of rule of law: the absence of the rule of law is attributable in no small part to the present state of intergovernmental relations. Therefore, if law does not matter for economic growth, it must fail to matter not only because property rights, contractual enforcement and independent judiciaries do not matter, but also because having rules for coordination and achieving compliance with government policies do not matter. Yet this conclusion – that coordination and policy implementation do not matter – is hard to make sense of. Suppose we accept that Chinese subnational government officials are highly incentivized to promote economic growth. How did they act on such incentives? How did they achieve economic growth if the system for transmitting and enforcing policy is constantly eroded? Without being able to envision such mechanisms, it seems that one would have to claim that whatever economic growth was achieved, was achieved regardless of (much) government policy. The opposite would seem more plausible: if Chinese intergovernmental relations had a less inhibitive effect on the development of the rule of law, enormous productive potential would have been unleashed. The perspective of law, therefore, casts doubt on the explanatory power of federalism, Chinese-style for economic growth.

The account of this chapter also has fundamental implications for the literature on the development of the rule of law in China. Notably, current literature on the rule of law is founded on two assumptions. First, it is assumed that the term "rule of law" stands for a set of legal institutions that are prominent in the legal systems of developed countries, including especially a competent and independent judiciary. Although there has been a lively debate on whether developments in the Chinese legal system should be measured by a thick or thin conception of the rule of law,[34] it is still common for legal scholars and commentators to associate the rule of law with particular legal institutions and to either blame the failure of the rule of law on the features of these institutions or to pin hopes for a wider conception of the rule of law on changes to these institutions. These instinctive causal inferences are not unique to Chinese legal studies,[35] yet over time they increasingly stretch credulity. For example, is there any evidence that the manpower and budgetary changes proposed in 2013 for the judiciary will have a decisive impact on the Chinese legal system? The details of such arrangements are rarely regarded as central to the functioning of judiciaries elsewhere.[36] Similarly, those who believe that the rule of law means the judiciary's ability to constrain government advocate for purportedly "idealistic" pro-plaintiff provisions (such as less stringent standing requirements and the possibility of anticipatory adjudication) in the revision of the Administrative Litigation Law, when

[34] See, e.g., Randall Peerenboom, *China's Long March toward Rule of Law* (Cambridge: Cambridge University Press, 2002).

[35] Hadfield and Weingast argue that "the great majority of academic and policy work takes the concept for granted, generally equating it with the institutions and practices in those (relatively few) parts of the world where the rule of law has been largely achieved." Gillian K. Hadfield and Barry R. Weingast, "Microfoundations of the Rules of Law," *Annual Review of Political Science* 17 (2014): 21.

[36] Increasing vertical control and providing better professional incentives to government employees are hardly new initiatives even in China.

such provisions are hardly regarded as necessary or even desirable in developed legal systems.[37]

A second assumption in the existing literature is that the CCP's preferences determine the development of the rule of law. It is almost uniformly accepted that the Chinese government embraces an instrumentalist conception of law; the Chinese government only promotes the rule of law when and only when it is in the CCP's own interest. Thus China has witnessed some progress toward the rule of law because that is in the CCP's interest; but there has not been greater progress, because that would have threatened to undermine the CCP's self-interest. The flaws of this kind of narrative as social scientific explanations are patent.

The connection drawn in this chapter between intergovernmental relations and the rule of law in China departs from both of the above assumptions. First, a wide range of institutions, social practices, and individual behavior determine whether there is a legal order or not. Conversely, the absence of legal order often has nothing to do with courts. For example, if regulators and regulated subjects achieve mutually acceptable outcomes extra-legally (e.g., sufficient revenue is collected regardless of what the tax law says), neither party will litigate. It will then be wrong to blame low litigation volumes on the lack of judicial independence. Moreover, if potential plaintiffs refuse to litigate, the rule of law cannot be enhanced by empowering the judiciary to monitor administrative agencies.[38] Indeed, whether legal order is maintained or not often does not even depend on the government alone. If a regulated subject decides not to hire a lawyer or otherwise learn the law, but instead puts in an inquiry with a low-level government employee, it is he (the citizen and not the government employee) who initiates the informal transaction. Finally, whether an adequate supply of legal rules is available may depend not on the relation between the legislative and executive branches (an institutional configuration frequently emphasized by rule of law advocates) but on the relationship between higher and lower tiers of government.

Second, this chapter has also shown that the extent of rule of law may not be determined by the preferences of the (single) ruling political party. Even if radical legislative centralization is seen as the preference of the Chinese authoritarian government – with the caveat that it also appears

37 See William Landes and Richard Posner, "The Economics of Anticipatory Adjudication," *Journal of Legal Studies* 23 (1994): 683.

38 Likewise, if statutes and formal regulations are most often vague and lacking in details, most judges will have no choice or incentive but to defer to agency interpretations.

to be the preference of the dominant majority of Chinese law scholars however otherwise liberal-minded – radical administrative decentralization is much more likely to be exogenous to such preferences. Chinese politicians are products of such a system, not the other way around.

VI Conclusion

I believe that my arguments are novel, even contrarian, in a number of important ways. From a normative and legal perspective, they are unorthodox both doctrinally and in their policy implications. As Part I discussed, the error that most scholars of Chinese law, as well as much social scientific scholarship that passively accepts the Chinese legal discourse, fall prey to is conflating law and centralized law.[39] Under the prevailing conception, "law" is what the central government announces, whereas "real practice" – enforcement or nonenforcement, compliance or noncompliance – is what happens "locally." Whereas the distinction between law on paper and law in practice holds everywhere in the world, this distinction is often aligned with the "central/local" divide in China. This conflation has even led some to postulate a conflict between decentralized experimentation and the rule of law. The perspective advanced in this chapter, however, suggests that this mode of discourse originates in an unreflective acceptance of a political ideology that promotes excessive centralization. Breaking free of the shackles of this confounding discourse is necessary just to get the descriptions of many phenomena in Chinese law right.

From a social scientific perspective, the arguments of this chapter offer fresh insights, empirically as well as theoretically. Recognizing what an outlier China is (relative to the legal systems with which China is normally compared) in terms of legislative centralization and administrative decentralization should prompt a range of empirical reclassifications. Provincial policy making, for example, should often be seen as centralized, not decentralized, policy making. This chapter also opens avenues for new historical inquiries, e.g., into how the anomalous pairing of radical legislative centralization and radical administrative decentralization came about. More importantly, in terms of theorizing about legal systems, the connections I draw between federalism and the rule of law is based on the demand for and supply of legal rules and the relevant actors'

[39] In contrast, Upham notes that ultra vires rules are not "law" but "order." Upham, Chapter 5.

ability and incentives to acquire knowledge of legal rules. In analyzing how the rule of law has developed in China, I do not place specific institutions, such as courts or property right regimes, on a pedestal. While the study of Chinese law – and the study of legal systems in developing or transitional economies more generally – has traditionally dwelled upon these institutions, it has been suggested recently that this approach is mistaken. Instead, legal theorists are now calling for explorations of the micro-foundations of the rule of law.[40] The arguments in this chapter can be seen as answering that call.

[40] Hadfield and Weingast, "Micro-foundations of the Rules of Law," 22.

5

Lessons from Chinese Growth

Rethinking the Role of Property Rights in Development

FRANK K. UPHAM*

This chapter addresses two questions that arise from China's more than thirty years of economic growth without a robust property rights regime. First, should social scientists rethink the conventional wisdom about the economic role of property rights? Second, if so, can China's experience with property law serve as a model for other developing countries? In other words, does it make sense to think in terms of a "Beijing Consensus" on the role of property rights in development that would replace the Washington Consensus, which dominated development economics from the 1980s to the turn of the century? To cut to the chase, my answers are yes and not really.

The chapter proceeds as follows. Part I reviews the current conventional wisdom on property and development. Part II summarizes the evolution of China's formal property law over the high-growth period. Part III compares the actuality of law's role in China with the role that conventional wisdom would predict with particular attention to three areas. The first area is the interaction between what I call bureaucratic order and formal law; the second area is the nature of informal property rights in investment, one in the township and village enterprises of the early reform period and the other in foreign direct investment in contemporary China; the third area is the creation and sustainability of informal and illegal land markets in Chinese cities. Part IV discusses whether the deviations from social science theory found in Part III represent simply a variation on expected general patterns or are so different in nature that they demand a fundamental rethinking of the doctrine. Part IV

* Research for this chapter was supported by the Filomen D'Agostino and Max E. Greenberg Research Fund at NYU School of Law. Many thanks to Ms. Jean Lee for her research and editorial assistance.

concludes provisionally that China presents a fundamental challenge to the status quo of development theory, at least as that theory has been put into practice by the vast majority of first world law reform practitioners. Part V addresses the fundamental question surrounding this publication: should social scientists use the data of Chinese economic growth to create a "Beijing Consensus"?

I What Is Orthodox Theory of the Role of Property Rights in Development?

The World Bank in 1996 summarized the conventional wisdom on the role of property rights and growth as follows:

> Property rights are at the heart of the incentive structure of market economies. They determine who bears risk and who gains or loses from transactions. In so doing they spur worthwhile investment, encourage careful monitoring and supervision, promote work effort, and create a constituency for enforceable contract. In short, fully specified property rights reward effort and good judgment, thereby assisting economic growth and wealth creation.[1]

In this view of the world, property rights are linked with contract rights and an independent, honest, and competent judiciary that will effectively enforce both. Property rights determine who has control over assets; contract law enables market participants to exchange those assets in complicated transactions among strangers; and the courts enable market actors to plan by resolving disputes predictably, efficiently, and in accordance with public and unambiguous legal rules. While legally unenforceable exchange can occur in networks and communities with high levels of trust, complicated transactions among strangers, upon which large-scale growth depends, cannot take place without these elements.

This focus on courts and property rights has its home in institutional economics and traces its origins to *The Problem of Social Cost* by Ronald Coase[2] and *Toward a Theory of Property Rights*[3] by Harold Demsetz. Summarizing the ideas of these thinkers in a few words is impossible, but suffice it to say that Coase argued that a core function of the government in

[1] World Bank, *World Development Report 1996: From Plan to Market* (New York: Oxford University Press, 1996), 48–49.
[2] R. H. Coase, "The Problem of Social Cost," *Journal of Law & Economics* 3 (1960): 1
[3] Harold Demsetz, "Toward a Theory of Property Rights," *The American Economic Review* 57 (1967): 347.

a market economy was to enforce property and contract rights. Demsetz went a bit further to argue that property rights should in most instances be individual and private so that owners will internalize the costs and benefits of their actions. In such a universe, or at least one without debilitating transaction costs, private parties would use contract rights to bargain to efficiency regardless of the initial distribution of resources, and the enforcement of property rights would ensure that the social costs and benefits of economic activity would be borne by the private owners. The result would be efficient growth.

The third figure in the institutional pantheon is Douglass North.[4] He emphasized what had been implicit in the work of his predecessors: none of the wonderful results of contract and property rights or the advantages of individual over commonly held property would materialize without institutions to enforce them. It is important to note that for both Demsetz and North, "institutions" include formal and informal rules as well as organizations like courts or governments that are the more familiar referent of the term. Demsetz captured the essence eloquently:

> Property rights are an instrument of society and derive their significance from the fact that they help a man form those expectations which he can reasonably hold in his dealings with others. These expectations find expression in the laws, *customs* and *mores* of a society [emphasis added].

Unfortunately, this broad definition has not survived the transition from theory to practice, and the term "institutions" has come to mean the statutes, courts, judges, and lawyers of a country's formal legal system. It is in this narrower sense of the term that China's experience presents a challenge.

Consistent with these beliefs, the past three decades have seen a massive expansion of legal reform projects aimed at engendering economic growth in poor countries by creating "market-friendly" legal rules and

[4] See, for example, Douglass C. North, *Institutional Change and Economic Performance* (Cambridge: Cambridge University Press, 1990); and Douglass C. North, *Structure and Change in Economic History* (New York: W. W. Norton, 1981). Mancur Olson is another economist associated with institutional economics. See Mancur Olson Jr., "Big Bills Left on the Sidewalk: Why Some Nations Are Rich, and Others Poor," *Journal of Economic Perspectives* 10 (1996): 3. Olson uses contract and property rights to explain why people in poor countries fail to "realize the largest gains from specialization and trade: They do not have the institutions that enforce contracts impartially, and so they lose most of the gains from those transactions . . . that require impartial third-party enforcement. They do not have institutions that make property rights secure over the long run, so they lose most of the gains from capital-intensive productions." Olson, "Big Bills Left on the Sidewalk," 22.

enhancing the judiciary's role in their enforcement. As of 2004, the World Bank alone had sponsored as many as six hundred judicial reform projects in more than one hundred countries.[5] The operative assumptions underlying these projects are well captured by remarks of the chief counsel of the World Bank's Legal and Judicial Reform Practice Group: "A free and robust market can thrive only in a political system where individual freedoms and property rights are accorded respect and where redress for violations of such rights can be found in fair and equitable courts."[6] The emphasis on courts has remained constant within the world of law and development despite changes in the wider development community that have led to at least a rhetorical rejection of the one-size-fits-all template for reform, a recognition that informal norms play a crucial role in market performance, and the widespread acceptance that development should include poverty reduction, attention to the status of women and indigenous communities, popular participation in goal setting, and other dimensions of development sometimes lumped together as "the social."[7]

II The Evolution of Chinese Property Law since "Reform and Opening"

Despite the leading role of the industrial proletariat in Marxist theory, the CCP came to power in 1949 on the backs of poor tenant farmers and immediately rewarded them with a thoroughgoing land reform. Article 3 of the Common Program, the new regime's provisional constitution, declared that the state "must systematically transform the feudal and semifeudal land ownership system into a system of peasant land ownership."[8] A thoroughgoing redistribution of land followed under the Land Reform Act of 1950. By 1953, 40 percent of Chinese land had been

5 Alvaro Santos, "The World Bank's Uses of the 'Rule of Law' Promise in Economic Development," in *The New Law and Development: A Critical Appraisal*, David M. Trubek et al. (eds.) (Cambridge: Cambridge University Press: 2006), 253.

6 Maria Dakolias, "A Strategy for Judicial Reform: The Experience in Latin America," *Virginia Journal of International Law* 36 (1995–1996): 168.

7 See generally Kerry Rittich, "The Future of Law and Development: Second-Generation Reforms and the Incorporation of the Social," in *The New Law and Development: A Critical Appraisal*, David M. Trubek and Alvaro Santos (eds.) (Cambridge: Cambridge University Press: 2006), 203, 205.

8 Article 3 of the Common Program of the Chinese People's Political Consultative Conference as enacted on September 29, 1949. "Modern History Sourcebook: The Common Program of The Chinese People's Political Consultative Conference, 1949," *Fordham University*, http://legacy.fordham.edu/halsall/mod/1949-ccp-program.html.

redistributed to 60 percent of the population, and almost 300 million farmers had received approximately 700 million *mu* (1 hectare = 15 *mu*) of agricultural land.

In 1954 the first constitution of the PRC ratified the land reform and established four forms of ownership: state, individual worker, capitalist, and collective. The last encompassed rural land and foreshadowed the eventual elimination of individual landownership. The collectivization process had begun in 1948 with voluntary Mutual Aid Teams, went through various forms of decreasingly voluntary cooperatives, and eventually culminated in 1958 in the transfer of all remaining private rights to the People's Communes of which the farmers were members. From 1958 to Deng Xiaoping's "reform and opening" (*gaigekaifang*) of 1978, the People's Communes constituted de facto the only form of landownership in rural China, although it was not until the constitutions of 1975 and 1978 that the four ownership forms of the 1954 Constitution were legally reduced to the state and collective forms that constitute constitutional property today.

The commune system dramatically decreased agricultural productivity,[9] but continued unchallenged until 1978 when Xiao Gang Village in Anhui Province began leasing land to families for cultivation outside of the commune system. The experiment, initiated with some trepidation by Xiao Gang farmers, was hugely successful and adopted as the Household Responsibility System (HRS) by the central government in a 1980 CCP Central Committee declaration entitled Several Issues Concerning Strengthening and Improving the Agricultural Production Responsibility System.[10] Within a year of promulgation, 97.7 percent of collectives had adopted the system[11] and were contracting out land to individual families for periods that began as fifteen years but that have lengthened progressively until the present where the default period is thirty years with the full, if de facto, expectation of indefinite renewal. Security of tenure had strengthened along with contract terms.

[9] See Justin Yifu Lin, "Collectivization and China's Agricultural Crisis in 1959–1961," *Journal of Political Economy* 98 (1990): 1228–29, 1238.

[10] "Zhongyang zhongyang yinfa 'Guanyu jinyibu jiaqiang he wanshan nongye shenchan zerenzhi de jige wenti'" [Central Committee Announces a 'Notice on Several Issues Concerning Strengthening and Improving the Agricultural Production Responsibility System'], *Xinhua News*, September 27, 1980, http://news.xinhuanet.com/ziliao/2005–02/04/content_2547020.htm.

[11] Wei Du and Shanming Huang, *Shidi nongmin quanyibaozhang de jingjixue yanjiu* [The Economic Research on the Guarantee of the Displaced Farmers' Interest] (Beijing: Kexue Chubanshe, 2009), 69–73, 78.

Initially, villages commonly re-allocated land to address changes in family populations such as births, deaths, and the departure or return of a married or divorced daughter. By the end of the century, however, such re-allocations were limited to natural disasters and similarly extraordinary events, and households enjoyed in practice, if not in law, indefinite tenure.

Although the jurisprudential distinction between de facto and de jure land use rights may have meant little to a farmer,[12] especially in a context where courts typically refused to accept land cases, the legal niceties of the evolution of the HRS system deserve our attention because they illustrate the interaction between formal law and nonlegal policy that has characterized Chinese property law – indeed virtually all forms of law – throughout the history of the PRC. We must note, therefore, that not only did the Xiao Gang experiment have no legal basis, but the same might also be said of the Central Committee's 1980 declaration that led to the immediate and nationwide transformation of land tenure practices. Not only was there no statute authorizing the policy change, but the HRS also directly contradicted Article 7(2) of the 1978 Constitution, which stipulated that individual households could possess land only for residential and family use. It was not, in other words, only the Xiao Gang villagers who were acting illegally but also the Central Committee. In China, however, such deviations from formal law are standard practice. If a new policy direction is successful, law can follow, as it did in this instance with the recognition in Article 11 of the 1982 Constitution that the private sector constitutes "an important component of the socialist market economy."[13]

[12] The full clarification of what constitutes "law" as opposed to less formal government-imposed norms in regard to Chinese land is a daunting jurisprudential task that is beyond our ken, but it is important to note that tangible evidence of land use rights in the form of administrative documents describing land allocations is highly prized by Chinese farmers, regardless of whether they can be vindicated in court. For example, see Landesa Rural Development Institute, "Summary of 2011 17-Province Survey's Findings," www.landesa .org/china-survey-6/.

[13] Article 11 of "Constitution of the People's Republic of China"(PRC Constitution): The non-public sectors of the economy such as the individual and private sectors of the economy, operating within the limits prescribed by law, constitute an important component of the socialist market economy. The State protects the lawful rights and interests of the non-public sectors of the economy such as the individual and private sectors of the economy. The State encourages, supports and guides the development of the non-public sectors of the economy and, in accordance with law, exercises supervision and control over the non-public sectors of the economy. See Constitution of the People's Republic of

Although Article 6 of the 1982 Constitution still states that the "basis" of the Chinese economy is the "socialist public ownership of the means of production,"[14] the constitutional legitimation of private property begun in 1982 has continued in a series of amendments from 1988 to 2004. The first in 1988 allowed the transfer of land use rights "according to law" and for state protection of the "lawful rights and interests of the private sector of the economy."[15] A more fundamental step came in 1993 with the replacement of "socialist public ownership economy" by "socialist market economy,"[16] declaring unequivocally China's departure from central planning to voluntary exchange premised implicitly on private property. The amendment also eliminated People's Communes and formally recognized the HRS and individual contracting for land use rights. The year 2004 saw the most recent advancement of constitutional law where property rights are concerned.[17] Article 13 now states that "[c]itizens' lawful private property is inviolable"; that "the State, in accordance with law, protects the rights of citizens to private property and to its inheritance"; and that the state may only expropriate private property in the "public interest and in accordance with law" and with compensation.

A plausible reading of this evolution of property norms would put the constitutional status of private property on a par with that of the United States, Japan, and other developed countries. While technically accurate, such a reading would be seriously misleading. An initial reason of overriding importance is that Chinese courts are not effective guarantors of

China, effective December 4, 1982, www.npc.gov.cn/englishnpc/Constitution/2007–11/15/content_1372963.htm.

[14] Article 6 of PRC Constitution: The basis of the socialist economic system of the People's Republic of China is socialist public ownership of the means of production, namely, ownership by the whole people and collective ownership by the working people. The system of socialist public ownership supersedes the system of exploitation of man by man; it applies the principle of "from each according to his ability, to each according to his work." In the primary stage of socialism, the state upholds the basic economic system in which the public ownership is dominant and diverse forms of ownership develop side by side and keeps to the distribution system in which distribution according to work is dominant and diverse modes of distribution coexist.

[15] Articles 10 and 11 of PRC Constitution. [16] Article 6 of PRC Constitution.

[17] There was also a series of changes in 1999 that inter alia declared that China shall be governed "according to law" and that China will be developed as "a Socialist country under the rule of law," but did not directly affect property rights significantly. See Chuanhui Wang, *The Constitutional Protection of Private Property in China: Historical Evolution and Comparative Research* (Cambridge: Cambridge University Press, 2016). This addition forms the first paragraph of Article 5 of the 1982 Constitution. The 1999 Amendment was enacted on March 15, 1999. www.npc.gov.cn/wxzl/wxzl/2000–12/10/content_7075.htm.

private property, both because of institutional incapacity and because official policy has been to settle property disputes, especially social conflict over land, extra-judicially. However, it would also be misleading to rely on constitutional norms for the simple reason that the Chinese Constitution is not self-executing. In other words, courts may not directly apply constitutional provisions in interpreting statutory law and deciding cases.[18] Direct application of the constitution depends on prior statutory incorporation of constitutional norms, which has often been slow in coming. The individual household contracting rights of the HRS, for example, were not statutorily recognized until the 1986 passage of the Land Administration Law and were not fully elaborated until the Rural Land Contracting Law of 2002, which provides for 30 year renewable terms for arable land, 30 to 50 year terms for grazing land and 30 to 70 year terms for forest land.

Urban land has followed a distinct but parallel path. Private property rights in urban land were effectively eliminated by the collectivization movement begun in the late 1950s, then formally nationalized by the 1975 Constitution, only to be gradually re-legitimated since, although limited to ownership of use rights. The process, however, has been much more straightforward and has gone much farther toward total liberalization than rural land. The virtually total dependence of city residents in 1978 on either their local government or state-owned employer for housing began to be dismantled immediately in 1979 on an experimental scale and "housing commercialization" became national policy when transfers "according to law" were constitutionally recognized in the 1988 constitutional amendments. The process continued in 1994 with the passage of the Law on Urban Real Estate Administration (LUREA).[19] The LUREA provides two methods to acquire land use rights from local governments. The first is government allocation, which is mainly used for land to be put to public use. The second is leasing, which is the main way that individuals and enterprises acquire land use rights. For residential use, the maximum term is 70 years, for industrial use 50 years, and for commercial use 40 years. The result is an urban land market that resembles in practice, if

[18] The few instances where courts have referenced the Constitution or appeared to do so, such as the right to education case, have been discussed widely but they remain both rare and inconclusive. See, for example, "Qi Yuling v. Chen Xiaoqi Case of Infringement of Citizen's Fundamental Rights of Receiving Education under the Protection of the Constitution by Means of Infringing Right of Name," *Zuigao Renmin Fayuan Gongbao* 5 (2001): 158.

[19] This section on urban land is drawn from Wang, *Constitutional Protection of Private Property*.

not in legal form, similar markets where allodial landownership is the norm.[20]

The most recent significant step in the evolution of formal property law was the passage by the National People's Congress of the Property Law in 2007. Despite the ambitious title, the legislation did not change much. It did clarify such weighty matters as whether owners of ground floor condominium units must contribute to elevator maintenance or whether the developer or homeowner association owns the parking spaces in residential subdivisions. More generally, however, the 2007 Property Law left most of the pressing issues alone. The reason for the law's reticence was simple: land has been officially cited as the greatest source of "mass social conflict" in contemporary China and is arguably the most controversial and most fundamental legal and policy issue facing the government and CCP today. The Property Law's recognition that private property enjoyed the same protected status as public property was already intensely contentious.[21] To go further and decide unresolved fundamental questions would have delayed the law's passage indefinitely, and, as we have seen, the national legislature is emphatically not where legal decisions are initially made, but where they are ratified after they have already become national policy.

III The Absence of Property Rights in Chinese Economic Growth

If China did not possess legally defined property rights enforceable in the courts, some other social processes enabled economic actors, whether they were Chinese farmers or multinational corporations, to "form those expectations which he can reasonably hold in his dealings with others."[22] A full description of what those processes were is well beyond the scope of this chapter, but a quick tour of five sociolegal phenomena can provide an overview.

A No "Law" at All?

Even this summary account of the role of property law in China's transition from a planned economy and collectivist society to a market economy

[20] Donald Clarke, "China's Stealth Urban Land Revolution," *American Journal of Comparative Law* 62 (2014).

[21] Frank Upham, "Demsetz to Deng: Speculations on the Implications of Chinese Growth for Law and Development Theory," *International Law and Politics* 41 (2009): 551.

[22] Harold Demsetz, "Toward a Theory of Property Rights," *The American Economic Review* 57 (1967): 347.

and consumerist society raises three questions about the role of law in society. First is the preliminary question of what constitutes "law" in contemporary developing countries. The second is a function of the first: what social institutions played the role conventionally attributed to property law in China's growth, and could similar institutions play that role in contemporary poor countries? The third and most fundamental question asks what conclusions we should draw from three decades of rapid economic growth without legislated legal norms enforced as promulgated by an independent and effective judiciary.

As the reader will have noted, policies and practices precede law in contemporary China. The communes were instituted despite the 1954 Constitution's provisions for private ownership of farmland. They were not legally authorized until the 1975 and 1978 constitutions, which were almost immediately violated by the introduction of the HRS. The HRS was not legalized until the 1982 Constitution and not fully articulated in statute until the 2002 Rural Land Contracting Law. The process of normative change has been similar for the liberalization of urban land use rights, and we can expect any future legal reformulation of rural land use rights to follow a similar pattern of regional bureaucratic experimentation, national adoption of successful measures through executive policy announcements, and statutory ratification only well after full implementation.[23]

From one positivist perspective – the perspective adopted here[24] – only statutes passed by the National People's Congress qualify as *falü* or "law" in Chinese. It follows that in this sense much of Chinese government action is lawless. It does not follow, however, that it is informal in the sense that much of what happens in both the public and private spheres in poor countries is informal or that it reflects some Chinese version of customary order.[25] The transitions from private ownership of land to collectivization and then back again may not have been legal in our narrow usage, but it proceeded in response to and was intended by political leadership. To

[23] Indeed, Guangdong Province is already experimenting with rural liberalization, although it is far from clear that it will have the transformative effect of Xiao Gang's experiment of 1978. See Shitong Qiao, *Chinese Small Property: The Co-Solution of Law and Social Norms* (JSD diss., Yale University, 2015), and Shitong Qiao and Frank Upham, "China's Changing Property Law Landscape," in *Research Handbook on Comparative Property Law*, M. Graziadei and L. Smith (eds.) (Edward Elgar, forthcoming).

[24] And perhaps one similar to a strict reading of H. L. A. Hart's rule of recognition.

[25] Robert Ellickson, *Order without Law: How Neighbors Settle Disputes* (Cambridge, MA: Harvard University Press, 1991).

put it glibly, it may not have been *law*, but it was *order* and a far cry from the lack of centralized normative order that occurs in many developing countries, particularly in relation to land.[26]

The consistent maintenance of relative public order raises the question of whether we should take a positivist approach when discussing China's changing property law or whether we should rather identify the order created by the administrative system as "law." My conclusion is that the narrow usage is preferable. China itself recognizes the distinction between the bureaucratic order I have described and the legal order of National People's Congress (NPC) legislation. Indeed, during the Fourth Plenum in October 2014, the Central Committee of the CCP emphasized, inter alia, the development of China's *formal* legal system including the strengthening of the judiciary. This was a clear indication that the PRC leadership not only sees the difference between bureaucratic order and formal law, but also that it recognizes the value of the latter. That said, as we see in the next four parts of this chapter, China's "lawlessness" usually includes a degree of order and stability that can effectively play the role typically attributed to a robust formal legal system.

B Ownership Rights in Township and Village Enterprises

Township and village enterprises (TVEs) were the "growth engine" of reform in China until the 1990s[27] and "Exhibit A" in most commentators' discussion of China's ambiguous property rights.[28] They varied greatly in structure and operation, but their defining commonality was collective ownership by the residents of the village or township in which they were located. Ownership was in name only, however, as TVEs were controlled by local government and CCP leaders who in turn delegated day-to-day operation to managers. Local officials were in turn accountable to their superiors in the state apparatus, not to the local residents who were the legal owners. The presence of this agency slack did not mean, however, that the residents/owners did not benefit. Most employees were residents, and most revenues went toward the provision of public goods such as

[26] Daniel Fitzpartrick, "Evolution and Chaos in Property Rights Systems: The Third World Tragedy of Contested Access," *Yale Law Journal* 115 (2006): 996.

[27] See Barry Naughton, *The Chinese Economy: Transitions and Growth* (Cambridge, MA: MIT Press, 2007), 275. Naughton calls TVEs the "'motor' for the entire transition process."

[28] D. L. Wank, "Producing Property Rights: Strategies, Networks, and Efficiency in Urban China's Nonstate Firms," in *Property Rights and Economic Reform in China*, Jean Oi and Andrew Walder (eds.) (Stanford, CA: Stanford University Press, 1999), 248–53, 260–72.

schools, transportation, and infrastructure. The community was not in legal control, however, either through some form of shareholding or elections.

De jure ownership, in other words, was virtually irrelevant, at least in the commonly used sense of defined and enforced property rights. This ephemeral nature of formal law is eloquently described in Chih-jou Jay Chen's study of property rights in two villages with dramatically different economic and political structures.[29] Shuang Village in Jiangsu Province was dominated throughout the reform period by CCP cadres. Hancun Village in Fujian Province, by contrast, was characterized by preliberation family firms that resisted effective state control. Even the privatization of Shuang's TVEs was controlled by local officials while the most that the local government in Hancun could achieve was forcing the private firms to "wear a red cap," i.e., to accept rhetorically collective ownership, and pay tribute to the township treasury.

A few general observations are possible despite the differences. First, property rights were ambiguous and judicially unenforceable, and yet both places enjoyed spectacular economic growth. Second, the state played a role that was at times parasitic – corruption and rent seeking were rampant – but the state did not do what many economists argue every state will do if not prevented by formal property rights: it did not steal all the wealth of successful businesses. Officials may well have been motivated by personal ties to the community, but their opportunism was also limited by political and social structures – not legal ones – that made it undesirable, impossible, and unnecessary for the state to kill the golden goose that was doing so well for the local economy, the local society, and ultimately local government and party bureaucrats.

The TVE story is important but there are many reasons to doubt the broader applicability of any "model" that might be gleaned from it. TVEs thrived in the earliest days of reform before large-scale legal construction; however one might define "law" in the developing world, there was little of it in the early days of reform. Second, TVEs constituted the initial primitive stage of China's transition to markets; they were small, local, and oriented toward taking advantage of short-term market opportunities and lacked the long-term perspective required for sustained market success. Indeed most existing TVEs have been at least partially privatized, and the economic form is no longer a prime driver of the PRC

[29] Chih-jou Jay Chen, *Transforming Rural China: How Local Institutions Shape Property Rights in China* (London: Routledge, 2004).

economy. Third, as the examples of Shuang and Hancun demonstrate, their nature was highly contingent on local circumstances, making generalization extremely difficult. In other words, although I would not endorse such a characterization, one might argue that TVEs were an idiosyncratic, perhaps incoherent, response to economic anarchy. (See also Tan, Chapter 3, on Singapore's response to postwar economic hardship by embracing the corporate form "government-linked company.") While they might be of some relevance to very poor countries at the earliest stages of economic growth, the TVE experience has little or nothing to say about what is necessary to get beyond the immediate goal of alleviating desperate poverty in the rural hinterlands. For a more contemporarily relevant account of the role of property rights and perhaps one that can be abstracted out of the localized circumstances of individual Chinese villages and applied to the broader world, we now turn to the role of property law in foreign direct investment.

C Foreign Direct Investment

China is now the world's leading recipient of foreign direct investment (FDI), meaning that non-PRC individuals and businesses have invested vast amounts of money in China without the close personal ties and geographical proximity that undoubtedly contributed to the security of TVE investments.[30] If they have done so without the formal legal institutions conventionally assumed to be required, it will not only indicate that the TVE experience should not be lightly dismissed as idiosyncratically limited to a specific time and place, but it will also provide persuasive evidence that the conventional wisdom that formal property law is indispensable for arm's length, large-scale, sustained commercial transactions is at least incomplete if not simply wrong.

I believe that the magnitude and nature of capital flows into China provide precisely such evidence. Recent work on Chinese FDI by Weitseng Chen demonstrates that "substitutes established by foreign investors for formal property institutions fulfill various functions that are otherwise supplied by a state-backed property regime."[31] Foreign investors use these "institutional substitutes"[32] to provide three fundamental attributes of property law: security of tenure, alienability, and dispute

[30] Weitseng Chen, "Arbitrage for Property Rights: How Foreign Investors Create Substitutes for Property Institutions in China," *Washington International Law Journal* 24 (2015): 47.

[31] Chen, "Arbitrage for Property Rights," 48. [32] Ibid., 91.

resolution.[33] These are provided by a range of jury-rigged legal and non-legal, formal, and informal structures that, although not as particularistic and contingent as those supporting TVEs, defy easy summary but that can, nonetheless, provide another example of the myriad alternatives to developmental orthodoxy.[34] Although he notes the existence of classic informal practices such as hiring local officials for no-show jobs[35] and relying on reputational networks,[36] Chen stresses the innovative use of legal forms such as contract and corporate structure to provide substitutes for property rights institutions and an effective judiciary. Some of these workarounds are illegal, such as the "subcontracting manufacturing factories" that allow foreign firms to "unlawfully lease land . . . and begin their export-oriented manufacturing."[37] Others such as joint ventures [JVs] are formally legal but have been adopted, not for their intended purposes, but to accomplish ends normally achieved through property institutions and functioning courts. As Chen puts it, "[w]ithout a functional judiciary to enforce various contracts, foreign investors may reduce legal risks by transforming numerous business deals into internal business decisions of a JV company."[38]

[33] The investors investigated by Chen are largely overseas Chinese, which raises the possibility that it is a shared culture and language that enable commercial transactions without the standard legal institutions. He argues, however, that such culturally created trust is intertwined with and cannot exist without institutions and, further, gently implies that to discuss trust in the Chinese context alone suffers from a tinge of Orientalism: "[a] rational American is unlikely to trust a British stranger and set up a business with her simply because they both speak English and know who William Shakespeare is. It is unlikely that those who share a common Chinese culture are any different." Ibid., 53.

[34] Chen argues that because some of the "institutional substitutes" are based on formal legal institutions such as contracts and corporate form, China does not "overrule the orthodox view" about "the indispensable role of property rights in economic growth." Ibid., 47. Since he amply documents not only the innovative nature of the use of formal law in these practices but also its frequent illegality and at times criminality, I believe that his assertion that the orthodox view remains unscathed can be true only if we take the orthodoxy as the original broad approaches of Demsetz and North, i.e., that institutions and hence in this context "law" include informal norms. We will return to this issue and the idea of "law" as a spectrum in the conclusion.

[35] Ibid., 61. The practice is hardly limited to China. See, for example, Joe Draper, "NYRA Chairman, Anthony Bonomo, Is Taking a Leave of Absence," *New York Times*, June 2, 2015, B14.

[36] One of these is the Taiwanese merchants associations, which Weitseng Chen describes as a "workable substitutes to compensate for its (PRC) institutional deficits." Ibid., 89.

[37] These contracts with local governments were illegal at least until the late 1980s. Ibid., 59, 61.

[38] Ibid., 67.

The FDI story demonstrates that formal legal institutions, if not property law institutions per se, have not been absent in Chinese growth. The use of contracts and the JV form to substitute for effective property rights show that formal law and imaginative lawyering are relevant to protecting investment even if their function has been far from that anticipated by conventional wisdom. Before we discuss whether and how this use of law factors into the broader questions of this chapter, however, we examine in the next two parts two instances where its absence has affected ownership and use of land, undoubtedly still the most important form of property in contemporary China: first, the expropriation of rural farmland by expanding cities, where formal legal institutions have been employed to their intended end if not consistently or faithfully, and, second, the "small property rights" real estate market, an instance where vibrant markets exist in direct defiance of formal law.

D The Transfer of Agricultural Land to Urban Use

Chinese cities must find room for hundreds of millions of new residents over the next few decades. To do so, large areas of rural land must be converted to urban use, which could be simply and quickly done if there were a functioning legal market in land use rights, but there is not. On the contrary, the sale of rural land use rights for nonrural use is prohibited. Rural land is collectively owned by village residents in a way similar to TVEs and is limited to agricultural use. For it to be used for urban purposes, it must first be formally expropriated by the local municipality and converted to state-owned urban land, after which the city can sell use rights at market prices.

Expropriation must satisfy certain legal criteria. It must be in the public interest; those affected must be consulted; and compensation must be paid.[39] The requirements of public interest and consultation are similar to American doctrine, but the measure of compensation throughout most of this period departed substantially from both American practice and law and development orthodoxy. First, it was unclear who should receive the compensation, the collective that owns the land or the individual member

[39] Patrick A. Randolph Jr. and Jianbo Lou, *Chinese Real Estate Law* (The Hague: KluwerLaw International, 2000), 73, 84. For a detailed explication of these procedures in a concrete case, see Eva Pils, "Land Disputes, Rights Assertion, and Social Unrest in China: A Case from Sichuan," *Columbia Journal of Asian Law* 19 (2005): 244–59.

households who own the rights to use it. The law seemed to choose the former and rely on the collective to ensure that individual households were in turn compensated. Second, the compensation award was largely based on the discounted value of the usufruct right for agricultural use. Since the duration of the usufruct right went from fifteen to thirty years during this period, the amount increased similarly from the discounted value of fifteen years of crops to thirty.

The problem with the process should be obvious: the total disconnect with market value. Since rural land could not be legally sold for nonagricultural use, there was no existing legal market but one can be assured that, had sales been legally possible, a market would immediately have developed and produced a price close to that which the local government received when it transferred the land to developers. In fact there was and is an illegal market, which we will discuss in the next part but expropriation remains the only legal way to transfer land to urban use, and the effect is to guarantee that urban governments get the land at a small fraction of its market value.

The weaknesses of this legal framework from a Demsetzian perspective are substantial, but actual practice was often much worse and was exacerbated by the inaction of the courts. No one will be surprised to learn that local village officials colluded with municipal officials and real estate developers; that required consultations with collective residents did not always take place; that the full pro-rata share of compensation did not always make it to the dispossessed farmers; that promised urban employment and housing often did not materialize; and that money went missing on a massive scale. It is impossible to state with confidence how often irregularities occurred, but land disputes were often cited as the primary cause of social conflict. What is important for our purposes, however, is that the courts generally opted out of these disputes. They simply would not accept the cases.[40] The reason was simple: the cases were too politically charged for local courts to intervene against local governments. (See also, e.g., Liebman, Chapter 9, for a discussion on "politically charged" cases in local courts.) Some observers might condemn this passivity as a dereliction of the courts' most important role;

[40] See Xin He, "Administrative Law as a Mechanism for Political Control in China," in *Constitutionalism and Judicial Power in China*, Stephanie Balme and Michael W. Dowdle (eds.) (New York: Palgrave Macmillan, 2009); Pils, "Land Disputes, Rights Assertion, and Social Unrest in China," 259–73.

others might consider it a cautious and pragmatic strategy that preserves the limited power and autonomy that the courts currently enjoy.

We do not have to make a judgment. For our purposes all that matters is that no one was enforcing property rights, and yet China grew faster than any other significant economy in the world. Would China have grown faster if property rights were enforced? No one can answer that question, but it seems highly unlikely. Indeed, the lack of property rights arguably accelerated the transfer of valuable factors of production, specifically land, from relatively unproductive agriculture to highly productive urban uses. Carefully enforcing the substantive and procedural requirements of requisitioning rural land would likely have dramatically slowed the process and added significantly to total economic costs. Since local cities had a monopsony in rural land, they could already effectively set the price. Once one factors in the virtually total lack of legal oversight by courts and political oversight from either the central government above[41] or a democratic electorate below, the shift from the lower productivity of agriculture to the vastly higher productivity of industry, commerce, and urban housing became even simpler and faster than if the PRC had granted individual farmers alienable property rights and allowed them to negotiate arm's length sales to willing buyers. All those political, social, and economic factors that delay, raise the cost of, and sometimes prevent altogether such transfers in rule of law capitalist economies were simply not an issue. As Chen put it from the foreign investor's point of view, "a one-party Leninist regime . . . may reduce the transaction cost tremendously."[42] Does this ease of process mean that ignoring property rights was a good thing? Of course not. It simply means that property rights were not necessary for economic growth. If we want to justify property rights, at least in contemporary China, we must find a noneconomic rationale for doing so.

E *Small Property Rights: Vibrant Land Markets without Rights*

The rigidity of Chinese land law, specifically the legal inability of collective owners to use land nonagriculturally, has spawned a second phenomenon

[41] While the central government did not effectively monitor the practice of local expropriations of farmland, it did limit its frequency as part of a policy of agricultural self-sufficiency, as we shall see in the discussion of small property rights in the next section.

[42] Chen, "Arbitrage for Property Rights," 73.

that is less politically prominent but that poses a more complicated question for reformers than abusive expropriation: the illegal development of rural land on a massive scale. Known as "small property rights" to denote their inferior nature in comparison to fully legal "big property rights," this form of informality is ironically caused not by expropriation, but by the failure of cities to expropriate often enough.[43] Because of the social and political issues discussed above and because the central government limits conversion of agricultural land in the name of national food self-sufficiency, expanding cities have not taken enough land to come close to meeting the demand. The result has been the emergence of a broad and deep illegal market in virtually all major Chinese cities. We will use Shenzhen to illustrate the scope of that market.[44]

Situated immediately north of Hong Kong, Shenzhen is China's fourth largest city, and the symbolic heart of the Chinese economic miracle.[45] It is also the city with the largest and most dynamic market in illegal land and buildings and the highest ratio of small-property buildings: 47.57 percent of its total floor space, compared to 30 percent in Xi'an and 20 percent in Beijing.[46] These illegal buildings are concentrated in 320 intracity

[43] See, e.g., Fu, Chapter 10, for a discussion on corruption in relation to land expropriation; Cui, Chapter 4, on the role of local government in regional land markets.

[44] Small property rights in Shenzhen is very much a community phenomenon with the village administrations playing a central coordinating role, but small property rights can be an individual phenomenon as well, and in those individual cases, courts have been willing to respond. A quick review of one case (Ma haitao yu li yulan fangwu maimai hetong jiufen shangsu an [The Appeal of Ma Haitao v Li Yulan in a Property Contractual Dispute] (2007) Second Intermediate People's Civil Court Final Judgment No. 13692 (Beijing Second Intermediate People's Court Civil Judgment, October 20, 2008) will illustrate not only how the market developed but also its legal nature. The case began in 2002 when Li Yulan, a Beijing artist, purchased a house in the suburban "painters' village" of Songzhuang from farmer Ma Haitao. Village authorities recognized the sale and Li later applied for and received official permission to renovate the house. The deal soured in 2006 when Ma realized that land values in Songzhuang were appreciating rapidly and that there was a chance of formal annexation of the area by Beijing, which would mean a large compensation award. Ma accordingly demanded the house back and, when Li refused, sued for its return on the basis that the original contract was void because it was in direct violation of the law. The court agreed, vacated the sale, and awarded ownership to Ma, but required Ma to compensate Li for the renovations and increases in the market value of the house.

[45] See, for example, Howard W. French, "Chinese Success Story Chokes on Its Own Growth," *New York Times*, December 19, 2006, www.nytimes.com/2006/12/19/world/asia/19shenzhen.html?pagewanted=1&_r=1&ex.

[46] "Xiaochanquanfang meiyou zhuanzheng 'tequ'" [No Special Economic Zone for the Legalization of Small-Property Houses], Renminwang, July 4, 2012, http://theory.people.com.cn/n/2012/0704/c112851–18443279.html.

"villages" whose land is still legally classified as rural despite being in the middle of a city of more than 10 million inhabitants. Small property residences host most of the 8 million migrant workers in Shenzhen and are the main source of income for the more than 300,000 original villagers. It is important to note, however, that they are not characterized by the low quality slums evoked by the stereotype of informal housing in the developing world but include modern buildings of high quality.

This market has resulted from the huge gap between the land's agricultural value and its value when used, even illegally, for other purposes.[47] It is sustained by the changing economic, political, social, and legal relations among villagers, government agencies, and real estate developers. In particular, a network of market participants has grown from participants with strong ties with each other to those with weaker ties, and eventually to participants with no preexisting relationship whatsoever. In other words, Shenzhen's small property market extends outwards from bounded communities to unbounded parties, including foreign investors, and all without a framework of enforceable legal rules. The property arrangement that a villager or a group of villagers can and does make is determined by their unique positions in the social network, but the direct involvement of professionals like lawyers and real estate brokers, commercial institutions like banks, and even different levels of the local government has allowed a market of close knit parties to open to strangers with no more than commercial connections to the original village. The scope, magnitude, and continuity of this market challenge the conventional wisdom that only official institutions implementing legal rules can create the lasting security necessary for sustained economic growth, but it also poses a pragmatic future issue for Chinese leaders: how to integrate small property into the legal system.

Their options can be portrayed as a spectrum. At one end would be the vindication of the law whereby all illegally constructed buildings would be demolished and their developers punished. The scale of illegality, however, all but precludes this option. Although informality does not dominate China's urban landscape as it does some Latin American and African cities where a majority of residents live illegally, 20 percent of Beijing, 30 percent of Xi'an, over 45 percent of Shenzhen, and similar numbers across China would mean a lot of demolition, resettlement, and punishment. However, the problem is not solely one of scale. The

[47] Prices for small property apartments are significantly lower than those for "big property" apartments. See Qiao Shitong, *Chinese Small Property*, 7.

network of relationships that sustains small property markets goes way beyond the individual squatters and shady real estate developers that one associates with informal housing in poor countries. Brokers advertise the properties and bring the parties together. Lawyers certify that the resulting transaction has been entered into voluntarily by both parties and retain copies of relevant documents for subsequent review by later buyers or lessees. Local state-owned banks provide individual mortgages for ordinary buyers and large-scale financing for industrial parks, commercial malls, and high-rise apartment buildings built by foreign investors. Small property, in other words, is not a departure from the Shenzhen real estate market, but a core part of it on which large segments of the professional and middle class depend and in which many participate.

The complex and contradictory role of government is a last but not least reason to doubt the possibility of simply repudiating small property rights. Chinese municipalities are divided into three levels: the city, the district, and the subdistrict, and the scale and functions of illegal buildings have different implications for different levels of the Shenzhen government. The city and district governments are generally hostile to small property. They are responsible for aggregate economic development and prefer big investors to small ones, and hence to the shops or restaurants that serve middle- to low-income populations. Cheap and sometimes free land is the key incentive that the city has to offer large foreign investors, and officials worry that the more land used for illegal "rural" development, the less will be available to big investors. The subdistrict governments, on the other hand, daily face millions of ordinary people in the city and are directly involved in its routine management. Their work is centered on the housing and monitoring of millions of migrant workers and on overseeing the livelihoods of more than three hundred thousand indigenous villagers. They understand how crucial small property is to the normal operation of the city and are generally reluctant to punish or deter illegal transactions. In fact, some subdistrict governmental offices are located in small-property buildings.

Furthermore, for government agencies with specific missions such as health, safety, or sanitation, the daily reality of widespread illegality makes cooperation with small property owners essential. For example, the Bureau of Business Administration grants business licenses to enterprises (restaurants, factories, shops, etc.) located in small-property buildings on the condition that the village collective certifies that the buildings are appropriately rented or owned by the enterprises. Similarly, the City Office of Housing Renting (MOHR), which is one of the agencies with responsibility for public security and social stability, registers and assigns identification numbers to all small-property buildings in its system and cooperates with village collectives for purposes of taxation and the management of the migrant population. As a MOHR official once said: "[W]e knew these buildings were illegal. Our registration has nothing to do with illegality; we just want to maintain social stability by closely monitoring the migrant population, most of whom live in these buildings."[48]

This deep integration into public and private life makes the option of simply "saying no" to small property rights virtually inconceivable. What is left, therefore, is some place on the spectrum further toward the option of granting small property owners full "big property rights" in their assets. Where on the spectrum the eventual resolution will settle is well beyond the scope of this chapter. What matters for our purposes is not, however, what will happen to property rights in China's future economy, but the role that they have or have played in the past.

IV Does the Role of Law in Chinese Economic Growth Require a Rethinking of Orthodox Theory?

To answer this question, we must return to the putative sources of modern property rights theory: Demsetz and North. If we take what they wrote rather than how their ideas have been implemented, the answer is quite possibly no. As elaborated in Part III, China created a bureaucratic and social order that supported investment and sustained markets without the formal property rights that contemporary law and development practitioners proclaim to be necessary, but Demsetz and North did not claim that economic assets had to be protected by formal norms. Under the varying rubrics of customs, mores, mental models, and ideologies they specifically anticipated that informal norms could play the roles reserved for courts, legislatures, and lawyers by today's economists and rule of law reformers. It does not immediately follow, however, that the normative structures that provided order during China's growth period were consistent with the informal norms anticipated by Demsetz and North. In other words, maybe they too would be surprised by the nature of Chinese order.

Fortunately, we do not have to answer that question but only whether Chinese growth undermines the conventional wisdom that dictates

[48] Shitong Qiao, "Planting Houses in Shenzhen: A Real Estate Market without Legal Titles," *Canadian Journal of Law and Society* 29 (2013): 255.

attention to creating or reforming the institutions of poor countries' legal systems according to templates derived from Western models. Here, the answer seems to be yes, although there is evidence that some of China's formal legal institutions have played a significant role. Su Yang and He Xin[49] and Benjamin Liebman[50] have described how judges have left their chambers and turned the street into courtrooms to settle labor and other contentious disputes and have become the locus of dispute resolution when populist anger threatens social harmony. However, these authors demonstrate the social and political, not the legal, role of the judiciary. Indeed, their point was the deviance from the letter of the law, not its vindication. Similarly it was the rhetorical "red hat" of collective ownership worn by Chih-jou Jay Chen's Fujian merchants that secured their interests, not the law, which would have repudiated the very private ownership that their red hats protected. The story is the same with small property rights: legal institutions are involved but not in their expected roles. The lawyers facilitating the deals, after all, are doing so not only in direct defiance of law but also of the orders of the Guangdong bar association. Even in Weitseng Chen's description of the use of contracts and corporate structure in foreign direct investment to secure and transfer property interests in land, the forms and doctrines are found in unusual places playing roles not conventionally called "property rights." Property rights institutions, meanwhile, have been conspicuously absent.

So, even where legal institutions were involved, they played roles far from that expected by the orthodoxy. Moreover, in many instances such as the TVEs, they were totally absent. Furthermore, if we stick to our positivistic definition of law, most of the evolution of property rights over these decades was illegal and often in direct contradiction to the existing constitution. Even more fundamental has been the virtual absence of courts, which are central to the orthodox view of law and development and of property in particular. It is true that the courts were involved in a conventional manner in some small property rights cases, but those

[49] Yang Su and Xin He, "Street as Courtroom: State Accommodation of Labor Protest in South China," *Law and Society Review* 44 (2010).

[50] Benjamin Liebman, "Malpractice Mobs: Medical Dispute Resolution in China," *Columbia Law Review* 113 (2013); Benjamin Liebman, "A Return to Populist Legality? Historical Legacies and Legal Reform," in *Mao's Invisible Hand: The Political Foundations of Adaptive Governance in China*, Sebastian Heilmann and Elizabeth J. Perry (eds.) (Cambridge, MA: Harvard University Asia Center, 2011); Benjamin Liebman, "A Populist Threat to China's Courts?," in *Chinese Justice: Civil Dispute Resolution in Post-Reform China*, Margaret Y. K. Woo and Mary E. Gallagher (eds.) (Cambridge: Cambridge University Press, 2011).

were among individuals and not politically dangerous. When property is threatened by important social or government actors, the courts have looked the other way (see, e.g., Liebman's discussion of authoritarian courts in China, Chapter 9). Yet the economic interests of foreign and domestic investors in China have not been so violated that growth has stopped. Quite the contrary, and in that sense it seems to me impossible to deny the importance of the Chinese experience in re-evaluating the current dogma.

V Is There a Chinese Model/Beijing Consensus for the Role of Property Rights in Development?

The answer to this question is more difficult. To claim a "Beijing Consensus," one must be able to create a positive story of the role of property rights in Chinese development. By that I mean that one would have to identify what social institutions created what informal norms that substituted for the role of property rights in the orthodox model. It is not enough to assert, as I have just done, that the Chinese experience disproves (or weakens, or whatever phraseology one might choose along the negative spectrum) the orthodoxy. One must have a substitute explanation based on the Chinese experience, and that is just the first step. After one has determined with sufficient clarity and generality what provided security for investment and exchange in China, one must be able to claim that this new model or set of social or political institutions can be replicated elsewhere. Such, after all, was the role of the Washington Consensus: even if "one size fits all" was eventually repudiated, the core idea of a model of sufficient generality to fit Bolivia, Burundi, and Bangladesh with a modicum of adjustments must remain, or the idea of a model collapses. The point bears repeating. The idea that a model must fit "Bolivia, Burundi, and Bangladesh" is not simply alliterative exaggeration. What is required by a "model" is a template or recipe that can be applied universally with a degree of specificity that can guide concrete action in poor countries as different as Bolivia, Burundi, and Bangladesh.[51]

With China, I believe that even the first step of explaining its growth with clarity, generality, and precision will be very difficult, and the idea of

[51] See also Prado and Dowdle's debate about whether the Beijing Consensus is qualified as a "model," Chapter 1; and Kroncke's description of the Beijing Consensus as an "anticonsensus," Chapter 2.

applying it, even with adjustments, elsewhere seems extremely problematic. Indeed, even replicating it in some hypothetical re-run of the last 35 years seems unlikely. The variety of institutions and contexts that made growth possible without law is unlikely to be recreated even inside China, much less in other poor countries, each one of which has its own unique characteristics. One possibility is to broaden the perspective and claim that the "model" is some meta-characteristic of contemporary China. The usual suspects are Confucian culture or the CCP, but it is hard to call this approach either a model or a consensus. The point of both a model and a consensus in this context is to provide the basis for a general agreement on a course of action, and contemplating the creation of either Confucian culture or the CCP in other developing countries stops the conversation.

The failure to relocate the Washington Consensus to Beijing does not mean that we cannot generalize, however. Even if China's last three decades demonstrate that property rights are not necessary for economic growth, one might still draw some links connecting the legal nature of the Chinese experience and that of other countries that have grown rapidly. One is the tendency for countries to look for legal order even when it has been illegality or a-legality that has delivered growth. The examples are legion but we can begin with three: the English Enclosure Movement from the sixteenth to the nineteenth century, the transformation of American property law in the nineteenth century, and the Japanese land reform of 1945–1952. In each of these processes property rights were destroyed for the sake of development, in the first two for economic growth only, in the third primarily for political development. But in each instance, after the fruits of the destruction of property were harvested – economic growth and democracy, respectively – there was a re-building of property rights. If we look hard, we may be able to discern a similar process in the description of Chinese property rights in Parts II and III. Although more data is necessary, one might say that informality, illegality, and ad hoc institutional innovation have been followed by movement toward formality including legal formality. Such has been the case with the urban real estate market and the privatization of the TVEs. The Supreme People's Court has also ordered local courts to accept land cases, although whether it will be in the vein of "street as courtroom" in the service of social harmony or formal adjudication true to the legal rules remains to be seen. In other words, what we may be seeing is the role of property rights in the political development of China, as opposed to its economic growth.

Finally, to return to the question, I do not think that China will become a model for other poor countries looking to grow fast, but it is not because I consider China's growth to have been unique. It is because I consider each country's situation to be, if not unique, so contingent as to make "models" impossible and their advocacy at best worthless and all too often harmful.

6

Size Matters? *Renminbi* Internationalization and the Beijing Consensus

WEITSENG CHEN*

I Introduction

Internationalization of *the Renminbi* (RMB) has become a new buzzword, leading to various theories about its impact and prospects. "Currency War," a best seller in China that Chinese leaders have reportedly read, engages in a conspiracy theory depicting how the United States and its investment banks made the US dollar the international reserve currency. Commentators have therefore established that currency internationalization requires strong state action at a critical juncture. The British pound, for example, remained the dominant currency even after the United States replaced the United Kingdom as the biggest economy in the late nineteenth century. Not until after World War II did the United States spend nearly two decades pushing the US dollar to the pinnacle by using the post-war economic conditions in the United Kingdom to its advantage. It has also been argued that the transition to a high-growth economy requires exogenous "accidents and good fortunes" that break the path dependence and institutional equilibrium at a lower level of growth.[1] Interestingly, this sounds very similar to the recent comment of Zou Xiao-chuan, the President of the People's Bank of China (PBoC): "RMB internationalization requires luck and opportunity, and the [recent] global financial crisis is the one."[2]

* The author would like to thank Daniel Awrey, Michael Bridge, Christopher Bruner, Jedidiah Kroncke, Curtis Milhaupt, Tomoo Marukawa, Tjio Hans, Wei Cui, Dora Neo, Chien-Hsun Chen, Dan W. Puchniak, Alex Loke, and Florian Gamper for their helpful discussions and comments.

1 Gary Becker, Kevin Murphy, and Robert Tamura, "Human Capital, Fertility, and Economic Growth," *The Journal of Political Economy* 98 (1990): 14.

2 Chen Fashan and Liu Caiping, "Renminbi guojihua bu shixian anpai sudu jiezhou shidian" [Pace, Number of Steps and Timeline Regarding the Internationalization of

The long-term goal of the RMB internationalization scheme (the "Scheme") is to make the Chinese yuan an international settlement, investment, and reserve currency. With the RMB as the settlement and investment currency, China no longer needs to accumulate large amounts of foreign reserve due to foreign exchange; rather, foreign direct investment (FDI), as well as overseas revenues of Chinese export firms, could flow directly into domestic markets in RMB without conversion. Chinese firms will also be free from currency exchange risks. At present, to manage its immense foreign reserve, China has no better option than to purchase US treasury bonds, thereby subjecting the value of its assets to the fluctuations of the dollar and US monetary policy. Perhaps more importantly, if the RMB becomes an international reserve currency, China may resort to printing RMB to diffuse its own economic risks, similar to what the US Federal Reserve did during the 2008 financial crisis. There is no doubt that China would be able to exert more influence on the global stage with a genuinely internationalized RMB.

Considering its revolutionary goal, does the Scheme construct any part of the Beijing Consensus (i.e., the Chinese Model) that my fellow contributors of this book aim to unpack? How and to what extent does the Scheme overrule the policy prescriptions made by the Washington Consensus based on neoliberal economics? Are the policies that China has been implementing for the Scheme so unique that one may claim that the Beijing Consensus exists? With these questions in mind, this chapter examines the Beijing Consensus and searches for the Chinese Model for law and economic development in the context of RMB internationalization.

The balance of this chapter proceeds as follows: Part II reviews the recent developments of RMB internationalization, aiming to frame issues from the perspective of law and development. Part III goes on to identify the challenges confronting the Scheme and argues that internationalization of the RMB is more of a domestic project than an international one in terms of implementation. The major challenges are caused by China's extremely large-scale economy and significant regional variations in market conditions. Part IV analyzes China's approach to coping with these challenges by way of legal engineering, dealing with size disadvantages by leveraging size advantages, in particular. This chapter concludes in

the Renminbi Not Predetermined], *Caixin*, March 11, 2014, http://finance.caixin.com/2014-03-11/100649710.html.

Part V by offering a tentative view on whether the Beijing Consensus exists in the context of RMB internationalization.

II RMB Internationalization and Law and Development

A Recent Developments

To pave the way for RMB internationalization, China has implemented a number of ambitious policies. To begin with, a set of initiatives has significantly increased the total amount of RMB circulated offshore, with the aim of increasing the global demand for Chinese yuan. For example, with legal constraints first lifted in 2007 and then again in 2010, domestic and Hong Kong banks are able to issue RMB-denominated bonds traded outside China, commonly known as "dim sum" bonds, which have dominated the Asian capital markets ever since.[3] Furthermore, to improve the liquidity of offshore RMB, the PBoC has signed bilateral currency swap agreements with thirty-three countries as of 2015, creating a number of offshore RMB settlement and trading centers in places such as Australia, Hong Kong, Korea, London, Malaysia, Singapore, and Taiwan.[4] Previously, such settlement was not legal unless done through designated domestic banks or banks in Hong Kong. In Europe, a huge "Euroyuan" market is expected to pick up in a way similar to how in the 1970s the offshore US dollar created the Eurodollar markets that have played a major role in the global capital markets ever since.[5]

Following a similar rationale of promoting the use of RMB internationally, Beijing made a few bold, if not controversial, moves more recently. The New Development Bank (formally referred as the BRICS Development Bank operated by Brazil, Russia, India, China, and South Africa),

[3] Weitseng Chen, "Institutional Arbitrage: China's Economic Power Projection and International Capital Markets," *Columbia Journal of Asian Law* 26 (2013): 347; Terry E. Chang, "Slow Avalanche: Internationalizing the Renminbi and Liberalizing China's Capital Account," *Columbia Journal of Asian Law* 25 (2011): 62.

[4] Ulrich Volz, "RMB Internationalization and Currency Co-operation in East Asia," Working Paper No. 125 (Universität Leipzig Wirtschaftswissenschaftliche Fakultät, 2013): 6.

[5] Beginning in 2014, the British pound was being traded with RMB directly. This is said to be a milestone in establishing the "Euroyuan," like the "Eurodollars" decades ago. Other currencies that are allowed to trade directly with the yuan include the US dollar, Japanese yen, Australian dollar, New Zealand dollar, Russian ruble, and Malaysian ringgit. This unlocks a great deal of potential for the investment community. Jeanny Yu, "Yuan to Trade Directly with UK Pound: Today's Change Replaces System of Referencing the Two Currencies' Rates against US Dollar," *South China Morning Post*, June 19, 2014, www.scmp.com/business/banking-finance/article/1535833/yuan-trade-directly-uk-pound.

the Asian Infrastructure Investment Bank (AIIB) and the Silk Road Fund were all created between 2014 and 2015 and have the potential to diversify China's foreign reserve management and expand the offshore reserve of RMB. The United States and its allies such as Canada, Australia, and Japan tried to boycott the AIIB but failed in the end.[6] Claiming the move as a "diplomatic triumph," Beijing launched the AIIB, committing up to $100 billion with the reported aim of competing with, if not replacing, the Asian Development Bank. Since it was created, the AIIB had been reported to likely use RMB for its loans and foreign aid. Eventually, the AIIB selected USD, but it still has a strong capacity to facilitate the use and circulation of RMB in the region.[7] As such, the AIIB "represents the first serious institutional challenge to the global economic order established at Bretton Woods 70 years ago," according to a former senior economic advisor for the Obama administration.[8]

Another high-profile initiative is the Shanghai Free Trade Zone (SFTZ) established in 2013, which was accompanied by unprecedented deregulation of the banking sector and foreign exchange markets. Private banks have been incorporated and foreign banks can provide full services within the zone subject to limited capital controls. These reforms have changed the dynamics of China's state-dominated banking sector. To introduce more competition into the allegedly inefficient banking industry, Beijing lifted the controls on bank lending rates nationwide in July 2013, and it plans to liberalize savings rates too in due course.[9]

Thus far, the Scheme appears to be bringing about rapid changes in the institutional configurations of several cornerstones of Chinese state capitalism: the banking sector, corporate governance, and securities and capital market regulations.

[6] Daniel Runde, "AIIB and US Development Leadership: A Path Forward," *Forbes*, April 30, 2015, www.forbes.com/sites/danielrunde/2015/04/30/aiib-us-development-leadership/; Yelin Hong, "The AIIB Is Seen Very Differently in the US, Europe, and China," *The Diplomat*, May 8, 2015, http://thediplomat.com/2015/05/the-aiib-is-seen-very-differently-in-the-us-europe-and-china/.

[7] "AIIB to Issue Loans in US Dollars, Attract Capital in Other Currencies," *Sputnik International*, January 17, 2016, https://sputniknews.com/business/201601171033266847-aiib-loans-us-dollars/.

[8] "China Launches New World Bank Rival," *RT Network*, October 24, 2014, http://rt.com/business/198928-china-world-bank-rival/.

[9] In the short term, the overhaul is also seen as an effort to help China's economy, because lifting the control of lending rates could prompt banks to inject more capital into the economy.

B The Washington Consensus Revisited

On account of RMB internationalization, has the Scheme shed any light on the idea of the Beijing Consensus? Yes, but perhaps in a reverse manner. As a matter of fact, it is difficult to find an overarching policy that carries out more policy prescriptions from the Washington Consensus in one go than the Scheme. Reflecting neoliberal economics, the Washington Consensus suggests, for example, that the state liberalize interest rates and make exchange rates competitive, and that fiscal discipline be in place to reduce the need for governmental subsidies that distort the banking system. The Washington Consensus also suggests that the state should welcome FDI and lift capital account control, and that FDI needs to be channeled to industries monopolized by state-owned enterprises (SOEs) to improve efficiency. The past three years have seen the PBoC implementing all of these prescriptions by way of the Scheme.

In fact, the PBoC is even more liberal than some veterans of neoliberal economics. In a recent paper, Ronald McKinnon of Stanford University, the economist famous for his theory about the sequence of financial and banking reforms in developing countries, advised against China's rapid liberalization policy (especially regarding exchange rate control) as part of the Scheme.[10] Interestingly, Chinese scholars disagree and argue for aggressive reforms for internationalizing RMB.[11] Policymakers in China and liberal economists in the West have switched positions this time, with the Scheme appearing to reinforce the value of the Washington Consensus, rather than a Chinese Model.

Different scholarly perceptions of RMB internationalization account for this change in position. Academics in the West generally think that

[10] Ronald McKinnon and Gunter Schnabl, "China's Exchange Rate and Financial Repression: The Conflicted Emergence of the RMB as an International Currency," *China & World Economy* 22 (2014): 1.

[11] Yong-Ding Yu, "Comment from the Editor-in-Chief," *China & World Economy* 22 (2014): 32. The underlying disagreement is an empirical one. Yu, among other Chinese scholars, suggests that the current level of the RMB has been close to equilibrium and there exists little room for further significant appreciation. In comparison, McKinnon disagrees and suggests that the RMB will appreciate significantly if the capital controls are lifted. McKinnon thinks that drastic appreciation of RMB will trigger appreciation of other currencies in Asia and greatly impact the Asian economy as a whole. See McKinnon and Schnabl, "China's Exchange Rate and Financial Repression"; "People's Republic of China: 2010 Article IV Consultation – Staff Report," Country Report No. 10/238 (IMF, 2010), www.imf.org/external/pubs/ft/scr/2010/cr10238.pdf; Nicholas R. Lardy, *Sustaining China's Economic Growth: After the Global Financial Crisis* (Washington, DC: Peterson Institute for International Economics, 2012), 105.

the Scheme will not advance without causing economic volatility in China and the region in the short term, such as sudden fluctuation in the exchange rate of the Chinese yuan owing to investors' expectations and speculation.[12] It remains questionable in the long term whether it will overturn the dominance of the dollar. One less drastic solution suggested is to reform the problem of dollar dominance and imbalance within the current dollar-centered settlement and reserve system.[13] In comparison, despite fierce debates about implementation strategies, Chinese academics generally think that the Scheme is not only viable but also necessary, especially considering China's advantageous market condition – the extremely large-scale economy. The following section aims to examine the pros and cons of this condition from a law and economic development perspective.

C *Development Theories of RMB Internationalization*

It is not too difficult to conclude that the Scheme, if successful, will significantly change the global balance of power, politically and economically. On account of the revolutionary outcome, academics have established various theories of currency internationalization and therefore foresee different prospects for the RMB as international currency. Many of these analyses resonate with classical law and development debates about the relationship between development, democracy, and the rule of law.

The first theory is that only countries with advanced Western capitalist economies may make their currency international reserve currency, the reason being that full currency convertibility and deep capital markets are the prerequisites for currency internationalization. The former allows both foreign and domestic investors to freely convert currency without any restrictions, whereas the latter helps channel capital inflow into various investment markets rather than speculative areas, such as real estate markets that would lead to asset bubbles. Both prerequisites rest on various institutions that are only available in a mature capitalist economy, including market transparency, a solid financial sector, good corporate

[12] McKinnon and Schnabl, "China's Exchange Rate and Financial Repression." As a matter of fact, the exchange rate of the RMB indeed depreciated dramatically after China's stock market crash in summer 2015 and raised great concern about China's quick liberalization of capital account and other initiatives under the Scheme. In January 2016, Japan's central bank governor even unorthodoxically called on Beijing to impose more stringent capital controls to stem massive outflows of hot money from China and stabilize its currency.

[13] Ibid.

governance, and effective law enforcement.[14] From this perspective, unless China streamlines its state–private relationship, strengthens its banking sector, and improves its corporate and capital market regulations, it will not be able to introduce full currency convertibility and push the RMB to become an international reserve currency. Otherwise, it will harm China's economy eventually since domestic markets may fail to digest such immense capital inflow. As such, it is unlikely that the RMB will become an international reserve currency anytime soon.

The second theory, with a focus on the political system, suggests that only a democratic country may make its currency international reserve currency.[15] Foreign investors will not have their wealth denominated by the currency of a country that is politically unstable due to lack to transparency, accountability, and checks and balances. Since the early nineteenth century, the leading international currencies have been those of countries with democratic political systems where there are constraints on the executive, that have built a durable political climate, and where creditors are well represented.[16] The choice of international reserve currency manifests the trust of global communities in a specific country's polity, which does not and will not manipulate its markets or currency even in the face of variations in its domestic political and economic climate. One example of such trust is that the value of the US dollar remained stable even after the US federal government was forced to shut down due to budget deficits and a political stand-off between the Democrats and Republicans in 2013. As such, unless the value of RMB has the capacity to remain stable even if the Chinese government is compelled to shut down for some reasons, RMB is unlikely to become an international reserve currency. This theory is not arguing that China has to become a democracy, but it does suggest that significant political reforms are necessary for the Scheme.

Interestingly, there has been little discussion of one factor that the Chinese often bring up in the context of China's economic development; that is, the large-scale economy: whether such a scale is necessary and advantageous for internationalizing the currency. The immense market scale of the United States, Japan, and the European Union (EU) are vital

[14] Chen-yuan Tung, Guo-chen Wang, and Jason Yeh, "Renminbi Internationalization: Progress, Prospect and Comparison," *China and World Economy* 20 (2012): 63.

[15] Barry Eichengreen, "Number One Country, Number One Currency?," *The World Economy* 36 (2013): 363.

[16] Ibid.

for maintaining the US dollar, yen, and euro as international reserve currencies, respectively. However, this theory is a bit ambiguous because of an outlier: the Swiss Franc of Switzerland, one of the favorite international reserve currencies issued by a small economy with less than half of the population of Shanghai alone – fewer than eight million people.[17] Nevertheless, this theory addresses a commonly shared view that has not been systematically scrutinized in law and development literature: the size factor. How does the size factor play itself out in the process of policymaking and implementation of development policies such as the Scheme? To what extent does this size factor constitute a Chinese Model? Conversely, the size factor may make China's experiences too unique to be a general development model but rather Chinese exceptionalism.

D Size Matters, but How?

Commentators often attribute China's economic success and influence to the large size of its economy and workforce.[18] National champions, as the biggest Chinese SOEs such as SinoPec, China Mobil, and the big four banks are referred to, have been created by corporate restructuring and soon became the dominant market players in both domestic and international markets.[19] For instance, mega IPOs of the Industrial and Commercial Bank of China, the Agricultural Bank of China and, recently, Alibaba.com, broke financial history records in less than a decade. Continuing expansion of the domestic consumer market provides Chinese firms with new markets, unlike the firms of other leading East Asian economies that need to go abroad to find new customers.

17 The Swiss franc is legal tender only in Switzerland, the tiny principality of Liechtenstein, the Italian enclave of Campione d'Italia, and the German town Büsingen, with a population of fewer than two thousand residents.

18 Romeo Orlandi, "China, Size Matters," *Alberto Forchielli*, May 22, 2014, www.albertoforchielli.com/2014/05/22/china-size-matters/; D. Daniel Sokol, "Law and Development – The Way Forward or Just Stuck in the Same Place?," *Northwestern University Law Review Colloquy* 104 (2010): 242.

19 Weitseng Chen, "From the Middle East to the Far West: What Can Chinese Overseas Investments Tell Us about Law and Development and Global Regulatory Regimes?," in *Converging Regions: Global Perspectives on Asia and the Middle East*, Nele Lenze and Charlotte Schriwer (eds.) (London: Ashgate, 2014), 25–54; Peter Nolan, *Is China Buying the World*? (Cambridge: Polity Press 2013); Li-Wen Lin and Curtis J. Milhaupt, "We Are the (National) Champions: Understanding the Mechanisms of State Capitalism in China," *Stanford Law Review* 65 (2013): 697.

Historically, however, academics often regard large size as a negative factor for the development of a national economy and political power. One of the most prominent views is expressed by Fernand Braudel, famous for his theory of civilization and capitalism. Braudel pointed to France's large size as a major obstacle to France becoming a dominant power.[20] The large size dispersed limited financial resources, created difficulties in coordination, and increased various governance costs such as those for the military and transportation.[21]

Other theories about the development of various institutions also share a similar view. Corporate organization theorists, for example, point out that large firms are usually responsive to institutional innovation, but they respond at a slow pace. Some large Japanese firms are often referred to as cases in point.[22] Additionally, social norms and relational contract theories suggest that in an economy where firms and individuals rely on network or reputation mechanisms to enforce contracts, the expansion of markets would cause such mechanisms to fail due to the increase in the costs of maintaining networks or acquiring information.[23] Similarly, a large-scale economy may also make a centralized regulatory regime that primarily functions to coordinate between market players less effective.[24]

In Chinese financial history, the immense size of market has also served as a negative factor for governance. Leading up to the nineteenth century, numerous dynasties faced extreme difficulties in issuing sufficient currency made of a consistent quality of copper, especially after the southern economy boomed. The limited reserve of copper led to a dilemma: an insufficient money supply would obstruct cross-border business transactions in a large economy, but to issue more currency containing less

[20] Fernand Braudel, *The Wheels of Commerce* (*Civilization and Capitalism: 15th–18th Centuries*, vol. 2) (New York: University of California Press, 1992).

[21] Ibid.

[22] For example, Christina Ahmadjian and Patricia Robinson found that the larger the firms were, the less likely they were to respond to the Japanese recession in the 1990s by downsizing and deinstitutionalizing Japan's well-known permanent employment system. Ahmadjian and Robinson, "Safety in Numbers: Downsizing and the Deinstitutionalization of Permanent Employment in Japan," *Administrative Science Quarterly* 46 (2001): 622.

[23] E.g., Weitseng Chen, "Arbitrage for Property Rights: How Foreign Investors Create Substitutes for Property Institutions in China?," *Washington International Law Journal* 24 (2015): 87–88; Eric A. Posner, *Law and Social Norms* (Cambridge, MA: Harvard University Press, 2002).

[24] Curtis Milhaupt and Katharina Pistor, "The China Aviation Oil Episode: Law and Development in China and Singapore," in *Law and Economics with Chinese Characteristics: Institutions for Promoting Development in the Twenty-First Century*, David Kennedy and Joseph E. Stiglitz (eds.) (Oxford: Oxford University Press, 2013), 329.

copper would incentivize the private sector to store old currency of better quality and make illegal currency because of lowered costs.[25] As a result, many emperors were compelled to tolerate privately made currency in order to sustain the economy.[26] A similar challenge confronted both Chinese emperors and French kings: the difficulty in aggregating limited resources in a few financial centers, unlike Venice, Sienna, or Amsterdam at the time. Max Weber also pointed to this financial constraint as one major reason why capitalism did not emerge in premodern China.[27] How are we to reconcile conflicting views about the size factor in the Chinese context?

The size factor poses two major challenges to the state and other market players: coordination problems in an extremely large-scale country and the difficulty in finding a proper governance model that can accommodate significant variations in market conditions among regions. To begin with, coordination failure leads to fragmentation of power, giving rise to incoherent policymaking and inefficient law enforcement and policy implementation.[28] Coordination problems can nonetheless be largely dealt with by legal engineering, albeit not entirely, since the function of law is not only to protect rights but also to coordinate market players. As Milhaupt and Pistor argue, the function of law in transitional countries like China is more about coordination than rights protection.[29]

Secondly, significant variations in market conditions may cause a centralized and generalized rule-based governance regime to fail. Michael Dowdle argues that North Atlantic capitalism developed the modern rule of law system as a response to the need to govern their economies based on mass manufacture of standardized products to be distributed in largely hegemonic markets.[30] However, China is different because its markets are not only extremely large but also significantly vary between regions.[31]

[25] Zhu Jia-Ming, *Cong ziyou dao longduan: zhongguo huobi jingji liangqiannian* [From Laissez-Faire to Monopoly: The Monetary Economy of China – Past and Present], vol. 1 (Taipei: Yuan-Liou, 2012), 130.

[26] Ibid. [27] Ibid., 70 and 80.

[28] Daron Acemoglu and James A. Robinson, *Why Nations Fail: The Origins of Power, Prosperity and Poverty* (New York: Crown, 2012).

[29] Curtis J. Milhaupt and Katharina Pistor, *Law and Capitalism: What Corporate Crises Reveal about Legal Systems and Economic Development around the World* (Chicago: University of Chicago Press, 2008).

[30] Michael Dowdle, "China's Present as the World's Future: China and 'Rule of Law' in a Post-Fordist World," in *Chinese Thought as Global Theory*, Leigh K. Jenco (ed.) (Albany, NY: SUNY Press, 2016).

[31] Ibid.

Deviations from the conventional rule-based legal system are therefore unavoidable and necessary in order to govern China's economy.[32] All in all, whether China may benefit from its large-scale economy depends on the capacity of its legal institutions to solve the problems of coordination between the center and the regions, SOEs and private firms, foreign and local firms, offshore and onshore markets, and the state and market mechanisms, and whether it is able to develop a suitable governance model to accommodate the extreme variations in market conditions.

Coordination problems and variations in market conditions happen to be the two major challenges confronting the Scheme. For example, one prerequisite of RMB internationalization is full currency convertibility, which incentivizes investors to store their assets in large denominations of RMB without liquidity concerns.[33] However, the introduction of RMB's full convertibility requires the lifting of capital controls and would affect every aspect of China's monopolistic financial and business sectors, which currently vary across regions and render coordination extremely challenging. The lifting of capital controls would also invite speculative investors and hot money would flow into shallow investment areas such as the real estate market, which are prone to asset bubbles. Regions whose growth relies on fixed-asset investment (e.g., construction of official buildings and residential complexes) would be particularly vulnerable.[34] Additionally, informal financial sectors could be further fed by cheap capital. Provinces with problems of underground banking, which is unregulated and

[32] Ibid. See also Bob Jessop and Ngai-Ling Sum, *Beyond the Regulation Approach: Putting Capitalist Economies in Their Place* (Cheltenham, UK: Edward Elgar, 2006).

[33] Full convertibility here refers to full convertibility of capital account. China has achieved full convertibility on all current account transactions and the government approves all bona fide requests for foreign exchange for current payments and transfers. *People's Republic of China-Selected Issues: IMF Staff Country Report No. 97/72* (IMF, 1997); Javier Kurien and Bernard Geoxavier, "Roadmap for the RMB Internationalization: Navigating the Rise of China's Currency," *Harvard Kennedy School Review*, May 2, 2013, http://harvardkennedyschoolreview.com/a-roadmap-for-rmb-internationalization-navigating-the-economic-and-political-challenges-to-the-rise-of-chinas-currency/.

[34] Yasheng Huang points out that, beginning in the 1990s, regional governments reversed their early policies of encouraging the private sector and began favoring fixed-asset investments (FAIs). This policy reversal severely damaged China's private sector and entrepreneurship as a whole. Also, FAIs in land, assets, and buildings controlled by governments (excluding investments in SOEs) more than tripled from 2.3 percent of the total FAIs in the 1990s to 7.2 percent in 2002. Yasheng Huang, "Debating China's Economic Growth: The Beijing Consensus or the Washington Consensus," *The Academy of Management Perspectives* 24 (2010): 41.

nontransparent, could be hit badly should a liquidity crisis occur. Moreover, capital flight would be fueled by full convertibility, especially from regions with problems of rampant corruption and corporate irregularities. Overall, more developed cities such as Beijing, Shanghai, and Guangzhou may benefit from the open policies of the Scheme, but peripheral cities and provinces that have heavily relied on the support of state-owned banks will not, at least in the short term. More sophisticated SOEs and private firms that are competitive and export-oriented (and therefore bear more currency exchange risk) may benefit, but small and mid-sized companies that are less competitive and focus on domestic rather than export markets will not.

In short, the size factor is not as positive as would be expected; to the contrary, it usually creates great difficulties for rising powers. The next section examines the strategies that Beijing has adopted to cope with the problems of coordination in its large-scale economy and extreme variations in market conditions in order to proceed with RMB internationalization.

III Challenges for RMB Internationalization

A Challenges from within Rather than from Abroad

In terms of implementation, internationalization of RMB is more of a domestic than an international project. To pave the way for the Scheme, a great deal of reforms are required at home. However, the problems of coordination and extreme variations in market conditions pose tremendous challenges for such reforms.

In contrast, the Scheme has gone relatively smoothly at the international level, if not too fast. This is primarily because of the view shared by central bankers around the world that alternative reserve currency serves their best interest. Eswar Prasad uses the phrase "Dollar Trap" to describe the frustration of many central banks with the dominance of the US dollar.[35] As the US dollar remained the safest means of hedging risk and storing values even in the midst of the 2008 financial crisis, compared to other options, foreign investors were compelled to subject the value of their assets to the United States's expansionary monetary policy and dollar fluctuation at the time. As a result, many countries such as India,

[35] Eswar S. Prasad, *The Dollar Trap: How The US Dollar Tightened Its Grip on Global Finance* (Princeton, NJ: Princeton University Press, 2014).

France, and Russia started to turn their heads toward the RMB as a possible alternative to the greenback.[36] Many global central banks and regulators also offer a welcoming climate for the Scheme. From having an insignificant share of the global market in 2011, the RMB has since overtaken at least twenty-two currencies to claim the spot behind the US dollar, the euro, the British pound, and the Japanese yen as the fifth most widely used payment currency internationally as of 2014.[37] International progress seems to have been achieved much faster than expected.[38] The question is, however, whether the institutions at home will be able to catch up in order to support the fast progression.

B Large-Scale Dilemma

On the one hand, China's extremely large market provides the Scheme with a huge advantage; on the other, it faces the problems of coordination and market variations. The experiences of the United States and the EU are two similar cases in point. In the eighteenth century, the British tried to stop colonial New England from printing its own paper bills, lest British banks lose their markets to trade, settle, and lend British pounds in New England.[39] The response from the US founders was the consensus that the thirteen states be united to create a large enough market to confront the political and economic challenges from Britain. A more recent case is the creation of the euro zone. The EU began as a political project to integrate small European states and then proceeded as more of a monetary project to create a market large enough to support its new single currency. The outcome is the massive EU economy, which accounts for about 31 percent of world output.[40]

[36] Todd Buell, "China Currency Set for International Role, Says ECB Board Member," *The Wall Street Journal*, February 26, 2014, http://online.wsj.com/news/articles/SB10001424052702303801304579406612508072596.

[37] Anjani Trivedi, "Use of Yuan as Global Payment Currency Fails," *The Wall Street Journal*, March 26, 2014, http://online.wsj.com/news/articles/SB10001424052702304688104579462870399966210.

[38] From the speeches given by top policy makers, one can easily tell that Beijing has been satisfied, and somehow surprised, with the outcome.

[39] Claire Priest, "Currency Policies and Legal Development in Colonial New England," *Yale Law Journal* 110 (2001): 1303.

[40] Lim Ewe-Ghee, "The Euro's Challenge to the Dollar: Different Views from Economists and Evidence from COFER (Currency Composition of Foreign Exchange Reserves) and Other Data," Working Paper 06/153 (IMF, 2006): 10, www.imf.org/external/pubs/ft/wp/2006/wp06153.pdf.

In both cases, the size of the market was crucial for the adoption of the new currency, because the costs of switching to a new currency would be less if market scale could amplify the benefits of switching, such as diversifying the government's finance options and facilitating cross-state transactions. However, the costs of creating a large market are not minor. Aside from the military and economic confrontation in the United States in the eighteenth century, tremendous integration costs were incurred in the EU, legally and economically. For instance, the German constitutional court needs from time to time to scrutinize issues such as the constitutionality of delegating monetary power to the European Commission.[41] A recent case is Greece's debt crisis in the summer of 2015.

In the case of China, it fortunately has the natural benefit of a sizeable market, facing neither blunt military and economic threats such as those that colonial New England received, nor the financial and legal integration costs that the EU has been painfully coping with. Its immense market creates a large demand for the RMB, not only from the booming domestic economy but also from foreign investors that aim to benefit from China's consumer market. However, as discussed, the obstacles to the internationalization of the RMB come primarily from large and heterogeneous domestic markets, not from abroad.

As a matter of fact, these domestic challenges concern not only the policy prescriptions of the Washington Consensus but also one of the biggest criticisms of the Washington Consensus: the lack of a sequence for implementing its varying policy recommendations. The Scheme is associated with a wide range of regulations regarding banking, securities, capital markets, and currency exchanges, and no other areas of policy debates are more sequence-oriented than the reforms therein. Empirical evidence shows that, if the sequencing goes wrong, hyperinflation (e.g., Latin America), staggering recession (e.g., Japan) or even economic crisis (e.g., Iceland or Greece) may follow.[42] However, the more variations in market conditions there are, the more complex the sequence of policy implementation tends to be.

The other core policy of the Scheme – lifting of capital controls – has faced great challenges of a similar nature concerning sequencing. Global

[41] Carsten Gerner-Beuerle, Esin Küçük, and Edmund Schuster, "Law Meets Economics in the German Federal Constitutional Court: Outright Monetary Transactions on Trial," *German Law Journal* 15 (2014): 281; Christian Hofmann, "A Legal Analysis of the Euro Zone Crisis," *Fordham Journal of Corporate and Financial Law* 18 (2013): 519.

[42] Volz, "RMB Internationalization and Currency Co-operation."

financial crises have caused the conventional wisdom about the liberal policy of capital control to be questioned. The IMF and the World Bank, together with numerous economists, used to advocate fiercely for the lifting of capital controls as a key approach to ensuring that developing countries benefit from foreign investment. However, the 2008 financial crisis, together with subsequent crises in Europe, demonstrate that free capital flow allows speculative investors to create various asset bubbles in emerging economies and then quickly pull their money before bubble bursts. In light of this hard lesson, the IMF has finally recognized that the variations in domestic market conditions matter and therefore modified its position – a certain level of capital controls may be desirable for developing countries as a complementary regulatory tool.[43] By contrast, the Scheme in China seems to be moving in the opposite direction of this paradigm shift.[44]

C Heterogeneous and Fragmented Markets

Aside from regional and sectoral variations, problems of extreme market variations can also be observed in specific markets and their respective regulatory structures pertinent to the Scheme: capital markets, foreign exchange markets, and banking sectors. Whether the Scheme is viable depends on how China deals with such complex and diverse market conditions in these markets.

To begin with, China's capital markets, which are tied to the success of the Scheme, are very segmented due to capital controls: there is the market of A shares, denominated in RMB, available only to Chinese citizens; the market of B shares, denominated in foreign currency, originally reserved

[43] Naoyuki Yoshino, Sahoko Kaji, and Tamon Asonuma, "Dynamic Transition of Exchange Rate Regime in China," *China and World Economy* 22 (2014); Jonathan D. Ostry et al. (eds.), "Managing Capital Inflows: What Tools to Use?," IMF Staff Discussion Note SDN/11/06 (IMF, 2011), www.imf.org/external/pubs/ft/sdn/2011/sdn1106.pdf; Volz, "RMB Internationalization and Currency Co-operation," 369. For example, in his talk given at NUS in November 2014, Martin Wolf also suggested that Indonesia consider capital controls to deal with immense hot money as a result of expansionary monetary policies in the US, Japan, and China.

[44] In January 2016, in the midst of quick, surprising depreciation of the RMB, the IMF managing director Christine Lagarde did not reject the suggestion by Japan's central bank that Beijing impose stringent capital controls to stabilize the RMB. This demonstrated the IMF's change in position. Chris Giles, "Kuroda Calls for China to Tighten Capital Controls," January 23, 2016, *Financial Times*, www.ft.com/intl/cms/s/0/03395bdc-c1c4–11e5–808f-8231cd71622e.html#axzz3yJWfT4bg.

for foreign investors, although Chinese citizens may now hold these shares as well; and the market of H shares, which are shares listed by Chinese firms on the Hong Kong stock exchange.[45] As a result of establishing this structure, Chinese policymakers can collect household savings through capital markets but also tap into foreign investment without exposing the domestic economy to destabilizing capital flows.[46]

This segmentation stemmed from the inconvertibility of the RMB and was based on the logic of erecting firewalls between foreign and domestic markets, reflecting the policymakers' response to extreme variations in market conditions. While the firewalls prevent a potential chain reaction in the face of systemic risks caused by existing institutional deficiency and exposure to speculative investment, large-scale markets nevertheless allow each market unit sufficient economies of scale that can make a significant change. However, the problems with China's fragmented capital markets have been well-documented, and include immense arbitrage, insider trading, and weak and inefficient law enforcement.[47] In the absence of well-functioning institutions, lifting capital controls under the Scheme may lead to market inability. In fact, it has been reported that deregulating capital controls as a result of the Shanghai-Hong Kong Stock Connect served as the major factor leading to the dramatic collapse of China's stock markets in the summer of 2015.[48]

Secondly, the foreign exchange rate markets pose a challenge of coordination to Chinese policymakers.[49] RMB internationalization requires

[45] Additionally, "S-chip," "Red-chip," and "P-chip" refer to overseas Chinese firms that are listed and traded on foreign exchanges (e.g., S-chips are Chinese firms listed on Singapore Stock Exchange).

[46] Barry Naughton, *The Chinese Economy: Transitions and Growth* (Cambridge, MA: MIT Press, 2007), 470–71.

[47] See, e.g., Donald C. Clarke, "Law without Order in Chinese Corporate Governance Institutions," *Northwestern Journal of International Law and Business* 30 (2010): 131; Lay-Hong Tan and Jiangyu Wang, "Modeling an Effective Corporate Governance System for China's Listed State-Owned Enterprises: Issues and Challenges in a Transitional Economy," *Journal of Corporate Law Studies* 7 (2007): 143; Satyananda J. Gabriel, *Chinese Capitalism and the Modernist Vision* (Oxon, UK: Routledge, 2006); Yong Kang, Lu Shi, and Elizabeth D. Brown, "Chinese Corporate Governance: History and Institutional Framework," Rand Corporation Technical Report TR-618-RC (Rand Corporation, 2008), www.rand.org/pubs/technical_reports/TR618.html.

[48] Yi-Huan Du, "Zuihou jiule zhongguo gushi de shi gonganbu" [It is the Ministry of Public Security That Saved China's Stock Markets], *Common Wealth Magazine*, July 9, 2015, www.cw.com.tw/article/article.action?id=5069089#.

[49] The conflict between RMB internationalization and foreign exchange rate control can be best explained by the "impossible trinity," a trilemma that every central bank faces. The trilemma means that any state can only choose two of the three policy options:

liberalization of the foreign exchange rate because full currency convertibility cannot coexist with foreign exchange rate control. Although this control is a rather centralized policy set by the central bank, liberalizing and replacing it with a market-oriented regime would involve every level of the regulatory system and requires complex legal and financial engineering. Tasks include, for example, how to create foreign exchange markets with a functional pricing mechanism to determine the exchange rate, how to select banks that have capacity to operate the markets, or how to create and coordinate varying monitoring mechanisms and regulatory bodies to supervise the markets.

The challenge for the Scheme, then, is whether the PBoC can coordinate its financial institutions and local governments in order to create a market environment that allows banks to price their foreign exchange transactions. Currently, the largest state-owned banks monopolize about 95 percent of foreign exchange transactions, with the exchange rate largely decided by the PBoC.[50] As such, before they are given clearance to participate in this market, all banks need to acquire the capacity to run this new business. In other successful cases, this liberalization has appeared to be a long journey. For example, Taiwan adopted a capital control and foreign exchange policy very similar to China's throughout its economic take-off period. Taiwan's Central Bank began experimenting with the free foreign exchange market in 1979.[51] It took this much smaller economy ten years to coordinate and train banks to operate this new foreign exchange market.[52] This could serve as an indicator of the coordination challenges that the PBoC faces.

fixed exchange rate, free capital flow, and independent monetary policy. If the state intends to maintain a fixed exchange rate, it has to compromise either free capital flow or independent monetary policy; neither is desirable under the RMB internationalization scheme.

50 Zhu, "Cong ziyou dao longduan: zhongguo huobi jingji liangqiannian," 386.

51 At the beginning of the process, five selected banks were allowed to create a foreign exchange market among banks and established a joint committee to decide their own exchange rate. Four years later the Central Bank of Taiwan expanded this institutional experiment by setting the once-centralized exchange rate based on the rates determined by the five selected banks. Finally, in 1989, the Central Bank abolished foreign exchange rate control entirely in the belief that the banks had obtained the skills necessary to decide foreign exchange rates for themselves. Hsu Cheng-Ming, "You jinrong ziyouhua yu guojihua de guocheng tan jinrong jianli" [Financial Liberalization, Internationalization and Supervision], Policy Reports 090-039 (National Policy Foundation, 2001), http://old.npf.org.tw/PUBLICATION/FM/090/FM-R-090-039.htm.

52 One reason for the long duration of currency reform in Taiwan is that its economy depended more on domestic capital than FDI, compared to that of China. In China, FDI

Thirdly, the other fragmented sector is the banking system. Top Chinese banks have gone through significant reforms in the past decade through internationalization. However, regional banks are slow to adapt to changes. Nicholas Lardy points out that the banking sector is one exception to an overwhelming trend of privatization across industries in China between 2008 and 2013, and that this sector remains inefficient.[53]

Banking is all about risks: how to assess and distribute the risks. Before RMB internationalization lifts capital controls, banks need to obtain expertise in order to evaluate their risk portfolio, as well as the capacity to operate in a relatively free market environment without the government's subsidies. Without such capacity, banks may not be able to carry out a vital task that the Scheme requires: to determine interest rates. As a result, the lifting of capital controls is probably the perfect recipe for failure in the banking sector. In the face of negative savings rates, for example, Chinese households would withdraw their savings from state banks and hold their assets in foreign currency or deposit them elsewhere (e.g., informal financial institutions, private banks, or foreign bank branches in China that offer higher savings rates) if they are given the option. This would lead to a liquidity crisis. Nevertheless, banks' capacity varies across the country and even within the same bank. A bank's branch offices in tier-one cities may be very different from those in tier-three cities in terms of capacity to evaluate borrowers' creditworthiness, assess the risks of their own financial products, and develop diverse and competitive revenue sources.

To sum up, the immense and fragmented capital markets, foreign exchange market and banking system pose great challenges to RMB internationalization. In particular, lifting of capital controls has historically and empirically proven to be a risky and difficult process. The orthodox solution, as a rich body of literature suggests, centers on identifying the sequence for implementation; for example, liberalization of lending rates should happen earlier than that of savings rates, deregulation for institutional investors prior to individuals, or outbound FDI prior to

as well as securities investors from overseas have injected immense capital into the banking sector, thereby granting more leverage for the regulators to carry out reforms. One case in point is the successful reform of non-performing loans in the 2000s through injecting foreign capital into the banking system.

[53] Nicholas Lardy, *Markets over Mao: The Rise of Private Business in China* (Washington, DC: Peterson Institute for International Economics, 2014).

inbound FDI.[54] In this regard, a number of East Asian countries such as Japan, Korea, and Taiwan have arguably demonstrated the "right" sequence of financial and banking reforms.[55]

However, the sequence approach assumes that each policy being implemented paves the way for subsequent ones, which can "wait" and are largely segregated from the impact of previous reforms. This linear assumption is more likely to stand in a small economy, or a large but hegemonic economy. In contrast, in large or heterogeneous markets, various sectors and policies are usually far more interdependent. The larger or more fragmented the market is, the less likely it is that such linear assumptions can stand. Coordination may also become more costly and ineffective, making the implementation of such sequential reforms difficult and distorted. The "right" sequence would therefore be difficult to identify or may not even exist.

IV China's Response by Leveraging the Scale

To implement the Scheme, as discussed, China needs to cope with three challenges: (1) extreme variations in market conditions; (2) coordination difficulties; and (3) systemic risks magnified by a large-scale economy. In response, China seems to have adopted a number of shrewd strategies commonly seen in *Taiji*, the Chinese martial art: coping with problems of scale by leveraging the scale.

A Institutional Diversification

China's first response to heterogeneous market conditions was to diversify institutional settings rather than adopt a general rule-based regulatory regime. To begin with, institutional experimentation is being conducted

54 Ronald I. McKinnon, *The Order of Economic Liberalization* (Baltimore: The Johns Hopkins University Press, 1991). Justin Yifu Lin, the Peking University economics professor and former Vice President of the World Bank, also expressed a similar view: "Although the yuan will be playing an increasingly important role . . . its ascendance to fully fledged reserve currency status must await substantial reform of its financial markets." Justin Yifu Lin, *Against the Consensus: Reflections on the Great Recession* (New York: Cambridge University Press, 2013), 170.

55 Hsu, "You jinrong ziyouhua yu guojihua de guocheng tan jinrong jianli."

in various regions as a response to regional variations. The most high-profile experiment is the SFTZ, which covers a combined area of nearly thirty square kilometers in Shanghai. It aims to "explore new routes and systems for China's opening-up policies, to accelerate the transformation of how government functions . . . [and] to pioneer innovative ideas that can be replicated in the future in other parts of the country."[56] In August 2013, the National People's Congress passed an unprecedented resolution, suspending major corporate law regulations on matters relating to foreign firms' investment within the SFTZ for three years: "After three years, new institutions that have proven workable may continue; otherwise the original regulations should be restored and resume."[57] Additionally, the State Council also suspended twenty-seven regulations with respect to specific industries (e.g., shipping and car manufacturing), corporate entities (e.g., joint venture and wholly foreign-owned enterprises), and administrative procedures (e.g., approval of manufacturing license or market entry).[58] Other measures necessary for the Scheme have also been adopted within the SFTZ, including lifting of capital account restrictions, legalization of private banks, and liberalization of banking savings and lending interests through which banks will be able to freely assess their risk exposure and reflect such risks to the interest rates free from government intervention.

Moreover, other pilot zones with different institutional settings catering to different regions have been created. Qianhai Pilot Zone is most representative. Established in 2011 and located next to Hong Kong, Qianhai Pilot Zone aims to develop an onshore RMB financial center by replicating Hong Kong's institutional environment. It replicates Hong Kong's

56 "Introduction," China (Shanghai) Pilot Free Trade Zone, http://en.china-shftz.gov.cn/About-FTZ/Introduction/.

57 "Decision of the Standing Committee of the National People's Congress on Authorizing the State Council to Temporarily Adjust the Relevant Administrative Approval Items Prescribed in Laws in the China (Shanghai) Pilot Free Trade Zone," China (Shanghai) Pilot Free Trade Zone, http://en.china-shftz.gov.cn/Government-affairs/Laws/General/62.shtml.

58 "Guowuyuan guanyu zai zhongguo (Shanghai) ziyoumaoyi shiyanqu nei zanshi tiaozheng shishi youguan xingzheng fagui he jing guowuyuan pizhun de bumen guiding de zhunru tebie guanli cuoshi de jueding" [The Decision of the State Council on Adjusting Temporarily Administrative Approval Items and Special Administrative Measures for Access Prescribed by Related Administrative Regulations], announced September 4, 2014, www.china-shftz.gov.cn/PublicInformation.aspx?GID=c39042c4-eac2–4d94–9766–2443119d7346&CID=953a259a-1544–4d72-be6a-264677089690&MenuType=1&navType=1.

low tax regime, invites professionals and consultants from Hong Kong to join the management teams, models its dispute resolution institution (i.e., arbitration) on Hong Kong's and hires legal professionals from Hong Kong.[59] While the SFTZ is conducting comprehensive experimentation, Qianhai Pilot Zone is focusing more on financial services.[60]

Institutional diversification exists not only geographically but also caters to specific business groups or sectors. To deal with the fragmented capital markets, the Scheme's solution is to drill several holes in the firewalls of capital controls. These mechanisms (i.e., the holes) include, for example, the Qualified Foreign Institutional Investors (QFII) and the Renmibi Qualified Foreign Institutional Investors (RQFII), which was introduced more recently.[61] As a way to selectively lift capital controls, QFII and RQFII grant direct access to China's fragmented capital markets to foreign institutional investors that meet certain qualifications. Due to the desire of offshore investors to benefit from China's markets, the capital flowing in through these tiny holes is nevertheless immense – so China is now benefitting from the scale advantage.

In short, institutional diversification makes the best use of scale advantages. While each unit of diversification may address varying institutional demand by region and by sector, each is nonetheless large enough to maintain sufficient economies of scale.[62] The aggregation of such economies of scale in turn provides greater leeway for policy choices and institutional design.

59 "Qianhai shengang xiandai fuwuye hehuoqu" [Qianhai Shenzhen-Hong Kong Modern Service Industry Cooperation Zone], Government of Shenzhen, www.szqh.gov.cn:81/ljqh/qhjj515/qhdsj/.

60 The development of the Qianhai Pilot Zone has triggered debates in Hong Kong. Some commentators, including HK legislators, hold the view that Qianhai is being developed by the central government in order replace Hong Kong, of which Beijing does not have a full control. "Ling jian jinrong chengshi qianhai qudai xianggang" [Qianhai: Creating a New Financial Center to Replace Hong Kong?], *Hong Kong Economic Journal*, http://forum.hkej.com/node/60537.

61 QFII and RQFII are mechanisms adopted by the Scheme to recycle offshore RMB back to domestic markets, so that offshore RMB can substantively contribute to Chinese economy. Such recycling is prominent and crucial for offshore USD and the US economy. The success of the USD relies on effective recycling mechanisms. For example, oil dollars in the Middle East can be recycled back to the US market through the sovereign wealth funds in the Middle Eastern countries.

62 Michael Dowdle, "On the Public-Law Character of Competition Law: A Lesson of Asian Capitalism," *Fordham International Law Journal* 38 (2015): 301.

B Pluralist Capitalism

Institutional diversification further denotes the idea of pluralist capitalism in China. Take the SFTZ and the Qianhai Pilot Zone as examples: both are created by the state in order to advance the internationalization of RMB and provide guidance for future reforms. Literature often refers to this interventionist approach as state capitalism. Nevertheless, multiple state capitalisms seem to coexist here as the two pilot zones represent different models of capitalism.

For one, the Qianhai Pilot Zone is modeled on Hong Kong, a classical model of laissez-faire capitalism. The British colonial government implemented the "positive nonintervention policy," under which business decisions are left to the private sector with minimal governmental intervention in the form of tax incentive packages. Competition law, for example, has developed slowly, and market monopolies are largely tolerated.[63] Milton Friedman described his meeting in 1963 with the architect of the nonintervention policy, then financial secretary John Cowperthwaite. In response to Friedman's query about the paucity of statistics, Cowperthwaite described his firm belief in laissez-faire capitalism: "If I let them compute those statistics, they'll want to use them for planning."[64]

In comparison, the SFTZ appears to model Singapore, the opposite model to that of Hong Kong. Singapore's interventionist approach is summarized by Goh Keng Swee, the former Deputy Prime Minister and Singapore's economic architect: "[the laissez-faire policies of the colonial era] had led Singapore to a dead end, with little economic growth, massive unemployment, wretched housing, and inadequate education . . . thus [we] had to try a more activist and interventionist approach."[65] For example, the Economic Development Board, set up in 1961, geared Singapore's industrial strategies, labor policies, and education system toward meeting Singapore's economic goals by way of tax incentives, investment in strategic industries, and global network building. In its heyday, there were more than 600 state-owned enterprises and government-linked

[63] The Hong Kong government passed its first ever antitrust law in 2012. Nevertheless, it is still not uncommon for monopolies to perform evil tactics like attempting to eliminate competitors by predatory pricing.

[64] Milton Friedman, "The Hong Kong Experiment," *Hoover Digest*, July 30, 1998, www.hoover.org/research/hong-kong-experiment.

[65] Devan Nair, *Socialism That Works: The Singapore Way* (Singapore: Federation Publications, 1976), 84.

companies, many of which were run on commercial principles and were profitable and internationally competitive from the outset.[66]

Interestingly, Chinese policymakers for the SFTZ and commentators are not shy about expressing their ambition to replace Singapore eventually. China has been sending their officials and senior bank managers to Singapore for professional training at universities, government-linked companies and sovereign wealth funds. In fact, companies from Singapore are the SFTZ's primary targets to attract: as of September 2014, nearly six hundred companies from Singapore have established subsidiaries and branch offices in the SFTZ.[67] Singapore's model of state capitalism is behind the SFTZ's institutional design for the implementation of the Scheme.

Again, experimentation with multiple capitalisms evidences the way in which China leverages its scale advantage. Both the "Hong Kong model" in Qianhai Pilot Zone and the "Singapore Model" in the SFTZ aim to improve China's institutional capacity to run a genuine market economy for the sake of the implementation of the Scheme. Reforms necessary for the Scheme are being carried out within the zones, but the state remains present to ensure that the model of pluralist capitalism serves the Scheme well.

C *Bridging and Institutionalization*

To cope with the problems of coordination in large-scale and fragmented markets, Chinese regulators try to bridge multiple markets, foreign markets included, and institutionalize certain market experimentations at the regional level.[68]

Bridging occurs in different forms. For example, to bridge onshore and offshore RMB markets, Beijing has been signing currency swap agreements with foreign jurisdictions. Under these swap agreements, foreign

[66] Boon Siong Neo and Geraldine Chen, *Dynamic Governance: Embedding Culture, Capabilities and Change in Singapore* (Singapore: World Scientific, 2007), 92.

[67] "Xinjiapo jin 600 qiye ruzhu shanghai zimaoqu" [Nearly Six Hundred Singapore Firms Joined Shanghai Free Trade Zone], Economic and Commercial Counsellor's Office of the Embassy of the People's Republic of China in the Republic of Singapore, http://sg.mofcom.gov.cn/article/fuhua/tzdongtai/201410/20141000768457.shtml.

[68] A number of strands of literature use different labels to coin this working relationship between regulators at the central and regional levels. E.g., Wei Cui, in Chapter 4, discusses "federalism, Chinese style" proposed by Gabriella Montinola, Yingyi Qian, and Barry Weingast. See Gabriella Montinola, Qian Yingyi, and Barry R. Weingast, "Federalism, Chinese Style: The Political Basis for Economic Success," *World Politics* 48 (1996): 50.

regulators may exercise their swap rights in the face of increasing demand for the RMB and then inject more RMB into foreign markets. The total amounts of such swap rights to be granted by the PBoC constitute bargaining power between China and its foreign partners.

Another recent bridging initiative is the Shanghai-Hong Kong Stock Connect. The rationale is that the larger the capital markets are, the more liquidity the markets possess, and therefore they are more efficient and better economies of scale can be created. In theory, China has a number of models to choose from for bridging domestic and foreign stock exchanges, including secondary listing, cross-listing and a national security market model used by American regulators for the market linkage between Europe and the United States. Given China's size and lower integration costs, Beijing regulators chose the most aggressive model: a direct linkage between China and offshore markets.[69] The next steps are probably to link to Singapore, and thereby to the ASEAN markets in the south, as well as to the Taiwan Stock Exchange in the east.[70]

In comparison to bridging, institutionalization occurs at the domestic and regional levels. As discussed, China needs to liberalize its interest rates to reduce opportunities for arbitrage and speculative investments after lifting capital account restrictions. It could be risky if such liberalization goes too fast, because banks will not yet have the capacity to decide on optimal market savings rates by evaluating their risk portfolios fairly. As such, the central government has chosen to assist localities in institutionalizing existing practices.

For example, Wenzhou, a city once famous for informal banking, is where the experimentation of free interest rates is being conducted at the moment. Beginning in 2012, private lenders and financial institutions in Wenzhou were allowed to determine their own savings rates, while the government is only playing a coordinating role.[71] Numerous

[69] David Donald, "Beyond Fragmentation: Building a Unified Securities Market in China (and Asia)," in *Finance, Rule of Law and Development in Asia: Perspectives from Hong Kong, Singapore and Shanghai*, Jiaxiang Hu, Matthias Vanhullebusch, and Andrew Harding (eds.) (Leiden, Netherlands: Brill, 2016).

[70] Ibid. Also, Singapore and China began integrating their securities markets in 2013. See "SGX and China Securities Regulatory Commission Establish Direct Listing Framework," WongPartnership, www.wongpartnership.com/index.php/files/download/1134.

[71] Shangguan Shasha and Han Chi, "Zhou xiang quanguo de 'wenzhou zhishu' wei lixi shichanghua toushiwenlu" [Wenzhou Index and National-wide Marketization of Interest Rates], *Wenzhouwang*, November 3, 2011, http://news.66wz.com/system/2014/11/03/104261941.shtml.

working units, established in Wenzhou and in other partner cities where Wenzhou's financial institutions have a strong presence, collect a variety of information concerning savings rates (e.g., mortgages, collateral, pledges, and other security packages). A centralized system set up by the Wenzhou regulators computes and publicizes these statistics every day. The government is not currently deciding the rates but allows them to be predictable and stable by releasing market information.[72] Market players appear to adapt themselves quickly to this nascent market mechanism. Private lenders depend on this disclosure system to determine interest rates when lending to their family members, relatives, and business partners. Given the experiment's initial success, the Wenzhou government has vowed to establish roughly one hundred private micro-lending firms with estimated capital of RMB 80 billion.[73]

D Risk Sharing and Cost Bearing

The sheer size of the Chinese economy magnifies any systemic risk. The success of reforms therefore also rests on sufficient risk-sharing institutions, which may encourage risk-taking, innovation, and institutional experimentation. In their paper analyzing why China once led but fell far behind England economically after the sixteenth and seventeenth centuries, Avner Greif et al. argue that the configurations of various risk-sharing institutions (e.g., patent and social welfare systems) account for the distinctive growth trajectories and outcomes in the two ancient empires.[74] In the context of RMB internationalization, two general approaches are adopted to deal with large systemic risks: (1) to contain the risks in smaller, closed subsystems; or (2) to distribute the risks to an even larger pool.

First, the pilot zones are subsystems that can contain the risks within the zones. Private banks, for example, are only allowed within the zones.

[72] In a way, this approach is very similar to the role the US Federal Reserve plays. The Fed does not explain its policies but allows these policies be predicable by releasing signals and communicating with the private sector regularly. See Janet Yellen, "Speech: Vice Chair Janet Yellen at the Society of American Business Editors and Writers," Board of Governors of the Federal Reserve System, April 4, 2013, www.federalreserve.gov/newsevents/speech/yellen20130404a.htm.

[73] Chen De Rong, "Wenzhou jinrong gaige zaichufa" [The Restart of Wenzhou's Financial Reform], *China Reform* no. 340, March 2012.

[74] Avner Greif, Murat Iyigun, and Diego L. Sasson, "Social Institutions and Economic Growth: Why England and Not China Became the First Modern Economy," (2012), http://dx.doi.org/10.2139/ssrn.1783879.

Their more competitive lending and savings rates will therefore not draw clients and drain cheap capital away from state-owned banks outside of the zones. Enforcement of anti-money-laundering regulations has been strengthened accordingly to prevent speculators from abusing the free capital account within the SFTZ.[75] In fact, some commentators advocate a higher financial firewall between SFTZ and the rest of China so that speculators will not use the lifting of capital controls within the zone to their advantage. Such a firewall approach creates an inherent dilemma: it will not be effective in isolating risks if the firewall is too soft, but if the firewall is too high and stands for too long, the scale of the SFTZ will not itself be large enough a pool to support the internationalization of the RMB.[76] This dilemma explains why foreign investors and banks, instead of calling for stronger firewalls, have started complaining about the slow progress of deregulation.[77]

The second approach is to distribute risks to a larger pool.[78] Global capital markets serve as a key mechanism of international risk sharing, as they distribute the risks of a specific foreign issuer to international investors.[79] As discussed, the Scheme is more about domestic reforms. Whereas deregulation of the domestic banking and foreign exchange markets requires a gradual approach to improving the capacity of banks and related market players, capital markets appear to be easier to strengthen in a quick fashion. Chinese firms have also been aggressively accessing international capital markets to compensate for their domestic governance deficiencies and to facilitate their capacity building.[80] Overall, China's attempt to

[75] In the SFTZ, residents, individuals, and corporate entities alike can apply for resident accounts that allow them to freely wire capital in and out without approval in advance.

[76] McKinnon and Schnabl, "China's Exchange Rate and Financial Repression."

[77] Michelle Chen, "Reform Paralysis, Slow Progress Cloud Shanghai Free Trade Zone Project," *Reuters*, September 15, 2014, www.reuters.com/article/2014/09/14/china-shanghai-ftz-idUSL3N0RB1JR20140914.

[78] In fact, one major function of making a currency an international reserve currency is to enable the country of the currency (e.g., the US or China) to distribute domestic economic risk internationally, if necessary. While expansionary monetary policy may be used to bail out domestic firms and boost domestic economy, it leads to depreciation of the currency and hence decreases the value of assets denominated in that currency and held by global investors. See also Katharina Pistor, "A Legal Theory of Finance," *Journal of Comparative Economics* 41 (2013).

[79] Shigeru Iwata and Shu Wu, "Stock Market Liberalization and International Risk Sharing," *Journal of International Financial Markets, Institutions and Money* 19 (2004): 461; Vadym Volosovych, "Risk Sharing from International Factor Income: Explaining Cross-Country Differences," *Applied Economics* 45 (2013): 1435.

[80] Chen, "Institutional Arbitrage."

overhaul and bridge multiple capital markets under the Scheme is in line with the theory of capacity building for risk sharing.

E Summary

All in all, China needs to strike a balance between efficiency and diversity when implementing the Scheme. Governance structure with too much diversity would be inefficient and thus make the economy inefficient, albeit highly resilient. Conversely, governance that puts too much emphasis on efficiency may indeed be highly efficient but will reduce diversity.[81] The literature on East Asian capitalism has unveiled a shared model of economic success in Asia in light of this dilemma. Compared to North Atlantic capitalism, Asian capitalism (primarily referring to the "Asian Tigers") focuses on productive adaptability to sudden market changes rather than on exploiting economies of scale based on mass production, standardized processes, and general rule-based governance structure.[82] In comparison, however, China's large-scale economy enables China to engage in both approaches, including multiple state capitalisms, to implement the Scheme.[83]

V A Chinese Model?

The large size factor indeed accounts for China's institutional design for the Scheme. China's extremely large-scale economy affects integration costs, diversification of institutions, the ability to bear inefficiency, the capacity for risk sharing, the freedom to conduct institutional experimentation, and the ways in which its legal system codifies and formalizes norms and market practices. For example, in terms of institutional diversification, while each unit may produce sustainable and minimally efficient economies of scale, the state shrewdly coordinates various market players to aggregate and leverage such economies of scale to further

[81] Michael Mainelli and Bob Giffords, "Size Matters: Risk and Scale," *The Journal of Risk Finance* 11 (2010).

[82] Jessop and Sum, *Beyond the Regulation Approach*; Dowdle, "On the Public-Law Character of Competition Law."

[83] Kanishka Jasuriya, "Institutional Hybrids and the Rule of Law as a Regulatory Project," in *Legal Pluralism and Development: Scholars and Practitioners in Dialogue*, Brian Z. Tamanaha, Caroline Sage, and Michael Woolcock (eds.) (Cambridge: Cambridge University Press: 2012), 145.

advance the Scheme. Some strategies such as linkage of foreign exchange rates and bridging capital markets are only possible in this kind of large-scale economy. In this way, China is able to borrow more time for difficult reforms, especially those involving lifting capital controls and introducing full currency convertibility.

However, the size factor is a common constraint that other economies have to deal with in the context of currency policy, too. Singapore, for example, initially chose a noninternationalization policy to prevent its small economy from speculative attacks. Even at a later point when Singapore decided to cease this policy and lift capital controls, the size factor led to the choice of its exchange rate–centric model to manage the full currency convertibility on the capital account, leaving interest rates to be determined freely by market forces.[84] The rationale for this lies in the small size of its economy. Having to coordinate with only a few major players in its banking sector, the authorities felt comfortable letting interest rates be decided by the market,[85] giving up the monetary tool of interest rate adjustment commonly seen in capitalist economies.[86]

In contrast to Singapore's exchange rate–centric model, Taiwan adopted a very different model to manage its capital account also because of the larger size of its economy: an interest rate–centric model.[87] Categorized as a typical Asian state capitalism along with Singapore, Taiwan nevertheless has to deal with more complex issues due to more market players, various levels of localities, and diverse institutional settings. Prior to its overhaul of the financial sectors in the 1990s, Taiwan faced very similar challenges to those faced by China at this time, including financial repression imposed in order to aggregate private capital for quick state-led

[84] Chong Tee Ong, "Singapore's Policy of Non-internationalization of the Singapore Dollar and the Asian Dollar Market," BIS Paper no. 15 (Bank for International Settlements, 2003), www.bis.org/publ/bppdf/bispap15l.pdf.

[85] DBS, one of the largest banks in Singapore, is a spin-off of the Monetary Authority of Singapore (MAS), the central bank of Singapore.

[86] Chong Tee Ong, "An Exchange Rate-Centered Monetary Policy System: Singapore's Experience," BIS Paper no. 73 (Bank for International Settlements, 2013): 308, www.bis.org/publ/bppdf/bispap73w.pdf; Chow Hwee Kean, "Managing Capital Flows: The Case of Singapore," ADB Institute Discussion Paper no. 86 (Asian Development Bank Institute, 2008): 15, www.adb.org/sites/default/files/publication/156725/adbi-dp86.pdf.

[87] Compared to Singapore's exchange rate–centric model, Taiwan's interest rate–centric model is less clearly formed, as Taiwan's Central Bank still monitors and adjusts the exchange rate from time to time through open market operations.

industrialization, the inefficiency of the state-owned banks that dominated the financial sector, immense bad loans caused by the moral hazard inherent in the state banking sector, and underground banking where small and middle-sized firms obtained capital. Taiwan is geographically small but economically large enough to demonstrate institutional issues similar to those that China has to cope with. Its authoritarian political system also faced sufficient dissenting voices to make the state continually pursue reforms, albeit incrementally, in order to minimize potential backlash.

In fact, many of the policies adopted by the SFTZ are identical to those Taiwan implemented to refine its banking sectors in the 1980s and 1990s, including the negative list, QFII, and an open policy with respect to private banks. Like China, Taiwan was aware of the need to reform the domestic banking institutions before introducing full currency convertibility. Both were also under similar and tremendous pressure from the international community, especially the United States, regarding alleged manipulation of the currency exchange rate. Effective experimentation was conducted in Taiwan too, but on a much smaller scale.[88]

The EU is another example of the scale effect. The euro is also based on the immense scale of the EU's economy. However, the EU remains incapable of fully maximizing the synergies due to various obstacles to the integration of nonhomogeneous economies in Europe.[89] The rocky integration of small economies is the source of the problem, as member states remain independent and are guided by different policies. In this regard, the EU faces difficulties with respect to regional variations among member states similar to those in China. All in all, the size factor does not

[88] For example, Taiwan established one of the earliest special economic zones in the world to diversify its institutional settings. Frederic C. Deyo, "Addressing the Development Deficit of Competition Policy: The Role of Economic Networks in Asian Capitalism and the Regulation of Competition," in *Asian Capitalism and the Regulation of Competition: Towards a Regulatory Geography of Global Competition Law*, Michael W. Dowdle, John Gillespie, and Imelda Maher (eds.) (Cambridge: Cambridge University Press, 2013), 283.

[89] For example, while debts are denominated in euros, they are issued by separate nation-states that have varying credit quality and liquidity risks and are subject to different legal procedures. There is also no benchmark euro asset like the US treasury bonds; instead, twelve different issuers participate in the euro government securities market. Lim Ewe-Ghee, "The Euro's Challenge to the Dollar," 14; Gabriel Galati and Phillip Woolridge, "The Euro as a Reserve Currency: A Challenge to the Pre-eminence of the US Dollar?," *International Journal of Financial Economics* 14 (2009): 12.

seem to be unique to China and it is therefore difficult to claim a Chinese Model, or the Beijing Consensus, in the context of currency policy.

VI Conclusion

The size factor has often been mentioned by both scholars and practitioners as one of the most vital factors accounting for China's economic success and international influence. This theory sometimes shows its merit in fields beyond economics. A scholar of electrical engineering once told the author that China demonstrates an equation for innovation: a large-scale consumer market naturally leads to technological innovation. Size definitely matters for institutional innovation, too, but how it matters remains unclear and context dependent. RMB internationalization is arguably the most revolutionary scheme China is currently carrying out. As such, this chapter explores how China's unique size factor plays out in the Scheme, aiming to apply this scrutiny to shed light on the idea of the Beijing Consensus.

Given institutional constraints at home, the implementation of the Scheme has more to do with domestic reforms than an international agenda, and it faces more challenges from within than from abroad. The large-scale factor is not as positive as would be expected; rather, it poses great challenges to China, including problems of coordinating its unprecedentedly large economy, the governance problems that confront extreme market variations, and the resulting systemic risks that are amplified by such a large and heterogeneous economy. In essence, challenges result not only from the identification of reform measures but also from determining the sequence for implementing such measures, challenges that reflect the inherent limitations of the Washington Consensus.

In response, China appears to leverage its large-scale economy to compensate for and cope with the disadvantages of scale. China's extremely large economy enables it to diversify institutional settings while maintaining minimally efficient economies of scale in each unit of institutional experimentation, and to improve its ability to utilize risk-sharing institutions both domestically and internationally. By the same token, pluralist capitalism can be observed in the Scheme as well, as evidenced by the SFTZ in Shanghai aiming to replicate the Singapore Model and Qianhai in Guangdong Province mimicking the Hong Kong model. Experimenting with both of these policy designs simultaneously is probably only possible in a large economy.

Besides the implementation strategy, China needs to contemplate its responsibility as an issuer of a major international reserve currency. The RMB's impact on the global financial order would be enormous. For example, in the face of financial sanctions imposed after its intrusion in Ukraine and Crimea, Russia circumvented these bans, which prevent Russian firms from raising long-term debts in dollar-dominant capital markets, by prompting more companies to use the RMB.[90] The yuan-ruble trade on the Moscow Exchange therefore jumped tenfold in 2014.[91] If the RMB becomes as widely used as the US dollar, China, like the United States, will obtain extensive jurisdiction over foreign entities involved in RMB-related transactions, products, and services. It is extremely crucial to create a set of accountable, impartial, and transparent mechanisms for exercising such expanding regulatory power. Otherwise, the internationalization of the RMB would lead to increasing international disputes rather than financial stability and fairness. Backlashes against the RMB would occur, similar to what we have witnessed to date against the US dollar's dominant status.

All in all, does the scrutiny of RMB internationalization suggest a Chinese Model or construct any aspect of the Beijing Consensus? Indeed, China's experiences are in contrast to the conventional regulatory model, forged from the experiences of advanced industrialized nations where immense and economically coherent markets have led to abstract and rule-based regulations at the national level. China's unprecedentedly large and heterogeneous markets are likely to require highly diverse configurations of regulatory models. Nevertheless, in the context of the Scheme, the merits of China's various reform approaches are rather in line with the values of neoliberal economics underlying the Washington Consensus, as evidenced by the reform measures China is currently pushing in order to internationalize RMB.

This chapter also demonstrates that the size factor has played a role in determining currency policies, not only in China but also in other Asian countries during their transitions. While Singapore illustrates how a small-size economy led to its exchange rate–centric model, Taiwan

[90] Nevertheless, the "smart sanctions" based on Russian firms' need for US capital or USD assets seem to have harmed Russia's economy terribly. Kathrin Hille and Roman Olearchyk, "Plunging Rouble Raises Spectre of Fresh Financial Crisis for Russia," *Financial Times*, November 7, 2014, www.ft.com/intl/cms/s/0/6c059328-666d-11e4-9c0c-00144feabdc0.html#axzz3vbsuscAE.

[91] "Russia Turns to RMB to Thwart Western Sanctions," *China Daily*, November 14, 2014, www.china.org.cn/business/2014-09/25/content_33609143.htm.

provides a contrasting example as to how a mid-size economy gave rise to an interest rate–centric model. In essence, deviations from orthodox policy prescriptions are inevitable due to the local political economy, existing institutional settings, or the dynamics of the global balance of power. The question is, then, to what extent may we characterize these deviations as the Chinese Model, or mere path dependence?[92] Given the neoliberal nature of the Scheme and various other measures relating to the implementation of the Scheme, it is fair to conclude that Beijing in fact follows the policy prescriptions under the Washington Consensus for creating a potential game changer for the global financial world. In other words, this chapter opts for the latter interpretation – that is, the Chinese experience is mere path dependence as opposed to being a form of the Beijing Consensus.

[92] Mariana Mota Prado and Michael J. Trebilcock, "Path Dependence, Development, and the Dynamics of Institutional Reform," *University of Toronto Law Journal* 59 (2009): 341; Michael J. Trebilcock and Mariana Mota Prado, *What Makes Poor Countries Poor? Institutional Determinants of Development* (Cheltenham, UK: Edward Elgar, 2011).

7

A Chinese Model for Tax Reforms in Developing Countries?

JI LI

Effective taxation is essential for achieving sustained growth in third world countries as many lack adequate financial resources to provide basic public goods. Advice from international development agencies has recently shifted away from the Washington Consensus toward a model that stresses institutional building and contextualized tax policy making and implementation. Against that backdrop, this chapter reviews the tax reforms in China for the past three decades, explores their structural determinants, and attempts to draw lessons for the least developed countries seeking to strengthen their extractive capacity. The review indicates that in reforming its tax system, the Chinese government engages in constant pluralistic learning, target setting, and making incremental changes based on trial and error. The Chinese Model of tax reform, however, may not be broadly transferable as most other developing countries do not share its structural premise. Moreover, the model loses much of its glamour if examined from a comparative perspective. Nonetheless, the Chinese experience sheds light on several key questions regarding tax reforms in the least developed countries such as the role of the state, the importance of timing, and priority setting in institutional building.

I The Tax Components of the Consensuses

The Washington Consensus, when originally conceived, enshrined three basic policy tenets: "a market economy, openness to the world, and macroeconomic discipline."[1] Yet over time it took on a tone of market fundamentalism and inspired policy prescriptions for developing

[1] Narcis Serra, Shari Spiegel, and Joseph E. Stiglitz, "Introduction: From the Washington Consensus towards a New Global Governance," in *The Washington Consensus Reconsidered*, Narcis Serra and Joseph E. Stiglitz (eds.) (Oxford: Oxford University Press, 2008), 3.

countries that emphasize predominantly economic liberalization.[2] The market-centered campaign, however, gradually lost its momentum. Critics of the Washington Consensus observed that countries normally underperformed after blindly adopting the liberalization policies;[3] some even questioned the enterprise of providing development policy agenda based on international best practices as "appropriate growth policies are almost always context specific."[4]

As the Washington Consensus lost its appeal, scholars seeking a new development model naturally looked to China, the economy of which sustained remarkable growth despite policy deviations from market fundamentalism. The term Beijing Consensus was coined to encapsulate a development approach of "groping for stones to cross the river,"[5] and was later interpreted as stressing "the importance of second-best solutions, the need for experimentation and the diversity of possible end states."[6]

Since its creation, the concept of Beijing Consensus (or the Chinese Model) has stirred up no fewer debates than its Washington predecessor.[7] For many, the Chinese Model illustrates "a smart state with a light touch able to address deficiencies in the market and adopt a long-term perspective that facilitates sustainable growth."[8] Others doubt the replicability of the Chinese development strategy[9] or question the very existence of such a model.[10] Despite the lack of consensus, most acknowledge that the Chinese government plays an indispensable role in designing and implementing development policies, i.e., identifying and analyzing development problems, exploring multiple solutions, conducting tests and experiments, refining the solutions accordingly and implementing them in a way that allows for local flexibility.[11] The fast growing

[2] Ibid.

[3] Ibid.; Joseph E. Stiglitz, "Is There a Post–Washington Consensus Consensus?," in *The Washington Consensus Reconsidered*, Serra and Stiglitz (eds.), 46.

[4] Dani Rodrik, *One Economics, Many Recipes: Globalization, Institutions, and Economic Growth* (Princeton, NJ: Princeton University Press, 2007), 4.

[5] Joshua Cooper Ramo, *The Beijing Consensus* (London: Foreign Policy Centre, 2004), 4.

[6] Randall Peerenboom and Bojan Bugaric, "The Emerging Post Washington, Post Beijing Consensus: Prospects and Pitfalls," *UCLA Journal of Law & Foreign Affairs* 19 (2015): 100.

[7] Scott Kennedy, "The Myth of the Beijing Consensus," *Journal of Contemporary China* 19 (2010): 461.

[8] Peerenboom and Bugaric, "The Emerging Post Washington, Post Beijing Consensus," 102.

[9] Barry Naughton, "China's Distinctive System: Can It Be a Model for Others?," *Journal of Contemporary China* 19 (2010): 437.

[10] Kennedy, "The Myth of the Beijing Consensus."

[11] Peerenboom and Bugaric, "The Emerging Post Washington, Post Beijing Consensus," 101–2.

literature, however, has neglected one important subject – the relationship between development and tax policy and administration. This chapter attempts to fill the void.

Taxation is an important component of the Washington Consensus. First, the Washington Consensus specifically prescribes tax reforms that combine "a broad tax base with moderate marginal tax rates."[12] Such policy represents a sharp turn against the mainstream post-WWII fiscal advice for developing countries to rely primarily on income taxes of progressive and high rates.[13] Another core piece of the Washington Consensus, fiscal discipline, also relates to taxation.[14] Governments in third world countries run into huge deficits often because they fail to raise sufficient revenue through effective taxation. In addition, the Washington Consensus in emphasizing the importance of "secure property rights" implicitly requires predictable and equitable tax lawmaking as well as tax administration, i.e., no grave infringement on private property rights or expropriation through selective taxation or arbitrary tax-related prosecution. Finally, lawful taxation is also critical to the rule of law and good governance, two items topping the reform agenda of most international institutions that endorse the Washington Consensus.[15]

In comparison, in the post-Washington Consensus era, developing countries have been advised to structure their tax systems according to "the need and desire for increased public services, the capacity to levy taxes effectively, and preferences for such public policy goals as attaining a desired distribution of income and wealth and increasing the rate of growth."[16] The promoted tax policy package incorporates the objective of distributional equity through a shift from consumption tax, which widens the tax base in developing countries, back toward more direct taxes on income and land at progressive rates.[17] The shift in policy orientation to a great extent corresponds with the Chinese experience of reforming its tax system.

[12] John Williamson, "A Short History of the Washington Consensus," in *The Washington Consensus Reconsidered*, Serra and Stiglitz (eds.), 14.

[13] Richard M. Bird, "Foreign Advice and Tax Policy in Developing Countries," in *Taxation and Development: The Weakest Link? Essays in Honor of Roy Bahl*, Richard M. Bird and Jorge Marinez-Vazquez (eds.) (Cheltenham, UK: Edward Elgar, 2014), 103.

[14] Williamson, "A Short History of the Washington Consensus," 14.

[15] Peerenboom and Bugaric, "The Emerging Post Washington, Post Beijing Consensus," 91.

[16] Bird, "Foreign Advice and Tax Policy in Developing Countries," 103.

[17] Williamson, "A Short History of the Washington Consensus," 14.

II Three Decades of Tax Reforms in China

This section presents a chronological review of the Chinese reforms in tax law and administration for the past three decades. As will be demonstrated, the long-term trajectory of the changes largely follows the Washington Consensus,[18] yet major nonconformities exist. Part III will then analyze the structural factors that determine the features characterizing these tax reforms. The review covers the three decades between 1984 and 2014 as the foundation of the current Chinese tax system was laid during this period.

In the decade before 1994, Chinese tax policies and revenue collection methods went through frequent changes.[19] The government implemented the *li gai shui* (profit to tax) reform, replacing revenue extraction from state-owned enterprises with enterprise tax in order to incentivize management efficiency.[20] To induce local economic growth, the central government (or the Center) relied on a fiscal contract scheme according to which provincial governments collected taxes and remitted a negotiated amount to the Center. Provincial officials in turn would negotiate with local governments about the allocation of subprovincial revenues. Due to information asymmetry and the lack of administrative capacity, the negotiated allocation greatly favored the lower governments. The system resulted in a sharp decline of government revenue-to-GDP ratio, a contraction of central revenue relative to provincial revenue (see Figures 7.2 and 7.3), and high revenue volatility (see Figure 7.1), all of which were perceived as seriously threatening the Center's governance capacity.[21]

Following the policy guideline of "unifying tax laws, equalizing tax burdens, simplifying tax system, and rationalizing the allocation of tax authority,"[22] the central government in 1994 implemented a systematic fiscal reform that laid the groundwork for most subsequent development.

[18] Kennedy, "The Myth of the Beijing Consensus," 461–77.

[19] Stephen B. Herschler, "The 1994 Tax Reforms: The Center Strikes Back," *China Economic Review* 6 (1995): 239.

[20] Alfred Tat-Kei Ho and Meili Niu, "Rising with the Tide without Flipping the Boat? Analyzing the Successes and Challenges of Fiscal Capacity Building in China," *Public Administration and Development* 33 (2013): 29.

[21] Wang Shaoguang and Angang Hu, *The Chinese Economy in Crisis: State Capacity and Tax Reform* (Armonk, NY: M. E. Sharpe, 2001), 13–17.

[22] Deng Liping, *Shuishou zhidu lilun yu shiwu* [Theory and Practice of a Tax System] (Beijing: Higher Education Press, 2007), 91.

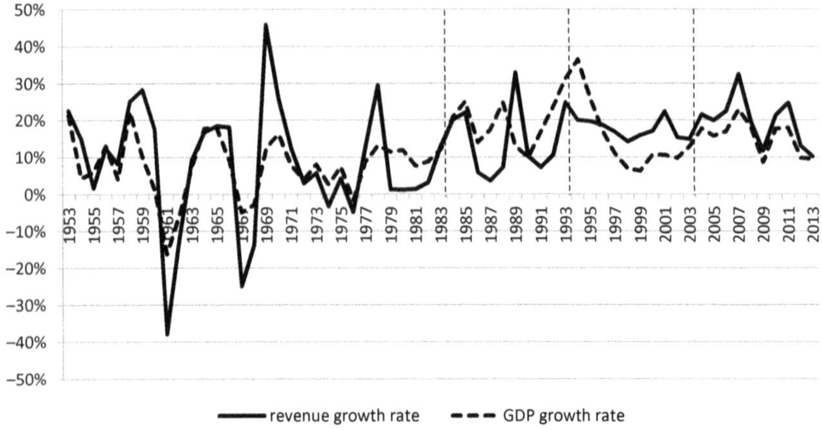

Figure 7.1 Revenue growth and GDP growth of sixty years (1953–2013). The volatility of the revenue growth rate in the 1994–2004 decade is significantly lower than in the previous decade. The increase in volatility in 2004–2014 is due mainly to the 2008 Global Financial Crisis and the drastic fiscal measures taken by the Chinese government in response.

The reform institutionalized the allocation of revenues between the central and local governments, greatly expanded the VAT to be the main revenue source and allocated the lion's share of the VAT to the Center.[23]

The post-reform taxes fit in three general categories: national taxes, taxes shared by the central and local governments, and local taxes.[24] National taxes include customs duty, consumption tax, income tax of central enterprises, income tax of banks, etc. Taxes shared between the central and local governments include the VAT, resource tax, and securities transaction tax. Seventy-five percent of the VAT, the major tax source after the reform, is allocated to the central government. Most other taxes belong exclusively to local governments, e.g., business tax, corporate income tax of local enterprises, personal income tax, and urban land use tax.

The 1994 reform also restructured the tax administration. To strengthen the Center's tax collecting capacity, the original subnational tax administration was split into two hierarchical agencies: a national agency (also known as the State Tax Bureau; STB) under the vertical leadership of the State Administration of Taxation (SAT) and local tax bureaus

[23] Jane K. Winn and Angela Zhang, "China's Golden Tax Project: A Technological Strategy for Reducing VAT Fraud," *Peking University Journal of Law School* 1 (2013): 1.

[24] Herschler, "The 1994 Tax Reforms," 239.

(LTBs).[25] The SAT existed prior to 1993, but it was mainly in charge of collecting taxes of some large SOEs paid to the central government.[26] The STB provides administrative guidance to provincial LTBs and inter-provincial coordination, and the provincial governments exercise direct leadership control over the LTB including the appointment of ranking officials. The subprovincial LTBs are subject to dual leadership of the higher tax bureaus and the corresponding local governments.

From 1994 to 2004, various legal and administrative reforms were implemented under the guiding policy of "unifying tax laws, equalizing tax burdens, simplifying tax system, and rationalizing the allocation of tax authority."[27] The number of taxes was further reduced from 32 to 18.[28] The State Council promulgated more regulations to standardize and unify tax collection. The STB adopted various measures to improve its administrative capacity, the most notable of which was building a computerized network for recording and cross-checking VAT invoices, an infrastructure critical to effective collection of the VAT.[29]

In the decade of 2004 to 2014, the Center's fiscal policy – "*simplifying the tax system, broadening the tax base, reducing the tax rate, and strengthening the tax administration*"[30] – bore close resemblance to the tax policy component of the Washington Consensus. To implement the policy, the Center unified the corporate tax rates for domestic companies and foreign-invested companies.[31] The VAT continued to be the focus of the new round of reforms. Gradual experiments and changes on the production-based VAT were made, eventually transforming it into the European model of consumption-based VAT in 2009.[32] As the Center's revenue sources expanded and stabilized, it could afford to reduce various tax rates. *Law on Individual Income Tax*, for instance, was amended three times to eventually exempt all taxpayers earning less than RMB 3,500 yuan a month. The agricultural tax was trimmed down and eventually

25 Ibid.

26 Zhang Le-Yin, "Chinese Central-Provincial Fiscal Relationships, Budgetary Decline and the Impact of the 1994 Fiscal Reform: An Evaluation," *The China Quarterly* 157 (1999): 115.

27 Deng, *Shuishou zhidu lilun yu shiwu*, 91.

28 Herschler, "The 1994 Tax Reforms," 239.

29 Jin Dongsheng and Jin Weifu, "On the Development Strategy of China's Value-Added Tax (VAT) Reform," *Journal of China Tax and Policy* 3 (2013): 226.

30 Deng, *Shuishou zhidu lilun yu shiwu*, 94.

31 Kanghua Zeng, Shan Li, and Qian Li, "The Impact of Economic Growth and Tax Reform on Tax Revenue and Structure: Evidence from China Experience," *Modern Economy* 4 (2013): 839.

32 Winn and Zhang, "China's Golden Tax Project," 1.

abolished in January 2006. Moreover, the Center initiated local experimentations with residential property tax and the conversion of business tax to VAT.[33] In terms of tax administration, noticeable improvements were made in this decade. The percentage of STB and LTB staff with college degrees grew, and more advanced technologies were applied to tax reporting and collection.

Congruent with the implicit policy advice in the Washington Consensus, the central government attempted to bring tax administration under the shadow of the law. The agents' administrative authority officially stems from the *Law on the Administration of Tax Collection*, and substantive laws including the *Law on Individual Income Tax* and the *Law on Enterprise Income Tax*. Like their peers in developed countries, the tax agencies are delegated certain legislative power. Under the current *Law on Legislation*, the national legislature may authorize the State Council to make tax regulations not covered by statutes,[34] or regulations about statutory enforcement.[35] In practice, the delegated legislative power is to a great extent exercised by the SAT and the Ministry of Finance.[36] Lower agencies also issue normative documents on tax administration. Although such agency documents may lack sound legal basis, their legality is rarely questioned by Chinese taxpayers and tax professionals.[37]

The 1994 reform produced formal procedures for tax compliance and administration that are substantially analogous to those in developed countries. Taxpayers register with relevant tax bureaus, report periodically tax-related information as required by the law, and pay taxes or claim refunds. Tax administration is departmentalized for purposes of specialization into compliance supervision, investigation of tax evasion, information gathering, and so on. Taxpayers may engage accountants and other tax professionals to assist in tax compliance and to resolve tax controversies.

As part of reforming the agency, the central government put in place a wide variety of monitoring and reviewing mechanisms to prevent abuse of

[33] Zeng et al., "The Impact of Economic Growth and Tax Reform on Tax Revenue and Structure."

[34] Article 9, *Legislation Law of the People's Republic of China*, effective September 1, 2000, http://english1.english.gov.cn/laws/2005–08/20/content_29724.htm.

[35] Ibid., Article 56.

[36] Qiu Dongmei, "Interpretation of Tax Law in China: Moving towards the Rule of Law?," *Hong Kong Law Journal* 44 (2014): 589.

[37] Wei Cui, "Two Paths for Developing Anti-Avoidance Rules in China," *Asia Pacific Tax Bulletin* 17 (2011): 1.

the delegated power and discretion, the most comprehensive one of which is probably the newly established administrative law regime.[38] After the enactment of the *Administrative Reconsideration Regulation*, which was later upgraded to a statute,[39] any concrete tax administrative action may be challenged through a petition for reconsideration by a designated body in the tax bureau or a higher bureau.[40] The reconsideration body may review both the *appropriateness* and the legality of the challenged act and the underlying rule.[41]

Once taxpayers have exhausted the administrative recourse for disputes over a tax matter, they may turn to the court. The defendant tax agency in general bears the burden of proof that the challenged administrative act is lawful.[42] The court may also conduct its own investigation. In theory, within three months of registering a case the court must render a decision, and unsatisfied parties may appeal the trial court decision.[43]

The enactments of the major administrative laws provide taxpayers a variety of formal channels to resolve disputes with tax agents in China. The formal legal regime, though containing some elements favorable to the tax agencies (e.g., the filing of an administrative reconsideration being conditioned on the payment of the assessed tax), affords Chinese taxpayers basic legal protection against abusive tax agents or misinterpretation of tax laws and regulations.

To sum up, after three decades of reforms the Chinese government has put in place a rather sophisticated tax system. Since 1996, government revenues have grown continuously, exceeding the pace of GDP growth by a large margin. Moreover, the volatility of both revenue growth and GDP

[38] In a very general sense, the administrative reconsideration mechanism resembles a typical administrative appeals institution in the United States.

[39] See *Law on Administrative Reconsideration*, effective October 1, 1999, www.gov.cn/banshi/2005–08/21/content_25100.htm.

[40] Petitions against bureaus of the STB are handled by the bureau of the next higher level. Petitions against an office of the LTB may be filed with either the corresponding local government or the bureau of a higher rank unless otherwise stipulated by regional rules. Petitions against the STB in Beijing may be filed with the bureau itself. Petitions should in general be filed, orally or in writing, within 60 days after knowledge of the concrete administrative action. See *Shuiwu xingzheng fuyi guize* [Rules Concerning Tax Administrative Reconsideration], Guojia shuiwu zongjuling di ershiyi hao [SAT Rule No. 21], effective April 1, 2010, www.chinatax.gov.cn/n8136506/n8136593/n8137537/n8138502/9563669.html.

[41] Article 35, *New Rulemaking Measures of the STB.*

[42] Article 32, *Administrative Procedure Law of the People's Republic of China*, effective October 1, 1990, www.china.org.cn/english/government/207335.htm.

[43] Ibid., Article 57.

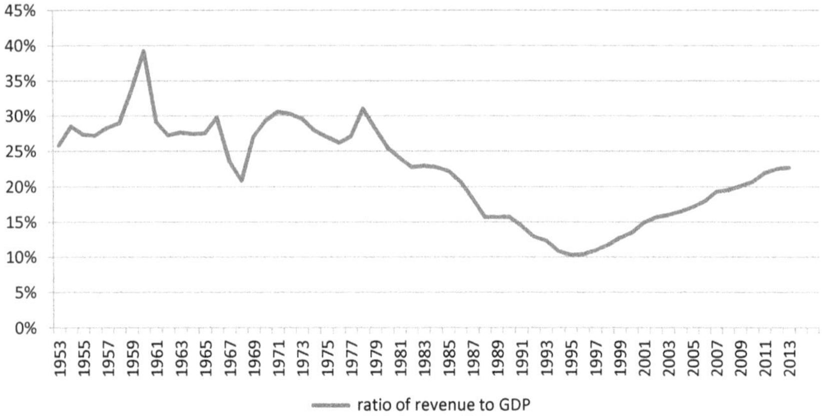

Figure 7.2 Government revenue-to-GDP ratio of sixty years (1953–2013). The ratio is much higher if disposable revenue is used for the calculation. But the general trend of decline from 1985 to 1995 remains unchanged as a result of revenue decentralization.

Zhang, "Chinese Central-Provincial Fiscal Relationships, Budgetary Decline and the Impact of the 1994 Fiscal Reform: An Evaluation."

growth declined (see Figure 7.1), indicating enhanced extractive capacity of the central government and consequently its greater ability to manage the economy with countercyclical fiscal tools. The Chinese tax reform has therefore been applauded as an exemplary success.[44] Although the Chinese case loses much of its glamour upon a close examination from a comparative angle (as will be discussed in Part IV), the quick rebound of the state's extractive capacity after 1994 nonetheless offers valuable lessons to the least developed countries striving to build a functional tax system. But before they duplicate the specific reform strategies described above, it is crucial to understand the major structural premise that enabled China to implement systematic reforms and to engage in incremental changes, learning, and experiments, which feature prominently in the newly advocated tax and development policy agenda.

III Structural Determinants of China's Tax Reforms

One may derive from the chronological review in the preceding section several features characterizing China's tax reforms: piecemeal changes, pluralistic learning, testing, and experimentation of possible solutions, as well as target setting and institutional improvements through trial

44 Bird, "Foreign Advice and Tax Policy in Developing Countries," 103.

and error. These procedural features have been incorporated in the post-Washington Consensus discourse. The Tax Development Model 3.0 currently promoted to developing countries attempting to upgrade their fiscal systems stresses the importance of "building up institutional capacity both within and outside governments to articulate relevant ideas for change, to collect and analyze relevant data, and to assess and criticize the effects of such changes as are made."[45] This chapter contends, however, that the value of this model hinges on the transferability of the structural factors enabling the Chinese tax reforms.

Three major structural factors shaped the Chinese tax reforms. First, the central government expects a rather stable political rule despite all the challenges it confronts.[46] Holding a relatively long-term prospect, the stable authoritarian state maximizes its interest by refraining from one-time over-extraction, and providing basic public goods and investing in the rationalization of various extractive institutions such as the tax agencies.[47]

The second structural factor is the fragmented nature of the authoritarian state, which causes the processes of policy and lawmaking to be heavily dependent on consensus building. Consequently, this explains the Center's tolerance of zealous representation by departmental and local interests.[48] This factor also explains the incremental nature of most tax reforms in China as major policy changes could not occur without a solid agreement among all powerful stakeholders.[49] Power fragmentation also determines that persuasion, not coercion, drives policymaking. In negotiating a reform and its terms, power-holders in China tend to collect and bring to the table supportive evidence carrying high persuasive power, such as data collected through experiments, past experiences from developed countries, expert opinions, technical advice from international organizations, and international conventions. This has led to the keen interest in experimentation and pluralistic learning shown by both the central and the local governments.

45 Ibid.

46 For a thorough analysis of the formidable challenges the government confront, see Susan L. Shirk, *China: Fragile Superpower* (New York: Oxford University Press, 2007); Minxin Pei, *China's Trapped Transition* (Cambridge, MA: Harvard University Press, 2006).

47 Mancur Olson, "Dictatorship, Democracy, and Development," *American Political Science Review* 87 (1993): 567.

48 Kenneth Lieberthal and Michel Oksenberg, *Policy Making in China* (Princeton, NJ: Princeton University Press, 1988), 22. Note that the causal chain here is not one directional. It is arguable that the revenue-sharing system contributed to the fragmentation of the political regime. See Zhang, "Chinese Central-Provincial Fiscal Relationships."

49 Lieberthal and Oksenberg, *Policy Making in China*, 22.

The third structural factor, which is related to the first one, is a central state apparatus capable enough to implement the core elements of a systematic tax reform, i.e., a comprehensive national VAT.[50] "Major change and improvement in both tax policy and administration in any country requires a solid analytical foundation in the form of a more systemic approach to assembling and analyzing data."[51] In other words, an agency of adequate competency is critical to the identification of problems, analysis of relevant data and information, and finding and implementing solutions. Although the government agencies at the central level do not fully qualify as Weberian bureaucracy (defined as predictable, rule of law–oriented, apolitical, impersonal public administration), scholars generally agree that Chinese central agencies boast of "capable and autonomous bureaucrats, who are capable of managing and coordinating sophisticated policies."[52] The small cohort of high-quality central bureaucrats may not possess all requisite information, knowledge, or skills for policy implementation, but the hierarchical political structure and the tight state-social relations enable them to solicit the assistance of experts and specialists from different agencies, lower-level governments, research institutes and even foreign countries.

This section elaborates on how these three structural factors interactively shaped China's tax reforms of the past three decades. Before proceeding to the detailed analysis, a brief description of the historical background is in order. From 1950, when the Chinese government established a centralized tax system, to 1979, the overall policy trend was to simplify the tax system as the state owned and managed most business enterprises.[53]

[50] For more on how the promotion system operates, see Pierre F. Landry, *Decentralized Authoritarianism in China: The Communist Party's Control of Local Elites in the Post-Mao Era* (New York: Cambridge University Press, 2008). For arguments that promotion is politics motivated, see Victor Shih, Christopher Adolph, and Mingxing Liu, "Getting ahead in the Communist Party: Explaining the Advancement of Central Committee Members in China," *American Political Science Review* 106 (2012): 166; Shih et al.'s study looks at the promotion of top-level officials. The findings do not apply to tax agents as they rarely advance to the central committee.

[51] Richard M. Bird and Pierre-Pascal Gendron, *The VAT in Developing and Transitional Countries* (New York: Cambridge University Press, 2007), 181.

[52] Randall Peerenboom, "Revamping the China Model for the Post-Global Financial Crisis Era," in *China in the International Economic Order*, Lisa Toohey, Colin B. Picker, and Jonathan Greenacre (eds.) (New York: Cambridge University Press, 2015), 18.

[53] In some years fiscal power was decentralized as the central bureaucratic machine was paralyzed during the Cultural Revolution and the regional governments bore more financial burden in preparing for a potential military attack from the Soviet Union.

Thus, by 1980 only ten types of tax remained.[54] As China transitioned from a Soviet-style planned economy to experimenting with state capitalism, the government gradually withdrew from micro-managing all economic activities. Against this historical background, the Center adopted the policy of "substituting tax payment for profit submission."[55] Reflecting the uncertainties and institutional disruptions inherent in the transitional period, three major tax reforms took place in the period between 1980 and 1984, establishing (with the assistance of US experts)[56] a more complex tax system dependent on turnover tax and income tax.[57]

As noted in Part II, a contract scheme was adopted for revenue collection as part of the overall decentralization policy.[58] The fiscal contract system soon proved problematic. First and foremost, it weakened the power of the central government vis-à-vis lower governments. As shown in Figure 7.3, the Center's share of tax revenues declined significantly during the period. In addition, the negotiations triggered a race to the bottom, as every provincial government tried to lower their share of revenue remittance. Meanwhile, local governments competed for business investments by granting tax subsidies, causing a sharp drop in aggregate government revenues relative to GDP (see Figure 7.2). Another serious drawback concerned high transaction costs. As tax was negotiated regularly at all levels, enormous amount of human resources were wasted in the process. A senior official of the Ministry of Finance reported to have spent about twenty days negotiating with his provincial counterparts on the proper amount of revenue remittance.[59] It also created great uncertainties in fiscal planning.

Cui Wei, "Shuishou lifa gaodu jiquan moshi de qiyuan" [The Historical Origin of High Concentration of Tax Legislative Power], *Peking University Law Journal* 24 (2012): 765.

[54] Before the market reform, the Central government relied mainly on profit remittance from the state-owned enterprises. Zhang, "Chinese Central-Provincial Fiscal Relationships, Budgetary Decline and the Impact of the 1994 Fiscal Reform"; Zeng et al., "The Impact of Economic Growth and Tax Reform on Tax Revenue and Structure."

[55] Winn and Zhang, "China's Golden Tax Project," 1.

[56] Jinyan Li, "Tax Transplants and the Critical Role of Processes: A Case Study of China," *Journal of Chinese Tax and Policy* 3 (2013): 85.

[57] Zeng et al., "The Impact of Economic Growth and Tax Reform on Tax Revenue and Structure."

[58] Xu Jian, "Fenshuizhixia de caiquan jizhong peizhi: guocheng ji qi yingxiang" [Concentration of Fiscal Power under the Tax Sharing System: Process and Influence], *Peking University Law Journal* 24 (2012): 802.

[59] Zhao Yining, "Woguo fenshuizhi juecebeijing lishi huifang" [Historical Background of the Tax-Sharing Reform], *Liaowang*, August 4, 2008, http://news.hexun.com/2008–08–04/107889818.html.

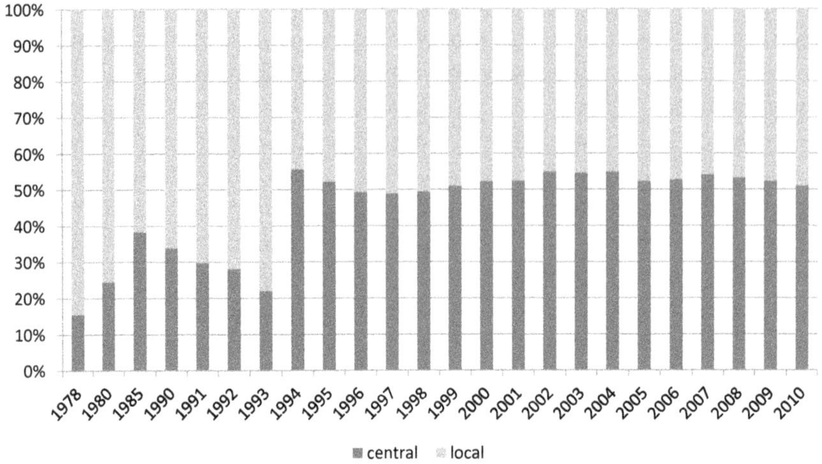

Figure 7.3 Changes in allocation of government revenues. Data are from Table 8–3, "Ratios of Central and Local Revenues to Total Revenues," *China Statistics Yearbook*, 2011.

Having identified the negotiated taxation as a major issue, the central government began to conduct local experiments of tax-sharing reforms.[60] It had attempted to introduce the tax-sharing system twice prior to 1993. The first proposal was shelved in 1985 because, based on an analysis of available data, the Center concluded the reform might cause a net revenue loss.[61] The second proposal in 1990 met with strong local resistance, so the Center decided to postpone its implementation for at least five years.[62] Meanwhile, to tackle the fiscal shortage the state sought alternative short-term solutions including borrowing from state-owned banks and provincial governments.[63] In 1992, Chinese state-owned banks extended credit to the Ministry of Finance to cover much of the RMB 100 billion yuan fiscal deficit of the Center.[64] In 1993, however, the Center was trying to overhaul the financial system by commercializing state-owned banks, and loans to finance the central government's expenses contradicted the objective. As a result, Premier Zhu Rongji rejected the request for loans.[65] Additionally, the financial situation of the state sector deteriorated due to the market reform, further aggravating the Center's revenue shortage.[66]

60 Zhao, "Woguo fenshuizhi juecebeijing lishi huifang."
61 Zhang, "Chinese Central-Provincial Fiscal Relationships," 115. 62 Ibid.
63 Zhao, "Woguo fenshuizhi juecebeijing lishi huifang." 64 Ibid. 65 Ibid.
66 Zhang, "Chinese Central-Provincial Fiscal Relationships."

To the surprise of some provincial officials expecting at least a postponed tax reform, the Standing Committee of the Politburo formed a resolute consensus to restructure the fiscal system.[67] The relatively short window of unity among the top power-holders opened up only after Deng Xiaoping sent a clear signal to the conservatives that tied their career prospects to economic liberalization.[68] Against this backdrop, the Third Plenary of the Fourteenth Central Committee of the CCP approved a broad plan to establish a "socialist market economy," a core component of which being a fiscal reform that would establish the tax-sharing system. Reasonably anticipating strong local resistance, Zhu Rongji travelled to sixteen provinces to promote the proposed reform.[69] As noted, consensus building plays a critical role in policymaking and implementation in the fragmented power structure. For a complex institutional reform to take effect, the Center had to obtain genuine support from provincial governments and adjust the proposal according to their vested interests.

The negotiations took two months and altered the substance of the deal.[70] The three structural factors shaped the course of this process. The fragmented nature of China's authoritarian state as well as the consensus-based making and implementation of major policies meant that the Center had to guarantee that local revenues would not diminish as a result of the reform. But because the Center had a longer time horizon, it could afford short-term loss in exchange for future revenue growth. In the 1990, most of the top party leaders anticipated a rule of two terms and likely longer as their influence and benefits typically extended beyond retirement. In contrast, the average length of tenure for provincial party secretaries and provincial governors were less than five and four years, respectively,[71] while lower-level officials rotated even faster, with an average tenure of about two and a half years for mayors in China.[72]

According to the initial proposal, provincial governments would receive postreform at least the same amount of revenues as they would have collected in 1992. But officials from Guangdong Province insisted

[67] Herschler, "The 1994 Tax Reforms."

[68] Ezra Vogel, *Deng Xiaoping and the Transformation of China* (Cambridge, MA: Harvard University Press, 2013), 677–79.

[69] Zhao, "Woguo fenshuizhi juecebeijing lishi huifang."

[70] Zhang, "Chinese Central-Provincial Fiscal Relationships."

[71] Cheng Li, "Political Localism versus Institutional Restraints: Elite Recruitment in the Jiang Era," in *Holding China Together: Diversity and National Integration in the Post-Deng Era*, Barry Naughton and Dali L. Yang (eds.) (Cambridge: Cambridge University Press, 2004), 29.

[72] Pierre Landry, "The Political Management of Mayors in Post-Deng China," *The Copenhagen Journal of Asian Studies* 17 (2005): 38.

that the baseline be the revenues collected in 1993, the year the negotiations were conducted. Zhu compromised on this point in order to win their support, which was crucial to the success of the reform given Guangdong's economic size.[73] As anticipated, many regional governments reported an abrupt increase in their 1993 revenues in order to boost their tax receipts after the tax-sharing reform. The Center dispatched work teams to investigate but found no obvious fraud.[74] Given its ability to focus on long-term return and the need to build regional support, the Center ignored the anomaly. Subsequent to the reform, revenues collected by the central government rose substantially (Figure 7.3). Yet because of the strategic actions taken by the provincial governments, the Center initially had to distribute more than it collected.[75] But as shown in Figure 7.2, the new system led to a surge in tax to GDP ratio after 1996.

The other structural factor, a central agency of adequate competency, played a key role in the reform's success. Taxation is a highly technical area, so from designing tax policies to negotiating with provincial officials, the top central leaders relied extensively on technocrats from the Ministry of Finance and other agencies.[76] The strong political will at the top ensured the pooling of human resources as many bureaucrats from a variety of agencies were temporarily transferred (*jiediao*) to work on the project. Adequate capacity in data collection, information analysis, and policy design enabled the comparison of multiple solutions and subsequent negotiation and implementation of the chosen policy to be based on informed decision making.[77]

As noted in Part II, the 1994 reform expanded the central bureaucratic apparatus by establishing the dual tax administration structure. The new structure provided the central government with the capacity to reach the local level for information gathering and revenue collection.[78] With eyes in local economic activities, the Center was able to detect policy violations or abuse of power and discretion by local governments (e.g., underreporting tax revenues).

The tax agency also played a critical role in implementing the new VAT. An effective VAT operates on business invoices.[79] In a country where

[73] Zhao, "Woguo fenshuizhi juecebeijing lishi huifang."

[74] Ibid. [75] Ibid. [76] Ibid. [77] Ibid.

[78] However, as Wei Cui points out in Chapter 4, central ministerial employees are also sometimes viewed as having limited information and capacity in administering the law.

[79] Winn and Zhang, "China's Golden Tax Project," 1.

business transactions were frequently conducted in cash and accurate book-keeping was lacking, the administration of a VAT faced daunting challenges. Mass production and use of phony VAT invoices posed an existential threat to the newly expanded tax. It became so rampant and serious that at one time the Center even considered abolishing the VAT and reverting to the product tax. Expressing his doubt, then vice premier Li commented to the head of the STB that its failure to curb invoice fraud would prove that the VAT might not suit China.[80]

In response to this challenge, the SAT explored multiple measures. Concurrent with the 1994 tax reform, it launched a computerized system called "golden taxation" that would enable cross-checking of taxpayers' information for VAT purposes.[81] The goal was to centralize invoice clearing and enable the government to timely detect and prevent invoice fraud.[82] The first trial failed and had to be aborted as it required manual input of large amounts of data.[83] The agency then analyzed the failure and made a second attempt, which reduced VAT invoice fraud significantly. The rate of suspected noncompliance declined from 0.227 percent in 2001 to 0.0002 percent in 2007 for certified VAT special invoices, and from 8.5 percent to 0.031 percent for inspected VAT special invoices.[84] The agency continued to improve on the "golden taxation" system and shifted more of taxpayers' compliance work online. The modernization of tax administrative system strengthened the state's capacity to raise revenues, manage tax agents, monitor economic activities, and analyze the effects of tax laws and policies.

The three structural factors also determine that the tax agency constantly engages in pluralistic learning from foreign countries and international organizations.[85] As noted earlier, because of the fragmented power distribution within the ruling elite, policymaking depends more on persuasion than coercion. Given the persuasive power of international conventions and experiences from developed countries, officials are incentivized to back up their proposals with such evidence. Thus, once a governance problem has been identified the central government typically dispatches groups of agents to foreign countries to study their solutions. For instance, in making the case for the tax-sharing reform,

[80] Dan Wenyuan, "Caishui gaige bukeyi zhiuqiu yibudaowei" [For Incremental Reforms of the Fiscal and Tax System], *Zhongguo caijing shibao*, November 3, 2014.

[81] Winn and Zhang, "China's Golden Tax Project," 1.

[82] Ibid. [83] Ibid. [84] Ibid.

[85] Studying the experience of foreign countries has been a major feature of the state's response to local problems. Kennedy, "The Myth of the Beijing Consensus."

the Center claimed that its comprehensive study indicated all countries but Yugoslavia and Canada had the budgetary revenue-to-GDP ratio and the central revenue-to-local revenue ratio above 40 percent and 60 percent, respectively.[86] Likewise, the provincial governments engaged in similar pluralistic learning in order to locate evidence in their favor. Thus, both central and provincial officials cited foreign precedents or international conventions in negotiating the terms of the tax reform.[87] This learning capacity is essential to a state capable of renewing itself in response to changing circumstances and challenges.[88]

The 1994 tax reform restructured the central-local government relations and strengthened the central government. With steady revenue increase, the Center had more policy tools at its disposal. Significant increase in spending on nationwide infrastructure and defense illustrated the central government's growing capacity. The structural factors that shaped the 1994 tax reform remained intact in the decade of 2004 to 2014. However, while the top leaders continued to enjoy a relatively long time horizon, and consensus among political stakeholders remained an important precondition for major policy changes including tax reforms, clear unity among the top power-holders ceased to exist.[89] Thus, the Center lacked the political will to implement any systematic reform of the tax system as it did in 1994. Meanwhile, the capacity and quality of the central tax agency remained on an upward trajectory. As a result, most of the new tax reforms during this period took the form of incremental adjustments, and the SAT played a more important role in formulating and implementing the reforms.

As noted in Part II, the guiding policy for the tax reforms in this decade was more in line with the Washington Consensus, i.e., "simplifying tax system, *broadening tax base, reducing tax rate*, and strengthening tax administration."[90] To implement this policy, the central government

86 Zhang, "Chinese Central-Provincial Fiscal Relationships."

87 Herschler, "The 1994 Tax Reforms."

88 Wang Shaoguang, "Xuexi jizhi yu shiying nengli: zhongguo nongcun hezuo yiliao tizhi bianqian de qishi" [The Learning Mechanism and Adaptive Capacity: Insights from the Transformation of China's Rural Cooperative Healthcare System], *Zhongguo shehui kexue* (2008): 111.

89 Cheng Li, "One Party, Two Factions: Chinese Bipartisanship in the Making?" (Paper presented at the Conference on "Chinese Leadership, Politics, and Policy," Carnegie Endowment for International Peace, November 2, 2005).

90 Wen Ren, "Yifa zhishui jiaqiang zhengguan – guojia shuiwu zongju juzhang xie xuren dajizhewen" [Strengthen Tax Administration in Accordance with Law – Director of SAT Answer Journalists' Questions], *Zibenshichang* (2003): 64–65.

unified the corporate tax rate for domestic and foreign-invested companies. Prior to the reform, corporate income tax was regulated by a dual system composed with the *Income Tax Law for Foreign and Foreign-Invested Enterprises* and the *Interim Regulations on Chinese Enterprises.* Both set the rate at 33 percent, but several provisions in the former significantly reduced the effective tax rates for foreign enterprises.[91] The reform set the rate for both domestic and foreign-invested companies at 25 percent. After the reform, the rate for many foreign companies that had enjoyed favorable effective tax rates was slightly increased, but the new law granted a phase-out period.[92] Because of the revenue growth subsequent to the 1994 tax-sharing reform, the Center could afford the anticipated revenue loss from a slight decrease of nominal corporate tax rates.

Individual income tax rate was also reduced during this period. The Ministry of Finance first proposed to reform the individual tax system in October 2003,[93] and Guangdong Province began to experiment with raising the exemption level for individual income tax.[94] Later that year the Standing Committee of the National People's Congress (SCNPC) approved the amendment to the *Individual Income Tax Law* and raised the exemption threshold to RMB 1,600 yuan. In December 2007 the SCNPC again increased the threshold to RMB 2,000 yuan. The amendment in June 2011 further raised the level to RMB 3,500 yuan. All these tax rate adjustments were made possible by the continuous growth of government revenues at rates exceeding the growth of GDP (see Figure 7.1).

The guiding policy also led to the conversion of business tax to the VAT. The 1994 reform left business tax intact in order to mitigate local resistance. But the policy goal of simplifying tax system and lowering tax rate necessitated further reforms of the business tax. In the past few years, the central government initiated local experimentations of the conversion in several provinces to evaluate its effects and prepare for nationwide

91 For example, certain foreign invested enterprises in special economic zones were subject to income tax rate of 15 percent. Also, the income of productive foreign-invested companies (with investment of more than ten years) was exempted from income tax for two years after the first year of profit, and the rate applied in the following three years was reduced by half. Sections 7 and 8, *Income Tax Law for Foreign* and *Foreign-Invested Enterprises,* effective July 1, 1991, available at www.china.org.cn/english/14960.htm.

92 Section 57, *Enterprise Income Tax Law of the People's Republic of China,* effective January 1, 2008, www.fdi.gov.cn/1800000121_39_3339_0_7.html.

93 Qi Yanbing, "Caizhengbu jianyi tigao geshui qizhengdian" [Ministry of Finance Proposes Raising Exemption Level for Individual Income Tax], *Beijing qingnian bao,* July 3, 2003.

94 Wei Xiaohang, "'Yuediaoyan' geshui qizhengdian tigao" [Guangdong Experiments Raising Income Tax Exemption Level], *Xinxi shibao,* December 14, 2004.

implementation.[95] Once again, to preempt strong opposition, the Center considered adjusting tax-sharing ratio for the VAT in favor of lower governments to compensate for their potential revenue losses from the conversion.

Meanwhile, the rationalization of tax administration continued. Various measures were taken to regulate revenue collection. As noted, the tax agencies played a crucial role in the interpretation and application of tax laws and regulations. Agency actions and agency-made normative rules, however, varied significantly across regions and administrative levels. To solve this problem and streamline tax administration, the SAT issued rules to regulate the procedure for agency lawmaking and revenue collection.[96] Furthermore, the tax agencies engaged in more active exchanges with their counterparts in developed countries and participated in international conferences to improve administrative knowledge and skills. While a decade ago most Chinese tax agents were incapable of handling sophisticated audits involving multinational corporations,[97] the knowledge gap has been closing, as evidenced by the increasing amount of revenue recovered from investigating tax evasion and aggressive tax planning.[98] Additionally, the agencies applied advanced technologies and encouraged taxpayers to report and pay tax online, reducing the role of local tax agents and curtailing their discretion.

The state's growing extractive capacity also enabled the use of taxation to facilitate the implementation of macro-level economic and political policies. The residential property tax may be used as an illustration. After the 1994 tax-sharing reform, local governments developed heightened reliance on real estate-related revenues and became heavily invested in the development of that sector.[99] Subsequent massive demolitions and relocations caused enormous social discontent. In addition, overinvestment in real estate and excessive local government borrowing against real assets posed serious risk to economic stability. The Center, concerned with

[95] Jin and Jin, "On the Development Strategy of China's Value-Added Tax (VAT) Reform."

[96] Qiu, "Interpretation of Tax Law in China."

[97] Chan K. Hung and Lynne Chow, "An Empirical Study of Tax Audits in China on International Transfer Pricing," *Journal of Accounting and Economics* 23 (1997): 83.

[98] Wu Qiuyu, "Fanbishui yinian gongxian shuishou 468 yi, bushao kuaguo qiye zhuanzhou lirun" [One Year of Anti-Tax Avoidance Enforcement Raises Revenue of 46.8 Billion. Many Multinational Companies Turn Profitable], *Renmin Ribao*, October 13, 2014.

[99] Sun Xiulin and Feizhou Zhou, "Tudi caizheng yu fenshuizhi: yige shizheng jieshi" [Land-Oriented Fiscal Policy and the Tax Sharing System: An Empirical Explanation], *Zhongguo shehui kexue* (2013): 41–43.

its long-term rule, began to experiment with policy solutions such as providing affordable public housing. In terms of tax reform, it allowed local governments to collect residential property tax. Judging by the results of the experiments, the tax would unlikely be a main source of local revenues. However, the central government appeared to focus on the equity and macro-level economic benefits of the tax.

As noted earlier, power was more dispersed among top leaders between 2004 and 2013, and none of the problems with the tax system appeared to critically threaten the regime. Thus, tax reforms adopted in this period were aimed largely at fine-tuning and optimizing the existing system. The structural factors enabled the tax agencies to regularly identify fiscal problems and inefficiencies, research relevant foreign experiences, design multiple solutions, and conduct local experimentations to analyze their viability and effects. When consensus is again reached at the top level, the Center can make informed decisions.

In 2014, as Xi Jinping completed the consolidation of his political power, new consensus began to form on the next major fiscal reform. The proposed reform reflects the piecemeal feature of China's policy changes. The central government first restructured the current government budgetary system by amending the *Law on Government Budget* according to the guiding policies of the Third Plenary Session of the Eighteenth CPC Central Committee.[100] The NPC proposed to amend the law in 1997 but the official process did not start until 2004. Because the amendment would implicate the power-holders, the proposals could not garner enough support to reach a consensus until the recent power consolidation at the top.[101]

Next comes the overhaul of the tax system, starting with the nationwide conversion of business tax to the VAT. The reforms will touch on six types of taxes: the VAT, consumption tax, resource tax, environmental tax, real estate tax, and personal income tax. The last phase of the systematic fiscal reform will amend the rules governing central-local revenue allocation. According to the Minister of Finance, the objective of the reform is to have the central government control revenues that are of high volatility, high redistributive nature, and unequal or highly transferrable tax basis, and to have the local governments collect taxes that require much local

[100] "Yusuan fa xiugai yu caishui tizhi gaige 'hepai'" [Amendment of Budget Law Match Fiscal System Reform], *Xinjingbao*, September 2, 2014, http://epaper.bjnews.com.cn/html/2014–09/02/content_532751.htm?div=0.

[101] Ibid.

information, impact local resource allocation, and have stable tax basis.[102] In short, the policy aspiration is to build a "modern fiscal system by 2020."[103]

In tax administration, the agencies have been stepping up their cooperation with developed countries and international organizations to combat the global trend of base erosion and profit shifting. Again, pluralistic learning assisted the government in designing and implementing the rules. China followed closely the OECD in the making of transfer pricing regulations (e.g., the definition of "associated enterprises" was similar to the one in US regulations).[104] China has entered into agreements with numerous countries to share tax information. The government readily experiments with new institutional tools that have proven effective in foreign countries to deal with tax compliance issues. For instance, the SAT established a special department to manage and serve large corporate taxpayers, and the model has been duplicated at local levels.[105] Meanwhile, the research branch of the agency has set the goal of future VAT reforms for the fourteenth Five-Year plan period (2021–2025), aiming at "reducing the tax rate and unifying the tax rate . . . to eventually establish China's modern VAT system."[106]

The ongoing revision of the *Law on Tax Administration* serves as a good illustration of the central tax agency's policy implementation capacity. Bearing the primary responsibility of drafting the amendments, the SAT took a number of steps to ensure the quality of the new draft, which included holding a conference in Shanghai dedicated to the discussion of the revision, consulting experts from Australia, the United States, the Netherlands, and the IMF on some complex issues, soliciting comments from provincial tax agencies, and convening a workshop for specialists to opine on the revised draft.[107]

[102] Shan, "Caishui gaige bukeyi zhuiqiu yibu daowei."

[103] Jie Han, Gao Li, and He Yuxin, "Yichang guanxi guojia zhili xiandaihua de shenke biange – caizhengbu buzhang lou xu wei xiangjie shenhua caishui tizhi gaige zongtifangan" [A Major Reform about Governance Modernization – Minister of Finance Lou Jiwei Details the Plan to Deepen Fiscal Reform], *Xinhuawang*, July 3, 2014, http://news.xinhuanet.com/fortune/2014–07/03/c_1111449207.htm.

[104] Chan and Chow, "An Empirical Study of Tax Audits in China."

[105] *Guojia shuiwu zongju daqiye shuishou fuwu he guanli guicheng (shixing)* [SAT Large Enterprises Tax Service Provision and Administration Rules (Trial)], *Guoshuifa* no. 71 (2011), effective July 13, 2011, www.lawinfochina.com/display.aspx?lib=law&id=11183.

[106] Jin and Jin, "On the Development Strategy of China's Value-Added Tax (VAT) Reform."

[107] Zhou Xiaoxiao, "Shuishou zhengguanfa xiuzhengan datiaozheng" [Major Changes to the Amendment of Tax Administration Law], *Shiji jingji baodao* 21 (September 22, 2014).

Thus far, this section has elaborated on the tax reforms of the past three decades and their structural determinants. The broad theme is that the hierarchical yet fragmented political structure and adequate bureaucratic capacity at the central level to administer a nationwide VAT set in motion a virtuous cycle of incremental tax reforms that were based on foreign experience, local experiments, and trial and error.

The tax reforms have strengthened the state's governance and extractive capacity. One may be curious as to why the powerful state and agents then refrain from exploiting their newfound strength. At the top level, the ruling elites are to a certain extent refraining from short-term over-extraction because of the expected long-term political rule and the concern with social discontent. At the local level, tax agents are held back from widespread abuse of power by multiple measures such as internal administrative mechanisms to detect and punish rogue agents. More importantly, local governments competing to attract and nurture business investment rein in local tax agents. As an experienced accountant in a southern city observed, county party secretaries would warn local tax agents not to bother local businesses with audits. Tax evasion and other forms of noncompliance are rampant and to a certain extent tolerated.[108]

For proponents of the Washington Consensus, what is missing from the picture is active judicial review of tax administration. As discussed in the preceding section, a rather sophisticated system of formal laws and regulations has been established for tax administration and the resolution of administrative disputes. Yet disgruntled taxpayers rarely use the formal channels to resolve disputes with tax agents, as evidenced by the mere 13,419 administrative lawsuits filed from 1998 to 2011.[109] Broad administrative discretion enjoyed by tax agents,[110] heavy reliance on local agents for tax compliance (see, e.g., Cui, Chapter 4), limited scope of judicial review,[111] and weak courts may all contribute to the marginal judicial role in restraining tax agents.[112] The recent amendment to the *Administrative Litigation Law* has lowered the barrier for plaintiffs to sue,[113] but no surge in lawsuits against tax agencies is likely to follow unless the structural

[108] Li Ji, "Dare You Sue the Tax Collector? An Empirical Study of Tax-Related Administrative Lawsuits in China," *Pacific Rim Law & Policy Journal* 23 (2014): 106.

[109] Qiu, "Interpretation of Tax Law in China."

[110] Ibid. [111] Ibid. [112] Ibid.

[113] For instance, the amendment allows plaintiffs to appeal if the first-instance court refuses to take their administrative cases. Section 52, *Amendment to Administrative Litigation Law*, effective May 1, 2015, www.npc.gov.cn/npc/xinwen/2014–11/02/content_1884662.htm.

context for tax compliance and administration changes. In sum, courts do not play a major role in the evolution of China's tax system, casting doubt on the implicit rule of law argument of the Washington Consensus.

IV A Model for Other Developing Countries?

The structural premise of the Chinese tax reform determines the transferability of the entire model.[114] Only in developing countries with hierarchical yet fragmented political structure and adequate bureaucratic capacity is the Chinese Model for tax reform potentially duplicable. But should it be duplicated? Although some view the Chinese tax reforms as an exemplary success,[115] a comparative analysis would suggest otherwise. Controlling for GDP per capita, China achieves no more than the predicted tax to GDP ratio; and when tax to GDP ratio is held constant, the Chinese government spends relatively less than the predicted government expenditure. In other words, the Chinese tax model merely achieves an average score. From a normative perspective, the Chinese reforms and the subsequent revenue allocation have generally favored the political and social elites in China because the VAT is a regressive tax. Personal income tax, though featuring a progressive rate, has been less effectively imposed on high-income individuals who do not rely on salaries. Tax on investment income is relatively low. The postponement of levying residential property tax and inheritance tax also favors the wealthy.

Although not an exemplary success positively or normatively, the Chinese tax reforms, enabling a quick rebound of the state's extractive capacity,[116] may nonetheless be used as an important case study that offers valuable lessons to other developing countries that have yet to establish a functional tax system. First, reforms can be carried out incrementally. Most tax reforms involve redistribution and will likely face strong resistance from powerful groups who have a vested interest in maintaining the status quo. The Chinese experience suggests that a major tax reform may succeed only if the reformers are able to assure power-holders of their vested interests and focus on the redistribution of future revenues.

Second, the government of a developing country should engage in pluralistic learning. Once a problem has been identified, the Chinese

114 Stiglitz, "Is There a Post–Washington Consensus Consensus?"

115 Bird, "Foreign Advice and Tax Policy in Developing Countries."

116 Even the quick rebound is not unprecedented, e.g., Turkey between 1984 and 2002 in Figure 7.4.

government usually studies the reactions of other countries with prior experience. It also actively participates in international exchanges. Selective reliance on nonstate or foreign expertise is almost a necessary condition for tax reforms in developing countries as the agencies generally lack adequate knowledge and skills. However, just as China is able to "select appropriate tax concepts, rules or principles that solve a specific tax problem and suit China's needs,"[117] other developing countries should acquire the basic capacity to assess different proposals and identify those best serving their needs.

Third, experimentation is critical to the success of tax reform. By now it must be obvious that not all models drawn from the best practices of developed countries or abstract public finance theories can produce the same anticipated results when transplanted to developing countries. Local tests and experimentation will enable better understanding about how a new policy or rule actually operates in specific political, social, and economic contexts and its revenue effects. The Chinese government, for example, even contemplated abandoning the VAT not long after its introduction because of rampant invoice fraud.[118]

Tax administration is as important as tax policies, especially in developing countries.[119] Much attention has been paid to strengthening and rationalizing tax agencies and making them independent from political influence, with some success.[120] The Chinese experience lends support to such efforts. Critical to the 1994 reform was a group of technocrats at the central level capable of administering a national VAT through trial and error. When resources are limited, prioritizing the rationalization of the central tax agency contributes more to state capacity.

Implicit in policies advocated by the Washington Consensus is the withdrawal of state from market. But as the Chinese tax reforms illustrate, the state plays an essential role in establishing a fiscal system that ensures steady government revenue. In other words, instituting a functional tax administration necessitates a minimum level of state capacity. Yet on

[117] Li, "Tax Transplants and the Critical Role of Processes."

[118] Zhao, "Woguo Fenshuizhi Juecebeijing Lishi Huifang."

[119] Bird, "Foreign Advice and Tax Policy in Developing Countries"; Charles Mansfield, "Tax Administration in Developing Countries: An Economic Perspective," *Staff Papers* 35 (Washington, DC: IMF, 1988): 181.

[120] Odd-Helge Fjeldstad and Kari K. Heggstad, "The Tax Systems in Mozambique, Tanzania and Zambia: Capacity and Constraints," CMI Report R 2011:3 (Chr. Michelsen Institute, 2011), www.cmi.no/publications/file/4045-taxation-mozambique-tanzania-zambia.pdf; Carlo Cottarelli, "Revenue Mobilization in Developing Countries" (IMF, 2011) www.imf.org/external/np/pp/eng/2011/030811.pdf.

the other hand, a functional tax system is considered a precondition for building state capacity.[121]

So, chicken first or egg first? The Chinese experience sheds some light on this question. To initiate a virtuous cycle of increasing tax revenues and empowering the state, certain minimal state capacity is absolutely necessary. The state should be capable enough to introduce an initial set of tax policies that fit its socio-economic context, win the support of powerful vested interests, and implement the policies relatively effectively. The success of the initial policies will raise state revenue and strengthen its capacity to carry out further tax reforms that may subsequently generate more revenues at lower administrative costs. The question that naturally follows is how to achieve the minimal level of state capacity in a fragile developing country, as most of them "are struggling to build effective public sectors in the absence of a tradition of strong technocratic bureaucracy."[122] In other words, given extreme resource constraints, where do we begin?

Tax agencies in China play a critical role in tax policymaking and implementation. The central level agencies are capable of basic long-term planning, gathering data and information, conducting experiments, and proposing policy solutions. With accumulated expertise, the agencies are able to facilitate major tax reforms in time of political consensus, which rarely occurs even in a fragmented authoritarian state. In new democracies or transitional states where political environment tends to be unstable, a functional tax agency at the national level with long time horizon is even more important. Therefore, the first step should be to use limited resources to set up a tax agency at the central level with adequate competency to implement a basic VAT. International organizations have begun to recognize the importance of basic extractive capacity of developing countries and have assisted some to form efficient and merit-based tax agencies. Those that succeeded have reported encouraging results.[123]

Moreover, political will is essential to any major tax policy change.[124] Thus, reformers should pay special attention to timing because strong and unified political will to push through a systematic reform tends to

[121] Deborah Brautigam, Odd-Helge Fjeldstad, and Mick Moore, *Taxation and State-Building in Developing Countries: Capacity and Consent* (Cambridge: Cambridge University Press, 2008), 1.

[122] Peerenboom and Bugaric, "The Emerging Post Washington, Post Beijing Consensus," 108.

[123] Cottarelli, "Revenue Mobilization in Developing Countries."

[124] Li, "Tax Transplants and the Critical Role of Processes."

be evanescent, as illustrated by the Chinese experience. The practical lesson for weak states striving to build rudimentary fiscal infrastructures is the following: international organizations and domestic reformers should closely coordinate with competent domestic tax agencies in identifying core fiscal problems and testing multiple potential institutional solutions, then wait for an opportune moment to implement the best feasible solution in the specific economic and political context, leaving incremental improvements for the future. As weak states with segregated constituencies usually lack uniform political interests, reformers should take full advantage of any crisis that enables major legislative change and bureaucratic reorganization.[125]

V Conclusion

The Chinese tax reforms of the past three decades reflect an incremental "process of policy and legal transplants in the name of modernization."[126] Upon a casual glance, the tax component of the Washington Consensus appears to have its mirror image in Chinese tax policies, especially after the tax-sharing reform had resolved the central government's fiscal crisis. But a close examination reveals that most of these reforms were built on fiscal solutions fully adjusted to accommodate China's political and economic situations, and were carried out at a gradual pace. China's success revealed the flaws of the Washington Consensus, which paid inadequate attention to necessary processes for implementing locally the propagated policy package.[127]

The Chinese experience also challenges the market fundamentalist interpretation of the Washington Consensus, i.e., the message of restraining the state and letting the market allocate resources. Adequate state capacity is essential to establishing a basic tax system. Moreover, the Chinese reforms suggest that powerful and independent courts, implicitly recognized in the Washington Consensus as vital for development but generally lacking in developing countries, may not be a necessary condition for the initial rationalization of tax administration.

Having recognized the deficiency of the Washington Consensus, scholars recently proposed a process model that echoed the Chinese experience in tax reforms. Developing countries are encouraged to experiment

[125] Dara Kay Cohen, Mariano-Florentino Cuellar, and Barry R. Weingast, "Crisis Bureaucracy: Homeland Security and the Political Design of Legal Mandates," *Stanford Law Review* 59 (2006): 678.

[126] Li, "Tax Transplants and the Critical Role of Processes." [127] Ibid.

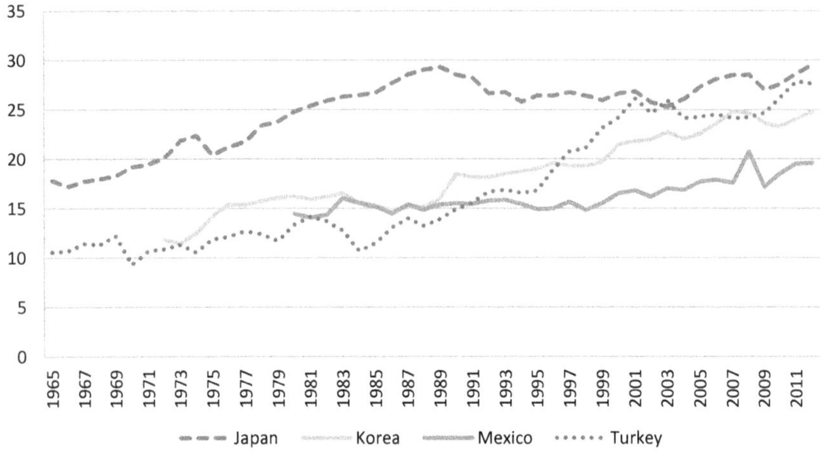

Figure 7.4 Total tax revenue as percentage of GDP (1965–2012). Data are from Table 2, "Tax Policy Analysis," OECD Center for Tax Policy and Administration, www.oecd.org/ctp/tax-policy/table2totaltaxrevenueasofgdp1965–2012en.htm.

with multiple fiscal solutions and implement those fitting their domestic context.[128] But the process model,[129] if promoted and understood simply as "best procedural practices" in reforming a tax system, will likely fail to address the problems left by the Washington Consensus. In order to duplicate the Chinese "success" in reforming its tax system, one has to understand its requisite structural premise. A central level tax agency of adequate competency, political consensus for major institutional reforms, and a central government with a relatively long time horizon are all critical to incremental and rational tax policymaking and implementation necessary to build an effective tax system from scratch. Countries without such a structural environment should focus on setting up an effective central tax agency with adequate competency to administer a broad VAT and on choosing the right timing for reform proposal and implementation.

[128] Stiglitz, "Is There a Post–Washington Consensus Consensus?"; Dani Rodrik, "Goodbye Washington Consensus, Hello Washington Confusion? A Review of the World Bank's Economic Growth in the 1990s: Learning from a Decade of Reform," *Journal of Economic Literature* 44 (2006): 973.

[129] For a discussion on a procedural and process model inspired by Chinese experiences, see Dowdle and Prado, Chapter 1.

8

The Chinese Model for Securities Law

YINGMAO TANG

I Introduction

The Washington Consensus prescribes that financial reform and a liberal market are preconditions for economic development in developing countries.[1] In stark contrast to this position is the development of the Chinese securities market. As opposed to liberalizing her securities market, China has subjected her securities market to extremely tight control. For over two decades since the opening of the national stock exchanges in the 1990s, the Chinese securities market has been heavily regulated by the China Securities Regulatory Commission (CSRC), and this is likely to be the case even in the future.

Where the development of securities markets is concerned, law and finance literature largely agrees with the ideas promulgated under the Washington Consensus. Still, some differences remain. While law and finance jurisprudence suggests certain links between the strength of securities markets and the protection of minority shareholders, it nevertheless argues that some amount of governmental intervention is necessary (and inevitable) before minority shareholders can be adequately protected. Governmental intervention takes the form of formulating securities disclosure rules, reviewing securities offering applications, and enforcing securities liabilities.[2]

[1] Yasheng Huang, "Debating China's Economic Growth, the Beijing Consensus or the Washington Consensus," *Academy of Management Perspective* 24 (2010): 40. I am not aware of any literature that provides a meaningful discussion of the Washington Consensus, addressing the development of the securities market. To the extent that the Washington Consensus requires financial liberation, a less interventionist government and strong market players, China is certainly not a model for the development of a securities market according to the Washington Consensus.

[2] Rafael La Porta, Florencio Lopez-de-Silanes, Andrei Shleifer, and Robert Vishny, "Legal Determinants of External Finance," *Journal of Finance* 52 (1997): 1131; Rafael La Porta, Florencio Lopez-de-Silanes, Andrei Shleifer, and Robert Vishny, "Law and Finance," *Journal of Political Economy* 106 (1998): 1113; Rafael La Porta, Florencio Lopez-de-Silanes,

The role of the CSRC, however, is much more expansive and intrusive than what law and finance theorists propose. For example, while public offerings are subject to the CSRC approval just like in other countries, private offerings, which are exempted from approval or registration in many countries, are also subject to the CSRC approval or registration, depending on a number of factors such as whether an issuer is a listed or unlisted company. This has been the case for almost two decades since the promulgation of the PRC Securities Law (the "1998 Securities Law") in 1998.[3] Similarly, not only are offerings to investors within mainland China subject to the CSRC's approval, which is in line with international practice, offerings to investors outside of mainland China are also subject to the CSRC's approval under the existing laws.[4]

The interventionist role of the CSRC in the Chinese securities market has not yet been adopted as a model for developing securities markets in other countries. There has not been any literature which discusses the Beijing Consensus in the context of the securities markets and their development. In fact, this chapter argues that the development of China's securities markets does not necessarily indicate that China's experience can be model for economic development, namely, the Beijing Consensus.

While it is undeniable that the growth of the Chinese securities market has been rapid, it is far from clear whether this market can be considered to be a successful one. No one would deny the rapid development of the Chinese securities market in the past 25 years. The number of listed companies in China (excluding those listed in Hong Kong) grew from zero in 1990 to about 2,600 in 2014,[5] and the market capitalization of listed

and Andrei Shleifer, "Corporate Ownership around the World," *Journal of Finance* 54 (1999): 471.

3 The Securities Law was promulgated in China in 1998 and amended in 2005. The Securities Law is silent with respect to the definitions of public offerings or private offerings of securities. Article 13 of the Securities Law as amended in 2005 (the "2005 Securities Law") provides that nonpublic offerings of listed companies are subject to the approval by the CSRC. In addition, department was established within the CSRC to handle the registration of non-public offerings in China by Chinese companies. Securities Law of the People's Republic of China, effective January 1, 2006, www.npc.gov.cn/englishnpc/Law/2007-12/11/content_1383569.htm.

4 Article 238 of the 2005 Securities Law provides that any offering of securities or any listing of securities outside of mainland China by a domestic enterprise directly or indirectly shall be subject to the approval by the securities regulator.

5 There were 2,592 listed companies in mainland China according to the monthly statistics of the CSRC. These statistics are available on the CSRC's website. "2014 Nian 11 yue tongji shuju" [Data of November 2014], China Securities Regulatory Commission, www.csrc.gov.cn/pub/zjhpublic/G00306204/zqscyb/201412/t20141219_265231.htm.

companies ranks second in the world, only behind the United States.[6] However, scholars have yet to form a consensus regarding the success of the Chinese market. Notably, a seasoned scholar had once referred to the Chinese stock market as a casino.[7] In addition to being viewed as a gambling house, China's securities market also appears to be extremely inefficient. Nearly 500 hundred Chinese companies are currently waiting for the CSRC to approve their applications for initial public offerings (IPOs).[8] In fact, national champions, such as China Mobile in the 1990s and Internet giants such as Alibaba in 2014, all chose listings outside of mainland China rather than in Shanghai or Shenzhen.

If a distinctive Chinese Model exists in the securities market, the key feature of this regulatory model (the "Chinese Model") is probably the strong intervention of the regulator in almost every aspect of a securities offering. For example: prospectus disclosure rules are heavily shaped by the CSRC; share pricing is controlled or influenced by the CSRC; due diligence process of investment banks are tightly regulated by the CSRC; even the format and content of legal opinions is subject to detailed regulation as laid down by the CSRC. The CSRC is everywhere. This chapter will show how this is the case.

Furthermore, prevalence of the CSRC in the Chinese Model will persist despite the recent reform regarding share registration. This reform is intended to reduce the intrusion of the CSRC, and to make the Chinese Model closer to the United States's. Nevertheless, the interventionist role of the regulator is likely to continue into the future.

[6] The combined market cap of listed companies in the Shanghai Stock Exchange and the Shenzhen Stock Exchange accounted for 9.45 percent of the total market cap of all listed companies in the world at the end of 2014. The US is the country where market cap of listed companies is larger than China. The calculation is based on the statistics of the World Federation of Exchanges. "Monthly Reports of December 2014," World Federation of Exchanges, www.world-exchanges.org/home/index.php/statistics/monthly-reports.

[7] On January 14, 2001, Mr. Jinglian Wu commented in the CCTV Dialog Show that "the Chinese stock market is very much like a casino . . . casinos have rules, you are not allowed to see others people's cards. However, in our stock market, some people can see the cards of others." Bin Xiao, *Gu Shi Feng Yun* [Stock Market Storms] (Beijing: China Machine Press, 2010), 2–32.

[8] According to the data released by the CSRC, on April 23, 2015, the CSRC has accepted 562 applications for IPOs, of which 485 companies are still waiting to be approved. "Xingzheng xuke shixiang: faxing jianguanbu shouci gongkai faxing gupiao shenhe gongzuo liucheng ji shenqing qiye qingkuang" [Supervision Department: The IPO Audit Work Processes and the Situation of Enterprises], China Securities Regulatory Commission, www.csrc.gov.cn/pub/zjhpublic/G00306202/201504/t20150424_275570.htm.

The rest of this chapter is organized as follows. Part II discusses the key features of the Chinese Model. Part III then proceeds to argue that the Chinese Model will not mirror the United States's despite the recent reform regarding share registration in China. Part IV concludes.

II Key Feature of the Chinese Model

The key feature of the Chinese Model is the expansive and intrusive role of the CSRC compared to the marginal role of investors and the judiciary.

A Extensive Approval Power

The CSRC's authority is quite extensive compared to the authority of regulators in other markets. A share offering to public investors is subject to the CSRC's approval. This is consistent with other key markets such as that of the United States. However, a private offering in China before 2015 would also be subject to approval or registration with the CSRC depending on whether the issuer is a listed company.[9] This is different from the United States, where a private placement is exempted from registration with the Securities Exchange Commission (SEC).

Furthermore, an offering to investors outside mainland China by a China-based issuer is also subject to the approval by the CSRC,[10] even if no mainland China investors are involved in the offering.[11] This is odd because, in theory, the rationale behind such approval requirement is that securities law of a jurisdiction is intended to protect investors of that jurisdiction. Yet, no Chinese investor is involved here. Also, such approval

[9] See 2005 Securities Law. It is expected that offerings to qualified investors will be exempted from approval in the proposed amendment to the Securities Law. See also the discussion in Part II of this chapter.

[10] Article 238 of the 2005 Securities Law. It is expected that offering to investors and listings outside mainland China will be subject to filing with rather than approval by the CSRC in the proposed amendment to the Securities Law. See also discussion in Part II of this chapter.

[11] The State Council Special Regulation regarding Overseas Offerings and Listings of Joint Stock Companies issued by the State Counsel on August 4, 1994 (the "The 1997 State Council Special Regulation") confers authority upon the CSRC to require approval for foreign IPOs. China Telecom is a joint stock company incorporated under the Chinese Company Law. The 1998 Securities Law also grants the CSRC the authority to approve foreign IPOs. The 1998 Securities Law contains an article similar to Article 238 of the 2005 Securities Law, which requires CSRC approval of any "direct" overseas' offering and listing by a Chinese domestic enterprise.

is required in addition to other approval or registration requirements of the jurisdiction where the offer is to be made.

For example, the IPO of China Telecom to investors in Hong Kong and the United States in 2002 was subject to the approval by the CSRC in addition to the approval of the regulators in Hong Kong and the United States. Similarly, Alibaba Group's IPO in the fall of 2014 in the United States was also subject to approval by the CSRC in addition to the registration requirement imposed by the SEC. Alibaba Group, whose IPO is the largest in the history of the world capital market, is a Cayman Island-incorporated company that has operational subsidiaries in mainland China.[12]

The CSRC has enjoyed an expansive role in approving a securities offering for over two decades, regardless of whether an offer is private or public, or whether an offer is domestic or international. This is quite different from the role of securities regulators in the United States and many other markets, where distinction is generally made between public and private offerings, and between domestic and international offerings when deciding the jurisdiction and the powers of approval of securities regulators.

B Merit-Based Approval Authority

The power of the CSRC to approve a particular offering is merit-based and discretionary. This is different from the US model, under which the

[12] The CSRC takes the view that an offering and listing outside of mainland China by a Cayman Island company which has operational subsidiaries in mainland China would be viewed as an "indirect" offering and listing by a Chinese domestic enterprise, which according to Article 238 of the 2006 Securities Law is subject to the approval by the CSRC. On August 8, 2006, six PRC regulatory agencies, including the Ministry of Commerce, the State-Owned Assets Supervision and Administration Commission, the State Administration of Taxation, the China Securities Regulatory Commission and the State Administration of Foreign Exchange, also jointly adopted the Regulations on Mergers and Acquisitions of Domestic Enterprises by Foreign Investors, which came into effect on September 8, 2006, and which was also amended on June 22, 2009. This rule includes, among other things, provisions that purport to require any offshore special purpose vehicle formed for the purpose of an overseas listing of securities of a PRC company to obtain the CSRC approval prior to the listing and trading of such special purpose vehicle's securities on an overseas stock exchange. As disclosed in its IPO prospectus, however, Alibaba was able to rely on its PRC counsel opinion that the CSRC approval is not required because of certain facts specific to Alibaba. See Alibaba's 424B4 prospectus (filed with the SEC, Sept. 22, 2014), at 54. "*Alibaba's* 424B4 prospectus," US Securities and Exchange Commission, www.sec.gov/Archives/edgar/data/1577552/000119312514347620/d709111d424b4.ht.

regulator focuses on disclosure rather than merits. Furthermore, the SEC's power to declare effective an offering registration statement is also much less discretionary in my view.

The regulator under the US model focuses on disclosure rather than merits. The key focus of the SEC in declaring effective a registration statement is whether the disclosure is accurate and adequate. The US Securities Law of 1933 does not impose any qualitative or quantitative criteria for a public offering other than requiring such offering to be registered with the SEC. The rules, regulations, or forms of the SEC do not generally impose additional criteria either. The touchstone is therefore the accuracy and completeness of disclosure in a registration statement.

On the other hand, the Securities Law of Mainland China as amended in 2005 (the "2005 Securities Law") imposes cumbersome requirements on a potential issuer. These requirements include, for example, a requirement that an issuer has "complete and sound internal organizations"; that an issuer has the "capability to make profits continuously" and that an issuer does not have "material illegal conducts."[13] The CSRC has issued a number of rules to elaborate these criteria. One key rule is the Initial Public Offering Administration Measures issued in May 2006 (the "IPO Review Rule").[14] This 70-article rule adds many more qualitative and quantitative requirements. For example, a company has to make profits for each of the preceding three years before it can conduct an IPO in China.[15] This has been strongly criticized by scholars and professionals in recent years when China-based Internet giants such as Baidu.com and Alibaba.com decided to conduct their IPOs outside of mainland China. Baidu and Alibaba chose to be listed in the United States because they were not qualified under this rule to do an offering in their home country.

Other examples of stringent requirements are abundant. For example, a potential issuer needs to demonstrate that it has not received any material

[13] See Article 13 of the 2005 Securities Law.

[14] The IPO Review Rule applies to applications for IPOs and listings on the main board of the Shanghai Stock Exchange. In 2009, the CSRC issued the Growth Board Initial Public Offering and Listing Administration Measures (the "Growth Board IPO Review Rule") to apply to applications for IPOs and listings on the growth board of the Shenzhen Stock Exchange.

[15] The Growth Board IPO Review Rule has nevertheless lowered certain criteria. For example, an applicant is required to make profits for the preceding two years rather than three. However, the overall standards are still quite high compared to the listing standards of other stock exchanges such as NASDAQ that allows listings of companies that do not make any profits prior to their listings.

penalties from a long list of government agencies such as those regulating matters of environment, tax, and customs. In practice, this means that a potential issuer will have to obtain certificates from these authorities to prove its innocence in front of the CSRC. Not only does it take a long time to obtain these certificates, certain certificates are also extremely difficult to obtain.[16]

C Prospectus Disclosure with the CSRC Style

No one would dispute the importance of the disclosure of information in a securities market. This is the foundation of securities law in almost every market. Securities regulators play a critical role in enforcing information disclosure, and are endowed with commensurate powers to play this crucial role. For example, the US Securities Law of 1933 has emphasized for more than seventy years since its enactment, that the SEC has the power to formulate forms regarding the format and content of information to be included in a registration statement and a prospectus.

The Chinese Model has generally followed the US model in this regard. The CSRC has formulated a significant number of rules, regulations, and forms regarding information disclosure. For example, the CSRC has issued rules, regulations and forms regarding prospectuses for IPOs and follow-on offerings,[17] regarding postlisting periodic or ad hoc reports

[16] It is difficult for foreigners to understand why and how a government agency would be able to issue certain certificates required by the CSRC at all. For example, an applicant is required to obtain certificates from the tax authorities confirming that the issuer has fully paid taxes. In many developed markets, one assumption of the tax authority is that taxpayers may not have fully paid their taxes so there is generally a statute of limitation (i.e., six years) regarding how long the tax authority will be allowed to request a taxpayer to pay unpaid or underpaid taxes. In these markets, it would be difficult for a tax authority to issue any certificate to prove that a taxpayer has fully fulfilled its tax obligations. Despite the CSRC's request, the language used in tax certificates varies from city to city in mainland China. This significantly undermines the original purpose of providing tax certificates, and the provision of tax certificates instead becomes a procedural burden on applicants.

[17] See, e.g., *Gongkai faxing zhengquan de gongsi xinxi pilu yu geshi zhunze diyihao – zhaogu shuomingshu* [Information Disclosure Form and Content Requirements No. 1 for Companies Conducting Public Securities Offerings – Prospectuses] (issued by the CSRC on May 18, 2005) (hereinafter the "*Disclosure Rule No. 1*"); *Gongkai faxing zhengquan de gongsi xinxi pilu geshi zhunze dishiyihao – shangshi gongsi gongkai faxing zhengquan muji shuomingshu* [Information Disclosure Form and Content Requirements No. 11 for Companies Conducting Public Securities Offerings – Listed Companies Public Offering Securities Prospectuses] (issued by the CSRC on May 8, 2005).

(i.e., annual reports, semiannual reports, major event reports, etc.),[18] financial reports and legal opinions.[19]

It is beyond the scope of this chapter to compare information disclosure rules between China and other countries. However, one key difference is that the United States as well as international practice generally allows an issuer to adopt a materiality approach or threshold in deciding what information should be disclosed to investors.[20] For example, an issuer is required to disclose its principle shareholders (i.e., 5 percent) in its IPO prospectus rather than every single shareholder under the US disclosure rule. The same materiality approach applies to other information such as an issuer's subsidiaries, investee companies or information in general (i.e., whether an event is material or not). The Chinese approach, on the other hand, requires the issuer to disclose every single item of a particular piece of information.

Under the Chinese disclosure rules, for example, an issuer is required to submit to the CSRC a complete list of its trademarks, patents, land use rights, house ownership rights, and mining rights.[21] The principle of materiality does not apply here. I was once told by a senior securities

[18] See, e.g., *Gongkai faxing zhengquan de gongsi xinxi pilu yu geshi zhunze dierhao – niandu baogao de neirong yu geshi* [Information Disclosure Form and Content Requirements No. 2 for Companies Conducting Public Securities Offerings – Annual Report Content and Format] (amended by the CSRC on December 17, 2007); *Gongkai faxing zhengquan de gongsi xinxi pilu yu geshi zhunze disanhao – banniandu baogao de neirong yu geshi* [Information Disclosure Form and Content Requirements No. 3 for Companies Conducting Public Securities Offerings – Semi Annual Report Content and Format] (amended by the CSRC on June 29, 2007); *Gongkai faxing zhengquan de gongsi xinxi pilu yu geshi zhunze dierhao – jidu baogao de neirong yugeshi* [Information Disclosure Form and Content Requirements No. 13 for Companies Conducting Public Securities Offerings – Quarterly Report Content and Format] (amended by the CSRC on March 26, 2007).

[19] See, e.g., *Baojianren jinzhi diaocha gongzuo zhunze* [Sponsor Due Diligence Working Guidelines] (issued by the CSRC on May 29, 2006) (hereinafter "*Sponsor Due Diligence Rule*"); *Gongkai faxing zhengquan de gongsi xinxi pilu yu geshi zhunze dishierhao – gongkai faxing zhengquan de falv yijian shuhe lvshi gongzuo baogao* [Information Disclosure Form and Content Requirements No. 12 for Companies Conducting Public Securities Offerings – Public Securities Offering Legal Opinions and Lawyer Work Report] (amended by the CSRC on March 26, 2006).

[20] "International Disclosure Standards for Cross-Border Offerings and Listings by Foreign Issuers," International Organization of Securities Commissions, www.iosco.org/library/pubdocs/pdf/IOSCOPD81.pdf.

[21] Item 9–1, *Gongkai faxing zhengquan de gongsi xinxi pilu yu geshi zhunze dijiuhao – shouci gongkai faxing bing shangshi shenqing wenjian* [Information Disclosure Form and Content Requirements No. 9 for Companies Conducting Public Securities Offerings – Initial Public Securities Offering and Listing Application Documents] (amended by the CSRC on March 19, 2006).

lawyer that not many years ago the CSRC required an issuer to submit to the CSRC for its review the original copies of all of the above rights and certificates in addition to the required list of every single right and certificate that the issuer has ever obtained. In one case, the staff of one large SOE had to hire two cars to deliver these certificates to the CSRC, which subsequently realized that there was not enough room to store these original documents.

In addition, a Chinese reader can frequently find in a prospectus a ten or twenty-page long disclosure about every single shareholder of an issuer. The current CSRC rule requires the disclosure of every single shareholder rather than principal or major shareholders.[22] In comparison, under the US disclosure rule, a one- or two-page-long chart of an issuer's principal shareholders would typically suffice. Numerous examples of this kind exist.

The fundamental difference between the Chinese Model and the US model about disclosure rules is whether an issuer is allowed to make a judgment about what information is important to investors, and which judgment is subject to judicial review later. In many jurisdictions such as the United States, the judgment is made mainly by investors or by the market in a broader sense. In China, the CSRC dominates such decisions and leaves little room for private enforcement.[23]

[22] For example, Article 31 of the Disclosure Rule No. 1 requires an issuer to disclose information on each change to its share capital since the incorporation rather than changes to the share capital in the latest three or five years as in other countries. In practice, certain issuers had to disclose all of the changes to each shareholder's shareholdings as long as there is any change to the issuer's share capital. The Everbright Bank uses more than ten pages to disclose every single change to the shareholding percentage of each of its 230 shareholders. "The IPO prospectus of the Everbright Bank," Shanghai Stock Exchange, 49, www.sse.com .cn/disclosure/listedinfo/announcement/c/2010-07-30/601818_20100730_2.pdf.

[23] As decided by the CSRC, China's courts can hear cases brought by investors on the ground of inaccurate prospectuses (based on a judicial interpretation of the Supreme People's Court in 2002) only when the prospectus contains false disclosure. As a result, the courts play a marginal role in enforcing securities disclosure liabilities compared to the role of the CSRC and that of American courts. The role of market forces (e.g., securities firms, lawyers, financial press) is less important compared to the role of state institutions (e.g., courts and regulators). See Donald C. Clarke, "Law without Order in Chinese Corporate Governance Institutions," *Northwestern Journal of International Law and Business* 30 (2010): 131.That said, Liebman and Milhaupt also examined the public criticism of listed companies on the two stock exchanges in China and pointed out its effect on listed companies and executives. This illustrates the role of the media and informal mechanisms that affect corporate governance and economic growth in China. Benjamin L. Liebman and Curtis J. Milhaupt, "Reputational Sanctions in China Stock Market," *Columbia Law Review* 108 (2008): 929.

The Chinese Model is able to function well in China because her courts do not hear civil disputes regarding misleading disclosure in prospectuses.[24] Unlike the US model, there is currently no class action against false or misleading prospectus disclosure in China. The role of the judiciary is kept to a minimum in enforcing securities law and disclosure rules.

In summary, the expansive role and authority of the CSRC in formulating disclosure rules, in enforcing disclosure rules, and in granting approval to a securities offering is completely opposite to the role of securities regulators in the United States and other developed markets. The Chinese Model is peculiar and is certainly not aligned with the financial liberation and deregulation proposed by the Washington Consensus. Given the weak institutional configuration of China's capital markets, the CSRC is likely to keep playing a heavy role and the Chinese securities market will continue to be subjected to heavy regulation. The recent stock market crash in the summer of 2015 also suggests that the performance and sustainability of the Chinese Model is questionable.

III Recent Share Registration Reform

A Share Registration Reform

In 2012, a share registration reform was initiated by the Chinese government.[25] One key feature of this reform is that China plans to follow the US model to regulate share offerings. Under the US model, a share offering is subject to registration with the SEC, rather than its approval. The concept of registration implies that instances of issuers seeking approval from the regulator are set to decrease and that the regulator will less likely intrude into the IPO process. The share offering

[24] According to the Several Provisions of the Supreme People's Court on the Trial of Civil Compensation Cases Arising from False Statements in the Securities Market, which was promulgated by the Supreme People's Court in 2002, a plaintiff (investor) must provide a court with a decision or an announcement made by a governance agency (i.e., the CSRC) imposing administrative liabilities or a court judgment imposing criminal liabilities upon a defendant before that court accepts a civil suit brought by the plaintiff. This requirement in practice means that administrative or criminal liabilities are a precondition for determining civil liabilities.

[25] Item 12 of Section 2 of *Zhonggong zhongyang guanyu quanmian shenhua gaige ruogan zhongda wenti de jueding* [Decisions of the China Communist Party Central Committee Regarding Several Key Issues of Deepening and Expanding Reforms] (issued by the China Communist Party Central Committee on November 15, 2013).

reform is thus labeled as "share registration reform" in China. In 2013, the CSRC Chairman indicated that the 2005 Securities Law was to be amended accordingly.[26] The amendment was expected to be passed by the National People's Congress in 2015, but was postponed due to the stock market crash in the summer of 2015.[27]

An aggressive agenda for reform is on the way and the overall theme is to significantly reduce the requirement of CSRC approval by amending the Securities Law. For example, certain types of share offerings, such as those made to qualified investors, are likely to be exempted from the approval by the CSRC. This is similar to the idea of private offerings. Also, share offerings to investors outside mainland China will probably not be subject to the approval by the CSRC. Instead, an issuer would only be required to make a filing with the CSRC after the completion of such offering.

It is also expected that the IPO qualification criteria will be significantly lowered. For example, an IPO issuer may not be required to demonstrate that it is capable of "continuously making profits."[28] Most importantly, the CSRC's authority of reviewing IPO applications may be delegated to stock exchanges.[29]

It is difficult to speculate at this stage what will exactly come out of the reform and the amended Securities Law. The label of "share registration reform" appears to suggest that China is seeking to steer its securities markets toward that of the United States. The proposed amendment to the Securities Law also demonstrates that the Chinese Model is heading toward a model that is in line with the spirit of the Washington Consensus. Having said so, does this mean that the Washington Consensus prevails and will China become more like the United States as far as the regulation of the securities market is concerned? My answer is, not quite yet.

Amending the Securities Law is certainly a big step forward. It will certainly help reduce the interventionist role of the CSRC. Certain proposed amendments and reform measures, if adopted, will no doubt have a

26 Wu Lihua, "Xiaogang: zhuajin xiuding 'zhengjuanfa'" [Xiao Gang: Pay Close Attention to the Amendment of "Security Law"], *Economic Information*, August 2, 2013, http://jjckb.xinhuanet.com/2013-08/02/content_459153.htm.

27 Xiang Bo, "China Expected to Revise Securities Law in 2015," *English.news.cn*, March 10, 2015, http://news.xinhuanet.com/english/2015-03/10/c_134055479.htm.

28 "China Focus: New IPO System Aims to Create Healthy Capital Market," *English.news.cn*, January 19, 2015, http://news.xinhuanet.com/english/indepth/2015-01/19/c_133930487.htm.

29 "News Analysis: Stock Issue Reform Still on the Way," *English.news.cn*, November 20, 2015, http://news.xinhuanet.com/english/china/2014-11/20/c_133803626.htm.

profound impact on the future development of China's securities market. For example, if securities offerings to investors outside mainland China are no longer required to obtain CSRC approval, companies will find it less cumbersome to list in overseas markets like Hong Kong or the United States.

However, amending the Securities Law is only part of the solution. Successful implementation of the amended Securities Law is another problem. To say the very least, it will take time, probably much more time than one would expect, to implement the necessary reforms required to reduce the interventionist role of the CSRC. More importantly, given that many CSRC rules or IPO practices were developed customarily, despite the lack of any basis under the Securities Law, amending the Securities Law may not be as helpful as one might be led to anticipate.

For example, neither the 1998 Securities Law nor the 2005 Securities Law provides explicitly or implicitly that the CSRC has a role in controlling or influencing the pricing of an offering. However, this is certainly one of the important roles of the CSRC. Similarly, both the 1998 Securities Law and the 2005 Securities Law lack provisions that authorize the CSRC to impose rules regarding due diligence on part of an investment bank or legal counsel. Yet the CSRC has issued extensive rules to regulate the processes of investment banks and the opinions that lawyers draft regarding IPOs.

There are reasons why the CSRC acts in such a manner, and, in spite of any change in the law, the CSRC is likely to continue in its ways in the future. This chapter will not go into details of these reasons. In any case, given the immense level of market intervention, one should be skeptical about what the share registration reform will achieve and the actual convergence between the Chinese Model and international practices.

B Controlling Share Pricing

The CSRC has a number of ways of controlling the pricing of a share offering as exemplified by two examples. First, the CSRC has issued rules since 2004 to regulate the price discovery and road show activities of underwriters or investment banks.[30] These rules set forth detailed requirements regarding marketing activities of investment banks and a target number

[30] See *Guanyu shouci gon kai faxing shixing xunjia zhidu de tongzhi* [Circular Regarding Pilot Implementation of Price Inquires of Initial Public Offerings] (issued by the CSRC on December 7, 2004).

of potential investors upon which an investment bank is then required to issue a price inquiry notice. These rules also stipulate the way in which price inquiry and road show activities are conducted.

Second, the CSRC uses "window guidance" (*chuangkou zhidao*) to informally influence the pricing of share offerings. Under the guise of providing guidance to investment banks, the CSRC influences the timing, pricing, and overall offering structure of a share offering.[31] This has the effect of creating informal rules to cap the pricing of an offering, which in turn suppresses high price-earnings ratios or listing prices in the secondary market.[32] Crucially, the CSRC has a record of suspending a particular offering after granting an approval certificate, and has even suspended the entire IPO market for over a year between 2005 and 2006.[33]

This is obviously different from the US model. The SEC would not attempt to control or even try to influence the pricing of a particular offering, let alone the suspension of the entire market. The road show activities are conducted by investment banks following the general market practice. The most recent attempt of the SEC to regulate road show and pricing activities is to require fair and open allocations by investment banks of IPO shares in the wake of scandals surfacing after the Dot.com bubble burst in 2000. Other than this, pricing is entirely a market activity conducted by market players.

The CSRC's influence over pricing has a resulted in a series of chain effects on the role of various market players. As pricing is essentially handled by the CSRC, investment banks have shifted their focus away

[31] "Window guidance" is not a legally defined term. An IPO issuer and its underwriters will conduct marketing activities after receiving approval from the CSRC. Underwriters will generally consult the CSRC on key terms of an offering. For example, the CSRC started to allow existing shareholders of an issuer to sell shares to the public during an IPO of the issuer in early 2014. Underwriters have been reported by news articles this year to discuss with the CSRC and receive its feedback on the percentage of shares to be sold by existing shareholders in an IPO compared to the percentage of shares to be newly issued by the issuer. "Zhengjianhui jiu aosaikang shijian chuju jingshihan" [The CSRC Issued a Warning Letter to Aosaikang], *Xinhuawang*, June 14, 2014, http://news.xinhuanet.com/fortune/2014-06/14/c_126618283.htm.

[32] *Guanyu xingu dingjia xiangguan wenti de tongzhi* [Notice on Issues Related to the Pricing of IPO] (issued by the CSRC on May 23, 2012), Section 6.

[33] The CSRC has suspended the IPO market a number of times in the past ten years. For example, the IPO market was suspended between 2005 and 2006 in order to allow the CSRC to implement reforms regarding fully tradable shares. In September 2012, the IPO offerings were suspended until early 2014. After the stock crash in summer 2015, the IPO offerings were suspended again.

from marketing share offerings. Instead, investment banks undertake the responsibilities of drafting prospectuses. This is a good way for banks to prove their value to issuers, however, it also leads to the poor quality of information disclosures.

In the United States, disclosure documents such as registration statements and prospectuses are typically prepared by lawyers.[34] I have not heard any case where a prospectus is drafted by an investment bank in the United States. To the contrary, investment banks would try to stay out of the prospectus drafting process because they are afraid of assuming liability. They would rather review a prospectus prepared by the legal counsel of an issuer and use the reviewing and commenting process as a tool to conduct due diligence on the issuer.

In short, the Securities Law offers no basis regarding the CSRC's role in controlling or influencing share pricing. It nevertheless has been quite common for the CSRC to do so. Neither does the Securities Law provide guidance as to what investment banks should or should not do in terms of pricing and prospectus preparation. In other words, these rules and distorted practices have been developed outside the law. Amending the Securities Law is unlikely to address these issues in any significant way.

C Regulating Due Diligence of Investment Banks

Not only are the marketing activities of investment banks heavily regulated, their other activities are also subject to detailed regulation by the CSRC. For example, the CSRC issued a set of regulations to set forth detailed requirements for due diligence by investment banks in their capacities as sponsors, a regime that the CSRC borrowed from Hong Kong.[35] This 77-article regulation is divided into eleven chapters that cover areas or issues regarding the issuer's business history, shareholders, employees, business, management, corporate governance, and financials. This more or less corresponds to the various chapters in a prospectus. For each subject matter, this rule lays out details regarding how a sponsor should conduct due diligence on a particular issue, what information it should review and how a review should be conducted. This rule amounts

[34] John C. Coffee, "The Attorney as Gatekeeper: An Agenda for the SEC," *Columbia Law Review* 103 (2003): 1302. The professionals (lawyers) typically have the principal role in the drafting of disclosure documents.

[35] The Sponsor Due Diligence Rule.

to an operating manual, or a textbook in a sense, for the practice of business and for the due diligence required in a prospectus.

Regarding the due diligence required of suppliers, the 77-article regulation requires a sponsor to, among other things, "investigate an issuer's major raw materials, major auxiliary supplies and energy supplies by communicating with an issuer's purchasing employees and suppliers"; to "gather information on at least ten suppliers, calculate the purchasing amounts of key suppliers for the last three years and decide whether the issuer relies on any single supplier"; to "obtain long-term supply contracts for key suppliers, analyze terms of these contracts and conclude whether supply is stable"; and also to "have meetings with both purchasing employees and employees from the manufacturing side, calculate the turn-over days for raw materials and conduct on-site visits to investigate whether there is any unused or poor quality supplies."[36] This is only a summary of one out of the seventy-seven articles of the CSRC Sponsor Due Diligence Rule. A sponsor is required to comply with all of these detailed requirements when conducting due diligence on an issuer and then submit a due diligence report, issued in its own name, to the CSRC as part of the issuer's IPO application documents.

In light of these requirements, it does not appear necessary or helpful for a sponsor in China to engage a legal counsel to conduct legal due diligence on its behalf. As a result, sponsors or investment banks in China do not have their own legal counsel.[37] In comparison, underwriters in the United States typically engage their own counsel to prove that they have conducted reasonable investigation that meets prevailing legal standards. What is shocking, however, is that the Chinese practice unwittingly lowers the quality of prospectuses since prospectuses are not drafted by legal counsel. This practice is unheard of in the United States, where investment banks self-regulate as required by the Financial Industry Regulatory Authority (FINRA), a broker-dealer association. It would probably be thought of as a joke if the SEC plans to issue a set of regulations telling investment banks how to conduct business or how to fulfill due diligence requirements as regards a potential issuer.

[36] Article 20 of the Sponsor Due Diligence Rule.

[37] See *Lvshi shiwusuo congshi zhengquan falv yewu guanli ban fa* [The Administration Measures for Law Firms Engaging Securities' Legal Service] (issued by the CSRC, May 7, 2007), Article 11, which prohibits law firms from delivering legal opinions to both the issuer and issuer's underwriters/sponsors.

Unlike rules or practices regarding pricing or prospectus drafting, the regulation of due diligence conducted by investment banks in China has its institutional basis in the Securities Law. The Securities Law has a chapter regarding the regulation of securities companies or investment banks. The CSRC has established an internal department to regulate the more than one hundred investment banks in the country. The regulation of investment banks' working product (i.e., due diligence reports) is a natural extension of the CSRC's authority and interest in regulating banks. Therefore, it is difficult to imagine any fundamental change made to investment banking practices without effecting any corresponding changes in the CSRC's regulation of investment banks.

D Regulating Lawyers

The CSRC also regulates legal opinions delivered by lawyers pursuant to share offerings. Unsurprisingly, this approach diverges from the approach adopted in the United States as well. In the United States, the SEC has never attempted to regulate lawyers or legal documents delivered pursuant to share offering. The only requirement regarding a legal opinion for a share offering is Item 601 in Regulation S-K that requires the issuer's legal counsel to opine on the legality of shares to be issued to the public. This can be covered by a legal opinion of less than one page. Everything else is left to the market.

Furthermore, underwriters in the United States typically engage their own counsel to conduct due diligence on an issuer. The underwriters' counsel would deliver a legal opinion to underwriters at the closing of an offering to reflect the due diligence done. Underwriters also typically require the issuer's counsel to deliver a legal opinion at the closing of a share offering. Generally, the legal opinion of the issuer's counsel is substantially the same as the legal opinion of the underwriters' counsel. The format and content of these legal opinions are subject to negotiation between underwriters and these counsels. This is not something that the SEC is concerned about.

On the contrary, the CSRC has regulated the legal profession in respect of share offerings since the commencement of the Chinese securities market. It attempted to regulate the legal profession at both the institutional level as well as the individual level. For example, the CSRC once created the title of "securities lawyers" to set an entry barrier for lawyers practicing securities law in addition to setting forth detailed requirements for the format and content of a legal opinion delivered by an issuer's counsel. The "securities lawyer" qualification was abandoned a few years ago but the detailed requirements for legal opinions continue to exist.

The CSRC's regulation on legal opinions has fifty-four articles. Like the CSRC's regulations on due diligence reports by investment banks, the CSRC's regulations on legal opinions sets forth details for what should be included in a legal opinion and what should be included in a so-called lawyers' work report, which are similar to legal due diligence reports. Crucially, both the legal opinion and the lawyers' work report are made available for public inspection. I do not plan to elaborate the details of these regulations in this chapter. However, suffice it to say that lawyers' work reports can easily be four or five hundred pages long. It is even longer than a prospectus. This aptly demonstrates the excessiveness of the CSRC's regulations concerning legal opinions and lawyers' work reports. Regulatory review and oversight of legal opinions is also unheard of in the US model.[38] The inexperience and unprofessionalism of the legal profession in China is the main concern that leads CSRC to intervene in this manner.

The Chinese bar is still young. China did not have private law firms until the early 1990s. The emergence of big Chinese law firms such as King & Wood Mallesons or Dacheng Denton is only a recent phenomenon. Hence, it makes sense for the CSRC to play a role in guiding, advising, or even baby-sitting lawyers given the youth of the legal profession in China. CSRC's intervention in the production of legal products has its deep roots in the weak legal institutions that support the development of capital markets.

[38] Ronald J. Gilson views lawyers as a "reputational intermediary" or a "transaction cost engineer" while Reinier H. Kraakman and John C. Coffee views lawyers as gatekeepers. Ronald J. Gilson, "Value Creation by Business Lawyers: Legal Skills and Asset Pricing," *The Yale Law Journal* 94 (1984): 239; Reinier H. Kraakman, "Gatekeepers: The Anatomy of a Third-Party Enforcement Strategy," *Journal of Law, Economics, & Organization* 2 (1986): 53; John C. Coffee, "The Attorney as Gatekeeper," 1293. However, neither Gilson nor Kraakman addresses the questions of whether and why lawyers should be regulated. Coffee discusses the regulation of securities lawyers by the SEC under Section 307 of the Sabanes-Oxley Act after the Enron scandal. Section 307 of the Sabanes-Oxley Act authorizes the SEC to prescribe minimum standards of professional conduct for attorneys appearing or practicing before it. However, Section 307 only contemplates reporting obligations that are "up-the-ladder" as regards securities lawyers who found to be in material violation of law. This is thus different from the CSRC's regulation of lawyers, legal opinions or lawyers' work reports as discussed in this chapter.

In short, an amendment of the Securities Law is unlikely to curtail the expansive reviewing powers that the CSRC exercises over legal opinions. The Securities Law does not say what a law firm should or should not say in its legal opinion. The unique legal opinion practices in share offerings have been developed outside the law, and have its institutional basis. Amending the Securities Law is helpful but may not bring about the expected changes.

IV Conclusion

It is probably too early to say that amending the Securities Law is not enough. It remains to be seen what hurdles will be removed, what control measures will be maintained and how market players will respond to the new regime. However, preliminary evidence shows that amending the Securities Law is far from enough, as manifested by the recent development of the "New Third Board."

The New Third Board is similar to over-the-counter markets in the United States such as the Over-the-Counter Bulletin Board (OTCBB). Both the Shanghai Stock Exchange and the Shenzhen Stock Exchange have a main board for listing large and blue-chip companies. The Shenzhen Stock Exchange opened a growth board in 2009, as known as the second board. The name "New Third Board" is to show the importance of this new board, which is second only to the two national stock exchanges.

To promote the New Third Board, the CSRC has significantly reduced the requirements for companies to be listed on the New Third Board. The review process has largely been streamlined, and the CSRC's authority to review securities transactions is delegated to the company operating the board. This is similar to the idea proposed by the amendment of the Securities Law – the review of IPO applications will be delegated to the two stock exchanges rather than the CSRC. The CSRC even considers it a pilot program to try out the share registration reform before making any amendments to the Securities Law. As a result of these measures, more than two thousand companies have been listed on the New Third Board within less than two years since its inception in early 2014. In short, this board has proven to be quite efficient.

However, nothing appears to have changed even with the New Third Board's arrival. Investment banks, rather than the issuers, continue to draft prospectuses, and the poor quality of prospectuses continues to be a problem as highlighted by the regulator and professionals.[39] Furthermore, unlike the extensive requirements for legal opinions delivered for companies listed on the Shanghai or Shenzhen stock exchanges, the requirements governing legal opinions issued on behalf of companies seeking to list on the New Third Board are very limited in number. This is intended to reduce the interventionist role played by the regulator. Ironically, law firms still voluntarily follow the extensive requirements applicable to issuers listed on the Shanghai and Shenzhen stock exchanges when preparing legal opinions for companies to be listed on the New Third Board. In other words, one still can easily find legal opinions that are over a hundred pages long for companies who seek to be listed on the New Third Board despite legal counsel not being required to do so.

A separate paper is required to explore the reasons why market players in the New Third Board behave as such. For example, it would be interesting to find out why legal counsel and law firms expose themselves to much higher risks by delivering opinions that they are not required. For the purpose of this chapter, it is sufficient to note that the development of the New Third Board has achieved everything that reformists aspire to achieve: less regulation and control, an issuer-friendly and decentralized review process and a staggering number of companies listed within such a short time, which is remarkable. These were achieved without amending the Securities Law. However, the distorted practices of market players continue to exist despite the amendments to the Securities Law, and these practices are likely to persist into the future.

In sum, it is incorrect to interpret the recent reform on share offer registration as a sign of China adopting the United States's share registration regime. The distorted role of the regulator and the excessive intervention of the government, which reflect the deep distrust on part of the regulator as regards market forces, cannot be fixed within a short period of time. The path-dependent nature of the industry practice, as a result of the heavy regulation of market players and their products by the CSRC, will likely make changes to the industry practice in the near future difficult. Detailed due diligence reports required of underwriters, extensive lawyer work reports required of issuers, the nonexistence of legal counsel for underwriters and other practices with "Chinese characteristics" would never exist under in the United States. Yet, these practices are not based

[39] "Xin sanban xinpi jidai guifan: zhaochao wangnian baioshu diji cuowu binxiang" [New Third Board Needs Standardization: Low-Level Errors are Frequently Seen], *Xinhuawang*, April 12, 2011, http://news.xinhuanet.com/fortune/2011-04/12/c_121294589.htm.

on the rules promulgated under the Securities Law but were developed outside the law. In my view, these practices will very much continue to exist despite the recent share offering reform and amendment to the Securities Law.

The Chinese Model has its own features.[40] One key feature is the strong intervention of the regulator in the development of the securities market. This feature distinguishes the Chinese Model from the models that embody or make reference to the Washington Consensus, and the US model which features lower levels of governmental intervention.

If I have to predict what the Chinese Model will look like in the next ten years or so and whether it will converge with the US model, my prediction would be that the Chinese government will eventually cease to intervene in the securities market but the cessation will take a longer time than expected.

[40] The development of the securities market in China is different from her experience with property rights. As illustrated by Upham in Chapter 5, formal property law institutions did not exist when property rights were being developed in China. In contrast, the CSRC was explicitly given extensive authority over the approval of IPOs in the 1998 and 2005 Securities Law. In other words, bureaucratic control exerted by the CSRC is not illegal; instead, this control is grounded in black-letter law. The developmental trajectory of the Chinese securities market is also different from the developmental trajectory of Chinese corporate law. As illustrated by Milhaupt in Chapter 11, state capitalism in China has several distinct features, one of which is Party centrality. While Party centrality may be one of many features characterizing the development of the securities market in China, Party centrality plays a much more muted role. While the CSRC can be said to be an extension of the Chinese Communist Party's will, its regulation of the securities market has largely been technical. Therefore, the Chinese Communist Party's influence on the CSRC or on China's securities market is not as obvious as in other fields.

PART III

Revisiting the Beijing Consensus

9

Authoritarian Justice in China

Is There a "Chinese Model"?

BENJAMIN L. LIEBMAN*

Most recent Western popular and scholarly writing on legal reform in China has focused on two apparently contradictory trends. Since coming to power in 2012 China's new leadership has significantly curtailed the limits of permissible legal activism, highlighted most clearly by the detention and prosecution of numerous leading lawyers and academics. The Party-state has also increased oversight and control over legal education and has explicitly rejected the relevance of Western models of legality for China, including concepts such as judicial independence. At the same time, China's leadership has announced some of the most significant legal reforms in decades, in particular in the courts, and has staked its future legitimacy on its ability to fight corruption and to "govern the nation according to law" (Decision of the Third Plenary Session of the Eighteenth CCP Central Committee 2013, IX). The Decision issued by the Central Committee of the Communist Party following its Fourth Plenum in October 2014 reflects this tension, providing an extensive roadmap for reform while at the same time reaffirming political control over the legal system. The repeated emphasis on Party oversight in both the Communiqué issued immediately following the Plenum and in the more detailed Plenum Decision (Decision of the Fourth Plenary Session of the Eighteenth CCP Central Committee 2014, hereinafter "Plenum Decision")[1] has led many to question whether China's leadership is serious about legal reform and

* This chapter was researched and written with support from the Stanley and Judith Lubman Fund, the Peter Drut Faculty Research Fund, and the Madsen Family Faculty Research Fund, all at Columbia Law School.

1 "Xinhuashe: Zhonggong shibajie sizhong quanhui jueding quanwen" [Xinhua Agency: Full Text of the Decision of the Fourth Plenary Session of the Eighteenth CCP Central Committee], *Xinhuashe*, October 29, 2014. www.cunet.com.cn/gaozhao/HTML/212606.html.

whether significant reforms are possible given the political confines in which China's legal system, and in particular China's courts, exist.

Far less attention has been devoted to another emerging trend: the attempt to define a Chinese Model of legal development. Although officials and scholars in China have long written of China's efforts to construct a "socialist rule of law system,"[2] in the past most such writings were aimed at explaining why the Chinese legal system needed more time to develop or why China did not conform to or accept liberal Western paradigms.[3] Serious scholarly (or official) efforts at defining the uniqueness of China's approach to legal development or at identifying specific characteristics of China's approach were rare. In contrast, a number of recent scholarly efforts have sought to identify distinctive aspects of China's approach to legal development, particularly in the courts and dispute resolution.[4] Some official[5] accounts have likewise begun to argue that China has adopted a unique approach to legal development and have sought to identify key characteristics of China's approach. Some such claims also begin to develop a normative claim that the Chinese Model is better for China and may also be better for other developing countries. An emerging line of scholarly and official arguments in China seeks not only to reject Western legal models but also to construct a model that is better for China and, perhaps, for other developing countries.

This chapter examines recent trends in legal reform in China with a focus on identifying what may constitute a Chinese Model of legal development, particularly in the context of the courts. The evolution of China's courts over recent years challenges both Western rule of law development models and also some common understandings about the role of law in authoritarian systems. Recent developments highlight this

[2] Writing on the topic became prevalent in particular following the Fifteenth Party Congress's endorsement of the concept of "Socialist Rule of Law" in 1997 and the addition of the phrase "ruling the country according to law" to the Constitution in 1998. "Jiang Zemin zai zhongguo gongchandang di shiwu ci quanguo daibiao dahui shang de baogao" [Report of Jiang Zemin at the Fifteenth National Congress of the Communist Party of China], *Xinhuawang*, September 12, 1999, http://news.xinhuanet.com/zhengfu/2004-04/29/content_1447509.htm.

[3] Much Western writing on China likewise has focused on how China's legal system functions compared to other developing or developed legal systems.

[4] Xiong Qiuhong, "Sifa gaige zhong de falun wenti" [Methodological Questions in Judicial Reform], *Fazhi yu shehui fazhan* 6 (2014): 25; Hou Meng, "Zhongguo de sifa moshi: chuantong yu gaige" [The Chinese Judicial Model: Tradition and Reform], *Fashang yanjiu* 6 (2009): 59.

[5] I recognize that the line between what is official and what is scholarly is blurred, in particular as former legal scholars assume prominent official positions in the legal system. Nevertheless, I believe a general distinction can and should be drawn.

nonconformity and also provide insight into both the potential reach of China's legal reforms and their limitations. My goal is not to prove or disprove the singularity of the Chinese approach; rather, it is to highlight the ways in which China's recent and likely future legal development continues to draw on multiple sources. The uniqueness of China's approach, if any, is that it continues to embrace aspects of both Western liberal legality and China's own imperial and revolutionary legal traditions in the service of conventional goals of authoritarian legality, including social stability and political control.

I begin in Part I by providing a brief overview of the Plenum Decision and recent trends in court reform.[6] I then turn to discussing official and scholarly efforts to identify and define key aspects of a Chinese Model of rule of law. I also highlight important aspects of court development in China that these accounts overlook and that have been central to legal development in China since 1978. In Part II, I discuss how China's approach to legal and court development maps onto existing models of legal development in democratic and authoritarian regimes and discuss what, if anything, makes China's approach unusual or unique. I conclude in Part III by discussing the implications both for China and for efforts to conceptualize legal development more generally. I suggest that by focusing on centralized, top-down reforms, China may be turning away from reliance on flexibility and local experimentation that have contributed to the rapid development of the Chinese legal system in recent decades.

I Defining a Chinese Model of Legal Development

Since coming to power in late 2012, Xi Jinping has repeatedly embraced the concept of *fazhi zhongguo* (法治中国), translated by the official media as "Rule of Law China" but by many scholars as "rule by law China." Many within the Chinese legal community were initially optimistic about the potential for deepening legal reform. Such optimism dimmed in the wake of renewed emphasis on ideological oversight of legal institutions and law schools and the detention of numerous legal activists and academics. Nevertheless, signals also emerged that specific, targeted reforms

[6] As Yu Xiaohong has noted, courts are only one of many actors in the legal system. Procuratorates are of equal rank to the courts yet have attracted far less attention in English-language scholarship. Most reforms announced since the Fourth Plenum have focused on the courts, however, and China's Supreme People's Court appears to have moved much more quickly to begin reforms than have the Supreme People's Procuratorate or other legal institutions. Yu Xiaohong, "Judicial Empowerment within/out of the Political-Legal System in China?" (unpublished manuscript, 2014) (on file with the author).

were likely and possible, evidenced most clearly by the abolition of the Reeducation through Labor detention system in 2013 and the announcement of pilot court reform projects in Shanghai and five provinces in mid-2014.

It was not until the Third Plenum in 2013 and, more importantly, the Fourth Plenum Decision in October 2014 that the phrase *fazhi zhongguo* began to develop specific content. The Fourth Plenum Decision has been analyzed in depth elsewhere, and thus I do not provide a comprehensive overview of its contents here. In the context of the courts, however, the Plenum Decision makes clear that reform is possible but that reforms are not designed to alter the fundamental authority of courts. Courts and the legal system remain subject to Party leadership. The Plenum Decision and concurrent remarks from Xi Jinping make clear that a key goal of future reforms is to restrain power, but that such restraint will be exercised internally by the Party and not by granting new powers to legal institutions.

The focus on continued Party oversight and lack of new authority for the courts has drawn headlines in the West. Yet the Plenum Decision also provides a roadmap for an extensive range of technical and functional reforms. The cumulative effect of the reforms has the potential to make significant improvements to the legal system. The Plenum Decision aims to address problems in enforcement and in filing of cases, with courts no longer engaging in substantive review prior to filing.[7] Adjudication of cases and enforcement are to be separated, with the intent of placing the trial at the center of court adjudication.[8] Local protectionism will be addressed through the creation of "circuit courts" under the Supreme People's Court (the SPC) and potentially through cross-regional courts.[9]

The Plenum Decision also speaks of restricting interference in court decision making, both external (from officials and entities outside the courts) and internal (intervention by court leaders or superior judges into cases or judges seeking input from court superiors). The Plenum Decision appears moderately to expand the limited definition of judicial independence set forth in Article 126 of the Constitution. Whereas the Constitution speaks of courts being free from interference from any "administrative organ, public organization or individual," the Plenum

[7] "Xinhuashe: Zhonggong shibajie sizhong quanhui jueding quanwen" [Decision of the Fourth Plenary Session of the 18th CCP Central Committee], IV.2.

[8] Ibid. [9] Ibid.

Decision suggests that interference from Party leaders and entities is also impermissible.[10] Reforms will also focus on certain substantive issues. In criminal cases reforms will be designed to standardize the application of criminal law, addressing concerns about discrepancies in sentences across jurisdictions. In administrative cases defendant government departments will be required to appear in court.[11]

In other areas the Plenum Decision is more reserved. The Plenum Decision endorses judicial transparency but also makes clear that this transparency is limited, focusing on making the end product of the judicial process transparent, not the process itself. The Plenum Decision also speaks of ensuring standardized media reporting on the courts, suggesting that courts will continue to control media coverage of legal proceedings.[12] Although the Plenum Decision calls for separation of judicial functions (which include those of both the courts and the procuratorate) from other Party-state functions, there is also heavy emphasis on oversight of judicial personnel. The Plenum Decision thus speaks of fighting corruption, holding individual judges accountable for their decisions, and strengthening supervision systems within courts.[13]

In the months following the Fourth Plenum the Party's Central Committee and the SPC moved quickly to begin to implement a range of new reforms. Five sets of reforms announced or enhanced in the months following the Fourth Plenum appear to be most significant. First, building on pilot reforms announced before the Fourth Plenum, courts have begun to reform their appointment and finance systems. The SPC has set a target of reducing the number of individuals holding the rank of judge by 61 percent. The goal is to have those classified as judges focus on hearing cases and to separate administrative roles in the court system from adjudicatory roles. Concurrently, court finances and appointments are being centralized at the provincial level in an attempt to reduce local

10 Some senior officials within China's court system have articulated this argument; whether the Constitution will subsequently be amended remains to be seen. As noted below, such a change only targets direct intervention, not the myriad of other ways in which judges are influenced by Party guidelines and political leaders.

11 Other aspects of the reforms that are also important but less directly affect the courts include a renewed focus on constitutional supervision by the Standing Committee of the National People's Congress and the encouragement of public interest litigation by procuratorates.

12 "Xinhuashe: Zhonggong shibajie sizhong quanhui jueding quanwen" [Decision of the Fourth Plenary Session of the Eighteenth CCP Central Committee], IV.6.

13 Ibid.

government influence on the courts.[14] Intermediate and high court judges will largely be chosen from lower-level courts, with some new judges being selected from legally trained personnel outside the court system.

Second, courts have begun to reform their case filing systems by removing substantive review of claims from the case filing process. Under the reform, which began in May 2015, the filing of cases is to become a purely administrative action. In the past many cases, in particular administrative cases against state actors, were rejected at the case filing stage. Under the new reforms a greater number and percentage of cases should be decided on their merits. Court filing offices are to inform litigants if they are missing any documents required to initiate a case, but the filing office may not review the merits of litigants' claims.[15] Filing offices must also produce written reasons for their rejection of any cases.

Third, the General Office of the Central Committee of the CCP and General Office of the State Council issued a notice banning government and Party officials from interfering in court decision making.[16] Courts and judges are required to record any acts of interference and to report interference to superior courts and to Party political-legal committees. Some have expressed concern that courts may be reluctant to record interference. Yet the most important effect of the new rule may be the message it sends to local officials that interfering in court decision making is no longer permissible.[17]

Fourth, the SPC has announced experiments with cross-jurisdictional courts and has created SPC tribunals in Shenzhen and Shenyang. The SPC tribunals hear cases that otherwise would go to the SPC.[18] One of the tribunals' important roles appears to be to resolve some cases away from Beijing – most notably those that could result in petitioning. The

14 Supreme People's Court, "Guanyu quanmian shenhua renmin fayuan gaige de yijian" [Opinion on Fully Deepening Reforms to the People's Courts], effective February 4, 2015, www.chinacourt.org/law/detail/2015/02/id/148096.shtml.

15 Luo Sha, "Li'an dengji zhi gaige shouyue quanguo fayuan li'an chao baiwan" [In the First Month of the Reform to the Case Filing System the Number of Case Filings Nationwide Exceeded 1 Million], *Legal China*, June 4, 2015, www.china.com.cn/legal/lawyer/2015-06/04/content_35741410.htm.

16 "Penalties for Party Officials' Interference in Court Decision Making," *Xinhuawang*, March 30, 2015, http://news.xinhuanet.com/legal/2015-03/30/c_1114812232.htm.

17 The rule may also make it easier for local officials to refuse requests by third parties that they interfere in pending cases.

18 Hou Meng, "Zuigao fayuan xunhui fating: hequ hecong" [The Circuit Tribunal of the Supreme People's Court: What Course to Follow], *Beida falü pinglun* 16 (2015).

cross-jurisdictional courts that have been established exist at the intermediate court level and generally hear administrative cases.

Fifth, the SPC has implemented plans to increase the quantity of publicly available court opinions. The SPC has created a centralized database of court judgments,[19] with more than 22 million court judgments, mostly from 2014 and 2015, and thousands of new cases added daily.

Yet not all reforms are transparent. In February 2015 the SPC made public a Five-Year reform plan.[20] The following month media reports noted the existence of a general reform plan for the legal system, being drafted by the Politburo's Leadership Small Group on Legal Reform. That plan, which is likely to be the most important policy document guiding the implementation of the reforms announced at the Fourth Plenum, appears to have been drafted in secrecy. It has not been made public.[21]

Official media and Party journals have repeatedly applauded the Plenum Decision as a breakthrough for legal development in China. In the words of one official *People's Daily* commentary, China has entered a "new stage" of legal development.[22] Drawing a distinction from prior legal reform efforts, commentators have noted that the present effort will go beyond the construction of law and legal institutions and will focus on legal implementation, fairness, efficiency, and ensuring that all people respect the law. Commentators link the development of China's legal system to economic development, repeating phrases such as "a modern nation must first be a rule of law nation"[23] and that further legal reform is needed to ensure economic development and social stability.

[19] "Zhongguo Caipan Wenshu Wang" [China Judgements Online], http://wenshu.court.gov.cn/.

[20] Supreme People's Court, "Guanyu quanmian shenhua renmin fayuan gaige de yijian" [Opinion on Fully Deepening Reforms to the People's Courts].

[21] "Zhongban Guoban yinfa shishi fangan guanche luoshi sizhong quanhui jueding bushu jinyibu shenhua sifa tizhi he shehui tizhi gaige" [The General Office of the Central Committee of the Communist Party of China and the General Office of the State Council issued the Implementation Plan to Thoroughly Implement the Fourth Plenum Decision to Plan for the Further Deepening of Reforms of the Judicial and Social Systems], *Renminwang*, April 10, 2015, http://military.people.com.cn/n/2015/0410/c172467-26822645.html.

[22] Ren Zhongping, "Rang fazhi wei xiandai zhongguo huhang – lun quanmian tuijin yifa zhiguo" [Let Rule of Law Guard Modern China – Discussing Fully Pushing Forward Rule of Law], *Renmin Ribao*, December 3, 2014, http://paper.people.com.cn/rmrb/html/2014-12/03/nw.D110000renmrb_20141203_6-01.htm. "Ren Zhongping" is a name used by *People's Daily* to connote official commentaries.

[23] Ibid.

Although such arguments may resonate with Western scholarship linking law and development, such commentaries also explicitly reject Western models.[24]

Of more significance for this volume have been efforts to articulate the specific characteristics of the Chinese approach to legal development. Although there does not appear to be a comprehensive summary of what characteristics the Party-state conceives of as unique to China's approach, consistent themes have emerged following the Plenum. Thus, for example, commentators have noted that a key component of China's legal system is Party leadership and also legalization of Party rules and governance mechanisms.[25] Party leadership is defined as the essential prerequisite to the Chinese Model of rule of law.[26] The Party oversees the legal system, but there will be greater focus on legalization within the Party. Party rules thus are to be understood as part of the Chinese legal system.[27] (See also Fu's discussion in the context of the anticorruption campaign, Chapter 10.) The focus on Party rules also helps to explain how the Plenum's promise that all individuals and entities will be subject to law is to be carried out: as scholars in China have explained, in the context of the Communist Party this will be done internally, by self-restraint, rather than by external restraint through courts or other legal institutions.

Official explanations have also endorsed a link between China's legal tradition and contemporary law. In parallel with Xi Jinping's renewed emphasis on Confucian values, legal commentators have argued that China's own legal and moral tradition serves as an important foundation

[24] Commentators also retrospectively make the argument that in the reform era economic growth has been strongest in periods in which the Party-state has emphasized legal reform. Thus it is exactly because China has embraced rule-of-law principles that it has enjoyed economic success and social stability. Such arguments are a reversal of Western scholarship, which has argued that China challenges the "rights hypothesis" linking economic development to strong legal protections for property rights. Ibid.

[25] Ren Zhongping, "Rang fazhi wei xiandai zhongguo huhang – lun quanmian tuijin yifa zhiguo."

[26] Hu Yunteng, "Quanmian tuijin yifa zhiguo shenhua sifa tizhi gaige" [Deepen Reforms to the Judicial System in order to Fully Push Forward Rule of Law], *Zhongguo ganbu xuexi wang*, November 6, 2014, http://study.ccln.gov.cn/gcjw/zz/127570.shtml.

[27] This is not a new concept. See, for example, Shigong Jiang, "Written and Unwritten Constitutions: A New Approach to the Study of Constitutional Government in China," *Modern China* 36 (2010): 12. The Plenum Decision is also understood as evidence of the Party's internal legalization. Detailed accounts of how the document was drafted have described a painstaking process, overseen by Xi Jinping, which resembles legislative drafting, with two drafts reviewed and discussed by the Politburo and three drafts reviewed and discussed by the Politburo Standing Committee.

for China's contemporary legal system.[28] Such accounts should not be overstated; as Wenxian Zhang has noted, the most important base for China's approach to constructing a legal system continues to be China's own experience.[29] China also continues to borrow from the West and to draw on the experience of other socialist systems. Nevertheless, the explicit embrace of China's imperial legal traditions in official post-Plenum discussions as a foundation for China's model of socialist legality and as a precedent for rule of law without democracy appears to be novel. The uniqueness of China's approach is thus defined as legal development that draws on multiple sources: China's experiences since 1949, China's own legal traditions, socialist legal models, and selective borrowing from Western systems.[30]

Official accounts have mostly praised the Plenum Decision without significant questioning or have made reference to the uniqueness of China's approach only in general terms. In contrast, some Chinese scholars have begun to try to describe a Chinese Model of rule of law in more specific terms.[31] There is no single argument, and no scholar can be said to be fully representative. Thus, for example, scholars have argued that the Chinese Model of rule of law encompasses restraint of public power through a combination of Communist Party self-restraint, institutional design, and public supervision. The claim appears to be that this approach entails greater restraint of public power than has generally been found in other authoritarian systems and that restraint of public power is possible even in a system in which courts lack the power of judicial review. Continuity with tradition is also recognized, mirroring the recent shift in the official legitimacy narrative toward the embrace of China's Confucian tradition. The scholarly argument goes a step further than the official account, arguing that China's approach to supervision – relying on Party-state organs to supervise each other – is also consistent with China's own historical approach to supervision.

Other aspects of the Chinese Model articulated by scholars include explicit recognition that courts are not the only vehicle for delivering justice and are not the central mechanism for dispute resolution. Instead,

[28] Hu, "Quanmian tuijin yifa zhiguo shenhua sifa tizhi gaige."

[29] Zhang Wenxian, "Jianshe zhongguo tese shehui zhuyi fazhi tixi" [Constructing a Socialist Rule of Law System with Special Chinese Characteristics], *Faxue Yanjiu* 6 (2014): 13.

[30] Western scholars have long made similar arguments regarding the multiple sources of China's contemporary approach to legal reform.

[31] Much of this discussion draws on presentations at the International Forum on Rule of Law hosted by the Chinese Academy of Social Sciences in November 2014.

the state plays a more active role in preventing disputes and resolving social conflict before cases arise, with only a portion left over for court adjudication. This proactive Party-state role in managing disputes – not sitting back and allowing courts to play a neutral role – is necessary, it is argued, because ordinary people do not have the patience to wait for the court system to resolve disputes. China's approach to managing society and conflict thus is less law-centered than in the West, relying instead on Party entities to resolve conflict alongside the courts. Implicit in such accounts is the argument that both approaches are equally valid. Often left unsaid is the fact that significant coercion is involved in state efforts to manage disputes, evidenced in recent years by new restrictions on petitioning and the increased use of criminal sanctions to target petitioners who refuse to accept state offers of compensation.

Similarly, some scholars contend that under the Chinese Model individual rights must yield in some cases to concerns about social stability, that rights will be protected at a different level than in the West, and that stability and economic development are preconditions for creating a law-based system, not consequences that follow from legal development. Scholars also argue that China has embraced a form of judicial independence that is by design more limited than in Western democracies. In practice this means that judges continue to focus on a range of extra-legal factors in deciding cases, including the potential for unrest, the desire to appease individual litigants, as well as Party policies more generally. For some scholars these claims appear to be descriptive accounts of how the Chinese system functions: the social impact of decisions at times trumps legal correctness. For others such claims are normative claims that an approach that prioritizes stability and economic development is most appropriate for China.

Efforts to articulate a Chinese Model of rule of law remain relatively new and under-developed and at times beg the question of how "rule of law" is defined. There is obvious circularity in stating that rule of law in China is defined by Party leadership without engaging the question of whether Party oversight undermines the ability of legal institutions to follow the law. Although the Plenum Decision speaks of restricting the influence of individual Party-state officials, nothing in the document restricts the ability of the Party itself to intervene in the courts. Some have noted that the Plenum Decision may actually legitimize the continued involvement of Party political-legal committees in court decision making.[32] The reforms

[32] The focus on greater reliance on Party rules suggests the possibility that such influence may be subject to greater rules, not that Party oversight will decrease.

suggest the possibility of greater separation of court roles from those of other Party-state actors. Yet the reforms do little to change the reality of interconnectedness between courts and other Party-state actors, and in particular ties between court leaders and Party leadership at each level of the Party-state. Court leaders at each level of the government interact with Party leadership in a range of contexts, and norms governing the appropriate response to sensitive cases generally run deep. Court leaders and individual judges need little instruction regarding how to handle cases touching on Party-state interests.

Similarly, defining China's approach to rule of law as recognizing that law must consider and in some cases yield to "social effects" – meaning stability concerns – raises questions about what, if any, rules govern when law is applied or ignored. Scholars within China, for understandable reasons, have also not engaged the question of what separates what is legal in China from what Hualing Fu has described as "extra-legal" or "extra-extra legal."[33]

Nevertheless, recent scholarly efforts are important for their attempts to identify what is unique about China's legal development path and to engage and challenge Western literature and models. Implicit in some such arguments is also a shift from arguing that China needs more time to develop robust Western-style legal institutions to an argument that such Western institutions would be problematic given China's historical traditions and political environment. Chinese commentators are not alone in basing arguments for particular legal development models on assumptions regarding the ideal-type of political system in which such development occurs. Scholars making such arguments also are not necessarily seeking to justify Communist Party rule. Instead they are focusing on where there is space for development given the fact of such rule.

A related line of post-Plenum discourse is the emergence of arguments that China's model may be helpful for other developing countries. Thus scholars, officials, and other commentators have articulated arguments that reject Western liberal models of law reform and that assert that the Chinese Model may be useful to other developing legal systems. Official accounts make such arguments more implicitly. Such arguments run in parallel to efforts to boost China's role in training lawyers and legal scholars from around the world, to efforts to make "legal foreign relations"

[33] See also Hualing Fu, "Politicized Challenges, Depoliticized Responses: Political Monitoring in China's Transitions," University of Hong Kong Faculty of Law Research Paper No. 2013/014 (University of Hong Kong, 2013), http://papers.ssrn.com/sol3/papers.cfm?abstract_id=2250073##. Also Fu, Chapter 10.

a key element of China's foreign policy,[34] and to nascent efforts to assist with legal reform in other developing countries. China may not yet be in the rule of law export business, but some steps are being taken to ensure that China's experiences are shared with other developing or authoritarian legal systems.

My goal in this chapter is not to engage in detailed discussion of the merits of claims regarding the singularity (or lack thereof) of China's approach. Omissions from recent accounts of China's legal development may be more important than the substance of such accounts. As one commentator has noted, the Plenum Decision raises questions about whether key characteristics of China's legal development in recent decades – and arguably key factors explaining many of the successes of legal reform – will continue to predominate in the future.[35] A key aspect of China's approach to legal reform since 1978 has been the embrace of flexibility and local experimentation.[36] In contrast, the Plenum document places a much greater emphasis on top-down legal development. Experiments will continue – and are under way in select localities in the courts – but central authorities appear to be playing a greater role in overseeing such experiments than in the past.

The reliance on bottom-up experimentation in the reform era has not been problem-free: diversity of practice and innovation has also given rise to inconsistencies, short-term solutions, extra-legal behavior, and local protectionism.[37] In some cases local experiments appeared primarily

[34] Gu Zhaomin, "Zhongguo kaizhan falü waijiao de xianzhuang yu fazhan qushi yanjiu" [Research on the current State and Development Trends of China's Initiation of Legal Foreign Relations], *Xiandai faxue* 4 (2013): 173; Zhang Wenxian and Gu Zhaomin, "Zhongguo falü waijiao de lilun yu shixian" [The Theory and Practice of China's Legal Foreign Relations], *Guoji Zhanwang* 2 (2013): 1. The term "legal foreign relations," or 法律外交, generally refers to efforts to boost interactions between legal officials and academics in China and those elsewhere, with the apparent goal both of increasing knowledge of Chinese law abroad and of shaping international law.

[35] Xiong, "Sifa gaige zhong de falun wenti." Scholars in China have criticized both the speed and the scope of the reforms. Some have argued that reforms are being implemented too quickly, will be difficult for local authorities to implement, and fail to take into account local conditions. Others have criticized the reforms for the focus on the courts, not the relationship between courts and other institutions. Scholars have also criticized the decision for failing to address a range of other problems in the legal system, including lack of specialization within the judiciary, the failure to separate small claims from larger claims, and the evaluation systems for judges.

[36] Benjamin L. Liebman, "A Return to Populist Legality? Historical Legacies and Legal Reform," in *Mao's Invisible Hand*, Elizabeth Perry and Sebastian Heilmann (eds.) (Cambridge, MA: Harvard University Asia Center Press, 2011), 165.

[37] For a detailed discussion, see Cui, Chapter 4.

designed to advance the careers of individual officials. The emphasis on centralization in the Plenum Decision may reflect a desire to redress problems through greater emphasis on uniformity and legal consistency. The Plenum Decision may also reflect a belief that experimentation is less needed than in the past to fill the gaps left by unclear legislation. Yet there is also a sense that Party-state leaders see a need to take control in order to speed up legal development; there is frustration with the problems that continue to plague legal institutions in China. It remains to be seen whether a shift toward a more top-down model of legal reform will prove effective not only for ensuring greater oversight over legal institutions but also for building public confidence in such institutions.

Also missing from most post-Plenum accounts of proposed reforms is discussion of the role of populism in the Chinese legal system. Although some commentators have interpreted the Plenum Decision as marking a shift away from populist legality, these arguments appear primarily to reflect hopes about where the Chinese legal system will go, not assessments of the effects of changes under way. Tension between populism and professionalism continues to be present in the Plenum Decision, reflecting the authoritarian populist legality model that has characterized Chinese legal development throughout much of the reform era.[38] The Plenum Decision continues to embrace China's mass line tradition, speaking of the need to continue to protect the position of "the people" (Decision, I) while at the same time seeking to introduce modest new procedural rules concerning popular participation. The Plenum Decision explicitly endorses a continued role for the petitioning system even as it seeks to create new rules regulating petitioning to the courts. The Plenum document likewise speaks of a continued and perhaps expanded role for people's assessors (lay people who sit alongside judges in some cases); at the same time it restricts the role people's assessors play to determining facts, not law.[39] A continued commitment to populist legality is also reflected in the focus on the social consequences of legal decisions and on calls for popular participation in the legal system.

The continued emphasis on popular participation and populism may not be pernicious. Some of the most important pre-Plenum reforms in China came from local experiments in areas such as transparency, public access, and public participation that mixed populism and legal

[38] Liebman, "A Return to Populist Legality."

[39] Reforms announced since the Plenum Decision have called for expanded use of people's assessors.

reform.[40] Such reforms have been particularly noteworthy in Henan, where populism has in recent years been embraced to curb abuses in the courts and as a mechanism for boosting popular support for and thus the authority of the courts. Such efforts may continue to be crucial to building public support for legal institutions, perhaps as or more important as top-down reform. Yet it is unclear whether such forms of legal innovation will continue to be possible in a new era of centrally led reform.

The Plenum Decision similarly does not address other tensions that have characterized legal development throughout much of the reform era: tension between politics and technical ability, judicial restraint and activism, substantive and procedural justice, social effects and legal effects and between the need for short-term solutions and long-term reform.[41] Over time how the Party-state implements the scores of specific reform items in the Plenum Decision and in subsequently announced reform documents will provide insight into what Party-state leaders view as key aspects of China's approach to legal reform. The Plenum Decision reflects a long-term goal of improving the efficiency and fairness of the legal system subject to continued Party control, suggesting recognition that improving fairness is important to maintaining stability. Improving the quality of judges, placing greater emphasis on court-centered dispute resolution, and increasing the accountability of all actors in the legal system are all steps to be taken in pursuit of this goal. The Party-state has made clear, however, that this renewed emphasis on legal reform does not mean that all state actions will be subject to legal regulation or procedures, in particular when the Party-state is responding to perceived threats.

II Nonconvergence and the "Beijing Consensus"

The content and future path of legal development in China remain contested, both within the Party-state and in Chinese society. Despite the efforts of scholars to begin to define key aspects of a Chinese Model of legal development, it remains far too early to declare the creation of a "Beijing consensus" regarding a Chinese approach to law reform. China's experience with legal reform may, nevertheless, contribute to understandings of existing models of legal development. In this section I ask how

[40] Benjamin L. Liebman, "Leniency in Chinese Criminal Law? Everyday Justice in Henan," *Berkeley Journal of International Law* 33 (2015): 153; Benjamin L. Liebman, "Legal Reform: China's Law-Stability Paradox," *Daedalus* 143 (2014): 96.

[41] Xiong, "Sifa gaige zhong de falun wenti."

China's experience of court development may inform or be affected by three models of court and legal development: the often idealized American model; a model of judging most often equated with civil law countries of continental Europe and Japan; and models of courts in authoritarian systems. My discussion of these models is necessarily stylized and incomplete; my goal is not to critique the models but rather to question the uniqueness of China's legal development.

The American ideal-type of independent courts with individual judges at the center, courts playing a crucial role in adjudicating and governing, and courts deciding crucial issues of the day has often appeared to be the principal benchmark used to assess legal reform in China. This was particularly the case in the late 1980s and 1990s, due to the predominance of US actors in legal reform projects in China and to the influence of Chinese scholars trained in the United States. Comparisons tended to focus on the model of independent judges with life tenure that characterize federal judges in the United States. Little attention was paid to state courts, where most judges are elected and lack life tenure – and where most cases in the United States are filed and heard.

Implicit in many comparisons between the US and Chinese legal systems was the hope (and in some cases the belief) that over time the Chinese system would converge with, or at least move in the direction of, the US model. The project of "exporting the pursuit of happiness" has been critiqued elsewhere.[42] Today it is clear that whatever form China's legal development is taking, it is not moving toward the American model of strongly independent and authoritative courts. Nevertheless, China has drawn on the US system in many substantive areas, from securities and corporate law to property law to criminal procedure (and even for a brief period in the early 2000s in constitutional law). It is in substantive law and technical matters, not institutional design, that China appears to have made the most movement toward Western models.[43]

The American model appears most influential today as a foil for those who reject reforms that might move China more in the direction of Western democratic legal systems. Indeed it appears that the only people who believe that the American model has any chance of spreading to China are those on the left in China who view the American model as a threat to the

[42] William P. Alford, "Exporting the 'Pursuit of Happiness,'" *Harvard Law Review* 113 (2000): 1677.

[43] There are some exceptions. For example, China's decision to grant jurisdiction over administrative cases to ordinary courts appears to have drawn from the US example.

survival of the Communist Party and thus to stability and development in China. Hence we have seen repeated discussion of the danger that Western concepts such as "judicial independence" pose to China. Concern about the potential influence of such Western concepts help explain renewed calls for ideological oversight over judges, in particular after the Arab Spring.[44] Yet concerns that Chinese judges will gradually become subject to the influence of Western-style judicial independence appear vastly overstated given the weak authority of Chinese courts and that Chinese judges lack even the modest amount of independence that has been a prerequisite to the development of court challenges to authoritarian regimes elsewhere.

The second model against which court and legal reform in China is at times measured is a model associated with continental systems and Japan. In the model, judges in such systems serve as neutral arbiters, applying law to the facts before them. In contrast to the American system of strongly independent and political judges, continental judges are often characterized as being fair and independent rule-applying bureaucrats. Courts in such systems often (at least in theory) eschew political decisions, with political matters left to administrative tribunals or resolved through adjudication of abstract norms, not individual cases.[45] Distinctions between the American model and the continental model are overstated; judges in many continental jurisdictions are understood today to be both fiercely independent and deeply involved in resolving political questions. Yet it is the stylized model, not the actual practice of diverse continental courts, which has had the largest impact in Chinese academic discourse.

[44] Although initially perceived as an example of the US's desire and power to export its institutions abroad, the Arab Spring has come to be understood by some on the left in China as showing the failure of the American legal development model. One recent account cites Egypt as an example of how the export of American-style legal institutions has led to mass killings and chaos. See Zhi Zhenfeng, "Fazhi zhuanxing de 'guojia nengli beilun'" [The "Paradox of State Ability" in Rule of Law Transitions], in *Governing the Nation According to Law and Rule of Law China* (Chinese Academy of Social Sciences, 2014): 92–93. Concerns about Western influence are also manifest in China's new law regulating foreign nongovernment nonprofit organizations, which has the potential to restrict severely both foreign NGO activity in China and academic exchanges between China and other countries.

[45] As many have noted, continental European practice has moved away from this model as a result of European integration, the creation of a European legal architecture, and the growing importance of domestic constitutional courts.

The continental model has received much less attention than the American model in China as a possible end-point for judicial reform.[46] Nevertheless, aspects of the reforms announced in the Plenum Decision can be understood as moving China toward this model: emphasis on courts that apply the law to the facts before them fairly, transparency, and continual evaluation of judges to make sure they do their jobs correctly. Likewise, the Plenum Decision can be read as reflecting a commitment to fair and neutral courts that decide individual cases, not policy or political matters, and that play only a limited role in checking the actions of other state actors.

Chinese judges do in some cases act in ways that strongly resemble judges elsewhere. Judges in China are generally understood to apply the law, not create new law. Yet there are numerous examples of courts innovating to create new legal rules in China – as in both continental and common law systems. Likewise Chinese judges' practice of considering the "social effects" of decisions may actually bring them into line with courts elsewhere that have long been understood to be influenced by political factors, even if they do not acknowledge such influences. Chinese judges' roles are also increasingly being shaped by their own goals and understanding of the appropriate role of judges, not just what Party-state officials tell them are their roles.

Despite some similarities with judging in established democracies, China's legal development has the greatest potential to contribute to literature on courts in authoritarian systems. Chinese scholarship, largely influenced by the US ideal-type, almost entirely overlooks such models: none of the scholarly accounts that I have encountered place China's model in the context of past or present systems of authoritarian justice elsewhere.[47] Yet literature on authoritarian systems has long noted the possibility of significant development of courts in authoritarian systems.

[46] This is not due to lack of trying by European scholars and governments. Although most European-funded law reform programs began later than those funded by US foundations and the US government, European efforts have nevertheless been extensive.

[47] This is almost certainly due in part to the sensitivity of the topic and the fact that China does not acknowledge that it is an authoritarian system. Chinese scholars have noted that Singapore may serve as a model for China's court development and have argued that the experiences of Korea and Taiwan show the value of sustained periods of one Party rule as a precondition to developing a legal system. Yet such accounts largely ignore the literature on authoritarian legality more generally, and often focus more on arguments for and against democracy, not the functioning of courts in such systems.

Literature on courts in authoritarian systems tends to focus on two broad questions: what roles do courts play in such systems, and to what degree (and under what circumstances) do courts in authoritarian systems challenge or serve as checks on other political institutions? The first question has received extensive attention in literature on Chinese courts in recent years.[48] The second question, in contrast, remains largely inapplicable in China and has received much less attention.

In many respects courts in China play roles similar to those played by courts in other authoritarian systems.[49] Greater use of courts and the development of more competent courts in the reform era have served Party-state goals of economic development and addressing principal-agent problems. Chinese courts have likewise played supporting roles in furthering the Party-state's interest in social stability. Emphasis on court development in the reform era is also part of the Party-state's effort to build a legitimacy narrative that relies on rule-based governance. Social stability, legitimacy, and facilitating economic development have all been recognized as goals of authoritarian legal systems elsewhere.[50]

Existing literature on authoritarian courts has also noted prior attempts to construct legal systems that separate out political from nonpolitical cases and has detailed the roles courts may play within authoritarian systems. For example, one study of the courts in Spain under dictatorship noted that courts were able to develop a division between political and nonpolitical cases.[51] Courts were able to decide most ordinary cases fairly, while political cases were handled with different procedures or in different tribunals. A modest amount of writing has described legal systems in other authoritarian systems in similar terms. Some have suggested that China's legal system may be developing along a similar track, with routine cases handled by increasingly competent and fair courts, while political cases

[48] Liebman, "Leniency in Chinese Criminal Law"; Rachel E. Stern, *Environmental Litigation in China: A Study in Political Ambivalence* (Cambridge: Cambridge University Press, 2014); Yu, "Judicial Empowerment within/out of the Political-Legal System in China?"

[49] There are, of course, a wide range of authoritarian legal systems.

[50] For general discussion, see Baogang He and Mark E. Warren, "Authoritarian Deliberation: The Deliberative Turn in Chinese Political Development," *Perspectives of Politics* 9 (2011): 269; Tom Ginsburg and Tamir Moustafa (eds.), *Rule by Law: the Politics of Courts in Authoritarian Regimes* (New York: Cambridge University Press, 2008); Hilton L. Root and Karen May, "Judicial Systems and Authoritarian Transitions," *The Pakistan Development Review* 45 (2006): 1301.

[51] Jose J. Toharia, "Judicial Independence in an Authoritarian Regime: The Case of Contemporary Spain," *Law and Society Review* 9 (1975): 475.

result in extensive Party-state intervention in the courts or are handled outside the formal legal system.[52]

Yet conceptualizing cases in China as political/sensitive or routine/nonsensitive makes little sense. The millions of cases in Chinese courts each year mean that large numbers of cases are decided by the judge or judges trying the case without direct interference; it would be impossible for court or political leaders to intervene in most cases. But the scope of what is political, or sensitive, in China, remains large and constantly shifting. The scope includes not just what would be recognized as political cases in other authoritarian systems but also cases that touch on important economic interests, cases with the potential for escalation or unrest, and even cases in which a single individual threatens to protest. Cases in China may also be subject to different rules because of the mere possibility that the case could become sensitive in the future. Distinguishing between explicitly political cases, where court norms dictate that they adopt flexible interpretations of the law or ignore the law entirely, and cases where courts come under pressure from Party-state officials or those with connections to officials for other reasons, is difficult. We are left, instead, with an intuitive notion that in China the scope of sensitive or political cases appears larger than in other authoritarian systems, but with little empirical support for such a claim.

Chinese courts are both weak political actors and are extremely political. Chinese courts appear to play little role in resolving what might be thought of as political questions in other jurisdictions. In contrast to many courts in both democratic and authoritarian systems, Chinese courts virtually never decide cases touching on policy or political issues. Courts facing such questions either refuse to accept cases or simply never resolve the issue. The degree to which Chinese courts avoid deciding cases touching on political or policy issues appears unusual. This inaction reflects the fact that Chinese courts are weak political actors; courts do not dare touch questions that could be conceived of as political or policy questions. Yet Chinese courts' refusal or inability to resolve such questions does not reflect a move toward becoming nonpolitical actors that focus on legal questions. Instead, the aversion to resolving political questions reflects the fact that courts are embedded in the Chinese political system. Chinese courts have a clear understanding of their own limited roles; this

[52] As Par Cassel commented at a presentation of this chapter, this distinction also has antecedents in Chinese legal history in the different treatment of Palace Memorials regarding cases, which went straight to the emperor, and more routine disputes.

understanding leads them to avoid a range of policy or political questions that courts elsewhere routinely resolve. The fact that Chinese courts are highly politicized and remain an instrument of Party-state governance leads to an aversion to resolving or even considering political or policy issues.

The second question concerning the role of courts in authoritarian systems that has attracted extensive academic discussion in recent years is what factors or conditions lead courts in authoritarian systems to challenge or develop checks on other political actors. This literature, which largely focuses on high courts, demonstrates that functional and sometimes independent courts can coexist with authoritarian systems and that developing a legal system is often a rational choice for authoritarian leaders.[53] China does not fit easily into this framework: there is little evidence of China's SPC assuming such a role.

Most literature on court development in authoritarian systems equates court development with increased court authority or power. This focus is consistent with writing on Western systems, which has focused on increased judicialization, often as the result of political fragmentation and greater emphasis on rights protection, as an indicator of court development.[54] In China, in contrast, the central question facing the courts is not whether they can expand their authority in ways that allow them to challenge or serve as checks on other political institutions or resolve a wider range of policy questions. The central question facing courts is whether they can expand their ability to handle routine, non-sensitive, cases without external interference. The Plenum Decision hints at a desire to reduce the scope of such intervention with the creation of a recording and reporting system for impermissible interference, but there is unlikely to be any formal guidance as to how to distinguish permissible from impermissible interference.

Over time the ability of Chinese courts to act fairly and freely without external pressure in routine cases in China may be a greater indicator of China's ability to create a sustainable form of authoritarian legality than the ability to challenge or restrain other state actors. Court development

[53] For general discussion of the role of courts in authoritarian systems, see Tamir Moustafa, "Law and Courts in Authoritarian Regimes," *Annual Review of Law and Social Science* 10 (2014): 281; Ginsburg and Moustafa, *Rule by Law*; C. Neal Tate and Stacia L. Haynie, "Authoritarianism and the Functions of Courts: A Time Series Analysis of the Philippine Supreme Court 1961–1987," *Law & Society Review* 27 (1993): 707.

[54] John Ferejohn, "Judicializing Politics, Politicizing Law," *Law and Contemporary Problems* 65 (2002): 41.

in China cannot be measured in terms of the ability of courts to restrain other Party-state actors. Increased judicialization is not happening in China and is not a goal of Party-state court reform.

Recognizing that China does not fit easily into existing frameworks for understanding court development leads to a different set of questions. What are the sources of court development in China? How should court reform be assessed in a system in which increased authority or power is not a goal of court reform and in which court reform is a goal in itself, not a method for achieving other goals? Do the roles played by Chinese courts differ significantly from those of courts in other systems, democratic or authoritarian? Evaluating court development in China is difficult in part because the usual metrics used to assess court evolution – including willingness to challenge political authority, greater emphasis on rights protection, and greater respect for court judgments by other political actors – are not apparent in China. Similarly, rising caseloads tell us little about the roles courts actually play.

My aim in this chapter is not to answer these questions. Instead, my goal is to suggest that understanding the role of courts and the meaning of court development in China requires focusing less on what courts do not or cannot do and more on the roles they actually play. Examining key features of the Chinese system through the experience of everyday justice suggests key aspects of court evolution in China. Some features have been mentioned above: emphasis on flexibility and experimentation; the influence of populism; social stability concerns; and social effects. Courts at times operate in the shadow of protest and violence.[55] Courts innovate not to expand their own power but to insulate themselves from criticism, from the public and from Party-state superiors. The Chinese legal and political system demonstrates a very high degree of responsiveness to individual and popular concerns – what I have termed the "over-responsive state." This is reflected in a wide range of cases in which courts take account of popular or individual discontent. In some cases, including traffic accidents and medical cases, courts appear to be serving not as impartial adjudicators of disputes based on law but rather as administrative compensation agencies, with courts working to ensure that aggrieved plaintiffs are compensated even when the legal or factual basis for such compensation is questionable. Social norms also continue to play a strong role in influencing court outcomes, even when such norms are in

[55] Benjamin L. Liebman, "Malpractice Mobs: Medical Dispute Resolution in China," *Columbia Law Review* 113 (2013): 181.

tension with the law. Courts that play such roles and that take account of a wide range of factors, not just formal law, in making decisions are doing exactly what they are supposed to do in the Chinese political-legal system. The concerns of courts in China are the concerns of the Chinese political system.

Do such roles make Chinese courts fundamentally different from those in other authoritarian systems? The limited amount of scholarship on everyday judging in such systems makes such an assessment difficult. We are left with a sense that the practice of everyday law in China may also be different in many respects from other authoritarian systems, in part because of the strong emphasis on the wide range of nonlegal factors (not just explicitly political factors) in shaping outcomes. The scope of legal reform and the reliance on such reforms as a base for legitimacy in China also appear unusual compared to other authoritarian legal systems.

If there is a Chinese Model of court development, it is a model in which there is an increasingly complex legal framework with extensive borrowing of substantive norms from liberal democratic systems, emphasis on professionalization of judicial personnel, and a policy of bringing a wider range and volume of cases into the courts at the same time that courts continue to be constrained by and embedded within the Party-state. Court development in China thus means a larger role for courts and a greater emphasis on resolving cases fairly, not greater court authority or power. Court reform serves to strengthen courts' roles as bureaucratic institutions, not to challenge the authority of other institutions. Legal questions continue routinely to become political questions – not the reverse. Courts' roles may be sustainable, and not inevitably in tension with the functioning of a one-party state, because they remain constrained.

III Implications: Exporting the Pursuit of Stability?

China does not fit easily into any of the principal existing models of democratic or authoritarian legality. Yet claims that there is a "Chinese Model" are also unsatisfying, both because they leave unexamined differences between the Chinese approach and that of other authoritarian systems and because of such claims fail to examine the everyday practice of law within China. Many aspects of the Chinese system map on to various aspects of the models that predominate in Western discussions of court systems. This is not surprising; others have noted that differences among various legal systems are often overstated. Rather than conceiving of different models of courts in democratic or authoritarian systems, courts likely should be understood as operating on a continuum. China shows there may be areas of convergence, but that convergence may not come in areas where it is most expected.

The central question of this volume is whether and how the creation of a Chinese Model challenges existing Western understandings of legal development. My discussion above suggests that we should perhaps at the same time ask what the creation of such a model (if any) means for China. This discussion also raises three questions that will be central to determining not only whether there is a Chinese Model of legal development but also (and perhaps more importantly) what the shape of legal development in China will be in the coming years.

First, is China moving away from a model of legal development that has resulted in significant success to date – arguably the most rapid development of a legal system in history? There are many problems in the Chinese legal system and the system continues to result in grave injustices. At the same time, however, the combination of reliance on a range of models, top-down reform, local experimentation, and grass roots development has resulted in a system that is far more comprehensive and developed than most had believed possible when reforms started in 1978. Can the system continue to develop in an era of top-down legal development? Does a shift to a Party-state driven, centralized, and top-down model of legal reform in China risk ignoring many of the lessons of legal development elsewhere?

Second, where are challenges to China's renewed focus on legal development and reform likely to originate? Some reforms require only changing court procedures and are relatively easy to implement. Institutional and personnel changes within the courts are more difficult, as they impact the interests of a wide range of actors. Changes to the power of courts compared to other Party-state institutions are even harder to implement.

China's history of legal reform suggests that challenges and opposition may come from unlikely places. Some of the strongest opposition to reforms appears to be coming from the courts. Many had expected that judges would welcome court reforms in Shanghai and elsewhere designed to place greater emphasis on the quality of judging by reducing the roles of nonjudicial personnel in deciding cases and by placing the selection of judges in the hands of provincial-level authorities. Recent reports suggest resistance to such reforms from judges, in part because of concerns that younger judges, who often have the most extensive legal training, will lose their jobs or find their status lowered. Large numbers of judges have resigned or are seeking to leave the courts, largely in response to what they view as limited opportunities for career advancement under the reforms. In addition, judges may not welcome attempts to separate and insulate them from local authorities: the embedded nature of the Chinese judiciary means that judges also benefit from relationships with local authorities. Judges may welcome the protection from criticism that can result from local intervention and the opportunities local official involvement in court decision making provide for both legitimate and illegitimate forms of rent seeking.

Third, is the Chinese Model exportable? As noted above, more must be done to identify the contours of China's legal development model before considering whether the model could work elsewhere. To date most arguments that China's model has relevance elsewhere boil down to arguments that democracy is not a precondition to some form of rule of law. Over time the more important question may be not whether this top-down model can succeed elsewhere, but rather whether China's approach to handling routine, everyday cases has relevance for other developing legal systems.

There are reasons to be cautious in thinking that the Chinese approach will travel well. Many aspects of China's legal development model are unusual: a strong bureaucracy operating under the guidance of a strong Leninist Party; unprecedented economic growth; and a commitment to borrowing from a range of different legal systems and traditions. Although the promise of law without democracy will hold appeal to some at the top in other countries, efforts to export the Chinese Model seem unlikely to succeed absent more evidence that China can address fundamental problems with the system within China. The principal question thus is not whether China has created a model that may be relevant for other developing legal systems; the central question is whether the Chinese Model can work in China.

China's own experience suggests that the best model for legal reform may be no model at all. In seeking to define a Chinese Model of legal development Chinese authorities may be leaving behind the approach that has brought significant legal development to China in favor of an approach that has encountered difficulties elsewhere. One lesson learned, in China and elsewhere, is that rigid adherence to a model designed from the top with insufficient attention to the experience of everyday law in practice carries significant risks.

10

China's Striking Anticorruption Adventure

A Political Journey Toward the Rule of Law?

HUALING FU*

China is a high-corruption country and the ruling Communist Party ("the Party") has made anticorruption enforcement a top priority. China is also well known for her authoritarian decisiveness in policy making and her effectiveness in policy implementation with a centralized political control contrasting sharply with a decentralized economic policy. This chapter examines two key aspects of this formulation. First, how has the authoritarian characteristic affected China's anticorruption enforcement; and, second, how is China different from other countries, authoritarian or otherwise, in this regard?

There has been an ongoing debate between a "convergence theory" and a "divergence theory" on China's political-legal development. According to the convergence story, nations differ in their level of legal development largely because of the different levels of economic growth. China is significantly different from high-income countries because China, as a middle-income country, lacks resources and capacity to support an advanced system.[1] But as China progresses economically, social and legal changes are bound to follow. Consequently, gaps in the legal system will be filled, and the distance between a mature legal system and an emerging legal system will be narrowed. Substantive convergence is the destination of all legal systems even though it may appear in different forms. There is an incremental trajectory along which nations develop their legal

* The author would like to thank Albert Chen, Weitseng Chen, Richard Cullen, Hilary Josephs, and Ben Liebman for their valuable comments on the earlier versions of this chapter.

[1] Randall Peerenboom and Tom Ginsburg (eds.), *Law and Development of Middle-Income Countries: Avoiding the Middle-Income Trap* (New York: Cambridge University Press, 2013); Randall Peerenboom, *China Modernizes: Threat to the West or Model for the Rest?* (Oxford: Oxford University Press, 2008).

system, in a thin sense, and, while sequencing in a certain sense may be important,[2] all nations can achieve that trajectory once the necessary conditions are present. In the anticorruption field, the Party proves to be resolute and innovative in designing anticorruption strategies and has demonstrated both the will and ability to put corruption under effective control by resorting to measures that are not fundamentally different from international best practices.[3]

While the divergence theory has a long spectrum of arguments, its central argument is that China has a unique system that renders convergence impossible. In Minxin Pei's cynical formulation of a "trap thesis,"[4] China's political model suffers from fatal flaws and is not self-correcting. Following a liberal line of conceptualization, Pei argues that, without meaningful political competition, separation of powers, independent legal institutions and active participation from the civil society, China is unlikely to overcome its corruption problem that is inherent in the authoritarian system. As a result, the regime becomes increasingly fragile structurally as it sinks deeper into a trap. Any incremental reform, which may prolong regime survival, cannot lead to a fundamental political transformation. Consequently, Pei provides a provocative and dim view of political corruption in China. He concludes that corruption will continue to entrench itself and the anticorruption mechanisms that rely on the Party's internal disciplinary framework, without the support of law and legal institutions, will not be able to stop the further spread of the trend. As a result the regime must collapse on its own weight before any transformation can occur. Pei's trap thesis has been shared by many others who, in various ways, present a China-collapse thesis.

Others have turned Pei's thesis on its head and argued that what appears to be fatal for Pei is precisely where China's strength lies and contributes to China's authoritarian resilience.[5] Striking a positive note, many have

[2] Randall Peerenboom, "Rule of Law, Democracy and the Sequencing Debate: Lessons from China and Vietnam," in *Legal Reforms in China and Vietnam: A Comparison of Asian Communist Regimes*, John Gillespie and Albert Chen (eds.) (London: Routledge, 2010).

[3] Hualing Fu, "Stability and Anticorruption Initiatives: Is There a Chinese Model?," in *Politics of Law and Stability in China*, Susan Trevaskes et al. (eds.) (Cheltenham, UK: Edward Elgar, 2014), 176.

[4] Minxin Pei, *China's Trapped Transition: The Limits of Developmental Autocracy* (Cambridge, MA: Harvard University Press, 2008); Minxin Pei, "Is CCP Rule Fragile or Resilient?," *Journal of Democracy* 23 (2012): 27.

[5] Shigong Jiang, "Written and Unwritten Constitutions: A New Approach to the Study of Constitutional Government in China," *Modern China* 36 (2010): 12; Pan Wei (ed.), *Zhongguo moshi: jiedu renmin gongheguo de 60 nian* [China Model: A New Developmental

argued that, instead of converging into a Western political model, China may have discovered a distinct development model based on its effective and decisive political leadership or communitarian social structure. China's anticorruption efforts deliver precisely because it is led and controlled by the Party at the macro-level. This anticorruption model is legitimate and effective because it is embedded within the Chinese reality and the cultural milieu. Seen from this perspective, China's political system, including its anticorruption regime works effectively in these Chinese circumstances.

This chapter discusses China's anticorruption enforcement within the context of the convergence/divergence debate and examines the degree to which the Chinese anticorruption model converges or diverges from the prevailing "international best practice" that is commonly observed in the high-income/low-corruption countries. Specifically this chapter will also discuss whether China could develop an anticorruption system that operates within a rule-based legal framework. The principal argument is that China's anticorruption practice manifests certain core features that may be unique to the Chinese political context and those features show most strikingly at the height of an anticorruption campaign. But if we look beyond an exceptional "strike-hard campaign" that targets the "tigers," shift the focus to the more routine enforcement against "flies," and in particular, observe China's anticorruption enforcement for a longer time span, it becomes clearer that China does not operate an anticorruption model sui generis. As the anticorruption storm dies down (as it will naturally occur), the enforcement will become more routine, regularized, and institutional. When that happens, the Chinese anticorruption model, if any, will appear no different from models elsewhere.

The remaining chapter is divided into four parts. Following this introduction, Part I introduces, in broad strokes, the core features of the internal disciplinary inspection committee (*jiwei*) of the Party. *Jiwei* has come to political prominence in the Xi government and is becoming the most powerful force in the Party apparatus. This part explains the political meaning of Party discipline and the core institutional design that renders the mechanism effective. Yet, despite the ostensible politicization of anticorruption, the *jiwei* mechanism shares some core characteristics with the most successful anticorruption stories in other authoritarian systems that one may observe in Hong Kong or Singapore.

Model from the Sixty Years of the People's Republic] (Beijing: China Compilation and Translation Press, 2009).

Part II then moves beyond *jiwei* to study the much marginalized and neglected legal anticorruption system in China and its interaction with *jiwei*. While fundamental differences between the two systems remain, they have, over the years, moved closer to one another and have the potential to replicate each other's structure and *modus operandi*.

Part III examines the anticorruption mechanism from a historical perspective and offers insights on the degree to which law is relevant to anticorruption enforcement. Part IV concludes this chapter.

I The Party's Dominance

The Party's leadership role is entrenched in the state constitution. The Party has approximately 80 million members, and all key state posts in China are occupied by Party members.

There are different ways to conceptualize Party leadership. For Backer and Wang,[6] the Party Constitution and the State Constitution are both integral parts of the Chinese socialist constitutionalism and the Party is not itself constrained by the state constitution; instead, the Party operates legitimately above and beyond state laws. A more critical view simply accepts the political reality that, constitutional or not, the Party dominates the political process and can rule directly without transforming the Party's will into a particular form of law. As Zhu Suli and others have argued, the root of China's constitutional order is the rule of the Party, and such political order does not only precede the constitutional order in a historical sense but also in the form of the first order rule in a political sense.[7] The Party exercises its leadership through the constitution and the laws made by the lawmaking body that it controls. While state laws reflect the Party's will, the Party operates within the legal framework it has created.

Many scholars have moved beyond merely describing the Party's role in China's constitutional order. These scholars are now treating the Party's

[6] Larry Backer and Keren Wang, "The Emerging Structures of Socialist Constitutionalism with Chinese Characteristics: Extra-Judicial Detention (*Laojiao and Shuanggui*) and the Chinese Constitutional Order," *Pacific Rim Law & Policy Journal* 23 (2014): 251.

[7] Hualing Fu, "Autonomy, Courts and the Political-Legal Order in Contemporary China," in *Handbook of Chinese Criminology*, Liqun Cao, Ivan Sun, and Bill Hebeton (eds.) (London: Routledge, 2013), 76; Xin He, "The Party's Leadership as a Living Constitution in Reform China," *Hong Kong Law Journal* 42 (2012), 73; Jiang, *Written and Unwritten Constitutions*, 12; Suli Zhu, "'Judicial Politics' as State Building," in *Building Constitutionalism in China*, Stephenie Balme and Michael Dowdle (eds.) (New York: Palgrave Macmillan, 2009), 23.

monopoly of political power as a key component of an emerging Chinese Model and the essence of China's success.[8] A new generation of scholars has pointed out both the empirical and normative dimensions of an entrenched Party leadership, and the normative dimension, in particular, has gained currency in the public debate. Put simply, the Party does not only rule China. It should do so.

Within China's Leninist Party, political loyalty provides a foundation for the internal disciplinary system of the Party. It is a fundamental rule that individual party members profess a high degree of, if not absolute, loyalty to the Party. No matter how the Party and state relationship is conceptualized, this political system places Party rules over state laws, demands the submission of Party members to Party rules and punishes disloyalty or split loyalty based on religious belief, professional ethics, or other callings. In that Leninist tradition, Party members are first and foremost the fabric of the gigantic political machinery before they are citizens of the nation. Party members' loyalty to the Party trumps fidelity to profession, religion, ethnicity, and even nation.

According to this political logic, when Party members misbehave, the matter would be more politically significant than legally relevant and *jiwei* enjoys supremacy in investigating and punishing delinquent members.[9] The Party's anticorruption system serves primarily the objectives of reinforcing political discipline and enhancing political loyalty through punishing individual members.[10] Party discipline has its unique historical meaning and political significance. The first internal disciplinary department of the Party was set up in April 1927 in a direct response to the white terror perpetrated by the Nationalist government. On April 12, 1927, the Nationalist government launched a brutal attack on the young Chinese Communist Party, leading to mass murder and mass arrest. The brutality also led to defection of Party members on a massive scale. To regroup and to cope with an existential threat, the Party set up a high-level Supervisory Committee (*zhongyang jiancha weiyuanhui* 中央监察委员会) – a ten-member committee independent of, and parallel to, the Central Committee of the Party. Although the power and remit of the Supervisory Committee was substantially reduced in 1928, its legacy has remained to this day as a disciplinary mechanism, serving the powerful

[8] Pan, *China Model.* [9] Backer and Wang, "The Emerging Structures," 251.

[10] Hualing Fu, "Wielding the Sword: President Xi's New Anti-Corruption Campaign," in *Greed, Corruption, and the Modern State*, Susan Rose-Ackerman and Paul Felipe Lagunes (eds.) (Cheltenham, UK: Edward Elgar, 2015), 134.

function to eliminate Party members who have betrayed the Party and punish those who have violated Party rules.[11]

Whenever the Party perceives a major crisis, its disciplinary inspection department would come to the fore stage, gaining more political prominence and power and playing a more direct role in political control. In the postcultural revolution era, when the Party was determined to abandon revolution in favor of modernization, it restored and strengthened the Supervisory Committee to rebuild the Party's integrity and credibility.[12] In response to the political crisis in the aftermath of the 1989 student movement, the Party, in 1993, merged the Ministry of Supervision, which was in charge of administrative complaints, into the disciplinary system and also placed the entire anticorruption enforcement, including the legal institutions, under the Party's direct leadership. From that year onward, the Party, through the Central Committee for Disciplinary Inspection (CCDI), together with Committees of Disciplinary Inspection (CDI) at the local levels, has taken a hands-on approach in defining, controlling, and punishing corruption. The Xi's government used anticorruption as an effective entry point into a governance reform, and has once again enhanced the political power of *jiwei* in controlling Party members more effectively and directly.[13] Therefore, the more serious corruption is perceived to be, the more political power the CCDI is able to accumulate. It is in that context that one appreciates the symbolic value of Wang Qishan's visit, upon assuming the role as the CCDI Secretary, to the historical

[11] Han Feng (ed.), "90 nian lai dang de jijian jiancha zhidu de yange he tedian" [The Evolution and Characteristics of the Party's Disciplinary Inspection System in the past 90 Years], Sichuan University Marxism School (School of Political Science), November 11, 2011, www.scu.edu.cn/zzxy/dwgz/jjgz/webinfo/2011/11/1321924224398934.htm; Wu Meihua, "Zhongguo gongchandang jicha jigou de lishi yange ji qi zhineng yanbian" [Historical Evolution and Changing Functions of the Chinese Communist Party's Disciplinary Inspection Organs], *Zhongguo gongchandang xinwen wang*, May 6, 2009, http://dangshi.people.com.cn/GB/138903/138911/9249192.html.

[12] Ting Gong, "The Party Disciplinary Inspection in China: Its Evolving Trajectory and Embedded Dilemmas," *Crime, Law and Social Change* 49 (2008): 139; Li Ling, "The Rise of the Party Committee of Discipline and Inspection (1927–2012): Anti-corruption Investigation and Decision-making in the Chinese Communist Party," Working Paper 1/2015 (New York University Law School US-Asia Law Institute, 2015), www.academia.edu/10195921/The_Rise_of_the_Chinese_Communist_Party_s_Disciplinary_Institution_1927–2012_The_operation_of_the_Party_anticorruption_machine; Graham Young, "Control and Style: Discipline Inspection Commissions since the 11th Congress," *The China Quarterly* 97 (1984): 24.

[13] Fu, *Wielding the Sword.*

site of the first Supervisory Committee in Wuhan where he laid a wreath before the statues of the ten members of the 1927 committee.[14]

The Party is firmly in charge of the anticorruption institutions. It sets agendas, designs institutions, prioritizes issues, and determines the scope and pace of the enforcement. The Party's disciplinary institutions and measures, as demonstrated in the recent anticorruption campaign, have shown three institutional features.[15]

The first is the leading role of *jiwei* in investigating corruption cases that are committed by senior Party officials within the respective Party's hierarchy. *Jiwei* performs multiple functions in preventing corruption and enforcing Party discipline but a defining characteristic is its near monopoly over the investigation of corrupt officials of a certain rank and the disposal of those cases. With little exception, major corruption scandals are all first investigated by *jiwei*. In investigating major corruption cases, *jiwei* leads and legal institutions comply.

Jiwei reaches out to all Party and state organs. A significant recent development is extending the reach of the CCDI into core state institutions, including the State Council, the NPC, the Chinese People's Political Consultative Conference (CPPCC), and the key political institutions such as the powerful Organization Department. This extension has the potential to undermine a fragile functional separation of powers and to further expand the CCDI's political power. The CCDI regularly dispatches disciplinary officials to be stationed in ministries and, under the new initiative, the CCDI has been sending disciplinary officials directly to the highest organs of state and political power and placing those organs under the direct supervision of the CCDI. This is said to be an unprecedented move and which will significantly enhance the control of the Party over state bodies.[16]

The structured and systematic control is reinforced by the Central Inspection Groups (CIG), an ad hoc high-level working group dispatched from Beijing to review disciplinary matters of state entities at the provincial and ministerial levels. This is the second institutional feature. The CIG

14 "Wang Qishan: Wangji Guoqu Jiu Yiweizhe Beipan" [Wang Qishan: Forgetting the Past Means Betrayal], *Xinhuan Net*, November 24, 2013, http://news.xinhuanet.com/politics/2013-11/24/c_118270161.htm.

15 Fu, *Wielding the Sword.*

16 "Zhongjiwei jiangdui paizhu shixian quanmian fugai: kanzhu zhongyang dang zheng jiguan quanli" [CCDI Will Cover the Entire Dispatched Organs: Limiting the Powers of the Central Party and Government Organs], China Net, January 7, 2016, http://news.china.com.cn/2016-01/07/content_37479167.htm.

was originated in the 1990s to compensate for the institutional inertia on the part of the provincial/ministerial *jiwei*, and was aimed at catalyzing and reenergizing the anticorruption endeavors. The CIG was revitalized under Xi and under the able leadership of Wang Qishan. In a short period of time, the CIG has become a sharp instrument in breaking up corrupt networks and syndicates, real or perceived, within the Party and has the potential to effect substantial change within the political system toward a "clean" government.

If *jiwei* itself is an extraordinary anticorruption mechanism that is imposed on the legal mechanism, the CIG represents another layer of enforcement on the Party's own disciplinary mechanism. In that sense, the CIG is a noninstitutional mechanism at the disposal of the Party leaders to solve the agency problem, seeking policy compliance at the provincial level. As such, it is regarded as a disruptive intrusion into the regular exercise of disciplinary authority within the Party.

Briefly, the CIG serves three functions. First, it uncovers and investigates corruption cases within the powerful state organs and SOEs. The CIG's work is case driven – that is to receive complaints and conduct preliminary investigation in relation to those complaints. The CIG is able to uncover major corruption cases because as agents of the highest authority of the Party, CIG investigators wield significant political power to overcome local and bureaucratic resistance in conducting investigations, serving as an effective forward guard to exposing corrupt networks.

Second, the CIG is to create a downward political pressure and cascade effect so that *jiwei* at the provincial and subprovincial levels would be sufficiently incentivized to act more aggressively to pursue local corruption (just as the CCDI does at the provincial level). From this perspective, the CIG is not principally interested in any of the cases that come directly to its attention but to pressurize local actors through case investigation. This can be seen with responsibility mechanism that Wang Qishan posits: following a successful CCDI's investigation, the CCDI would take action against both the corrupt officials under investigation and the officials of the relevant CDIs for failure to take action. By holding local CDIs responsible, the CIG inspection is expected to incentivize local CDIs to act as aggressively as the CCDI.

Beyond holding local CDIs responsible, the CIG aims to reinforce the Party's political control over Party members. Through the high-profile inspection tours, the CIG enhances the power and status of the central authority, and ensures the smooth implementation of central decisions. It has been made clear that the anticorruption regime has served as the most effective tool in swinging the gravitas of political power firmly into Xi's hands.

Finally, there is the institutional feature of *shuanggui*[17] – the de facto detention for the investigation of Party officials above certain ranks for violating Party rules during which an explanation at a designated place and time will be demanded. *Shuanggui* is a highly controversial measure that has caused heated debate in China and abroad. Without doubt, *shuanggui* is a form of extra-legal detention and a clear violation of the state constitution and domestic law.[18] But is it justifiable and politically feasible?

There are various views on the legality of *shuanggui* depending on the particular conceptualization of the Party/state relationship. For Backer and Wang who are prepared to elevate the Party Constitution to a status equivalent to the state constitution,[19] *shuanggui is* a measure to discipline Party members to ensure the integrity of the Party in power. Thus, *shuanggui* is politically legitimate even if it is in clear violation of the state constitution and legal rules. For others who believe otherwise, the Party must operate under the state constitution, and *shuanggui*, as an aberration to be used to place corruption under control, can only be excused on the grounds of urgency and necessity. As corruption is an entrenched and persistent political problem touching the highest levels of the political power, it has posed an existential threat to the Party-state and must be dealt with forcefully and effectively. Legal institutions are weak facing powerful but corrupt syndicates and it takes the Party, with its wherewithal, to punish its powerful delinquent members. The urgency of the matter, coupled with weak legal institutions, creates the necessity for the Party to deal with the corruption expediently outside the legal

[17] *Shuanggui* (双规) is a Party disciplinary measure that requires a Party member under investigation to offer explanation for the alleged problem at a designated place and time. The rules governing shuanggui were promulgated by the Standing Committee of the CCDI. On January 28, 1994, and these rules came into effect on May 1, 1994. See Article 28, Section 3 of "Zhongguo gongchandang jilu jiancha jiguan anjian jiancha gongzuo tiaoli" [Measures Concerning the Investigative Work for Cases under the Disciplinary Inspection Organs of the Chinese Communist Party], Chinese Communist Party, http://cpc.people.com.cn/GB/33838/2539632.html. Alternatively, see Law of the People's Republic of China on Administrative Supervision (hereafter, Administration Supervision Law), effective May 9, 1997, and amended June 25, 2010, www.npc.gov.cn/englishnpc/Law/2007–12/11/content_1383546.htm.

[18] Flora Sapio, "Shuanggui and Extralegal Detention in China," *China Information* 22 (2008): 7.

[19] Backer and Wang, "The Emerging Structures," 251.

frameworks through *shuanggui* – a special and temporary power that is tailor-made to suppress corruption despite being itself an aberration.[20]

The combined effect of *jiwei*, CIG, and *shuanggui* makes anticorruption crackdowns an internal affair of the Party, and this may itself be a problem. Because of the highly political nature of high-profile cases, the enforcement is seen to be selective, secretive, largely extra-legal, and in any event politically biased, with a clear agenda of rooting out political adversaries and of legitimizing existing political power. Seen from this perspective, one may be tempted to note an emerging Chinese Model reflecting the unique political landscape of the Party-state.

What has been neglected, however, is the fact that this model, to be effective, shares some fundamental characteristics with certain admirable anticorruption models in other countries. Once the focus of the inquiry is shifted from legitimacy and legality to implementation and effectiveness, there is a different perspective on the disciplinary inspection mechanism.

In measuring the success of Hong Kong's well-known Independent Commission Against Corruption (ICAC), researchers have pointed out conditions that are necessary for a successful anticorruption institution: an independent anticorruption agency with strong political and financial support along with dedicated and professional staff.[21] Equally, international anticorruption practices emphasize the importance of independence, authority, resources, and the effectiveness of anticorruption bodies.[22]

In respect of China, the *jiwei* is certainly independent of the organizations and individuals they monitor, investigate, and punish; *jiwei* enjoys a high political status and exercises extensive powers. It is a very hierarchical system with rigid upward accountability. Local interference, while it continues to exist, is becoming increasingly difficult.[23] On top of its high political status and relative autonomy from local authorities, *jiwei* also has the resources needed to carry out investigations. As a Party organ, *jiwei* may have only limited legal powers and institutional capacity in

20 For a review of the debate in China, see ibid.

21 Richard Cullen and Xiaonan Yang, "Executive Government," in *Law of the Hong Kong Constitution*, Johannes Chan and Chin Leng Lim (eds.) (Hong Kong: Sweet & Maxwell, 2015), 321; Melanie Manion, *Corruption by Design: Building Clean Government in Mainland China and Hong Kong* (Cambridge, MA: Harvard University Press, 2004), 27.

22 Susan Rose-Ackerman, *Corruption and Government: Causes, Consequences, and Reform* (New York: Cambridge University Press, 1999).

23 Hualing Fu, "The Upward and Downward Spirals in China's Anti-corruption Enforcement," in *Comparative Perspectives on Criminal Justice in China*, Mike McConville and Eva Pils (eds.) (Cheltenham, UK: Edward Elgar, 2013), 390.

actual anticorruption investigations, but the real strength of *jiwei* is the leadership it commands over the entire political and legal apparatuses of the anticorruption. When needed, *jiwei* can pool together resources of state organizations. In most, if not all, of the *jiwei*'s operations, the CDI or CCDI heavily relies on the legal and law enforcement professionals, including the police, procurators, and judges, using the legal authority that these professionals may exercise to conduct the investigation. This centralized system, supported by the highest political authority and armed with effective investigative tools, has been effective in containing the spread of corruption in China. The achievement to date under Xi is impressive, representing the most serious purge since the end of the Cultural Revolution – all done in the name of, and through, the disciplinary inspection system.[24]

The point of departure, however, as the critics are quick in pointing out, is the context in which an anticorruption agency operates. In Hong Kong, the ICAC is embedded and operates within a legal framework in which the ICAC is made accountable to the legislature, the judiciary, and the community at large. Accountability is indeed an integral part of the ICAC's efficiency and is one of the reasons for the ICAC's effectiveness. The rule of law which constrains the ICAC also gives it credibility.

There is a sharp difference between the mainland's and Hong Kong's anticorruption regimes: China's anticorruption regime is intertwined with her political system, which is based on political expedience, while the Hong Kong's regime is steeped in her legal system, which is based on the rule of law. The question is, in the long run, can China's Party-driven anticorruption model evolve into something that is based on the rule of law and is legally accountable? Before we move to discuss that *possibility*, let us first examine China's dual anticorruption system.

II China's Dual Anticorruption System

The disciplinary inspection system, as powerful as it is, does not function in isolation. It is an elite part of a much larger anticorruption system. China operates a dual anticorruption system in which the Party's disciplinary mechanism co-exists with a legal system for anticorruption enforcement. These are distinct institutions with different historical origins and political ideology.[25]

[24] Fu, *Wielding the Sword*, 134.

[25] Backer and Wang, "The Emerging Structures," 251.

A dual system posits that regular and routine issues will be handled by the "ordinary" system while exceptional, and largely political, matters will be handled by the "extraordinary" system. Historically, the Maoist theory of contradictions conceptualizes two types of contradictions: the first is those among the people and the second is those between the people and their enemies. Indeed, this dualism is dictated by Article 1 of the Chinese Constitution[26] and is visible in both political and legal theories and practices. Pils has pointed out the co-existence between the "state of norms" and the "state of measures" in analyzing state repression of human rights lawyers;[27] and Sapio has offered a broader analytical framework between normal and exceptional states in exploring social ordering in China.[28] Distinct types of cases are treated differently because of their political sensitivity and ramification.

This dualism is firmly institutionalized in anticorruption enforcement: a political mechanism which is dominated by *jiwei* in enforcing Party rules and a legal mechanism which is operated by the procuratorate according to legal provisions. Each mechanism has its own sphere of influences, institutional design, operating procedures, and political logic. The anti-corruption dualism also demands that the two mechanisms interface with each other and in the process affect one another. While the disciplinary mechanism brings political factors to bear in the legal process, the legal mechanism also produces a legal impact within *jiwei*, affecting the organizational structure and the procedural rules of the latter. As well, legal actors strive to enforce anticorruption rules independent of the *jiwei* system. To better understand the "extraordinary" part of the system (that is, the political mechanism operated by *jiwei*), one therefore needs to study it in relation to the "ordinary" part of the system (that is, the legal mechanism enforced by the prosecutorate). A comprehensive theory of the Chinese legal system, including the anticorruption regime, needs to pay more attention to "ordinary" justice (see also Liebman, Chapter 9).

Largely due to the Soviet influence, the procuratorate investigates and prosecutes offenses committed by civil servants in their official capacity,

[26] Article 1 provides: "The People's Republic of China is a socialist state under the people's democratic dictatorship led by the working class and based on the alliance of workers and peasants. The socialist system is the basic system of the People's Republic of China. Sabotage of the socialist system by any organization or individual is prohibited."

[27] Eva Pils, *China's Human Rights Lawyers: Advocacy and Resistance* (Abingdon, UK: Routledge, 2014), 224.

[28] Flora Sapio, *Sovereign Power and the Law in China* (Leiden, Netherlands: Brill, 2010), 16.

including corruption. Between 1979 and 1993, China had built an anti-corruption regime within her legal system, which had operated in parallel to the political mechanism of the day (i.e., *jiwei*). Under the Criminal Procedure Law 1979, the procuratorate was in charge of the anticorruption investigation and a special investigative unit called "Economic Crime Unit" was set up within each level of the procuratorate to conduct anti-corruption investigations. While the level of institutionalization was low, and resources and institutional autonomy of the "Economic Crime Unit" were limited, the procuratorate, while under the firm leadership of the Party, nevertheless operated with a high degree of independence from the *jiwei* system. *Jiwei* restricted itself primarily to internal disciplinary matters within the Party and was not allowed to exercise any coercive powers, such as search, seizure, or detention, that are necessary for criminal investigation.[29]

In the aftermath of the June 4, 1989, bloodshed, the Party responded to the call for more effective anticorruption enforcement. Against a national anticorruption campaign, Guangdong Province proposed a new institution. Inspired by the success of the ICAC in Hong Kong, a young and ambitious Xiao Yang, a deputy procuratorate-general of Guangdong, proposed the creation of an independent anticorruption bureau – i.e., the Anti-Corruption Authority (ACA). This new bureau would bring the task of anticorruption enforcement into sharp focus and its enhanced status would give it more resources and power. In the aftermath of June 4 protest, there was strong support for institutional innovation from both the Supreme People's Procuratorate (SPP), especially from the then SPP President, Liu Fuzhi, and the Guangdong Party Committee. As a result, the ACA was set up within the Guangdong Procuratorate on August 18, 1989. Following Guangdong, anticorruption bureau were created in other parts of the country and, on November 10, 1995, the SPP set up the National Anti-Corruption Authority (NACA, 反贪污贿赂总局).[30] Clearly, the political control exerted by the CCDI over anticorruption enforcement did not prevent the gradual institutionalization of anticorruption enforcement within the legal system.

[29] Li, *The Rise of the Party Committee of Discipline and Inspection*, 3.

[30] In March 1995, five CPPCC members who were specially appointed procurators by the SPP tabled a motion for the establishment of a national anticorruption authority in the SPP at the third Plenum of the Eighth CPPCC Meeting. The motion was sent to the Human Resources Planning Commission which replied favorably within a month. By the end of 1995, nearly all the provinces, about half of the cities and about one third of counties had set up similar anticorruption authorities.

What is the actual working relationship between *jiwei* and the ACA? There are different ways to analyze the dependence of the legal system on the political mechanism. First, *jiwei* has the near monopoly of major cases, cases that involve senior officials – while the legal system handles relevantly minor corruption cases. Hence *jiwei* and its related institution, the CDI, is known for tackling the "tigers" while the legal system and its related institution, the ACA, handles the "flies." As such, serious cases of corruption are first investigated nearly in their entirety by *jiwei*.

In 1994, the Party authorized the *jiwei* to undertake coercive measures, including detention, on its own delinquent members during anticorruption investigations.[31] Relying on those coercive measures, *jiwei* has been able to exert its jurisdiction over most of the major corruption cases. Only a tiny percentage of cases are referred to the ACA for criminal investigation and prosecution.[32]

Most of the more routine corruption offenses committed by lower-ranking officials, especially at the intervals of major anticorruption campaigns, are routinely handled by the ACA. It is no surprise, however, that most corruption offenses occur at the basic level of the government and most prosecutions against corruption are initiated by the ACA at corresponding level. While *jiwei* has resources – the CCDI certainly has more resources than the NACA of the SPP in terms of political authority, manpower, and other resources – the CDI lacks resources at the lower levels of China's governmental and political hierarchy. Put simply, the institutional design allows the CCDI and the CDI at the provincial level to take on large and important corruption cases, but the Party has to rely on the ACA to mainstream the anticorruption initiatives and to take action against the vast majority of the corruption cases at the lower levels.

A second way to conceptualize the *jiwei*-ACA relationship is to place the ACA's operation within the long shadow of the CDI's leadership. From this perspective, the ACA and the entire legal system play a supplementary role in the grand anticorruption design of the Party.

There are different ways in which the ACA may play that supplementary role. As mentioned, *jiwei* may refer cases to the ACA for investigation and prosecution, and those cases are given priority in the procuratorate. *Jiwei* may also request the ACA's assistance, in particular to borrow the ACA's coercive powers, in cases that are under *jiwei* investigation. On the flip side, the ACA may proactively participate in a *jiwei* investigation so as to take

[31] Li, *The Rise of the Party Committee of Discipline and Inspection*, 3.
[32] Fu, *The Upward and Downward Spirals*, 390.

advantage of *jiwei*'s procedures (such as treating confessions extracted by the *jiwei* as its own in addition to giving confessions the necessary legal effect or relying on *shuanggui* detention to bypass the time limit placed on pretrial detention).

III Anticorruption Enforcement and the Rule of Law

The dual system thesis offers a useful perspective to understand the political role of the *jiwei* in the larger context of anticorruption enforcement. While this is so, is it sustainable in the Chinese political context? To answer this question, the following analysis places the evolution of the anticorruption regime in China within the larger context of China's fast-changing legal system.

As with China's governmental budget,[33] Chinese law also comes in different varieties. Broadly, there is the official/formal law made pursuant to the constitution. There is also quasi-formal extra-law with questionable legality and constitutionality. Parallel to law and extra-law, one also finds a visible layer of informal "extra-extra law," which has been developing a life of its own. There are two perspectives on those varieties of law. From an empirical perspective, they coexist and are simultaneously present in different areas of Chinese law, particularly public law and criminal law. In anticorruption enforcement, legal institutions are certainly at work but certain extra-extra law practices and mechanisms have become institutionalized. Still, it is extra-law that has played a leading role in the field and exerted overarching control.

The varieties can also be viewed in evolutionary terms. Over the past three decades, the space within which extra-law operates in every aspect of Chinese law has, in general, been shrinking while correspondingly, the space within which law operates has been expanding.[34] Extra-extra legal practices, while continuing to exist, have become largely exceptional. The following sections of this chapter will discuss the extra-extra law, extra-law, and law in the context of China's anticorruption regime.

[33] It is well known that the Chinese government's budgetary process is convoluted. The concept of a "budget" in China includes a formal and legal budget, an official but quasi-legal extra-budget, and an informal, occasionally illegal, extra-extra budget. The government budget is thus a complex mix of budgets of various sources and degrees of legality and legitimacy.

[34] Sarah Biddulph, *Legal Reform and Administrative Detention Powers in China* (New York: Cambridge University Press, 2007), 40.

A *Extra-Extra Law*

Extra-extra law comprises of government measures that exist in some dark space, seemingly unrelated to any legal framework and devoid of any legal authority. Extra-extra law is an informal political institution characterized by a total lack of legality. It is used to advance some predatory and repressive government policies which cannot be justified by any law or policies. As such, extra-extra law is mired in secrecy and operates without legal accountability. Except for occasional and indirect admissions, such as the quasi-official admission of the existence of "black jails" for petitioners and religious offenders,[35] extra-extra law does not officially exist, and, as such, it survives and sometimes thrives because it is effective in achieving certain policy goals that cannot otherwise be achieved through law or extra-law. The legal system in China is regarded as weak and ineffective when it comes to sensitive issues, and, in these situations, extra-extra law expedites the process to the extent that it has become indispensable.

Examples abound. "Black jails" have also been used to detain peasants in violation of family planning policies or those who fail to pay illicit levies; to detain and intimidate petitioners who air their grievances in Beijing; and, more recently, to detain Tibetan monks for their alleged challenges to the official policy on religions. These repressive policies are extra-extra law because powers are exercised by the government on an ad hoc basis without any legal authorization or procedure, and with little accountability. The forced disappearance of human rights lawyers in 2011 and those who openly supported Hong Kong occupying movement well illustrated official law's vulnerability and the readiness of the Party to resort to extra-extra law. Lawyers and other advocates were typically snatched by internal security authorities and detained in unknown places for interrogation and intimidation.[36]

There is a fundamental difference between disappearance (i.e., extra-extra law) and abuse of criminal procedure (i.e., law). When the government uses, or even abuses, the law, the government still signals a commitment to law. Using or abusing the law also eschews a degree of legal accountability, publicity, and responsibility. This is the reason why the incarcerated human rights lawyers and many others have demanded

[35] "China: Secret 'Black Jails' Hide Severe Rights Abuses Unlawful Detention Facilities Breed Violence, Threats, Extortion," *Human Rights Watch*, November 11, 2009, www.hrw.org/news/2009/11/11/china-secret-black-jails-hide-severe-rights-abuses.

[36] Verna Yu, "Tales of Torture: Time Spent in Chinese Police Custody Leaves Victims Permanently Scarred," *South China Morning Post*, June 27, 2015.

their day in court so that abuses could be brought to the attention of the law and public scrutiny. A mere legal trapping may not be sufficient to convert a political persecution to a fair legal process, but it is a necessary first step in developing legal accountability against arbitrary power.

Legal rhetoric is important in both justifying and constraining state powers. It may not be possible to reduce law to total irrelevance without incurring cost. The judicial interpretation of the Supreme People's Court (SPC) on the application of sedition and subversion to the 1989 democratic movement activists;[37] the legal trappings that the Standing Committee of the National People's Congress and the SPC painstakingly created to justify its prosecution of the Falun Gong;[38] and, the courtroom tension between judges and lawyers in some of the Falun Gong trials[39] are all examples that law matters even at a repressive moment. The mere fact that a criminal charge is mounted necessarily means a degree of accountability. The path of law is a tortuous one, but as long as this is the path to tread, there exists some degree of legal control and accountability that cannot simply be swept away.

Another reason as to why law is important is because extra-extra law serves a fundamentally different objective. Enforced disappearance or "black jails" differs from criminal punishment in fundamental ways. In criminal punishment, the law addresses past offenses and the objective is to punish the wrongdoers. In enforced disappearance, the focus is instead on the "risk" that an individual poses, regardless of the offenses he or she may or may not have committed. Extra-extra law is thus applied not for the purpose of punishing past offenses but to reduce future risk, with targeted measures taken against individuals to maximize intimidation.

Torture, for example, may also be used in both law and extra-extra law. But in law, torture is typically used to extract confession to establish criminal liability; while in extra-extra law, it is to inflict fear so that those who are tortured would not speak or act out. Intimidation is therefore at the core of the extra-extra law. As such, in the enforced disappearance cases, no general norms apply; instead, the users of extra-extra law apply particularized stratagems, tailor-made for each individual

[37] Hualing Fu, "Sedition and Political Dissidence: Towards Legitimate Dissent in China?," *Hong Kong Law Journal* 26 (1996): 210.

[38] Randall Peerenboom, *China's Long March toward Rule of Law* (New York: Cambridge University Press, 2002), 55.

[39] Hualing Fu, "Human Rights Lawyering in Chinese Courtrooms," *Chinese Journal of Comparative Law* 2 (2014): 270.

case. With intimidation at the center of the equation, we see a quantitative change in the method of repression with a sudden turn against law.[40]

On the anticorruption front, internal discipline has been a core instrument to maintain Party integrity and reinforce Party loyalty. Historically, the *jiwei* had the much broader remit in enforcing party rule and had been ruthless in doing so. The Party's disciplinary mechanism is not to enforce the criminal law but to deal with the risk party members might pose to the Party. The mechanism is to apply Party's rules in a highly political fashion. This is a fundamental difference between legal enforcement of anticorruption law and the Party's application of internal rules.

The application of extra-extra law may be surgical and limited in its scope of application and in the degree of brutality. But these may not be the core issues. The core question is: is China moving toward a different doctrine of governance in the name of the a "Chinese Model" where legal constraints are regarded as redundant and ineffective and power is unconstrained so long as objectives are to be achieved?

Repressive episodes are recurring events in the post-Mao era, and each generation of leaders have their repressive moments during their terms, especially toward the end of their terms when they hand power over to the next generation of leaders. Deng Xiaoping sent tanks to suppress the 1989 democratic movements and Jiang Zemin smashed the Falun Gong and wiped out the China Democracy Party (CDP), incarcerating most of the CDP members for lengthy terms. Similarly, Hu Jingtao crushed the Chartist movement in 2008 and then the so-called Jasmine Revolution and took a generally repressive approach toward governance in the name of harmony and stability.[41] Xi is most forceful in silencing dissent political or otherwise. In contrast, new leaders, as they emerge to power, appear to be politically open and reform minded. This appearance enhances expectations and invites challenges.[42] Once that happens, however, the new leaders typically move decisively to demolish the challenges, creating their repressive moments and leaving a conservative legacy.

[40] Hualing Fu, "Mediation and the Rule of Law: The Chinese Landscape," in *Formalisation and Flexibilisation in Dispute Resolution*, Joachim Zekoll, Moritz Bälz, and Iwo Amelung (eds.) (Leiden, Netherlands: Brill, 2014), 108–29; Hualing Fu, "Challenging Authoritarianism through Law: Potential and Limit," *National Taiwan University Law Review* 6 (2011): 339; Carl F. Minzner, "China's Turn against Law," *American Journal of Comparative Law* 59 (2001): 935.

[41] Fu, *Challenging Authoritarianism*, 339.

[42] Fu, *Wielding the Sword*, 134.

B Extra-Law

The Party and the government have largely relied on extra-law to exercise their powers. Extra-law is a system and a normative order in which power is neither directly derived from clear legal rules and exercised through properly constituted authorities nor subject to independent oversight (judicial or otherwise) outside the Party. In contrast with law, extra-law does not allow deliberation, representation, transparency, or decision making that can be regarded as judicial. Extra-law has a strong political or policy orientation and the whole system is geared to informal practice, political expediency, or mere administrative convenience. China's legal reform in the past 30 years is characterized by a slow transition from extra-law to law. Yet, after more than 30 years of law reform and improved legality, the effect of extra-law still looms large, especially in core policy areas, such as criminal law and public law.

Examples of extra-law also abound. The first example is criminal law. A significant proportion of criminal justice matters are still governed by extra-law. There has been a large gray area when it comes to police powers to punish. Due to ideological commitment and historical legacy, criminal law punishes only "serious offenses," leaving "minor offenses" to the prerogatives of the police. While approximately 1 million criminal cases go through the criminal justice process each year, more than 10 million offenses of different severity and nature are dealt with administratively by the police in the name of punishment, treatment, or rehabilitation. The hodgepodge of administrative penalties targets prostitutes, drug addicts and a wide range of minor offenders, and the penalties may vary from a verbal warning to incarceration for prostitutes and those who visit prostitutes. This administrative punishment regime is characterized by relative severity in penalty, lack of representation and due process and, in some cases, uncertain legislative authorization.[43]

But rule by extra-law is not limited to the field of criminal law. Another example is media governance. Media governance is essentially a lawless business in China. China's legislature has yet to be allowed to pass a single law to govern the media, which is wholly state-owned and controlled tightly by the Party. Instead, the media is controlled through a well-established political mechanism, armed with strong organizations and detailed procedures, to guide and manage all media outlets in China

[43] Elisa Nesossi et al. (eds.), *Legal Reforms and Deprivation of Liberty in Contemporary China* (London: Ashgate, 2016).

on an ongoing basis. Media governance is particularly an area in which Party norms and organs, instead of legal rules and institutions, act as the ultimate authority.

Extra-law has also been extensively used in other regulatory fields, such as tax policy, state secrecy and securities regulation, in which significant issues such as imposition of tax, designation of state secrets, and regulation of insider trading, are subject to internal and often informal rules without clear legislative authorization, a degree of transparency and necessary legal accountability.[44]

The Party's anticorruption regime, including *jiwei*, the CIG and *shuanggui*, is a typical extra-law design. The Party's leadership rule is constitutionally entrenched and cannot be challenged through any legal measure. The supreme position of the Party necessarily means that the Party's rules have certain constitutional legitimacy even though these rules exist entirely outside the legal system of the state. Yet, when the Party has elevated its internal rules to the status of quasi-state law and has placed Party governance and state governance on a compatible footing, it is difficult to simply regard Party rules as constitutionally and legally irrelevant.[45]

C Law

The rule of law has once again become a rallying point for China's new round of political-legal reform with the Party pronouncing an unprecedented commitment to developing the socialist legal system.[46] With that new initiative as the backdrop, there has been renewed concern about the legality of the *jiwei* investigation, especially the use of *shuanggui* against

[44] Yongxi Chen, *Halfway to Freedom of Information: The Legislative and Judicial Protection of the Right of Access to Information in China* (London: Ashgate, 2016); Wei Cui, "What Is the 'Law' in Chinese Tax Administration?," *Asia Pacific Law Review* 19 (2011): 75; Nicolas Howson, "Enforcement without Foundation? – Insider Trading and China's Administrative Law Crisis," *American Journal of Comparative Law* 60 (2012): 955.

[45] Backer and Wang, The Emerging Structures. See also Larry Backer, "The Party as Polity, the Communist Party, and the Chinese Constitutional State: A Theory of State-Party Constitutionalism," *Journal of Chinese and Comparative Law* 16 (2009): 101.

[46] Randall Peerenboom, "The Future of Legal Reforms in China: A Critical Appraisal of the Decision on Comprehensively Deepening Reform" (2014), http://papers.ssrn.com/sol3/papers.cfm?abstract_id=2379161. Law is defined here as a constitutionally legal regime in which properly constituted authorities establish legal norms (in a legal format) and these legal norms are then applied fairly by independent tribunals. There is a credible process of legal representation and judicial deliberation, a degree of transparency and external accountability throughout the decision making process.

Party members without following legal procedures, and the effort to move the extra-legal practices into a more proper legal framework. Extra-law may be fit for crisis management during a transitional period. But it is not sustainable if used as a regular governance tool.

Nevertheless, China has been building a legal order based on law since the late 1970s, and the achievement is most pronounced in civil and commercial law. Chinese public law has also witnessed a gradual, albeit contradictory, process in enhancing regularity, transparency, and juridification. Even in criminal law which is traditionally police-centric and highly politicized, there has been a tendency toward increasing certainty, more effective judicial oversight, and stronger legal representation.[47] Building a legal order is a long endeavor and China has experienced periodical setbacks and frustration in the process. But the larger trend had been clear: the sphere of law had been expanding, reaching out to and occupying more fields;[48] and formal rules are occupying more commanding heights in governance in relation to extra-legal rules and practices. The Xi government has, in particular, encouraged the expansion and empowerment of legal institutions in dispute resolution so as to bring more social problems to effective legal resolution. As a result, the legal system is likely to be more autonomous and effective and, in the long run, while the Party will remain "hands-on" in politically sensitive cases, the Party's willingness and ability to intervene in the vast majority of cases are likely to diminish further.

There are several reasons that explain the possibility of a gradual but decisive shift from the *jiwei*-based political mechanism to a legal-centric mechanism in controlling corruption in China. The *jiwei* system as it stands is relatively new. As mentioned earlier, the current *jiwei*-centric model came into being as part of the crisis management in the aftermath of the 1989 student movement and it was specifically set up to address corruption. While the Party launched a brutal crackdown against the democratic component of the student movement, the Party kept the anticorruption component alive by launching one of the largest campaigns against corruption. As part of that campaign, the Party imposed the supremacy of Party in anticorruption matters by bringing the ACA and other related agencies under *jiwei*'s leadership. The clear objective was to

[47] Hualing Fu, "Institutionalizing Criminal Process in China," in *The Development of the Chinese Legal System: Change and Challenge*, Guanghua Yu (ed.) (London: Routledge, 2011), 26.

[48] Biddulph, *Legal Reform*, 40.

consolidate the diverse resources and to develop a stronger institutional capacity in both policy making and operation.

The current campaign was also made in response to a political crisis faced by the Xi government.[49] But as the political risk that corruption poses wanes, and as the crisis withers (as it naturally will happen), the Party is likely to shift its focus from combating corruption to a reformist agenda. Once the current wave of anticorruption investigation and prosecution diminishes, and once the "tigers" have been hunted down, corruption would be perceived as a lesser political risk and anticorruption would no longer attract the highest political attention. The investigation would be less proactive, focusing more on individuals than their political affiliations and on cases that have taken place at lower levels of the government. Thus, sooner or later, *jiwei* would declare its anticorruption campaign a victory and, with the number of corruption-related prosecutions declining, shift its priority from investigation to institution-capacity building with a focus on education and prevention. When that happens, anticorruption is likely to be less a highly charged political campaign and more of a matter of routine law enforcement.

There have been some subtle changes in *jiwei*'s operations, which indicate a certain surprising deference to the legal system. *Jiwei*, for example, has refrained from using terms such as "cases" to highlight the fact that what *jiwei* handles is no more than complaints. *Jiwei* has come out to state that while there is overlap between *jiwei* and the legal system, the former is not expected to replace the latter. Wang Qishan himself has, reportedly, made the philosophical concession that, "give back to the law the law and to the Party disciplinary system Party discipline."[50] *Jiwei*'s work is not to handcuff corrupt officials, according to Wang, but to enforce party discipline.

The gradual but visible legal-centric reform is also likely to shift the gravitas from *jiwei* to the ACA, while the latter is developing more credibility and capacity. For one, the ACA is likely to better its treatment of the persons it prosecutes. Part of the reasons why corrupt officials "voluntarily" stay with the *shuanggui* system is that *shuanggui* offers certain advantage and benefits that the legal system fails to offer: the food is better, the accommodation is more comfortable, there is little public

[49] Fu, *Wielding the Sword*, 134.

[50] "Jiedu: Wang qishan zuixin jianghua toulu chu de jiwei xindongxiang" [New Trend in *jiwei* Revealed in Wang Qishan's Speech], *Sina News*, July 11, 2015, http://news.sina.com.cn/c/2015-07-11/004132095831.shtml.

embarrassment, and there is much less chance for actual criminal prosecution beyond the Party discipline.[51] Of course, this is all possible because the CCDI is politically of higher status than the NACA and commands more authority.

The institutional advantage that the regular criminal justice system has in comparison with *shuanggui* is negligible. The first advantage is that, while there is no clear-cut time limit for detention under *shuanggui*, there is a time limit for detention in the criminal process. But this advantage is minor. Criminal detention could also be lengthy and the conditions in detention facilities are brutal. The second advantage is that while there is a no access to lawyer for *shuanggui*, an accused in the criminal process is entitled to legal advice and representation. But before legal representation becomes genuinely useful and effective, legal representation is limited at the pretrial stage.

If the ongoing legal reform can place the court at the center of the criminal justice system for the vast majority of the cases, the comparative advantages of *shuanggui* may diminish further and the comparative attraction of the legal system would increase. When more weight is given to lawyers' legal advice and representation, and when fair trials are ensured because courts are more independent, then the incentive structure would change and the gravitas will shift to court trials. This will lead to the decline of *jiwei* in anticorruption matters. The comfortable detention experienced by those put under *shuanggui* may even have a positive impact on the ordinary criminal justice system just as fortress confinement eventually enhanced the standard of criminal justice in the Europe.[52]

Another important reason to explain a possible shift from *jiwei* to the criminal justice system (i.e., ACA) is that the political system has started to resemble a legal system where the *jiwei*'s substantive rules and investigative procedures are concerned. The recent reform to promote the rule of law within the Party is likely to engender regularity, professionalism,

[51] Special detention facilities for the privileged are not new. A number of European countries historically operated "fortress confinement" – a comfortable detention facility for the more privileged members of their respective societies. This existed side by side with the harsh justice meted out for the less privileged members. According to Whitman, fortress detention eventually played a positive role in injecting a humanistic element into the whole criminal justice system in European countries. James Q. Whitman, *Harsh Justice: Criminal Punishment and the Widening Divide between American and Europe* (Oxford: Oxford University Press, 2004), 69.

[52] Whitman, *Harsh Justice.*

institutionalization, and, above all, compliance with constitutional and legal rules. The CCDI, for example, has limited the duration of *shuanggui* detention and made the time limit compatible with that under criminal procedure rules. The Party has also re-designed its disciplinary procedures to offer a degree of protection of the rights of individual Party members so that the Party's internal disciplinary process is similar in form, if not in substance, to the legal process.[53]

In many cases, the political mechanism is needed because it has some features that the legal mechanisms lack in order to effectively combat corruption. Those features, such as prolonged detention, are necessary to bypass the procedural constraints and have been shown to be effective in extracting confessions. The system allows the Party to hide behind the veil of Party disciplinary proceeding and to carry out an effective criminal investigation in the name of Party discipline. But if the *jiwei* system moves closer to the legal mechanism and when the Party's internal disciplinary process and the criminal process resemble each other in substance and in form, the disciplinary mechanism will lose its comparative advantage. The question then becomes, why rely on the political mechanism when a legal mechanism, which is equally effective and commands greater legitimacy, is available? This is not to say that *jiwei* will disappear. There is no doubt that the dualism as stated above will survive and *jiwei* will continue to be in charge of investigating a limited number of cases relating to high-level corruption. But the anticorruption gravitas is likely to shift to legal institutions for the vast majority of the cases as the current legal reform continues.

IV Conclusion

The Party is firmly in charge of China's anticorruption institutions with *jiwei* setting the agenda and leading the investigation of major corruption cases in the name of political expediency. In that largely political process, legal institutions play a marginal and supporting role. This chapter does not deny this political reality. What this chapter does is to provide a cautious reminder that *jiwei*, as powerful as it has been in the past two decades, is part of a larger anticorruption mechanism. While *jiwei*'s role may be conspicuous in governing a country in the face of a real or perceived political crisis, anticorruption enforcement has to achieve some form of normalcy where it will need to rely on legal institutions and procedures

[53] Backer and Wang, *The Emerging Structures*, 251.

once the crisis is over. A nation-state cannot be perpetually ruled on the presumption that the state is facing a crisis, and the Party has to allow the legal system to take over and to offer necessary predictability, certainty, and legitimacy. Corruption is a crime common to all human societies. While the syndrome of corruption may differ in different regime types, corruption can be uniformly explained by the lack of effective control over power and wealth and institutions designed to control corruption.[54] There are successful anticorruption institutional designs to enhance the accountability and control that have been well-tested and China, despite its unique characteristics, does not present an exceptional case in the long run.[55]

This chapter focuses on the cooperation and to a lesser degree the competition between the politically driven anticorruption system, or *jiwei*, and a more legal-centric anticorruption system, arguing for the possibility that, with some exceptions, China has the potential to develop fully a legal-centric anticorruption regime in the long run. There is no reason that China cannot create a single, unitary anticorruption body as independent, effective, and powerful as the ICAC in Hong Kong. The ACA can operate independently of the CDI on a rigid separation of powers and functions. Historically, the ACA operated with more political independence prior to the 1993 centralization and, at that point in time, there was a genuine effort on the part of the procuratorate to achieve more institutional autonomy on matters relating to anticorruption enforcement.

In the meantime, the procuratorate has struggled to maintain its institutional autonomy and integrity and indeed, the ACA has resiliently resisted further attempts by the *jiwei* of a more structural fusion. Given that the independence of the procuratorate and ACA from *jiwei* is constitutionally enshrined, this is the reason why attempts at incorporating the ACA into *jiwei* framework have not worked – and were never meant to work. The procuratorate may have humbly deferred to *jiwei*'s instructions where anticorruption policies and investigation is concerned, particularly in rendering assistance to *jiwei* when *jiwei* carries out its own investigations, but the ACA has always tried to maintain its institutional autonomy. Therefore, the ACA's own operations have never been replaced by the *jiwei*'s.

[54] Michael Johnston, *Corruption Contention and Reform: The Power of Deep Democratization* (New York: Cambridge University Press, 2014), 29.

[55] Fu, *Stability and Anticorruption Initiatives*, 176.

A single system, which allows *jiwei* certain discretion in enforcing Party discipline but leaves criminal investigation, at least for the vast majority of corruption cases, to the ACA, would be the most optimal design even for China's authoritarian system. There are earlier signs that China may be moving toward that direction. The newly revised Criminal Procedural Law has given the ACA the power to detain persons in major corruption cases, and this power was modeled precisely on *shuanggui* so that in cases where a genuine need to extend pretrial investigation exists the ACA could rely on clear legal authority instead of relying on *shuanggui*. Furthermore, the anticorruption legal institutions may be able to gain more political clout. Since the end of 2014, the ACA has undergone another round of institutional reform. With the endorsement of the Party, the SPP merged another two departments with the NACA to form an anticorruption agency at the vice-ministerial level.[56] Under the new design, the NACA is to have a higher administrative rank headed by a more senior procurator. It will also have more manpower and other resources in view of internal restructuring. Researchers need to pay more attention to the potential juridification of China's anticorruption regime in which law is prepared to fill the gap that the Party mechanism may eventually leave vacant.

[56] "'Shengjiban' Fantan Zhongju Jiangcheng Zhonggong Xin Fanfu Liji" [A New Anti-Corruption Authority Will Become a Sharp Weapon of the CCP], *Xinhuawang*, November 4, 2011, http://news.xinhuanet.com/politics/2014–11/04/c_1113115543.htm.

11

Chinese Corporate Capitalism in Comparative Context

CURTIS J. MILHAUPT*

> Capitalism will be much more robust if it's not a monopoly of the West, but flourishes in societies with different cultures, religions, histories, and political systems.[1]

I Introduction

The "Beijing Consensus" is a broad label applied to China's approach to economic governance, one in which the state plays a pervasive role and (at least in theory) markets serve the higher interests of national development. As such, the Beijing Consensus may be an alternative term for "state capitalism," a concept that has attracted considerable attention due to China's spectacular economic growth. These labels suggest something unique about China's developmental path. However, the Chinese economy shares with all other developed and developing economies a key feature: *corporate* capitalism. That is, the central actors in the Chinese economy are legal entities enjoying separate and perpetual existence, governed ostensibly by a board of directors and appointed managers, with ownership interests represented by shares held by the providers of capital.[2]

* Portions of this chapter are drawn from Li-Wen Lin and Curtis J. Milhaupt, "We Are the (National) Champions: Understanding the Mechanisms of State Capitalism in China," *Stanford Law Review* 65 (2013): 697. I received a wealth of stimulating comments on this chapter – more than I could fully respond to in such a short piece. Any shortcomings in the chapter remain in spite of the extremely helpful input I received from Jinhua Cheng, Ron Gilson, Jed Kroncke, Li-Wen Lin, Tomo Marukawa, Daniel Puchniak, Wentong Zheng, and participants at a workshop on Scaling the State at Columbia University and the Beijing Consensus workshop at National University of Singapore.

[1] Ronald Coase and Ning Wang, "How China Became Capitalist," *Cato Policy Report* 35 (2013): 1, http://object.cato.org/sites/cato.org/files/serials/files/policy-report/2013/1/cprv35n1-1.pdf.

[2] Of course, form does not necessarily mean function. Does a Chinese corporation – particularly a state-owned enterprise (SOE) – perform the same function as, for example, a US,

Using this fundamental commonality as a starting point, this chapter looks behind the "Beijing Consensus" or "state capitalism" by briefly examining Chinese corporate capitalism in comparative context, with particular reference to other countries that have influenced China's approach to economic organization: Japan, South Korea, and Singapore. It seeks to distill the common and distinctive features of China's approach to corporate capitalism, explain their existence in the context of the Chinese political economy, and examine the feasibility and normative appeal of replicating Chinese corporate capitalism in other developing countries. Simply put, the chapter asks what is unique about Chinese corporate capitalism and whether those unique elements can or should be transplanted elsewhere.

To briefly state the conclusions, the chapter argues that the organizational foundation of Chinese state capitalism is not particularly unique, because *state* capitalism is a species of *corporate* capitalism. The corporate form – with its inherent characteristics – lends a familiar structure even to a form of economic organization that looks novel (or sinister) to outside observers. Yet the chapter argues that Chinese corporate capitalism does have some distinctive features, namely "party centrality" and "institutional bridging" (concepts elaborated below), although they have rough functional parallels in the comparison countries. These distinctive features are mostly a matter of degree, yet they suggest shifting emphasis in the Chinese case from "state" capitalism to "party-state" capitalism. This is not a "model" system: even if the Chinese approach could be replicated elsewhere, at least in functional terms, the benefits of doing so are likely to be outweighed by the governance weaknesses and other costs engendered by this particular configuration of corporate capitalism. Nonetheless, undertaking a comparative analysis of Chinese corporate capitalism is useful because it appears to reinforce several important lessons about

German, or Japanese corporation in credibly constraining the behavior of its participants, particularly its majority shareholder? Or is the corporate form in China – again, especially as adopted by an SOE – simply a convenient means of organizing and accounting for the state's assets? A more direct version of this question is whether the corporate form meaningfully constrains the state from dictating the decisions of the SOE's managers and maximizing the state's (rather than the firm's) interests. As I suggest but do not fully substantiate here, I believe the corporate form in China is important both for its form and its function, though it probably constrains the behavior of its controlling shareholder more weakly than its counterparts in more institutionally robust, less state-centric economies. I am grateful to Ron Gilson for highlighting the importance of these questions in understanding the role of the corporation in Chinese capitalism.

economic development that have emerged from the collective experience of other countries.

Part II of the chapter highlights a basic but generally overlooked point in the burgeoning field of taxonomic classification of capitalism: all of the forms of economic organization being classified are species of *corporate capitalism*. This simple observation can be leveraged to clarify what "state capitalism" is and the dimensions along which it can be distinguished from other forms of corporate capitalism. Part III surveys the key features of Chinese state capitalism by mining the prosaic *corporate* underpinnings of this system of economic organization. It also places the Chinese system in comparative context, to highlight shared and distinctive traits vis-à-vis other systems. Part IV draws some possible lessons from the analysis for law and development literature.

II Varieties of Capitalism: The Prequel

Comparative scholarship on capitalist systems is a growth industry. Liberal Market Economy/Coordinated Market Economy... Shareholder Capitalism/Stakeholder Capitalism/Crony Capitalism... Market Capitalism/State Capitalism... Washington Consensus/Beijing Consensus... The taxonomy grows more extensive with each financial crisis and the appearance of each newly emerging economy on the world stage.

The object of this chapter is not to quarrel with the expanding taxonomies or to question the insights generated by debates about the efficiency, welfare effects, or sustainability of different approaches to economic organization. Rather, the aim is to explore the implications of an observation so obvious that it is generally overlooked: labels aside, virtually all viable economies today, regardless of size, stage of development, or political orientation – including most relevantly for this volume, China – take the corporate form as the central organizing device in the economy.[3] The bulk of economic activities in the global capitalist system

[3] I am mindful that other organizational forms, particularly the trust and the partnership, are also widely used in and important to global capitalism, but the corporate form would dominate a census of the most significant global economic actors. For example, a search of the suffixes (Corp., Inc., Partnership, Trust, etc.) of the names of the 3,281 firms listed on the New York Stock Exchange turns up only 1 partnership and 23 LLCs. Of the 2,426 firms listed on the London Stock Exchange, only about 200 have noncorporate suffixes; no firm in the CSI 300 (a capitalization-weighted index of firms listed on the Shanghai and Shenzhen exchanges) has a noncorporate suffix.

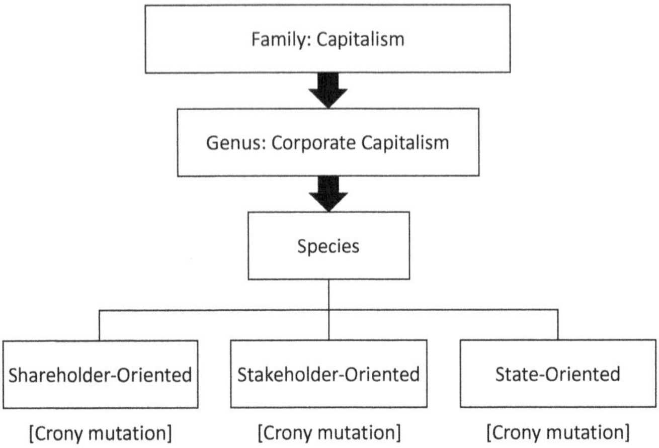

Figure 11.1 Taxonomy.

are conducted by or through the corporate form – a legal device enabled by the state, featuring separate and full legal personality; perpetual existence; limited liability for investors and managers; delegated management under a board of directors; and free transferability of shares.

The first point of the chapter is simply that Chinese "state capitalism" is a species of *corporate* capitalism (see Figure 11.1). This claim actually follows directly from the uncontroversial starting point of Hansmann and Kraakmann's controversial article, *The End of History for Corporate Law.*[4] That work is widely cited and often criticized for its muscular normative claim that intellectual convergence on the "shareholder-oriented model of the corporate form," working hand-in-hand with market forces, will erode differences among national corporate governance regimes and lead to convergence in economic systems. Generating virtually no comment, however, is the article's foundational descriptive claim: the *corporate* form has triumphed worldwide as a means of organizing capitalist economic

"Company List (NYSE)," NASDAQ, www.nasdaq.com/screening/companies-by-name.aspx?letter=0&exchange=nyse&render=download; "List of All Companies," London Stock Exchange, www.londonstockexchange.com/statistics/companies-and-issuers/companies-and-issuers.htm; "CSI 300," China Securities Index, www.csindex.com.cn/sseportal/ps/zhs/hqjt/csi/000300cons.xls.

[4] Henry Hansmann and Reinier Kraakman, "The End of History for Corporate Law," *Georgetown Law Journal* 89 (2001): 439.

activity.[5] Precisely why this is so need not detain us here, but I will return to this point later in the chapter.[6]

Figure 11.1 is a graphical depiction of two foundational points that animate the chapter: first, reality assuages doubts that China's state-oriented economic system is not capitalist because capitalism "is a form of economic activity dominated by *private* firms (emphasis added)" and profits are the "key test of a capitalistic enterprise."[7] This view of capitalism is ahistorical and perhaps US-centric: at an earlier state of economic and political development in the United States, the United Kingdom, and elsewhere, corporations were typically chartered as a grant of authority from the state to perform a specific purpose providing public benefits, such as to operate a railroad. Thus, the earliest corporations were public-private hybrids, serving as an organizational bridge between the state and the body public.[8] Stated differently, "[h]istorically, corporations, like states, have been used to achieve ends of government."[9] The British East India Company is a dramatic early example of this phenomenon. The conceptualization of the corporation as private property, and capitalism as a project of national development by means of the promotion of private property, emerged later and is most closely associated with American schools of thought. China's economic system, in which capital, labor,

[5] As one gauge of its usefulness, even North Korea, hardly a paragon of capitalism, uses the corporate form for the state's engagement with the economy, though tellingly, the state does not allow private entrepreneurs access to this powerful form of organization. John S. Park, "North Korea, Inc.: Gaining Insights into North Korean Regime Stability from Recent Commercial Activities," USIP Working Paper (United States Institute of Peace, 2009), www.usip.org/sites/default/files/North%20Korea,%20Inc.PDF.

[6] Much has been written about this subject. Suffice it to say that the combination of corporate attributes enumerated in the text has proven to be an extremely efficient device for pooling and investing capital while limiting and diversifying risk; while its drawbacks, mostly pertaining to externalization of risk and amplification of agency costs, are basically (though imperfectly) manageable through insurance and regulation (for risk) and governance and incentive mechanisms (for agency costs). The global policy choice implicit in the corporation's ubiquity is that the benefits to society from extensive use of the corporate form outweigh the costs. Of course, it is also possible that path dependence rather than economic efficiency explains the widespread adoption of the corporate form in China (and many other later-developing countries). That is, the corporate form may have been attractive to Chinese economic strategists, not because of its inherent superiority over possible alternatives, but because it had already been widely adopted elsewhere.

[7] Marshall W. Meyer, "Is It Capitalism?," *Management & Organization Review* 7 (2011): 8.

[8] Joshua Barkan, *Corporate Sovereignty: Law and Government under Capitalism* (Minneapolis: University of Minnesota Press, 2013).

[9] Ibid., 5.

goods and services are allocated (largely) in markets for profit,[10] is properly classified as capitalism, and since it is organized around the corporate form (as detailed below), it is properly classified as a species of corporate capitalism.[11]

A second foundational point, implicit from the figure, is that, due to its reliance on the corporate form, Chinese capitalism shares more traits in common with other species of capitalism than is commonly acknowledged, particularly by those who see in state capitalism something novel and potentially menacing.[12] Corporations everywhere have the same basic attributes, although the prominence of a given attribute in the overall constellation (for example, the priority assigned to ownership interests held by the providers of capital), may vary from country to country. This constellation of attributes offers the same basic advantages to everyone who utilizes the corporate form, and generates the same fundamental risks (insolvency being a key risk to shareholders and employees, and externalization of "public bads" such as financial contagion or environmental disasters being a key risk to society). Thus, the corporate form, by its very nature, powerfully channels the ways in which capitalism operates in every country. (As an important aside, the figure also depicts the reality that all species of corporate capitalism are susceptible to mutation into crony capitalism – whereby the operation or regulation of markets for capital, labor, or goods and services is corrupted by illicit relationships; this pathology is not uniquely identified with any particular species,

[10] Nicholas R. Lardy, *Markets over Mao: The Rise of Private Business in China* (Washington, DC: Peterson Institute for International Economics, 2014).

[11] Some commenters on an earlier draft suggested that all capitalism is properly classified as corporate, such that there is no meaningful taxonomic distinction between what I have labeled the family (capitalism) and the species (corporate capitalism). I think it is conceptually helpful to consider other genera of capitalism that do not rely on the corporate form, such as family capitalism, Islamic capitalism using the *wafq* and *mudaraba* organizational forms, and many other forms of proto-capitalism that emerged prior to the Industrial Revolution. Larry Neal and Jeffrey G. Williamson (eds.), *The Cambridge History of Capitalism: Volume 1, The Rise of Capitalism: From Ancient Origins to 1848* (Cambridge: Cambridge University Press, 2014). In any event, taxonomical precision for its own sake is not the objective of this chapter. Devoting attention to disambiguation highlights the important fact that all major "varieties of capitalism" today, including "state capitalism," are organized around a common organizational form. This development was not preordained and is testament to the power and adaptability of the corporate form.

[12] See, for example, Ian Bremmer, *The End of the Free Market: Who Wins the War between States and Corporations?* (New York: Penguin, 2010).

although of course the propensity and severity of the pathology may vary significantly across species.[13])

Advancing these basic claims about the prosaic features of Chinese state capitalism will contribute to the chapter's chief ambition: clarifying the ways in which the *state* species of *corporate* capitalism as practiced in China differs from the other species. I will argue that some of the differences are internal to the corporate form; others are external. The internal differences pertain to the way in which standard corporate structures and operations, such as the working of the board of directors, have been supplemented or altered by Chinese Communist Party organs. The external differences pertain to how the Chinese corporation is viewed and treated *as an actor* in the political economy, including the comparatively limited degree of autonomy it enjoys from the state, and the comparatively broad scope of objectives it may pursue, which extend beyond the corporation's first-degree stakeholders (shareholders, managers, and employees) to encompass "the citizens," "national interests," or "government/party policy." By developing these points, I hope the chapter will provide a novel perspective on Chinese state capitalism (or, if the reader prefers, the organizational DNA of the "Beijing Consensus").

III Chinese Corporate Capitalism

This section sketches key attributes of Chinese corporate capitalism as they have evolved in the reform era. Relevant features of other species of corporate capitalism, such as those of Japan, Korea and Singapore, are discussed for purposes of comparison. Several conjectures about the principal developmental consequences of Chinese corporate capitalism are then briefly discussed.

A Attributes

Corporatization of the Economy

Although Chinese "state capitalism" is not entirely synonymous with state-owned enterprises (SOEs), they are certainly of one of its principal

[13] Recent research suggests that rent seeking tends to be sector specific and appears not to be closely correlated with the strength of national institutions or varieties of capitalism. "The New Age of Crony Capitalism," *The Economist*, March 15, 2014, 13; "Planet Plutocrat," *The Economist*, March 15, 2014, 57.

mechanisms.[14] Consistent with the argument that the corporate form is the basic building block of all market-oriented economies, a crucial early move in China's reform process was "corporatization" of the economy.[15] This entailed transformation of the production arms of state agencies into joint stock corporations.[16] Through this process, production functions were formally separated from public regulatory functions and cloaked in an organizational form that is both prevalent and readily understood around the world. Shares were issued to the corporation's governmental owners (in theory, on behalf of the ultimate owners, the Chinese people). Ostensibly, at least, the newly formed corporations were imbued with the standard governance organs of boards of directors and shareholders meetings. A Corporate Law was enacted, very much with SOEs in mind,[17] to provide the norms of governance for and allocation of rights among the corporate stakeholders. Some of the best state assets were packaged into corporations which issued shares to minority public investors on Chinese and global capital markets. These listings, which would not have been possible without the transformation of state assets into an organizational form recognizable to international investors, provided capital, managerial expertise, and global visibility to the firms. The local Chinese governments were also integrally involved in the corporatization process. As Cheng states,[18] "local legislative experiments [with incorporation rules, public offerings and capital requirements] had significantly contributed to institutionalizing corporations and other business

[14] Benjamin Liebman and Curtis J. Milhaupt (eds.), *Regulating the Visible Hand? The Institutional Implications of Chinese State Capitalism* (New York: Oxford University Press, 2016).

[15] Several commenters pointed out that noncorporate entities, such as the TVE, were actually the first actors in China's movement toward a market-oriented economy. This is accurate, but the shift away from these entities in favor of corporatization reinforces the claim that the corporation proved to be a superior organizational form – perhaps not only economically but also from the standpoint of retaining the Communist Party's political control over the economy.

[16] Donald Clarke, "Blowblack: How China's Efforts to Bring Private-Sector Standards into the Public Sector Backfired," in *Regulating the Visible Hand*, Liebman and Milhaupt (eds.). Clarke persuasively argues that the corporatization project was driven by several misconceptions about what ailed China's state sector, and consequently about the potential for corporatization to remedy those ills. Nonetheless, there can be little doubt that corporatization was a necessary, if not sufficient, step in China's economic reform process.

[17] Donald Clarke, "Corporate Governance in China: An Overview," *China Economic Review* 14 (2003): 494–507.

[18] Jinhua Cheng, "Dual Intergovernmental Transformation and Economic Growth" (JSD diss., Yale University, 2011), 185.

organizations in transitional China," greatly reducing the costs of developing the national corporate economy.

Corporate Groups

Chinese SOEs, particularly at the national level, are organized into business groups comprised of numerous separate corporations arranged in hierarchical order. The decision to organize the firms into groups was a strategy based on observations of economic development elsewhere, particularly the high-growth economies of East Asia. Governmental encouragement of business group formation to foster the growth of national champions has been a common strategy around the developing world, followed by a wide range of governments pursuing diverse macroeconomic policies. Such countries include late-nineteenth-century Japan under the Meiji oligarchs, South Korea under military strongman Park Chung Hee in the early 1970s, and Chile under Pinochet in the late 1970s and 1980s. The Chinese leadership's decision to organize its corporatized SOEs into groups probably reflected the same motivations for business group formation found in these and other developing countries, including filling institutional voids in weak rule of law environments, internalizing capital markets, marshaling scarce resources (including both monetary capital and entrepreneurial human capital), and reducing the transaction costs of administering economic policy.

Business groups around the world have typically originated with family-founded enterprises. In China, group formation took place along a very different path, because there were no home-grown entrepreneurs in the immediate post-Mao era to serve as partners of government in the development project. Chinese economic strategists were intrigued by Japanese *keiretsu* and Korean *chaebol* business groups as models for promoting growth, but there was no shortcut available for replicating such groups in China. The SOE business groups in existence today are the result of a long process of experimentation with collaborative forms of production. Business alliances based on contract were tried first as a means of coordinating production and resource allocation, but they proved ineffective. In the next phase, in place of contracts, policy makers used organizational structures based on shareholding to link firms along the production chain and across complementary industries. Eventually, the business group concept was enshrined in regulations that permitted registration as a business group if it had certain required components and layers of entities. Registration as a business group afforded certain benefits, including most importantly eligibility to establish a finance company to handle intragroup lending, underwriting, cash management, and other financial functions that are otherwise prohibited on an intercompany level.[19]

In contrast to the main postwar Japanese *keiretsu* and Korean *chaebol* corporate groups, Chinese business groups are vertically integrated firms focused on a particular industry or sector, not diversified groups involved in a range of industries. Again in contrast to *keiretsu* and *chaebol* structures, shareholding is hierarchical: firms higher in the structure, particularly the parent company in which strategic and managerial decision making are concentrated, own downstream subsidiaries, but there is very little upstream or cross-ownership among group firms. Governance concerns – both corporate and political – are the primary reason for top-down ownership patterns. Parent companies have little use for upstream share ownership; top-down stock holdings reflect and reinforce the hierarchical structure of the groups. Moreover, given pervasive involvement of the Chinese Communist Party in group firms and other forms of party-state monitoring (discussed in the next subsection), the risk sharing and monitoring functions of cross-ownership performed in other countries, most prominently Japan, are not complementary to Chinese corporate group structures.

At least ostensibly, the controlling shareholder atop this giant web of corporate groups is an agency formed in 2003 called SASAC, the State-Owned Assets Supervision and Administration Commission. SASAC's formal role is to serve as the investor in the approximately 100 massive corporate groups under its supervision, on behalf of the Chinese state and people. But SASAC is a peculiar entity: part investor, part regulator and consolidated compliance department, part conduit for Party influence and government policy dissemination. While it formally "supervises" the central SOEs, it often must yield to the instructions of other ministries or to the prerogatives of the most politically well-connected SOEs themselves.

Holding Company Structure

Arguably the closest model for Chinese SOE reform and corporate structure, particularly following the formation of SASAC at the national level, can be found in Singapore. As in China, Singapore's development strategy has relied heavily on what are known in that country as government-linked

[19] Lin and Milhaupt, "We are the (National) Champions."

companies (GLCs). Shares of Singapore's GLCs are owned by a holding company, Temasek, which was formed in 1974 as a wholly owned subsidiary of the Ministry of Finance. Temasek took control of a number of companies that had been held by other government bodies, completing a separation of regulatory authority and enterprise ownership. These companies had already been formed into groups by the government, also in a manner reminiscent of the Korean *chaebol*, in order to foster national champions. Each of the companies in Temasek's portfolio is the head of its own corporate group with numerous affiliated companies.[20] According to Tan et al.,[21] 37 percent of Singapore's total stock market capitalization is comprised of companies in which the government is the controlling shareholder.

The basic structural similarities between Temasek and SASAC reflect similarities in the two government's motivations for adopting a state capitalist approach. Singapore's GLC-centered strategy, developed in the late 1950s and 1960s, grew out of "the ruling PAP government's perceived need to support the transformation of the Singapore economy," based on the conclusion that "control over key domestic markets and institutions [was] the most effective way to . . . meet the main planning objectives of absorbing surplus labour and promoting economic growth."[22] Moreover, in both countries, there is a strong link between economic success and political legitimacy. Particularly given the strength of these parallels and the success of Singapore's approach, it is not surprising that the Chinese Communist Party, along with many other analysts concerned with Chinese SOE reform, have continued to look toward Temasek as a model.[23]

[20] Grant Kirkpatrick, "Managing State Assets to Achieve Developmental Goals: The Case of Singapore and Other Countries in the Region" (Paper presented at the workshop on SOEs in the development process for the Organisation for Economic Co-operation and Development, OECD Conference Center, Paris, April 4, 2014).

[21] Cheng-Han Tan, Daniel Puchniak and Umakanth Varottil, "State-Owned Enterprises in Singapore: Historical Insights into a Chosen Model for Reform," *Columbia Journal of Asian Law* 28 (2015): 67.

[22] Ibid., 9.

[23] Boston Consulting Group and China Development Research Foundation, "Developing Mixed Ownership Structures and Modern Enterprise Systems" (Paper presented at the meeting for the China Development Forum, Beijing, China, March 22–24, 2014), www.bcg.com.cn/en/files/publications/reports_pdf/BCG_Developing_Mixed_Ownership_Structures_and_Modern_Enterprise_Systems_Mar2014_ENG.pdf; World Bank, *China 2030: Building a Modern, Harmonious and Creative Society* (Washington, DC: World Bank, 2013). Although the World Bank in the report (p. 119) does not explicitly reference Temasek, it argues: "It is critical . . . that SASAC confine itself to policy making and oversight, leaving asset management to the SAMCs [state asset management companies

But China adopted the Singapore holding company structure only selectively: SASAC is far from a copy of Temasek,[24] which has two closely related defining features that signal its role as a true holding company: (1) an unambiguously commercial orientation articulated in public documents and verified by its performance; and (2) a high degree of independence from direct political influence vis-à-vis the companies in its portfolio.[25] *Commercial orientation*: Temasek refers to itself as an active investor and steward of state assets. This claim is backed up by its performance. It has achieved a total shareholder return of 16 percent compounded annually since its inception in 1974. Temasek uses various devices to increase its financial discipline, such as issuing bonds (rated AAA by Standard & Poor's) and making detailed annual disclosures of its performance and portfolio. Market benchmarks are used to structure incentive compensation for managers. *Independence*: Temasek's board of directors is highly professional and nonpolitical in its orientation. The thirteen-member board (expanded from ten in January 2015) is presently comprised of a majority of independent private-sector directors, three of whom are non-Singapore nationals, including Robert Zoellick, former president of the World Bank. There is no ministerial representative on the board. To be sure, Temasek is not entirely free from political influence. Its current CEO is linked by marriage to modern Singapore's founding father Lee Kwan Yew. Members of the boards of both Temasek and its portfolio companies have historically been drawn from civil service and the military. Even today, the managers of Temasek's portfolio firms are chosen from the "ruling strata of Singapore. As a result, there [is] widespread agreement about the developmental objectives of the government, which has remained in the hands of the People's Action Party since independence."[26] As the quote suggests, the boards of directors of the GLCs themselves are not completely independent of the government in its role as controlling shareholder. But there is something of a "best of both worlds" quality to this arrangement: the presence of a controlling shareholder with incentives to monitor the portfolio firms,

that the World Bank recommends establishing to represent the government as shareholder and professionally manage the assets in financial markets]." The SAMCs contemplated by the World Bank are basically a description of Temasek.

24 See, for example, Ryan Rutkowski, "State-Owned Enterprise Reform: The Long Wait for a Chinese Temasek Continues ... " *Peterson Institute for International Economics*, January 23, 2014, http://blogs.piie.com/china/?p=3726.

25 The information in this paragraph is drawn largely from *Temasek Review*. Temasek Holdings (Private) Limited, *Temasek Review* 2014, www.temasek.com.sg/documents/download/downloads/20140707170404/Temasek-Review-2014-En.pdf.

26 Kirkpatrick, "Managing State Assets," 10.

but one whose overriding motive is maximizing the firms' economic outcomes, not extracting wealth from minority shareholders.

Party Centrality

Thus far, we have described a Chinese system that has parallels with group-oriented corporate capitalism elsewhere. But ending the description of Chinese corporate capitalism here would be highly incomplete, because the more or less universally recognizable features described thus far are supplemented (and perhaps functionally displaced) by some distinctive noncorporate features. The first I will call "Party centrality." This refers to the use of party organs and party structures to act as a shadow monitor of corporate actors as well as a personnel office for high-level managerial appointments in Chinese SOEs (and large private firms as well). In an extension of the Leninist approach to state organization, the Chinese Communist Party shadows *corporate* organizational structures in the same way that the Party shadows governmental structures. Every large firm in China has a party committee responsible for high-level managerial appointments and promotions.[27] These committees also appear to play an anticorruption/information and reporting role very roughly analogous to that of internal control structures in Western firms. The managerial elite of the SOEs (and again, many large, privately owned enterprises, or POEs) are overwhelmingly Party members,[28] and they simultaneously serve roles in Party and government bodies. The Party thus permeates Chinese corporate capitalism. Indeed, when focusing on large Chinese corporations, it may be more instructive to understand them as Party-linked companies rather than analyzing them within the standard state-owned versus privately owned (SOE-POE) dichotomy.

Institutional Bridging

Party centrality is closely associated with a second distinctive characteristic of Chinese corporate capitalism, a feature call "institutional bridging."[29]

[27] Large POEs have internal party committees just like SOEs, and their founders and/or controlling shareholders are often linked to party and governmental organs in the same fashion as SOEs managerial elites. Curtis J. Milhaupt and Wentong Zheng, "Beyond Ownership: State Capitalism and the Chinese Firm," *Georgetown Law Journal* 103 (2015): 665.

[28] In the national-level SOEs, 99 percent of the CEOs and 90 percent of the vice-CEOs are Party members. Li-Wen Lin, "Balancing Closure and Openness," in *Regulating the Visible Hand*, Liebman and Milhaupt (eds.).

[29] Lin and Milhaupt, "We are the (National) Champions," 726–27.

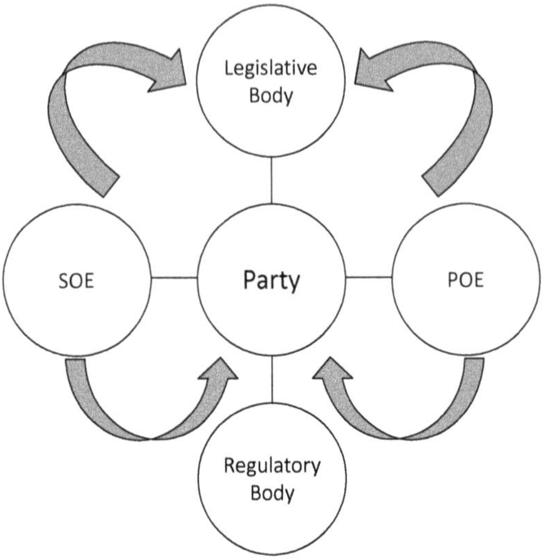

Figure 11.2 Party centrality and institutional bridging.

This refers to the way in which the various firms that comprise an SOE business group (as well as many large POEs) are extensively networked to the larger system of industrial organization and governmental authority, all of which are shadowed by the party. In effect, the party is the hub of a complex wheel whose spokes radiate out to business enterprise, banks, governmental organs, and other units of the state such as universities and research institutes (Figure 11.2).

Although the groups are legally and functionally distinct from each other, complementary groups are linked through joint ventures, strategic alliances, and intergroup equity ownership. The dense networks linking individual components of China's state sector were engineered by various means. Some, like the equity ownership linkages, make use of the corporate form and corporate law. Others are the result of personnel practices of the Party Organization Department and SASAC, in which senior managers are rotated within and among groups. Still others result from distinctive notions of representation in party and governmental organs, in which a number of seats are assigned to business leaders. These institutional bridges link the separate components of Chinese state capitalism into a complementary whole.

Since all of the parent companies of the national SOE groups are ultimately controlled, at least as a matter of formal law, by SASAC, the

Chinese group structure as a whole outwardly resembles the structure of a single Korean *chaebol*. That is, while individual corporate groups in China are vertically integrated along the production line and lack cross-shareholding among member firms, the groups under SASAC supervision, taken as a whole, resemble a giant diversified conglomerate under a single controlling shareholder, with extensive cross-ownership and other forms of collaboration, including extensive personnel rotation, among member firms. But the analogy should not be stretched too far: the SOEs themselves are quite heterogeneous, including in the degree to which they answer to SASAC as opposed to other regulators and political masters. And as Milhaupt and Zheng point out, there are many reasons to be skeptical of "the state's" ability to actually *control* state-owned enterprises in China.[30]

How might the structures just described have contributed to Chinese economic development? As Gilson and Milhaupt have noted, the alliances formed by the party-state with firms offering growth potential and the role of the party-state in funding, incentivizing and monitoring the managers of such firms is reminiscent of a private equity partnership: high-powered incentives for growth are provided by the party structure of rotations and job movement across the boundaries of business and politics.[31] Moreover, the integration of a large swath of the entrepreneurial population into the formal structures of party-state governance calls to mind Mancur Olson's concept of an "encompassing coalition" – a group representing a large enough segment of the population that it has incentives to grow the pie, as opposed to a "distributional coalition" representing a narrow segment of society.[32] By creating dense networks of managerial elites migrating across the spheres of politics, public governance and business in China, an encompassing coalition has been created with control over developmental policy formulation and implementation. The Chinese firm is but one component of party-centered economic and public governance – *Party-State, Inc.*, if you will. But again, the structure in operation is not one of simple top-down control, but rather loose linkages of firms (many of which are operating in competitive markets) and other state organs managed by elites enmeshed in, and responding to incentives flowing from, China's political system.

30 Milhaupt and Zheng, "Beyond Ownership."

31 Ronald Gilson and Curtis J. Milhaupt, "Economically Benevolent Dictators: Lessons for Developing Democracies," *American Journal of Comparative Law* 59 (2011): 262.

32 Lin and Milhaupt, "We are the (National) Champions," 702.

B *Assessing the "Corporate-ness" of Chinese Capitalism*

A short thematic chapter is not the place for an extended analysis of Chinese corporate law and governance in the context of the country's economic development. My aim in this subsection is simply to highlight the potential importance of the corporation to Chinese capitalism and to raise some questions about how the universal characteristics of the corporate form may be affected by Chinese state capitalism.

China's developmental experience is highly suggestive of the importance of the corporate form to economic development. The corporatization process was central to the hydraulics of industrial organization in the reform era: separating (incompletely and problematically, to be sure) the regulatory from the operational aspects of enterprise in the corporatization process was a crucial first step in the development of a functional state sector. The corporate form has proven to be extraordinarily useful in providing the Chinese party-state with a scalable, adaptable, and relatively anonymous[33] vehicle for investment and economic activity. It provided a template for the structure of the state sector and its scaling to globally important proportions. Its inherent features have provided an "off-the-rack" organizational device no less serviceable to the strategists of Party-State Inc. than to entrepreneurs in other economies.[34] The corporate form has also provided a template for the emergence of private entrepreneurship and a pathway for the possible retreat of the Party from direct involvement in business enterprise, should it ever choose to do so. (Note that the current SOE reform plan promoted by the Xi Jinping administration draws upon a standard corporate turnaround strategy – obtaining capital injections from investors capable

[33] Anonymity of the corporate form may be useful to state capitalists in masking the state operating behind the corporation. At the same time, however, this very masking can subject all firms operating out of a state capitalist system, whether closely linked to the state or not, to fears that they have non-commercial motives – a "suspicion tax" of sorts. This was most apparent in the case of two globally successful Chinese telecom firms Huawei and ZTE, which were the subject of a US House of Representatives investigation. Although the House committee found no conclusive evidence that the firms were affiliated with the Chinese state or Communist Party, it recommended that their future investment activity in the United States be blocked because they did not provide information sufficient to conclude that they were *not* linked to the state. In other words, the US politicians placed the burden of proof for demonstrating a 100 percent commercial orientation on the Chinese firms.

[34] This is particularly the case because, as noted above, China developed its corporate law with SOE reform, and the state as controlling shareholder, very much in mind. Clarke, "Corporate Governance in China," 494.

of improving managerial and financial performance – but falls short of true privatization.)

Yet throughout the reform period, Chinese economic strategists have chosen selectively from among the menu of corporate attributes, making extensive use of the corporation's hierarchical governance structure and separate legal existence in building networks of firms responsive to influence from party-state organs, and leveraging the power of the state in its ostensible role as controlling shareholder. At the same time, the universal, supreme decision making and oversight organ provided by the corporate form – the board of directors – has often been sidelined by the Party's own monitoring structures. Here the contrast with Singapore is instructive. Temasek is a professional asset management company in a high-quality institutional environment, pursuing commercial objectives, albeit in service of political legitimacy and preservation of national wealth and influence; SASAC is a holding company in form, but functionally it is a vehicle for pursuing two highly conflicting objectives: enhancing the performance and global reach of Chinese SOEs while maintaining the Party's direct influence over, and rent extraction from, important firms in the economy.

Thus, it may be instructive to briefly analyze how the universal attributes of the corporate form have been adapted to, and affected by, the ecology of Chinese capitalism:

Separate Legal Personality/Limited Liability

One of the principal concerns with SOEs everywhere is that they operate under a "soft budget constraint." That is, their managers do not fear financial failure because the state implicitly guarantees their debts and stands ready to cover deficits that arise in their operation. Under a soft budget constraint, and particularly given the personnel overlaps and rotations between SOE managers and party officials, one might conclude that neither separate legal personality nor limited liability carry the same import in China as in other species of corporate capitalism. However, as noted above, the separate, universally recognizable legal personality of the corporate form played a big role both in the internal re-arrangement of organizational actors during China's reforms and their scaling to global proportions. Limited liability may yet prove to be important, as Chinese growth slows and budget constraints harden.[35]

[35] China recently experienced its first bond default by an SOE.

Delegated Management

As argued above, the board of directors in SOEs is often bypassed by the Party system. Developing functional boards of directors of Chinese SOEs has been a relatively slow process. As long as Communist Party organs continue to parallel and shadow corporate organs in the state sector, and as long as the party-state retains direct influence over SOEs, Chinese corporate governance in the state sector will retain a distinctly shareholder-centric (that is, party-state-centric) bias in tension with the principle of delegated management.

Transferable Shares

Until recently, China maintained a share classification system that rendered shares of SOEs effectively nontransferrable to nonstate organs. Today, while all shares are transferrable as a formal matter and despite "mixed ownership" reforms to encourage more private investment in SOEs, the Chinese government shows no signs of relinquishing control over SOEs in sectors of the economy deemed to be critical. There is effectively no market for corporate control in China. On the other hand, creation of stock markets in the early 1990s was a major institutional step in China's developmental process, and it seems safe to conclude that liquidity facilitated by transferability of shares has been a major factor in foreign portfolio investments in China's state sector, including the banking sector.

Investor Ownership

SOEs, like all corporations, feature ownership by the providers of one factor of production – capital. But the state is unlike any other shareholder; and the Chinese party-state is unlike any other state. The distinctiveness of the state as shareholder is a defining feature of state capitalism, and the distinctiveness of the party-state sets Chinese state capitalism apart from that practiced in other countries,[36] at least as a matter of degree.

As this brief survey suggests, most universal corporate attributes are affected by state capitalism, including perhaps in particular China's subspecies of state capitalism. Thus, it is fair to ask whether the system should still be classified as a species of corporate capitalism. I believe the answer is affirmative. The basic corporate attributes are affected by and

[36] Mark Wu, "The WTO and China's Unique Economic Structure," in *Regulating the Visible Hand*, Liebman and Milhaupt (eds.), 313.

adapted to every species of corporate capitalism around the world. For example, few would question whether Japan evinces a species of corporate capitalism, notwithstanding the fact that Japanese managers, at least traditionally, have overwhelmingly placed the interests of employees over those of shareholders.

IV Lessons

A *What Is "State Capitalism" as Practiced in China (aka the Beijing Consensus)?*

The discussion thus far suggests that Chinese state capitalism is a species of corporate capitalism (1) featuring political involvement in, or at times displacement of, the standard corporate governance organs of the board of directors, professional managers, and shareholders meetings (the internal dimension); and (2) in which the corporation is treated by the state, or political actors closely identified with the state, as an integral part of the "Capital G" Governance apparatus and not simply as an object of regulation, as it is in (the idealized versions of) other species of corporate capitalism. Thus, its objectives are not limited to serving the interests of its first-degree stakeholders, but also encompass political and policy agendas (the external dimension). As a consequence, in state capitalism the firm is influenced by and influences public governance considerations to a larger extent than in other systems of corporate capitalism, and the unit of maximization is not the individual firm, but state interests as a whole (at least as those interests are defined by Party elites). Distinctiveness along what I have termed the external dimension suggests a potentially key tension between state capitalism and other species of corporate capitalism – but it is a tension that at least one other practitioner of state capitalism, Singapore, has managed to resolve, as discussed below.

The most distinctive quality of Chinese corporate capitalism as currently practiced is the degree to which political and managerial interests and incentives have been integrated in the state sector. A high degree of overlap between political and managerial interests may be common in a country's take-off stage of development. This raises the important question of whether Chinese corporate capitalism in its current *Party-State Inc.* form is transitional or enduring. I believe there are good reasons to think the latter (see below), but I defer extended discussion of this point to future work.

B Should Chinese Corporate Capitalism Be Regarded as a "Model," Such That Its Features Serve as the Basis for a New "Consensus" about How to Organize a Successful Economy? No.

As just discussed, the Chinese species of corporate capitalism does have several distinctive qualities, both internally and externally. But as argued throughout the chapter, Chinese "state" capitalism is not distinctive at its organizational core; the corporate building blocks are familiar to capitalists everywhere.

Even the distinctive aspects of the Chinese system have rough functional analogues in other countries. Close connections between political leadership and groups of favored business elites to transmit economic policy, finance industries deemed critical to national development, and manage competition were also a major facet of South Korea's and Japan's developmental paths, but other countries such as Taiwan and Brazil could also be mentioned. These interactions were institutionalized in Japan in the form of *amakudari* (descent from heaven), a practice in which high-level officials from the most powerful ministries parachuted into the private sector in mid-career. There they served as an important bridge between the government and the business and financial establishment, forming a network of managerial elites with shared backgrounds and basic values.[37] Chinese state-business interactions differ from most other examples on account of extensive state ownership of enterprise. But in the context of a developing economy, state versus private property ownership, of itself, may be relatively unrevealing of the proximity between corporations and political elites. In weak institutional environments that typify developing economies, the autonomy from governmental authority usually associated with private property ownership is often illusory; governments retain fairly extensive, unspecified residual control rights in all firms, whether state or privately owned, due to a lack of political accountability mechanisms and underdevelopment of institutions to secure private property against state incursions.

Thus, China is distinctive in the *extent* of state ownership of enterprise, the *degree* to which political considerations influence corporate decisions, particularly on managerial appointments, and the *degree* to which the managers of all major firms, regardless of equity ownership, are linked to a political party, particularly one with a monopoly on power.

[37] Richard A. Colignon and Chikako Usui, *Amakudari: The Hidden Fabric of Japan's Economy* (Ithaca, NY: Cornell University Press, 2003).

But it is very difficult to make the case that distinctiveness along these dimensions is beneficial to corporate performance and sound institutional development.[38]

C Even If the Chinese Species of Corporate Capitalism Does Not Merit Exalted Status as a "Model" or "Consensus" for Developing Countries, Does It Nonetheless Provide Lessons for Other Countries Seeking to Replicate China's Successful Growth Experience, If Not the Precise Means by Which It Was Achieved? Yes.

Why? Because China's growth story reinforces several basic lessons that emerge from careful analysis of other developmental success stories:

1. *Political will is crucial at the take-off stage*: As elaborated by Gilson & Milhaupt, China's experience confirms that "economically benevolent dictators" can achieve development even in the absence of strong formal institutions.[39] That is, in the admittedly rare circumstance in which a strong political leader prioritizes national development over personal enrichment, credible commitments to growth can be made even in the absence of strong formal institutions which allow a small-scale, relationship-based economy to be scaled up for linkage to the global economy. Indeed, twentieth-century experience suggests that political will engendering credible commitment to growth is more important to a country's developmental transformation than the pursuit of a particular macroeconomic strategy or the quality of its judiciary.
2. *Organizational forms matter*: While history indicates that countries can grow dramatically without strong formal institutions, no country in the last three hundred years has achieved significant development

[38] This conclusion merits more substantiation than I can provide in this short chapter. But for evidence of the negative impact of state ownership and political control on firm performance, see Marshall Meyer and Changqi Wu, "Making Ownership Matter: Prospects for China's Mixed Ownership Economy," *Paulson Institute Policy Memorandum*, September 18, 2014, www.paulsoninstitute.org/think-tank/2014/09/18/making-ownership-matter-prospects-for-chinas-mixed-ownership-economy/; Andrew Batson, "Fixing China's State Sector," *Paulson Institute Policy Memorandum*, January 9, 2014, www.paulsoninstitute.org/think-tank/2014/01/09/fixing-chinas-state-sector/. For the deleterious impact of China's SOEs on the legal system, see Lei Zheng, Benjamin Liebman, and Curtis J. Milhaupt, "SOEs and State Governance: How State-Owned Enterprises Influence China's Legal System," in *Regulating the Visible Hand?* Liebman and Milhaupt (eds.), 203.

[39] Gilson and Milhaupt, "Economically Benevolent Dictators."

except in reliance upon *corporate* capitalism. In other words, the corporate form is common to all national development stories. For all the discussion about varieties of capitalism and the law–finance connection, a particular legal form – the corporation – is an indispensable component of any functional national economic system, regardless of the legal family to which the country belongs, the left–right dimension of its politics, or the libertarian to authoritarian range of the roots of its political economy. Corporate capitalism has many species because adaptability is one of the key attributes of the corporate form. It serves as a template for businesses ranging from a family operated hardware store in Peoria to global technology behemoth Microsoft. The corporate form also has a chameleon-like ability to take on the characteristics of the political economy in which it operates. Witness the stakeholder orientation of German co-determination firms and the relentless focus on shareholder wealth maximization often found in publicly held US corporations. It is not surprising, then, that the corporate form has also been readily adapted to the Chinese party-state. The corporate form can be shareholder-centric, board-centric, employee-centric, or state-centric, depending on the institutional setting and political economy in which it is nested.

3. *Incentives matter*: The melding of political objectives and business enterprises in China has worked not only due to the adaptability of the corporate form, but also because corporate values and performance have been fitted into a complementary system for political advancement that generates incentives compatible with economic growth. To be sure, the current incentive structure also engenders rent seeking on a large scale, and most likely contributes to a host of public "bads," such as environmental degradation and corruption. To date, however, the negative effects of the arrangement have not completely overwhelmed the benefits produced by political will and growth incentives. (But see point 4 below.)
4. *Organizational forms shape institutions in the long run*: Corporations are not simply passive takers of rules and norms; they actively shape the institutional setting in which they operate.[40] National economic histories demonstrate the profound impact of corporations on

[40] As Barkan notes: "Once constituted, corporations and states share a range of techniques – from the consensual to the coercive – for establishing order within their institutional structures and across the places and territories in which they operate." Barkan, *Corporate Sovereignty*, 3.

> institutional development. This was true of the transformative period of US economic history in the nineteenth century. It also seems true of China in its first thirty years of experience with corporate capitalism – at least those portions of the experience shaped by SOEs.[41]

But here is where the claim to a new China "Model" or "Beijing Consensus" may fall flat. In the long run,[42] the Chinese version of corporate capitalism will likely prove to be unappealing because its distinctive internal dimension – direct political monitoring and selection of corporate actors, particularly by a party with a monopoly on power – is a poor substitute for robust corporate mechanisms of accountability based on law, markets, and media scrutiny. This is particularly so because the concomitant, distinctive external dimension of Chinese corporate capitalism – treating the corporation as an integral component of the party-state's governance network – leads to systematic distortion of the regulatory environment for corporate conduct.[43] Without a major retreat of the Party from Chinese corporate capitalism, the country's institutional arrangements are likely to become increasingly statist in their operation, regardless of whether they outwardly converge on global standards. As one commentator concludes, "[e]ven if governance institutions change, the thread of party influence will still run throughout China's economy as members continue to occupy key positions in the party, the government, and business hierarchies – often at the same time."[44]

It is of course possible that the Chinese Communist Party will find ways to continue improving the governance and global reach of SOEs while employing their profits to expand social expenditures for Chinese

[41] For a fascinating parallel analysis of national-local government institutional dynamics in relation to corporate capitalism in the nineteenth-century US and reform era China, see Cheng, "Dual Intergovernmental Transformation and Economic Growth."

[42] I will not hazard a prediction about how long "the long run" is, but China has already been growing at an exceptional rate for a historically unprecedented period of time. As Pritchett and Summers pointed out, "China's experience from 1977 to 2010 already holds the distinction of being the only instance, quite possibly in the history of mankind, but certainly in the data, with a sustained episode of super-rapid (> 6 ppa) growth for more than 32 years." Thus, a reversion to the mean in a time frame measured in years rather than decades seems rather likely. Lant Pritchett and Lawrence Summers, "Asiaphoria Meets Regression to the Mean," Working Paper 20573 (National Bureau of Economic Research, 2014): 36, www.nber.org/papers/w20573.pdf.

[43] Zheng et al., "SOEs and State Governance."

[44] Adam Hersh, "China's State-Owned Enterprises and Nonmarket Economics," 1 (Testimony before the US-China Economic and Security Review Commission, February 21, 2014).

citizens – in other words, to replicate and scale up Singapore's version of state capitalism. As Chua notes,[45]

> Should China, despite its severe deficit in all measures of democracy, be able to successfully transform [and] institutionalize its state capitalism, then neoliberal capitalism may be said to have met its other – a hegemonic single-party state with a strong state capitalist sector in a developed market economy which is an integral part of global capitalism, where the material life of a majority of its population is progressively improving. This status as the other of neoliberalism is one that the small island nation of Singapore could not claim.

But this sort of transformation would require major reform of the distinctive internal dimension of Chinese corporate capitalism – if not a complete withdrawal of the Party from the internal workings of SOEs, then at least the creation of a professional, arm's length relationship between the party-state in its role as controlling shareholder and the SOEs whose shares it holds for the benefit of the Chinese people.

V Conclusion

This chapter has attempted to understand what is unique about China's approach to economic organization. First, it has argued that Chinese "state" capitalism is a species of corporate capitalism, and as such, it shares fundamental traits with all other major systems of capitalism. Second, it has argued that Chinese corporate capitalism's distinctive qualities are manifest both internally and externally in relation to the corporate form. These distinctive features, like the distinctive features of every system of corporate capitalism, were cobbled together by trial and error over time and were heavily shaped by the domestic political economy; they did not spring forth fully formed from the minds of party strategists. Satisficing, not optimizing, characterizes China's developmental journey.[46] The not-very-surprising conclusion following from this analysis is that the "Beijing Consensus" is a fancy name for an un-fancy contraption – a successful one to date if measured by GDP growth and the alleviation of poverty – but one whose distinctive features are likely to have deleterious consequences for

[45] Huat Beng Chua, "State-Owned Enterprises, State Capitalism and Social Distribution in Singapore," *The Pacific Review* 28 (2015): 1, www.tandfonline.com/action/showAxaArticles?journalCode=rpre20.

[46] "They [Chinese officials] are satisficing," as stated by a senior US official with responsibility for China policy, in telephone discussion with author, regarding China's approach to SOE reform and development of market-oriented economic regulation.

the long-term global attractiveness of this particular species of corporate capitalism.

China has developed spectacularly over the past three decades. Its success is a function of many factors, including the navigational skills of its economic strategists and the growth focus of its authoritarian leadership. But if a "Consensus" is to be formed around Beijing's developmental miracle, it just might begin with the genius of a legal fiction available to dictators and democrats alike throughout the world – the corporation.

BIBLIOGRAPHY

I Books, Chapters in Books, Articles, and Papers

Acemoglu, Daron, and James A. Robinson. *Why Nations Fail: The Origins of Power, Prosperity and Poverty.* New York: Crown, 2012.

Acioly, Luciana, Eduardo Costa Pinto, and Marcos Antonio Macedo Cintra. "As Relações Bilaterais Brasil-China: A Ascensão da China no Sistema Mundia e os Desafíos Para o Brasil." *Comunicados do IPEA* 85 (2000): 249–68.

Ahdieh, Robert, Zhu Lee, Srividhya Ragavan, Kevin Noonan, and Clinton W. Francis. "The Existing Legal Infrastructure of BRICs: Where Have We Been and Where Are We Going?" *Northwestern Journal of Technology and Intellectual Property* 5 (2007): 503–24.

Ahlers, Anna L., and Gunter Schubert. "'Building a New Socialist Countryside' – Only a Political Slogan?" *Journal of Current Chinese Affairs* 38 (2009): 35–62.

Ahmadjian, Christina L., and Patricia Robinson. "Safety in Numbers: Downsizing and the Deinstitutionalization of Permanent Employment in Japan." *Administrative Science Quarterly* 46 (2001): 622–54.

Alford, William P. "Exporting the 'Pursuit of Happiness.'" *Harvard Law Review* 113 (2000): 1677–750.

Alibaba Group Holding Limited. *Alibaba's 424(B)(4) Prospectus.* IPO Prospectus 2014. www.sec.gov/Archives/edgar/data/1577552/000119312514347620/d709111d424b4.htm.

Anderlini, Jamil. "Big Nations Snub Beijing Bank Launch after US Lobbying." *Financial Times,* October 22, 2014. Accessed November 27, 2015. www.ft.com/cms/s/0/41c3c0a0–59cd-11e4–9787–00144feab7de.html#axzz3IZ1tBtWR.

Ang, James S., and David K. Ding. "Government Ownership and the Performance of Government-Linked Companies: The Case of Singapore." *Journal of Multinational Financial Management* 16 (2006): 64–88.

Ang, Yuen Yuen. "Counting Cadres: A Comparative View of the Size of China's Public Employment." *The China Quarterly* 211 (2012): 676–96.

Andrews, Matt. *The Limits of Institutional Reform in Development: Changing Rules for Realistic Solutions.* Cambridge: Cambridge University Press, 2013.

Arndt, H. W. *Economic Development: The History of an Idea.* Chicago: University of Chicago Press, 1989.

Arrighi, Giovanni, Beverly J. Silver, and Benjamin D. Brewer. "Industrial Convergence, Globalization, and the Persistence of the North-South Divide." *Studies in Comparative International Development* 38 (2003): 3–31.

Asongu, Simplice A. "How Has Mobile Phone Penetration Stimulated Financial Development in Africa?" *Journal of African Business* 14 (2013): 7–18.

Babb, Sarah. "The Washington Consensus as Transnational Policy Paradigm: Its Origins, Trajectory and Likely Successor." *Review of International Political Economy* 20 (2013): 268–97.

Backer, Larry, and Keren Wang. "The Emerging Structures of Socialist Constitutionalism with Chinese Characteristics: Extra-Judicial Detention (Laojiao and Shuanggui) and the Chinese Constitutional Order."*Pacific Rim Law & Policy Journal* 23 (2014): 251–341.

Backer, Larry. "The Party as Polity, the Communist Party, and the Chinese Constitutional State: A Theory of State-Party Constitutionalism." *Journal of Chinese and Comparative Law* 16 (2009): 101–68.

Banerjee, Abhijit V., and Esther Duflo. *Poor Economics: Barefoot Hedge-fund Managers, DIY Doctors and the Surprising Truth about Life on Less than $1 a Day.* New York: Penguin Books, 2011.

Barkan, Joshua. *Corporate Sovereignty: Law and Government Under Capitalism.* Minneapolis: University of Minnesota, 2013.

Batson, Andrew. "Fixing China's State Sector." Paulson Institute Policy Memorandum, January 9, 2014. Accessed May 21, 2015. www.paulsoninstitute.org/think-tank/2014/01/09/fixing-chinas-state-sector/.

Batson, Andrew. "Lin Urges Flexibility in Fighting Poverty." *Wall Street Journal*, February 29, 2008. Accessed January 30, 2016. www.wsj.com/articles/SB120422296784800317.

Becker, Gary, Kevin Murphy, and Robert Tamura. "Human Capital, Fertility, and Economic Growth." *The Journal of Political Economy* 98 (1990): 12–37.

Beeson, Mark, and Fujian Li. "What Consensus? Geopolitics and Policy Paradigms in China and the United States." *International Affairs* 91 (2015): 93–109.

Bertonha, João Fábio. "Modelos Para o Brasil. Final." *Revista Espaco Academico* 86 (2008): 1–5.

Biddulph, Sarah. *Legal Reform and Administrative Detention Powers in China.* New York: Cambridge University Press, 2007.

Bird, Richard M. "Foreign Advice and Tax Policy in Developing Countries." In *Taxation and Development: The Weakest Link? Essays in Honor of Roy Bahl*, edited by Richard M. Bird and Jorge Marinez-Vazquez, 103–46. Cheltenham, UK: Edward Elgar, 2014.

Bird, Richard M., and Pierre-Pascal Gendron. *The VAT in Developing and Transitional Countries: Capacity and Consent.* New York: Cambridge University Press, 2007.

Boas, Taylor, and Jordan Gans-Morse. "Neoliberalism: From New Liberal Philosophy to Anti-Liberal Slogan." *Studies in Comparative International Development* 44 (2009): 137–61.

Boin, Arjen, and Allan McConnell. "Preparing for Critical Infrastructure Breakdowns: The Limits of Crisis Management and the Need for Resilience." *Journal of Contingencies and Crisis Management* 15 (2007): 50–59.

Boston Consulting Group and China Development Research Foundation. "Developing Mixed Ownership Structures and Modern Enterprise Systems." Paper presented at the meeting for the China Development Forum, Beijing, China, March 22–24, 2014. www.bcg.com.cn/en/files/publications/reports_pdf/BCG_Developing_Mixed_Ownership_Structures_and_Modern_Enterprise_Systems_Mar2014_ENG.pdf.

Braudel, Fernand. *The Wheels of Commerce* (*Civilization and Capitalism: 15th–18th Centuries.* Vol. 2). New York: University of California Press, 1992.

Brautigam, Deborah, Odd-Helge Fjeldstad, and Mick Moore. *Taxation and State-Building in Developing Countries: Capacity and Consent.* Cambridge: Cambridge University Press, 2008.

Brautigam, Deborah. *The Dragon's Gift.* New York: Oxford University Press, 2009.

Bremmer, Ian. *The End of the Free Market: Who Wins the War between States and Corporations?* New York: Penguin, 2010.

Breslin, Shaun. "The 'China Model' and the Global Crisis: From Friedrich List to a Chinese Mode of Governance?" *International Affairs* 87 (2011): 1323–43.

Brooks, Bradley. "Cultural Clash Complicates China's Brazil Push." *Associated Press,* May 28, 2011.

Buckingham, Kathleen, Lars Laestadius, Aaron Reuben, Vera Lex Engel, Aurelio Padovezi, and Phil Covell. "Building BRICS in Restoration – The China Brazil Landscape Restoration Exchange." *WRI Blog,* December 9, 2014. Accessed January 16, 2016. www.wri.org/blog/2014/12/building-brics-restoration%E2%80%94-china-brazil-landscape-restoration-exchange.

Buell, Todd. "China Currency Set for International Role, Says ECB Board Member." *Wall Street Journal,* February 26, 2014. Accessed November 27, 2015. http://online.wsj.com/news/articles/SB10001424052702303801304579406612508072596.

Burawoy, Michael. "The Global Turn: Lessons from Southern Labor Scholars and Their Labor Movements." *Work and Occupations* 36 (2009): 87–95.

Cai, Hongbin, and Daniel Treisman. "Did Government Decentralization Cause China's Economic Miracle?" *World Journal* 58 (2006): 505–35.

Carnoy, Martin. "Higher Education and Economic Development: India, China and the 21st Century." Working Paper No. 297, Stanford Center for International Development, 2006. Accessed January 16, 2016. http://scid.stanford.edu/publications/higher-education-and-economic-development-india-china-and-21st-century.

Carvalho, Evandro Menezes de. "Lições do Modelo Chinês." *Folha de São Paulo*, April 26, 2014.

Cavens, Marcia. "Japanese Labor Regulation and the Legal Implications of Their Possible Uses in the United States." *Northwestern Journal of International Law & Business* 5 (1983): 585–625.

Chan, K. Hung, and Lynne Chow. "An Empirical Study of Tax Audits in China on International Transfer Pricing." *Journal of Accounting and Economics* 23 (1997): 83–112.

Chang, Ha-Joon. "Institutional Development in Historical Perspective." In *Rethinking Development Economics*, edited by Chang Ha-Joon, 499–522. London: Anthem Press, 2003.

Chang, Ha-Joon. *Kicking Away the Ladder*. London: Anthem Press, 2003.

Chang, Terry E. "Slow Avalanche: Internationalizing the Renminbi and Liberalizing China's Capital Account." *Columbia Journal of Asian Law* 25 (2011): 62–103.

Chapola, Ricardo. "Protesto Contra Dilma Fecha Parte da Avenida Paulista." *Estado Conteudo*, November 1, 2014. Accessed January 16, 2016. http://exame.abril.com.br/brasil/noticias/protesto-contra-dilma-fecha-parte-da-av-paulista.

Chen, Chih-jou Jay. *Transforming Rural China: How Local Institutions Shape Property Rights in China*. London: Routledge, 2004.

Chen, Christina. "The Politics of Labor Protection in Authoritarian Systems: Evidence from Labor Law and Enforcement in Post-Reform China." PhD diss., UC San Diego, 2011.

Chen, De Rong 陈德容. "Wenzhou jinrong gaige zaichufa" 温州金融改革再出发 [The Restart of Wenzhou's Financial Reform]. *China Reform* no. 340, March 2012.

Chen, Feng. "Privatization and Its Discontents in Chinese Factories." *China Quarterly* 185 (2006): 42–60.

Chen, Fashan 陈法善 and Liu Caiping 刘彩萍. "Renminbi guojihua bu shixian anpai sudu jiezhou shidian" 人民币国际化不事先安排速度节奏时点 [Pace, Number of Steps and Deadlines Regarding the Internationalization of Renminbi Not Predetermined]. *Caixin*, March 11, 2014. Accessed November 27, 2015. http://finance.caixin.com/2014–03–11/100649710.html.

Chen, Michelle. "Reform Paralysis, Slow Progress Cloud Shanghai Free Trade Zone Project." *Reuters*, September 15, 2014. Accessed November 27, 2015. www.reuters.com/article/2014/09/14/china-shanghai-ftz-idUSL3N0RB1JR20140914.

Chen, Weihua. "Labor Rights Make a World of Difference." *China Daily*, July 6, 2012.

Chen, Weitseng. "Arbitrage for Property Rights: How Foreign Investors Create Substitutes for Property Institutions in China." *Washington International Law Journal* 24 (2015): 47–97.

Chen, Weitseng. "From the Middle East to the Far West: What Can Chinese Overseas Investments Tell Us about Law and Development and Global Regulatory Regimes?" In *Converging Regions: Global Perspectives on Asia and the Middle East*, edited by Nele Lenze and Charlotte Schriwer, 25–54. London: Ashgate, 2014.

Chen, Weitseng. "Institutional Arbitrage: China's Economic Power Projection and International Capital Markets." *Columbia Journal of Asian Law* 26 (2013): 347–72.

Chen, Yongxi. *Halfway to Freedom of Information: The Legislative and Judicial Protection of the Right of Access to Information in China.* London: Ashgate, 2016.

Chen, Zhimin. "Soft Balancing and Reciprocal Engagement." In *China's Reforms and International Political Economy*, edited by David Zweig and Chen Zhimin, 42–61. Abingdon, UK: Routledge, 2007.

Cheng, Jinhua. "Dual Intergovernmental Transformation and Economic Growth." JSD diss., Yale University, 2011.

China Net. "Zhongjiwei jiangdui paizhu shixian quanmian fugai: kanzhu zhongyang dang zheng jiguan quanli" 中纪委将对派驻实现全覆盖：看住中央党政机关权力 [CCDI Will Cover the Entire Dispatched Organs: Limiting the Powers of the Central Party and Government Organs]. January 7, 2016. Accessed January 30, 2016. http://news.china.com.cn/2016–01/07/content_37479167.htm.

China (Shanghai) Free Trade Zone. "Decision of the Standing Committee of the National People's Congress on Authorizing the State Council to Temporarily Adjust the Relevant Administrative Approval Items Prescribed in Laws in the China (Shanghai) Pilot Free Trade Zone." Accessed November 27, 2015. www.china-shftz.gov.cn/PublicInformation.aspx?GID=9f8589db-cd96–4860-ad10–30f64c4076bb&CID=953a259a-1544–4d72-be6a-264677089690&MenuType=1.

China (Shanghai) Free Trade Zone. "Introduction." Accessed November 27, 2015. http://en.china-shftz.gov.cn/About-FTZ/Introduction/.

China-Brazil Business Council. *Brazilian Companies in China* (Rio de Janerio: CBBC, 2013).

China-Brazil Business Council. *Chinese Investments in Brazil* (Rio de Janerio: CBBC, 2013).

China.org.cn. "Communiqué of the Fourth Plenary Session of the 18th Central Committee of CPC." Last modified December 2, 2014. Accessed May 24, 2015. www.china.org.cn/china/fourth_plenary_session/2014–12/02/content_34208801.htm.

China Daily. "Russia Turns to RMB to Thwart Western Sanctions." November 14, 2014. Accessed November 27, 2015. www.china.org.cn/business/2014–09/25/content_33609143.htm.

China Securities Index. "CSI 300." Accessed May 21, 2015. www.csindex.com.cn/sseportal/ps/zhs/hqjt/csi/000300cons.xls.

China Securities Regulatory Commission. "Xingzheng xuke shixiang: faxing jianguanbu shouci gongkai faxing gupiao shenhe gongzuo liucheng ji shenqing qiye qingkuang" 行政许可事项：发行监管部首次公开发行股票审核工作流程及申请企业情况 [Supervision Department: The IPO Audit Work Processes and the Situation of Enterprises]. Accessed April 29, 2015. www.csrc.gov.cn/pub/zjhpublic/G00306202/201504/t20150424_275570.htm.

China Securities Regulatory Commission. "2014 nian 11 yue tongji shuju" 2014年11月统计数据 [Data of November 2014]. Accessed April 29, 2015. www.csrc.gov.cn/pub/zjhpublic/G00306204/zqscyb/201412/t20141219_265231.htm.

Chinese Communist Party. "Zhongguo gongchandang jilü jiancha jiguan anjian jiancha gongzuo tiaoli" 中国共产党纪律检查机关案件检查工作条例 [Measures Concerning the Investigative Work for Cases under the Disciplinary Inspection Organs of the Chinese Communist Party]. Accessed October 21, 2015. http://cpc.people.com.cn/GB/33838/2539632.html.

Chng, Mavis, and Michael W. Dowdle. "The Chinese Debate about the Adjudication Committee: Implications for What 'Judicial Independence' Means in the Context of China." *The Chinese Journal of Comparative Law* 2 (2014): 233–51.

Chow, Gregory C. "Economic Reform and Growth in China." *Annals of Economics and Finance* 5 (2004): 127–52.

Chow, Hwee Kean. "Managing Capital Flows: The Case of Singapore." ADB Institute Discussion Paper No. 86. Asian Development Bank Institute, 2008. Accessed January 24, 2016. www.adb.org/sites/default/files/publication/156725/adbi-dp86.pdf.

Chowdhury, Anis, and Iyanatul Islam. *The Newly Industrialising Economies of East Asia*. London: Routledge, 1993.

Chua, Beng Huat. "State Owned Enterprises, State Capitalism and Social Distribution in Singapore." *The Pacific Review* 28 (2015): 1–23. Accessed January 26, 2015. www.tandfonline.com/action/showAxaArticles?journalCode=rpre20.

Clarke, Donald. "Blowback: How China's Efforts to Bring Private-Sector Standards into the Public Sector Backfired." In *Regulating the Visible Hand? The Institutional Implications of Chinese State Capitalism*, edited by Benjamin Liebman and Curtis J. Milhaupt, 29–48. New York: Oxford University Press, 2016.

Clarke, Donald. "China's Stealth Urban Land Revolution." *American Journal of Comparative Law* 62 (2014): 323–66.

Clarke, Donald. "Corporate Governance in China: An Overview." *China Economic Review* 14 (2003): 494–507.

Clarke, Donald. "How Do We Know When an Enterprise Exists? Unanswerable Questions and Legal Polycentricity in China." *Columbia Journal of Asian Law* 19 (2005): 50–71.

Clarke, Donald. "Law without Order in Chinese Corporate Governance Institutions." *Northwestern Journal of International Law and Business* 30 (2010): 131–99.

Clarke, Donald. "'Nothing but Wind?' The Past and Future of Comparative Corporate Governance." *American Journal of Comparative Law* 59 (2011): 75–110.

Coase, Ronald. "The Problem of Social Cost." *Journal of Law & Economics* 3 (1960): 1–44.

Coase, Ronald, and Ning Wang. "How China Became Capitalist." *Cato Policy Report* 35 (2013). Accessed May 21, 2015. http://object.cato.org/sites/cato.org/files/serials/files/policy-report/2013/1/cprv35n1–1.pdf.

Coffee, John C. "The Attorney as Gatekeeper: An Agenda for the SEC." *Columbia Law Review* 103 (2003): 1293–316.

Cohen, Dara Kay, Mariano-Florentino Cuellar, and Barry R. Weingast. "Crisis Bureaucracy: Homeland Security and the Political Design of Legal Mandates." *Stanford Law Review* 59 (2006): 673–759.

Cohen, Jessica, and William Easterly (eds.). *What Works in Development? Thinking Big and Thinking Small.* Washington, DC: Brookings Institution Press, 2009.

Colignon, Richard A., and Chikako Usui. *Amakudari: The Hidden Fabric of Japan's Economy.* Ithaca, NY: Cornell University Press, 2003.

Colley, Chris. "China's Reforms at 30 and the 'Beijing Consensus.'" *Pambuzuka* 417 (2009): 1–5. Accessed January 16, 2016. www.pambazuka.net/en/category.php/africa_china/53757.

Cook, María. "Labor Reform and Dual Transitions in Brazil and the Southern Cone." *Latin American Policy and Society* 44 (2002): 1–34.

Costa, Claudia. "Brazilian Workers Buck Union Officials to Strike." *Labor Notes*, June 23, 2014. Accessed January, 16, 2016. http://labornotes.org/2014/06/brazilian-workers-buck-union-officials-strike.

Cottarelli, Carlo. "Revenue Mobilization in Developing Countries." IMF, 2011. Accessed December 29, 2015. www.imf.org/external/np/pp/eng/2011/030811.pdf.

Cui, Wei 崔威. "Dui qiyechongzu shuiwuguize qicaoguochengde fansi" 对企业重组税务规则起草过程的反思 [Reflections on the Making of the Income Tax Rules for Enterprise Reorganizations]. In *Shuifa panjue yu jieshi pingzh (di yi juan) 税法判例与解释评注 (第一卷)*, edited by Xiong Wei 熊伟, 163–82. Beijing: Law Press, 2010.

Cui, Wei 崔威. "Shuishou lifa gaodu jiquan moshi de qiyuan" 税收立法高度集权模式的起源 [The Historical Origin of High Concentration of Tax Legislative Power]. *Peking University Law Journal* 24 (2012): 762–81.

Cui, Wei 崔威. "Zhongguo shuiwu xingzheng susong shizheng yanjiu" 中国税务行政诉讼实证研究 [An Empirical Study of Tax Litigation in China]. *Qinghua faxue* 清华法学 (2015): 135–55.

Cui, Wei. "Administrative Decentralization and Tax Compliance: A Transactional Cost Perspective." *University of Toronto Law Journal* 65 (2015): 186–238.

Cui, Wei. "Fiscal Federalism in Chinese Taxation." *World Tax Journal* 3 (2011): 455–80.

Cui, Wei. "What Is the 'Law' in Chinese Tax Administration?" *Asia Pacific Law Review* 19 (2011): 75–94.

Cui, Wei. "Two Paths for Developing Anti-Avoidance Rules in China." *Asia Pacific Tax Bulletin* 17 (2011): 42–49.

Cui, Wei, and Zhiyuan Wang. "The Inefficiencies of Legislative Centralization: Evidence from Chinese Provincial Tax Rate Setting." *China: An International Journal* 13 (2015): 49–67.

Cullen, Richard, Yang Xiaonan, and Christine Loh. "Executive Government." In *Law of the Hong Kong Constitution*, edited by Johannes Chan and Chin Leng Lim. Hong Kong: Sweet & Maxwell, 2011.

Dahlman, Carl. "Innovation Strategies of Three of the BRICS: Brazil, India and China – What Can We Learn from Three Different Approaches?" Paper presented at the conference for the Sanjaya Lall Program for Technology and Management for Development, University of Oxford, Oxford, May 29–30, 2008.

Dan, Wenyuan 单文苑. "Caishui gaige bukeyi zhiuqiu yibudaowei" 财税改革不刻意追求一步到位 [For Incremental Reforms of the Fiscal and Tax System]. *Zhongguo caijing shibao* 中国经济时报, November 3, 2014.

Dasgupta, Partha, and Karl-Göran Mäler. "Wealth as a Criterion for Sustainable Development." *World Economics: A Journal of Current Economic and Policy* 2 (2001): 19–44.

Davis, Kevin E., and Mariana Mota Prado. "Law, Regulation, and Development." In *International Development: Ideas, Experience, and Prospects*, edited by Bruce Currie-Alder, David M. Malone, Ravi Kanbur, and Rohinton Medhora, 204–20. Oxford: Oxford University Press, 2014.

Dakolias, Maria. "A Strategy for Judicial Reform: The Experience in Latin America." *Virginia Journal of International Law* 36 (1995–1996): 167–231.

De Spinoza, Benedictus. *Ethics*, edited by Edwin Curley. New York: Penguin Books, 1996.

Deakin, Simon, Colin Fenwick, and Prabirjit Sarkar. "Labor Law and Inclusive Development." Working Paper No. 447, Centre for Business Research, University of Cambridge, 2013. Accessed January 16, 2016. www.cbr.cam.ac.uk/fileadmin/user_upload/centre-for-business-research/downloads/working-papers/wp447.pdf.

Demsetz, Harold. "Toward a Theory of Property Rights." *The American Economic Review* 57 (1967): 347–59.

Deng, Liping 邓力平. *Shuishou zhidu lilun yu shiwu 税收制度理论与实务* [Theory and Practice of a Tax System]. Beijing: Higher Education Press, 2007.

Deyo, Frederic C. "Addressing the Development Deficit of Competition Policy: The Role of Economic Networks." In *Asian Capitalism and the Regulation of Competition: Towards a Regulatory Geography of Global Competition Law*, edited by Michael W. Dowdle, John Gillespie, and Imelda Maher, 283–300. Cambridge: Cambridge University Press, 2013.

Dickson, Bruce. "Updating the China Model." *The Washington Quarterly* 34 (2011): 39–58.

Dirlik, Arif. "Beijing Consensus: Beijing 'Gongshi.' Who Recognizes Whom and to What End?" Accessed June 5, 2015. www.ids-uva.nl/wordpress/wp-content/uploads/2011/07/9_Dirlik1.pdf.

Dirlik, Arif. *Global Modernity: Modernity in the Age of Global Capitalism*. Boulder, CO: Paradigm, 2007.

Donald, David. "Beyond Fragmentation: Building a Unified Securities Market in China (and Asia)." In *Finance, Rule of Law and Development in Asia: Perspectives from Hong Kong, Singapore, and Shanghai*, edited by Jiaxiang Hu, Matthias Vanhullebusch, and Andrew Harding. Leiden, Netherlands: Brill, 2016.

Dowdle, Michael W. "China's Present as the World's Future: China and 'Rule of Law' in a Post-Fordist World." In *Chinese Thought as Global Theory*, edited by Leigh K. Jenco. Albany, NY: SUNY Press, 2016.

Dowdle, Michael W. "On the Public-Law Character of Competition Law: A Lesson from Asian Capitalism." *Fordham International Law Journal* 38 (2015): 303–86.

Dowdle, Michael W. "Public Accountability: Conceptual, Historical, and Epistemic Mappings." In *Public Accountability: Designs, Dilemmas and Experiences*, edited by Michael W. Dowdle, 1–32. Cambridge: Cambridge University Press, 2006.

Dowdle, Michael W. "Whither Asia? Whiter Capitalism? Whither Global Competition Law?" In *Asian Capitalism and the Regulation of Competition: Towards a Regulatory Geography of Global Competition Law*, edited by Michael W. Dowdle, John Gillespie, and Imelda Maher, 301–25. Cambridge: Cambridge University Press, 2013.

Drahos, Peter, and John Braithwaite. *Information Feudalism: Who Owns the Knowledge Economy*? London: Earthscan, 2002.

Draper, Joe. "NYRA Chairman, Anthony Bonomo, Is Taking a Leave of Absence." *New York Times*, June 2, 2015.

Du, Wei 杜伟 and Shanming Huang 黄善明. *Shidi nongmin quanyibaozhang de jingjixue yanjiu 失地农民权益保障的经济学研究* [The Economic Research on the Guarantee of the Displaced Farmers' Interest]. Beijing: Kexue chubanshe 科学出版社, 2009.

Dyer, Geoff. "Brazil's Lessons for China." *Financial Times*, March 3, 2008.

Du, Yi-Huan 杜易寰."Zuihou jiule zhongguo gushi de shi gonganbu" 最后救了中国股市的是公安部 [It Is the Public Security That Saved China's Stock Markets] *Tianxia zazhi* 天下雜誌, July 9, 2015. Accessed November 27, 2015. www.cw.com.tw/article/article.action?id=5069089#.

Emmott, Bill. "Can Brazil Emulate China?" *Exame*, October 2007. Accessed January 16, 2016. www.billemmott.com/article.php?id=116.

Ebel, Robert, and Robert Taliercio. "Subnational Tax Policy and Administration in Developing Economies." *Tax Notes International* 37 (2005): 919–36.

Economic and Commercial Counsellor's Office of the Embassy of the People's Republic of China in the Republic of Singapore 中华人民共和国和国驻新加坡共和国大使馆经济商务参赞处. "Xinjiapo jin 600 qiye ruzhu shanghai zimaoqu: xinjiapo meiti ping zimaoqu yunxing yinian chengxiao" 新加坡近600企业入驻上海自贸区：新加坡媒体评自贸区运行一年成效 [Nearly Six Hundred Singapore Firms Joined Shanghai Free Trade Zone: Singapore Media Reports That after One Year Shanghai Free Trade Zone is a Success]. Accessed November 27, 2015. http://sg.mofcom.gov.cn/article/fuhua/tzdongtai/201410/20141000768457.shtml.

Eichengreen, Barry. "Number One Country, Number One Currency?" *The World Economy* 36 (2013): 363–74.

Ellickson, Robert. *Order without Law: How Neighbors Settle Disputes*. Cambridge, MA: Harvard University Press, 1991.

Ellman, Michael. "Transition Economies." In *Rethinking Development Economics*, edited by Chang Ha-Joon, 179–98. London: Anthem Press, 2003.

English.news.cn. "China Focus: New IPO System Aims to Create Healthy Capital Market." January 19, 2015. Accessed January 20, 2016. http://news.xinhuanet.com/english/indepth/2015-01/19/c_133930487.htm.

English.news.cn. "News Analysis: Stock Issue Reform Still on the Way." November 20, 2015. Accessed January 20, 2016. http://news.xinhuanet.com/english/china/2014-11/20/c_133803626.htm.

Evans, Peter. *Embedded Autonomy: States and Industrial Transformation*. Princeton, NJ: Princeton University Press, 1995.

Fairbank, John, and Merle Goldman. *China: A New History*. Cambridge, MA: Harvard University Press, 2006.

Ferchen, Matt. "Whose China Model Is It Anyway? The Contentious Search for Consensus." *Review of International Political Economy* 20 (2013): 390–420.

Ferejohn, John. "Judicializing Politics, Politicizing Law." *Law and Contemporary Problems* 65 (2002): 41–68.

Fitzpatrick, Daniel. "Evolution and Chaos in Property Rights Systems: The Third World Tragedy of Contested Access." *Yale Law Journal* 115 (2006): 996–1048.

Fjeldstad, Odd-Helge, and Kari K. Heggstad. "The Tax Systems in Mozambique, Tanzania and Zambia: Capacity and Constraints." CMI Report R 2011:3, Chr. Michelsen Institute, 2011. Accessed December 29, 2015. www.cmi.no/publications/file/4045-taxation-mozambique-tanzania-zambia.pdf.

Fordham University. "Modern History Sourcebook: The Common Program of the Chinese People's Political Consultative Conference, 1949." Accessed July 16, 2015. http://legacy.fordham.edu/halsall/mod/1949-ccp-program.html.

French, Howard W. "Chinese Success Story Chokes on Its Own Growth." *New York Times*, December 19, 2006. Accessed July 16, 2015. www.nytimes.com/2006/12/19/world/asia/19shenzhen.html?pagewanted=1&_r=1&ex.

Friedman, Milton. "The Hong Kong Experiment." *Hoover Digest*, July 30, 1998. Accessed November 27, 2015. www.hoover.org/research/hong-kong-experiment.

Fu, Hualing. "Autonomy, Courts and the Political-Legal Order in Contemporary China." In *Handbook of Chinese Criminology*, edited by Liqun Cao, Ivan Y. Sun, and Bill Hebenton, 76–88. London: Routledge, 2013.

Fu, Hualing. "Challenging Authoritarianism through Law: Potential and Limit." *National Taiwan University Law Review* 6 (2011): 339–60.

Fu, Hualing. "Human Rights Lawyering in Chinese Courtrooms." *Chinese Journal of Comparative Law* 2 (2014): 270–88.

Fu, Hualing. "Institutionalizing Criminal Process in China." In *The Development of the Chinese Legal System: Change and Challenge*, edited by Guanghua Yu, 26–48. London: Routledge, 2011.

Fu, Hualing. "Mediation and the Rule of Law: The Chinese Landscape." In *Formalisation and Flexibilisation in Dispute Resolution*, edited by Joachim Zekoll, Moritz Bälz, and Iwo Amelung, 108–29. Leiden, Netherlands: Brill, 2014.

Fu, Hualing. "Politicized Challenges, Depoliticized Responses: Political Monitoring in China's Transitions." University of Hong Kong Faculty of Law Research Paper No. 2013/014, University of Hong Kong, 2013. Accessed January 30, 2016. http://papers.ssrn.com/sol3/papers.cfm?abstract_id=2250073##.

Fu, Hualing. "Sedition and Political Dissidence: Towards Legitimate Dissent in China?" *Hong Kong Law Journal* 26 (1996): 210–33.

Fu, Hualing. "Stability and Anticorruption Initiatives: Is There a Chinese Model?" In *Politics of Law and Stability in China*, edited by Susan Trevaskes, Elisa Nesossi, Sarah Biddulph, and Flora Sapio, 176–201. Cheltenham, UK: Edward Elgar, 2014.

Fu, Hualing. "The Upward and Downward Spirals in China's Anti-corruption Enforcement." In *Comparative Perspectives on Criminal Justice in China*, edited by Mike McConville and Eva Pils, 390–410. Cheltenham, UK: Edward Elgar, 2013.

Fu, Hualing. "Wielding the Sword: President Xi's New Anti-Corruption Campaign." In *Greed, Corruption, and the Modern State*, edited by Susan Rose-Ackerman and Paul Felipe Lagunes, 134–60. Cheltenham, UK: Edward Elgar, 2015.

Gabriel, Satyananda J. *Chinese Capitalism and the Modernist Vision*. Oxon, UK: Routledge, 2006.

Gadenne, Lucie, and Monica Singhal. "Decentralization in Developing Economies." *Annual Review of Economics* 6 (2014): 581–604.

Galati, Gabriel, and Phillip Woolridge. "The Euro as a Reserve Currency: A Challenge to the Pre-eminence of the US Dollar?" *International Journal of Financial Economics* 14 (2009): 1–23.

Gallagher, Mary, Song Jing, and Huong Trieu. "Bottom-Up Enforcement: Legal Mobilization as Law Enforcement in the PRC." Paper presented at the Annual Meeting of the American Political Science Association, September 2–5, 2010.

Gerner-Beuerle, Carsten, Esin Küçük, and Edmund Schuster. "Law Meets Economics in the German Federal Constitutional Court: Outright Monetary Transactions on Trial." *German Law Journal* 15 (2014): 281–320.

Gilson, Ronald J. "Value Creation by Business Lawyers: Legal Skills and Asset Pricing." *The Yale Law Journal* 94 (1984): 239–313.

Gilson, Ronald J., and Curtis J. Milhaupt. "Economically Benevolent Dictators: Lessons for Developing Democracies." *American Journal of Comparative Law* 59 (2011): 227–88.

Gilson, Ronald J., and Curtis J. Milhaupt. "Sovereign and Corporate Governance: A Minimalist Response to the New Mercantilism." *Stanford Law Review* 60 (2008): 1345–69.

Ginsburg, Tom, and Tamir Moustafa (eds.). *Rule by Law: The Politics of Courts in Authoritarian Regimes.* New York: Cambridge University Press, 2008.

Givens, John. "The Beijing Consensus Is Neither: China as a Non-ideological Challenge to International Norms." *St. Antony's International Review* 6 (2011): 10–25.

Goh, Keng Swee. *The Practice of Economic Growth.* Singapore: Federal Publications, 1995.

Gomes, Ana, and Mariana Mota Prado. "Flawed Freedom of Association in Brazil: How Unions Can Become an Obstacle to Meaningful Reforms in the Labor Law System." *Comparative Labor and Policy Journal* 32 (2011): 843–89.

Gong, Ting. "The Party Disciplinary Inspection in China: Its Evolving Trajectory and Embedded Dilemmas." *Crime, Law and Social Change* 49 (2008): 139–52.

Goodman, David. *Deng Xiaoping and the Chinese Revolution: A Political Biography.* London: Routledge, 2002.

Gouvea, Raul, and Manuel Montoya. "Brazil & China: Partners or Competitors?" *Asian Journal of Latin American Studies* 26 (2013): 1–23.

Government of Shenzhen. "Qianhai shengang xiandai fuwuye hehuoqu" 前海深港现代服务业合作区 [Qianhai Shenzhen-Hong Kong Modern Service Industry Cooperation Zone]. Accessed November 27, 2015. www.szqh.gov.cn:81/ljqh/qhjj515/qhdsj/.

Greif, Avner, Murat Iyigun, and Diego L. Sasson. "Social Institutions and Economic Growth: Why England and Not China Became the First Modern Economy."

Social Science Research Network, 2012. Accessed November 27, 2015. http://dx.doi.org/10.2139/ssrn.1783879.

Grenville, Stephen. "The IMF and the Indonesian Crisis." Background Paper 04/3, IMF, 2004. Accessed June 3, 2015. www.ieo-imf.org/ieo/files/completedevaluations/BP043.pdf.

Gu, Zhaomin 谷昭民. "Zhongguo kaizhan falü waijiao de xianzhuang yu fazhan qushi yanjiu" 中国开展法律外交的现状与发展趋势研究 [On the Current State and Development of China's Legal Foreign Relations]. *Xiandai faxue* 现代法学 4 (2013): 173–80.

Hadfield, Gillian K., and Barry R. Weingast. "Microfoundations of the Rules of Law." *Annual Review of Political Science* 17 (2014): 21–42.

Halegua, Aaron. "Getting Paid: Processing the Labor Disputes of China's Migrant Workers." *Berkeley Journal of International Law* 26 (2008): 254–322.

Halper, Stephan. *The Beijing Consensus: How China's Authoritarian Model Will Dominate the Twenty-First Century*. New York: Basic Books, 2010.

Han, Feng 韩枫 (ed.). "90 Nianlai dang de jijiancha zhidu de yange he tedian" 90 年来党的纪检监察制度的沿革和特点 [The Evolution and Characteristics of the Party's Disciplinary Inspection System in the Past 90 Years]. *Sichuan University Marxism School (School of Political Science)*, November 11, 2011. Accessed January 31, 2016. www.scu.edu.cn/zzxy/dwgz/jjgz/webinfo/2011/11/1321924224398934.htm.

Han, Jie 韩洁, Gao Li 高立 and He Yuxin 何雨欣. "Yichang guanxi guojia zhili xiandaihua de shenke biange – caizhengbu buzhang lou xu wei xiangjie shenhua caishui tizhi gaige zongtifangan" 一场关系国家治理现代化的深刻变革 – 财政部部长楼续伟详解深化财税体制改革总体方案 [A Major Reform about Governance Modernization – Minister of Finance Lou Jiwei Details the Plan to Deepen Fiscal Reform]. *Xinhuawang*, July 3, 2014. Accessed December 29, 2015. http://news.xinhuanet.com/fortune/2014-07/03/c_1111449207.htm.

Hansmann, Henry, Ronald J. Gilson, and Mariana Pargendler. "Regulatory Dualism as a Development Strategy." *Stanford Law Review* 63 (2011): 475–537.

Hansmann, Henry, and Reinier Kraakman. "The End of History for Corporate Law." *Georgetown Law Journal* 89 (2001): 439–68.

Hasmath, Reza. "White Cat, Black Cat or Good Cat: The Beijing Consensus as an Alternative Philosophy for Policy Deliberation?" Working Paper 14-02, Barnett Papers in Social Research, 2014. Accessed January 16, 2016. www.spi.ox.ac.uk/fileadmin/documents/PDF/Barnett_Paper_14-02.pdf.

He, Baogang, and Mark E. Warren. "Authoritarian Deliberation: The Deliberative Turn in Chinese Political Development." *Perspectives of Politics* 9 (2011): 269–89.

He, Xin. "Administrative Law as a Mechanism for Political Control in China." In *Constitutionalism and Judicial Power in China*, edited by Stephanie Balme and Michael W. Dowdle, 143–61. New York: Palgrave MacMillan, 2009.

He, Xin. "The Party's Leadership as a Living Constitution in Reform China." *Hong Kong Law Journal* 42 (2012): 73–94.

Heilmann, Sebastian. "Policy Experimentation in China's Economic Rise." *Studies in Comparative International Development* 43 (2008): 1–26.

Helleiner, Eric, and Troy Lundblad. "States, Markets, and Sovereign Wealth Funds." *German Policy Studies* 4 (2008): 59–82.

Henderson, Keith E. "Halfway Home and a Long Way to Go: China's Rule of Law Evolution and the Global Road to Judicial Independence, Judicial Impartiality, and Judicial Integrity." In *Judicial Independence in China: Lessons for Global Rule of Law Promotion*, edited by Randall Peerenboom, 23–36. Cambridge: Cambridge University Press, 2010.

Herschler, Stephen B. "The 1994 Tax Reforms: The Center Strikes Back." *China Economic Review* 6 (1995): 239–45.

Hersh, Adam. "China's State-Owned Enterprises and Nonmarket Economics." Testimony before the US-China Economic and Security Review Commission, February 21, 2014.

Hille, Kathrin, and Roman Olearchyk. "Plunging Rouble Raises Spectre of Fresh Financial Crisis for Russia." *Financial Times*, November 7, 2014. Accessed January 24, 2016. www.ft.com/intl/cms/s/0/6c059328-666d-11e4-9c0c-00144feabdc0.html#axzz3vbsuscAE.

Ho, Alfred Tat-Kei, and Meili Niu. "Rising with the Tide without Flipping the Boat? Analyzing the Successes and Challenges of Fiscal Capacity Building in China." *Public Administration and Development* 33 (2013): 29–49.

Hofmann, Christian. "A Legal Analysis of the Euro Zone Crisis." *Fordham Journal of Corporate & Financial Law* 18 (2013): 519–64.

Hong Kong Economic Journal 信报. "Ling jian jinrong chengshi Qianhai qudai Xianggang?" 另建金融城市前海取代香港? [Qianhai: Creating a New Financial Center to Replace Hong Kong?]. Accessed November 27, 2015. http://forum.hkej.com/node/60537.

Hong, Yelin. "The AIIB Is Seen Very Differently in the US, Europe, and China." *The Diplomat*, May 8, 2015. Accessed November 27, 2015. http://thediplomat.com/2015/05/the-aiib-is-seen-very-differently-in-the-us-europe-and-china/.

Hopf, Gregor. "Saving and Investment: The Economic Development of Singapore 1965–99." PhD diss., London School of Economics and Political Science, 2004.

Hou, Meng 侯猛. "Zhongguo de sifa moshi: chuantong yu gaige" 中国的司法模式：传统与改革 [The Chinese Judicial Model: Tradition and Reform]. *Fashang Yanjiu 法商研究* 6 (2009).

Hou Meng 侯猛. "Zuigao fayuan xunhui fating: hequ hecong" 最高法院巡回法庭 : 何去何从 [The Circuit Tribunal of the Supreme People's Court of China: What Course to Follow]. *Beida falü pinglun 北大法律评论* 16 (2015): 65–77.

Housing and Development Board, Singapore. "About Us." www.hdb.gov.sg/cs/infoweb/about-us/history. Accessed January 22, 2016.

Howson, Nicolas. "Enforcement without Foundation? Insider Trading and China's Administrative Law Crisis." *American Journal of Comparative Law* 60 (2012): 955–1002.

Hsu, Cheng-Ming 许振明. "You jinrong zhiyouhua yu guojihua de guocheng tan jinrong jianli" 由金融自由化与国际化的过程谈金融监理 [Financial Liberalization, Internationalization and Supervision]. National Policy Foundation Policy Reports 090–039, National Policy Foundation, 2001. Accessed November 27, 2015. http://old.npf.org.tw/PUBLICATION/FM/090/FM-R-090-039.htm.

Hsu, Immanuel. *The Rise of Modern China*. New York: Oxford University Press, 2000.

Hsu, Philip, Yu-Shan Wu, and Suisheng Zhao (eds.). *In Search of China's Development Model: Beyond the Beijing Consensus*. New York: Routledge, 2011.

Hu, Yunteng 胡云腾. "Quanmian tuijin yifa zhiguo shenhua sifa tizhi gaige" 全面推进依法治国深化司法体制改革 [Deepen Reforms to the Judicial System in order to Fully Push Forward Rule of Law]. *Zhongguo ganbu xuexi wang* 中国干部学习网, November 6, 2014. Accessed July 31, 2015. http://study.ccln.gov.cn/gcjw/zz/127570.shtml.

Huang, Yasheng. "Debating China's Economic Growth, the Beijing Consensus or the Washington Consensus." *Academy of Management Perspective* 24 (2010): 31–47.

Huang, Yasheng. "Rethinking the Beijing Consensus." *Asia Policy* 11 (2011): 1–26.

Huff, Greg W. *The Economic Growth of Singapore – Trade and Development in the Twentieth Century*. New York: Cambridge University Press, 1994.

Huff, Greg W. "What Is the Singapore Model of Economic Development?" *Cambridge Journal of Economics* 19 (1995): 735–59.

Human Rights Watch. "China: Secret 'Black Jails' Hide Severe Rights Abuses Unlawful Detention Facilities Breed Violence, Threats, Extortion." November 11, 2009. www.hrw.org/news/2009/11/11/china-secret-black-jails-hide-severe-rights-abuses.

Huntington, Samuel P. *Changing Societies*. New Haven, CT: Yale University Press, 2006.

International Confederation of Free Trade Unions. *Whose Miracle? How China's Workers Are Paying the Price for Its Economic Boom*. Brussels: International Confederation of Free Trade Unions, 2005.

IMF. *People's Republic of China: 2010 Article IV Consultation.* IMF Country Report No. 10/238, IMF, 2010. Accessed November 27, 2015. www.imf.org/external/pubs/ft/scr/2010/cr10238.pdf.

IMF. *People's Republic of China-Selected Issues.* IMF Staff Country Report No. 97/72, IMF, 1997.

International Organization of Securities Commissions. "International Disclosure Standards for Cross-Border Offerings and Listings by Foreign Issuers." Accessed September 5, 2015. www.iosco.org/library/pubdocs/pdf/IOSCOPD81.pdf.

Iwata, Shigeru, and Shu Wu. "Stock Market Liberalization and International Risk Sharing." *Journal of International Financial Markets, Institutions and Money* 19 (2004): 461–76.

Jasuriya, Kanishka. "Institutional Hybrids and the Rule of Law as a Regulatory Project." In *Legal Pluralism and Development: Scholars and Practitioners in Dialogue*, edited by Brian Z. Tamanaha, Caroline Sage, and Michael Woolcock, 145–61. Cambridge: Cambridge University Press, 2012.

Jessop, Bob, and Sum Ngai-Ling. *Beyond the Regulation Approach: Putting Capitalist Economies in Their Place.* Cheltenham, UK: Edward Elgar, 2006.

Jiang, Shigong. "Written and Unwritten Constitutions: A New Approach to the Study of Constitutional Government in China." *Modern China* 36 (2010): 12–46.

Jin, Dongsheng, and Weifu Jin. "On the Development Strategy of China's Value-Added Tax (VAT) Reform." *Journal of China Tax and Policy* 3 (2013): 226–37.

Jin, Hehui, Yingyi Qian, and Barry R. Weingast. "Regional Decentralization and Fiscal Incentives: Federalism, Chinese Style." *Journal of Public Economics* 89 (2005): 1719–42.

Jin, Zhouying. "Globalization, Technological Competitiveness and the 'Catch-up' Challenge for Developing Countries: Some Lessons of Experience." *International Journal of Technology Management and Sustainable Development* 4 (2005): 35–46.

Johnson, Chalmers. "Economic Crisis in East Asia: the Clash of Capitalisms." *Cambridge Journal of Economics* 22 (1998): 653–61.

Johnston, Michael. *Corruption Contention and Reform: The Power of Deep Democratization.* New York: Cambridge University Press, 2014.

Kaiman, Jonathan. "China's Toxic Air Pollution Resembles Nuclear Winter, Say Scientists." *The Guardian*, February 25, 2014.

Kahn-Freund, Otto. "On Uses and Misuses of Comparative Law." *Modern Law Review* 37 (1974): 1–27.

Kaplan, Ethan, and Dani Rodrik. "Did the Malaysian Capital Controls Work?" Institute of Advanced Study, School of Social Science, 2001. Accessed June 3, 2015. www.sss.ias.edu/files/pdfs/Rodrik/Research/did-Malaysian-capital-controls-work.PDF.

Kennedy, Scott. "The Myth of the Beijing Consensus." *Journal of Contemporary China* 19 (2010): 461–77.

Killion, M. Ulric. "Post-Global Financial Crisis: The Measure of the 'Beijing Consensus' as a Variety of Capitalisms." Social Science Research Network, 2010. Accessed January 16, 2016. http://dx.doi.org/10.2139/ssrn.1701868.

Kirkpatrick, Grant. "Managing State Assets to Achieve Developmental Goals: The Case of Singapore and Other Countries in the Regions." Paper presented at the workshop on state-owned enterprises in the development process for the Organisation for Economic Co-operation and Development, OECD Conference Center, Paris, April 4, 2014.

Korte, Guilherme José, and Sérgio Miranda-da-Cruz. "O Desafio do Desenvolvimento Sustentável e a Experiência Chinesa." *ConJur*, February 3, 2003.

Kraakman, Reinier H. "Gatekeepers: The Anatomy of a Third-Party Enforcement Strategy." *Journal of Law, Economics, & Organization* 2 (1986): 53–104.

Krause, Lawrence. "Government as Entrepreneur." In *Management of Success: The Moulding of Modern Singapore*, edited by Kernial Singh Sandu and Paul Wheatley, 436–52. Singapore: Institute of Southeast Asian Studies, 1989.

Kroncke, Jedidiah. "Property Rights, Labor Rights and Democratization." *NYU Journal of International Law and Politics* 46 (2013): 115–205.

Krugman, Paul. "Dutch Tulips and Emerging Markets: Another Bubble Bursts." *Foreign Affairs* 74 (1995): 28–44.

Kurien, Javier, and Bernard Geoxavier. "Roadmap for the RMB Internationalization: Navigating the Rise of China's Currency." *Harvard Kennedy School Review*, May 2, 2013. Accessed November 27, 2015. http://harvardkennedyschoolreview.com/a-roadmap-for-rmb-internationalization-navigating-the-economic-and-political-challenges-to-the-rise-of-chinas-currency/.

La Porta, Rafael, Florencio Lopez-de-Silanes, and Andrei Shleifer. "Corporate Ownership around the World," *Journal of Finance* 54 (1999): 471–517.

La Porta, Rafael, Florencio Lopez-de-Silanes, Andrei Shleifer, and Robert Vishny. "Law and Finance." *Journal of Political Economy* 106 (1998): 1113–155.

La Porta, Rafael, Florencio Lopez-de-Silanes, Andrei Shleifer, and Robert Vishny. "Legal Determinants of External Finance." *Journal of Finance* 52 (1997): 1131–150.

Labott, Elise. "Forced Labor Fuels Development." *CNN.com*, June 4, 2008. Accessed January 16, 2016. http://edition.cnn.com/2008/US/06/04/human.trafficking.

Lam, Raphael W., and Philippe Wingender. *China: How Can Revenue Reforms Contribute to Inclusive and Sustainable Growth*? Washington, DC: IMF, 2015.

Landesa Research Report. "Summary of 2011 17-Province Survey's Findings." Accessed July 31, 2015. www.landesa.org/china-survey-6/.

Landes, William, and Richard Posner. "The Economics of Anticipatory Adjudication." *Journal of Legal Studies* 23 (1994): 683–720.

Landry, Pierre. "The Political Management of Mayors in Post-Deng China." *The Copenhagen Journal of Asian Studies* 17 (2005): 31–58.

Landry, Pierre. *Decentralized Authoritarianism in China: The Communist Party's Control of Local Elites in the Post-Mao Era.* New York: Cambridge University Press, 2008.

Lardy, Nicholas R. *Markets over Mao: The Rise of Private Business in China.* Washington, DC: Peterson Institute for International Economics, 2014.

Lardy, Nicholas R. *Sustaining China's Economic Growth: After the Global Financial Crisis.* Washington, DC: Peterson Institute for International Economics, 2012.

Lau, Lawrence J., Yingyi Qian, and Gérard Roland. "Pareto-improving Economic Reforms through Dual-Track Liberalization." *Economics Letters* 55 (1997): 285–92.

Lee, Ching Kwan. *Against the Law.* Los Angeles: University of California Press, 2007.

Lee, Kuan Yew. *From Third World to First – The Singapore Story: 1965–2000.* Singapore: Times Editions, 2000.

Lee, Sheng Yi. "Public Enterprise and Economic Development in Singapore." *Malayan Economic Review* 21 (1976): 49–65.

Leonard, Mark. *What Does China Think?* New York: Public Affairs, 2008.

Lessig, Lawrence. "The Regulation of Social Meaning." *University of Chicago Law Review* 62 (1995): 944–1047.

Li, Cheng. "One Party, Two Factions: Chinese Bipartisanship in the Making?" Paper presented at the Conference on "Chinese Leadership, Politics, and Policy," Carnegie Endowment for International Peace, November 2, 2005.

Li, Cheng. "Political Localism versus Institutional Restraints: Elite Recruitment in the Jiang Era." In *Holding China Together: Diversity and National Integration in the Post-Deng Era,* edited by Barry Naughton and Dali L. Yang, 29–68. Cambridge: Cambridge University Press, 2004.

Li, Hongbin, and Li-An Zhou. "Political Turnover and Economic Performance: The Incentive Role of Personnel Control in China." *Journal of Public Economics* 89 (2005): 1743–62.

Li, Ji. "Dare You Sue the Tax Collector? An Empirical Study of Tax-Related Administrative Lawsuits in China." *Pacific Rim Law & Policy Journal* 23 (2014): 57–112.

Li, Jinyan. "Tax Transplants and the Critical Role of Processes: A Case Study of China." *Journal of Chinese Tax and Policy* 3 (2013): 85–139.

Li, Ling. "The Rise of the Party Committee of Discipline and Inspection (1927–2912): Anti-corruption Investigation and Decision-Making in the Chinese Communist Party." Working Paper 1/2015. New York University Law School US-Asia Law Institute, 2015. Accessed January 20, 2016. www.academia.edu/10195921/The_Rise_of_the_Chinese_Communist_Party_s_Disciplinary_Institution_1927-2012_The_operation_of_the_Party_anticorruption_machine.

Li, Shi, Hiroshi Sato, and Terry Sicular (eds.). *Rising Inequality in China: Challenges to a Harmonious Society*. Cambridge: Cambridge University Press, 2013.

Li, Xin, Kjeld Erik Brodsgaard, and Michael Jacobsen. "Redefining Beijing Consensus: Ten Economic Principles." Discussion Paper 29, Asia Research Centre, Copenhagen Business School, 2009. Accessed January 16, 2016. http://openarchive.cbs.dk/bitstream/handle/10398/7830/CDP%202009–029.pdf?sequence=1.

Lieberthal, Kenneth, and Michel Oksenberg. *Policy Making in China*. Princeton, NJ: Princeton University Press, 1988.

Liebman, Benjamin L. "A Populist Threat to China's Courts?" In *Chinese Justice: Civil Dispute Resolution in Post-Reform China*, edited by Margaret Y. K. Woo and Mary E. Gallagher, 269–313. Cambridge: Cambridge University Press, 2011.

Liebman, Benjamin L. "A Return to Populist Legality? Historical Legacies and Legal Reform." In *Mao's Invisible Hand*, edited by Elizabeth Perry and Sebastian Heilmann, 165–200. Cambridge, MA: Harvard University Asia Center Press, 2011.

Liebman, Benjamin L. "Leniency in Chinese Criminal Law? Everyday Justice in Henan." *Berkeley Journal of International Law* 33 (2015): 153–222.

Liebman, Benjamin L. "Legal Reform: China's Law-Stability Paradox." *Daedalus* 143 (2014): 96–109.

Liebman, Benjamin L. "Malpractice Mobs: Medical Dispute Resolution in China." *Columbia Law Review* 113 (2013): 181–264.

Liebman, Benjamin L., and Curtis J. Milhaupt (eds.). *Regulating the Visible Hand? The Institutional Implications of Chinese State Capitalism*. New York: Oxford University Press, 2016.

Liebman, Benjamin L., and Curtis J. Milhaupt. "Reputational Sanctions in China Stock Market." *Columbia Law Review* 108 (2008): 929–83.

Lim, Ewe-Ghee. "The Euro's Challenge to the Dollar: Different Views from Economists and Evidence from COFER (Currency Composition of Foreign Exchange Reserves) and Other Data." Working Paper 06/153. IMF, 2006. Accessed January 24, 2016. www.imf.org/external/pubs/ft/wp/2006/wp06153.pdf.

Lin, Justin Yifu. *Against the Consensus: Reflections on the Great Recession*. New York: Cambridge University Press, 2013.

Lin, Justin Yifu. "Collectivization and China's Agricultural Crisis in 1959–1961." *Journal of Political Economy* 98(1990): 1228–252.

Lin, Justin Yifu. *The Quest for Prosperity: How Developing Economies Can Take Off*. Princeton, NJ: Princeton University Press, 2012.

Lin, Li-Wen. "Balancing Closure and Openness." In *Regulating the Visible Hand? The Institutional Implications of Chinese State Capitalism*, edited by Benjamin Liebman and Curtis J. Milhaupt, 133–50. New York: Oxford University Press, 2016.

Lin, Li-Wen, and Curtis J. Milhaupt. "We Are the (National) Champions: Understanding the Mechanisms of State Capitalism in China." *Stanford Law Review* 65 (2013): 697–759.

Lin, Yi-min. "Economic Institutional Change in Post-Mao China: Reflections on the Triggering, Orienting, and Sustaining Mechanisms." In *China's Developmental Miracle: Origins, Transformations, and Challenges (Asia and the Pacific)*, edited by Alvin Y. So, 29–57. New York: Routledge, 2003.

Lindblom, Charles E. "The Science of 'Muddling Through.'" *Public Administration Review* 19 (1959): 79–88.

Liu, Mingwei. "Union Organizing in China: Still a Monolithic Labor Movement?" *Industrial and Labor Relations Review* 64 (2011): 30–52.

London Stock Exchange. "List of All Companies." Accessed May 21, 2015. www.londonstockexchange.com/statistics/companies-and-issuers/companies-and-issuers.htm.

Lou, Jiwei 楼继伟. "Xuanze gaigede youxiancixu" 选择改革的优先次序 [Choosing the Optimal Sequence of Reforms]. *Ershiyi shiji jingji baodao* 21 世纪经济报道, August 6, 2006.

Lou, Jiwei 楼继伟. "Yangdi guanxi zaichonggou" 央地关系再重构 [Restructuring Central and Local Relations Once Again]. Caijing 财经, April 2, 2012.

Luo, Sha 罗沙. "Li'an dengji zhi gaoge shouyue guanguo fayuan li'an chao baiwan" 立案登记制改革首月全国法院立案超百万[In the First Month of the Reform to the Case Filing System the Number of Case Filings Nationwide Exceeded 1 Million]. Legal China 法制中国, June 4, 2015. Accessed July 31, 2015. www.china.com.cn/legal/lawyer/2015-06/04/content_35741410.htm.

Lu, Aiguo. *China and the Global Economy since 1840.* London: MacMillan, 2000.

Malesky, Edmund, and Jonathan London. "The Political Economy of Development in China and Vietnam." *Annual Review of Political Science* 17 (2014): 395–419.

Mainelli, Michael, and Bob Gifford. "Size Matters: Risk and Scale." *The Journal of Risk Finance* 11 (2010): 344–48.

Mallen, Patricia. "Migrant Workers from Haiti Building 2014 World Cup Stadiums in Brazil Denounce Inhumane Conditions." *International Business Times*, February 4, 2014.

Manion, Melanie. *Corruption by Design: Building Clean Government in Mainland China and Hong Kong.* Cambridge, MA: Harvard University Press, 2004.

Mansfield, Charles. "Tax Administration in Developing Countries: An Economic Perspective. " Staff Papers 35, IMF, 1988.

McKinnon, Ronald. *The Order of Economic Liberalization.* Baltimore: The Johns Hopkins University Press, 1991.

McKinnon, Ronald, and Gunter Schnabl. "China's Exchange Rate and Financial Repression: The Conflicted Emergence of the RMB as an International Currency." *China and the World Economy* 22 (2014): 1–35.

McNally, Christopher. "The Challenge of Refurbished State Capitalism: Implications for the Global Political Economic Order." *Der Moderne Staat* 6 (2013): 33–48.

Mendonça, Luiz Carlos. "De Gastos, Ratos e Mercados." *Folha de São Paulo*, March 7, 2014.

Meyer, Marshall W. "Is It Capitalism?" *Management & Organization Review* 7 (2011): 5–18.

Meyer, Marshall, and Changqi Wu. "Making Ownership Matter: Prospects for China's Mixed Ownership Economy." *Paulson Policy Memorandum*, September 18, 2014. Accessed May 21, 2015. www.paulsoninstitute.org/think-tank/2014/09/18/making-ownership-matter-prospects-for-chinas-mixed-ownership-economy/.

Miao, Qingqing. "An Urge to Protect Is Not Enough: China's Labor Contract Law." *Tsinghua China Law Review* 2 (2010): 159–201.

Milhaupt, Curtis J., and Katharina Pistor. *Law and Capitalism: What Corporate Crises Reveal about Legal Systems and Economic Development around the World.* Chicago: University of Chicago Press, 2008.

Milhaupt, Curtis J., and Katharina Pistor. "The China Aviation Oil Episode: Law and Development in China and Singapore." In *Law and Economics with Chinese Characteristics: Institutions for Promoting Development in the Twenty-First Century*, edited by David Kennedy and Joseph Stiglitz, 329–57. Oxford: Oxford University Press, 2013.

Milhaupt, Curtis J., and Wentong Zheng. "Beyond Ownership: State Capitalism and the Chinese Firm." *Georgetown Law Journal* 103 (2015): 665–722.

Minzner, Carl F. "China's Turn against Law." *American Journal of Comparative Law* 59 (2001): 935–984.

Montinola, Gabriella, Yingyi Qian, and Barry R. Weingast. "Federalism, Chinese Style: The Political Basis for Economic Success." *World Politics* 48 (2006): 50–81.

Mote, Frederick W. *Imperial China 900–1800.* Cambridge, MA: Harvard University Press, 2003.

Moustafa, Tamir. "Law and Courts in Authoritarian Regimes." *Annual Review of Law and Social Science* 10 (2014): 281–99.

Mutalib, Hussin. "Illiberal Democracy and the Future of Opposition in Singapore." *Third World Quarterly* 21 (2000): 313–42.

Nair, Devan. *Socialism That Works: The Singapore Way.* Singapore: Federation Publications, 1976.

NASDAQ. "Company List (NYSE)." Accessed May 21, 2016. www.nasdaq.com/screening/companies-by-name.aspx?letter=0&exchange=nyse&render=download.

Naudé, Wim, Adam Szirmai, and Alejandro Lavopa. "Industrialization Lessons from BRICS: A Comparative Analysis." Discussion Paper No. 7543, Institute for the Study of Labor, 2013. Accessed January 16, 2016. http://repec.iza.org/dp7543.pdf.

Naughton, Barry. "China's Distinctive System: Can It Be a Model for Others?" *Journal of Contemporary China* 19 (2010): 437–60.

Naughton, Barry. *The Chinese Economy: Transitions and Growth*. Cambridge, MA: MIT Press, 2007.

Neal, Larry, and Jeffrey G. Williamson (eds.). *The Cambridge History of Capitalism*, vol. 1, *The Rise of Capitalism: From Ancient Origins to 1848*. Cambridge: Cambridge University Press, 2014.

Neo, Boon Siong, and Geraldine Chen. *Dynamic Governance: Embedding Culture, Capabilities and Change in Singapore*. Singapore: World Scientific, 2007.

Nesossi, Elisa, Flora Sapio, Sarah Biddulph, Susan Trevaskes, Yuwen Li, and Hualing Fu (eds.). *Legal Reforms and Deprivation of Liberty in Contemporary China*. London: Ashgate, 2016.

Ng, E-Jay. "GE 2011 Roundup and Analysis." *Sgpolitics.net*, May 8, 2011. Accessed January 26, 2016. www.sgpolitics.net/?p=6789.

Nolan, Peter. *Is China Buying the World*? Cambridge: Polity Press, 2013.

North, Douglass C. *Institutional Change and Economic Performance*. Cambridge: Cambridge University Press, 1990.

North, Douglass C. *Structure and Change in Economic History*. New York: W. W. Norton, 1981.

Novak, William. "The Myth of the 'Weak' American State." *American History Review* 113 (2008): 752–72.

Olson, Mancur, Jr. "Big Bills Left on the Sidewalk: Why Some Nations Are Rich, and Others Poor." *Journal of Economic Perspectives* 10 (1996): 3–24.

Olson, Mancur. "Dictatorship, Democracy, and Development." *American Political Science Review* 87 (1993): 567–76.

OECD. *Tax Administration 2013: Comparative Information on OECD and Other Advanced and Emerging Economies*. Paris: OECD, 2013.

Ogden, Suzanne. "Chinese Nationalism: The Precedence of Community and Identity over Individual Rights." In *China's Developmental Miracle: Origins, Transformations, and Challenges (Asia and the Pacific)*, edited by Alvin Y. So, 224–45. New York: Routledge, 2003.

Ong, Chong Tee. "An Exchange Rate-Centered Monetary Policy System: Singapore's Experience." BIS Papers No. 73. Bank for International Settlements 2013. Accessed January 24, 2016. www.bis.org/publ/bppdf/bispap73w.pdf.

Ong, Chong Tee. "Singapore's Policy of Non-Internationalization of the Singapore Dollar and the Asian Dollar Market." BIS Papers No. 15. Bank for International Settlements, 2003. Accessed January 24, 2016. www.bis.org/publ/bppdf/bispap15l.pdf.

Orlandi, Romeo. "China, Size Matters." *Alberto Forchielli*, May 22, 2014. Accessed November 27, 2015. www.albertoforchielli.com/2014/05/22/china-size-matters/.

Ortmann, Stephan. "The 'Beijing Consensus' and the 'Singapore Model': Unmasking The Myth of an Alternative Authoritarian State-Capitalist Model." In *China's Economic Dynamics: A Beijing Consensus in the Making?*, edited by Jun Li and Wang Liming. London: Routledge, 2014.

Ostry, Jonathan D., Atish R. Ghosh, Karl Habermeier, Luc Laeven, Marcos Chamon, Mahvash S. Qureshi, and Annamaria Kokenyne. "Managing Capital Inflows: What Tools to Use?" IMF Staff Discussion Note SDN/11/06, IMF, 2011. Accessed November 27, 2015. www.imf.org/external/pubs/ft/sdn/2011/sdn1106.pdf.

Ow, Chin Hock. "Singapore." In *The Role of Public Enterprises in National Development in Southeast Asia: Problems and Prospects*, edited by Truong Nguyen, 154–256. Singapore: Regional Institute of Higher Education and Development, 1976.

Pan, Wei (ed.). *China Model: A New Developmental Model from the Sixty Years of the People's Republic*. Beijing: China Compilation and Translation Press, 2009.

Pan, Wei 潘维. "Dangdai zhonghua tizhi – zhongguo moshi de jingji, zhengzhi, shehui jiexi" 当代中华体制：中国模式的经济、政治、社会解析 [The Contemporary Chinese System – An Analysis of the Economic, Political and Social of the China Model]. In *Zhongguo moshi: jiedu renmin gongheguo de 60 nian* 中国模式：解读人民共和国的60年 [The China Model: Interpreting Sixty Years of the People's Republic], edited by Pan Wei, 3–88. Beijing: Zhejiang renmin chubanshe 浙江人民出版社, 2009.

Pan, Wei 潘维. "*Zhongguo moshi: jiedu renmin gongheguo de 60 nian*" 中国模式：解读人民共和国的60年 [China Model: A New Developmental Model from the Sixty Years of the People's Republic]. Beijing: Zhongyang bianji chubanshe 中央编译出版社, 2009.

Park, John S. "North Korea, Inc.: Gaining Insights into North Korean Regime Stability from Recent Commercial Activities." USIP Working Paper, United States Institute of Peace, 2009. Accessed January 25, 2016. www.usip.org/sites/default/files/North%20Korea,%20Inc.PDF.

Peerenboom, Randall. "China and the Middle-Income Trap: Toward a Post Washington, Post Beijing Consensus." *The Pacific Review* 27 (2014): 651–73.

Peerenboom, Randall. *China Modernizes: Threat to the West or Model for the Rest?* Oxford: Oxford University Press, 2007.

Peerenboom, Randall. *China's Long March toward Rule of Law*. Cambridge: Cambridge University Press, 2002.

Peerenboom, Randall. "Revamping the China Model for the Post-Global Financial Crisis Era." In *China in the International Economic Order*, edited by

Lisa Toohey, Colin B. Picker, and Jonathan Greenacre, 11–26. New York: Cambridge University Press, 2015.

Peerenboom, Randall. "Rule of Law, Democracy and the Sequencing Debate: Lessons from China and Vietnam." In *Legal Reforms in China and Vietnam: A Comparison of Asian Communist Regimes*, edited by John Gillespie and Albert Chen, 29–50. London: Routledge, 2010.

Peerenboom, Randall. "The Future of Legal Reforms in China: A Critical Appraisal of the Decision on Comprehensively Deepening Reform." Social Science Research Network, 2014. Accessed January 30, 2016. http://papers.ssrn.com/sol3/papers.cfm?abstract_id=2379161.

Peerenboom, Randall, and Bojan Bugaric. "The Emerging Post Washington, Post Beijing Consensus: Prospects and Pitfalls." *UCLA Journal of Law & Foreign Affairs* 19 (2015): 89–112.

Peerenboom, Randall, and Tom Ginsburg (eds.). *Law and Development of Middle-Income Countries: Avoiding the Middle-Income Trap*. New York: Cambridge University Press, 2013.

Pei, Minxin. *China's Trapped Transition: The Limits of Developmental Autocracy*. Cambridge, MA: Harvard University Press, 2008.

Pei, Minxin. "Is CCP Rule Fragile or Resilient?" *Journal of Democracy* 23 (2012): 27–41.

Pessoa, Samuel. "Modelo de Desenvolvimento Brasileiro." *Poupanca* 63 (2009): 10–13.

Phongpaichit, Pasuk, and Chris Baker. *Thailand's Crisis*. Singapore: Singapore Institute of Southeast Asian Studies, 2000.

Pillai, Philip. *State Enterprise in Singapore: Legal Importation and Development*. Singapore: Singapore University Press, 1983.

Pils, Eva. *China's Human Rights Lawyers: Advocacy and Resistance*. Abingdon, UK: Routledge, 2014.

Pils, Eva. "Land Disputes, Rights Assertion, and Social Unrest in China: A Case from Sichuan." *Columbia Journal of Asian Law* 19 (2005): 235–92.

Prado, Mariana Mota, and Ana Chasin. "How Innovative was the Poupatempo Experience in Brazil? Institutional Bypass as a New Form of Institutional Change." *Brazilian Political Science Review* 5 (2011): 11–34.

Prado, Mariana Mota, and Michael Trebilcock. "Path Dependence, Development, and the Dynamics of Institutional Reform." *University of Toronto Law Journal* 59 (2009): 341–79.

Prasad, Erwar S. *The Dollar Trap: How The US Dollar Tightened Its Grip on Global Finance*. Princeton, NJ: Princeton University Press, 2014.

Priest, Claire. "Currency Policies and Legal Development in Colonial New England." *Yale Law Journal* 110 (2001): 1303–405.

Pritchett, Lant, and Lawrence Summers. "Asiaphoria Meets Regression to the Mean." Working Paper 20573, National Bureau of Economic Research, 2014. Accessed May 21, 2015. www.nber.org/papers/w20573.pdf.

Przeworski, Adam, Michael E. Alvarez, Jose Antonio Cheibub, and Fernando Limongi. *Democracy and Development: Political Institutions and Well-Being in the World*. Cambridge: Cambridge University Press, 2000.

Qi, Yanbing 齐雁冰. "Caizhengbu jianyi tigao geshui qizhengdian" 财政部建议提高个税起征点 [Ministry of Finance Proposes Raising Exemption Level for Individual Income Tax]. *Beijing qingnian bao* 北京青年报, July 3, 2003. Accessed December 29, 2015. www.southcn.com/news/china/zgkx/200307030260.htm.

Qian, Yingyi. "How Reform Worked in China." In *In Search of Prosperity*, edited by Dani Rodrik, 297–333. Princeton, NJ: Princeton University Press, 2003.

Qiao, Shitong. *Chinese Small Property: The Co-Solution of Law and Social Norms*. JSD diss., Yale University, 2015.

Qiao, Shitong. "Planting Houses in Shenzhen: A Real Estate Market without Legal Titles." *Canadian Journal of Law and Society* 29 (2013): 253–72.

Qiao, Shitong, and Frank Upham. "China's Changing Property Law Landscape." In *Research Handbook on Comparative Property Law*, edited by M. Graziadei and L. Smith. London: Edward Elgar, forthcoming.

Qiu, Dongmei. "Interpretation of Tax Law in China: Moving towards the Rule of Law?" *Hong Kong Law Journal* 44 (2014): 589–620.

Ramo, Joshua Cooper. *The Beijing Consensus*. London: Foreign Policy Centre, 2004.

Ramirez, Carlos D., and Tan Ling-Hui. "Singapore, Inc. versus the Private Sector: Are Government-Linked Companies Different?" Working Paper 03/156, IMF, 2003. Accessed June 3, 2015. www.imf.org/external/pubs/ft/wp/2003/wp03156.pdf.

Randolph, Patrick A., Jr., and Jianbo Lou. *Chinese Real Estate Law*. The Hague: Kluwer Law International, 2000.

Ravallion, Martin. "A Comparative Perspective on Poverty Reduction in Brazil, China and India." Working Paper No. 5080, World Bank Policy Research, 2009. Accessed January 16, 2016. www-wds.worldbank.org/servlet/WDSContentServer/WDSP/IB/2009/11/30/000158349_20091130085835/Rendered/PDF/WPS5080.pdf.

Ren, Zhongping 任仲平. "Rang fazhi wei xiandai zhongguo huhang – lun quanmian tuijin yifa zhiguo" 让法治为现代中国护航 – 论全面推进依法治国. [Let Rule of Law Flank Modern China]. *Renmin ribao* 人民日报, December 3, 2014. Accessed July 31, 2015. http://paper.people.com.cn/rmrb/html/2014-12/03/nw.D110000renmrb_20141203_6-01.htm.

Renminwang. "Xiaochanquanfang meiyou zhuanzheng 'tequ'" 小产权房没有转正"特区" [No Special Economic Zone for the Legalization of Small-Property Houses]. July 4, 2012. Accessed July 16, 2015. http://theory.people.com.cn/n/2012/0704/c112851-18443279.html.

Renminwang 人民网. "Zhongban guoban yinfa shishi fangan guanche luoshi sizhong quanhui jueding bushu jinyibu shenhua sifa tizhi he shehui tizhi gaige." 中办国办印发实施方案贯彻落实四中全会决定部署进一步深化司法体制和社会体制改革. [The General Office of the Central Committee of the Communist Party of China and the General Office of the State Council Issued the Implementation Plan to Thoroughly Implement the Fourth Plenum Decision to Plan for the Further Deepening of Reforms of the Judicial and Social Systems]. April 10, 2015. Accessed 19 October 2015. http://military.people.com.cn/n/2015/0410/c172467-26822645.html.

Rittich, Kerry. "The Future of Law and Development: Second-Generation Reforms and the Incorporation of the Social." In *The New Law and Development: A Critical Appraisal*, edited by David M. Trubek and Alvaro Santos, 203–52. Cambridge: Cambridge University Press, 2006.

Rodrik, Dani. "Goodbye Washington Consensus, Hello Washington Confusion?" *Journal of Economic Literature* 44 (2006): 973–87.

Rodrik, Dani. *One Economics, Many Recipes: Globalization, Institutions, and Economic Growth*. Princeton, NJ: Princeton University Press, 2007.

Rodrik, Dani. "The New Development Economics: We Shall Experiment, But How Shall We Learn?" In *What Works in Development? Thinking Big and Thinking Small*, edited by Jessica Cohen and William Easterly, 24–47. Washington, DC: Brookings Institution Press, 2009.

Root, Hilton L., and Karen May. "Judicial Systems and Authoritarian Transitions." *The Pakistan Development Review* 45 (2006): 1301–21.

Rose-Ackerman, Susan. *Corruption and Government: Causes, Consequences, and Reform*. New York: Cambridge University Press, 1999.

Rossi, Clóvis. "A China Pode Ser um Modelo?" *Folha de São Paulo*, June 5, 2014.

Rossi, Clóvis. "Emergentes Para Sempre." *Folha de São Paulo*, December 22, 2013.

RT Network. "China Launches New World Bank Rival." October 24, 2014. Accessed November 27, 2015. http://rt.com/business/198928-china-world-bank-rival/.

Rudra, Nita. *Globalization and the Race to the Bottom in Developing Countries: Who Really Gets Hurt?* Cambridge: Cambridge University Press, 2008.

Runde, Daniel. "AIIB and US Development Leadership: A Path Forward." *Forbes*, April 30, 2015. Accessed November 27, 2015. www.forbes.com/sites/danielrunde/2015/04/30/aiib-us-development-leadership/.

Rutkowski, Ryan. "State-Owned Enterprise Reform: The Long Wait for a Chinese Temasek Continues . . . " Peterson Institute for International Economics, January 23, 2014. Accessed May 21, 2015. http://blogs.piie.com/china/?p=3726.

Sahoo, Pravakar, Ranjan Kumar Dash, and Geethanjali Nataraj. "Infrastructure Development and Economic Growth in China." IDE Discussion Paper No. 261, Institute of Developing Economics, 2010. Accessed January 16, 2016. www.ide.go.jp/English/Publish/Download/Dp/pdf/261.pdf.

Santana, Marco, and Ruy Braga. "Brazil: The Swinging Pendulum between Labor Sociology and Labor Movement." *Work and Occupations* 36 (2009): 96–109.

Santos, Alvaro. "The World Bank's Uses of the 'Rule of Law' Promise in Economic Development." In *The New Law and Development: A Critical Appraisal*, edited by David M. and Alvaro Santos, 253–300. Cambridge: Cambridge University Press, 2006.

Sapio, Flora. "Shuanggui and Extralegal Detention in China." *China Information* 22 (2008): 7–37.

Sapio, Flora. *Sovereign Power and the Law in China.* Leiden, Netherlands: Brill, 2010.

Saxenian, AnnaLee, and Charles Sabel. "Roepke Lecture in Economic Geography Venture Capital in the 'Periphery': The New Argonauts, Global Search, and Local Institution Building." *Economic Geography* 84 (2008): 379–94.

Schuman, Michael. "Is the Chinese Yuan Becoming a Rival to the Dollar?" *Business Times*, February 15, 2011. Accessed November 27, 2015. http://business.time .com/2011/02/15/is-the-chinese-yuan-becoming-a-rival-to-the-dollar/.

Scott, Alan J. *Regions and the World Economy: The Coming Shape of Global Production, Competition, and Political Order.* Oxford: Oxford University Press, 1998.

Sen, Amartya. *Development as Freedom.* Oxford: Oxford University Press, 1999.

Serra, Narcis, Shari Spiegel, and Joseph E. Stiglitz. "Introduction: From the Washington Consensus Towards a New Global Governance." In *The Washington Consensus Reconsidered*, edited by Narcis Serra and Joseph E. Stiglitz, 3–13. Oxford: Oxford University Press, 2008.

Shangguan, Sha Sha 上官莎莎 and Han Chi 韩驰. "Zou xiang quanguo de 'wenzhouzhishu' wei lixi shichanghua toushiwenlu" 走向全国的"温州指数"为利率市场化投石问路[Wenzhou Index and National-wide Marketization of Interest Rates]. *Wenzhouwang* 温州网, November 3, 2014. Accessed November 27, 2015. http://news.66wz.com/system/2014/11/03/104261941.shtml.

Shanghai Stock Exchange. "The IPO prospectus of the Everbright Bank." Accessed April 29, 2015. www.sse.com.cn/disclosure/listedinfo/announcement/c/2010–07–30/601818_20100730_2.pdf.

Sheehan, Jackie. *Chinese Workers: A New History.* New York: Routledge, 1998.

Shih, Victor. *Factions and Finance in China: Elite Conflict and Inflation.* New York: Cambridge University Press, 2008.

Shih, Victor, Christopher Adolph, and Mingxing Liu. "Getting Ahead in the Communist Party: Explaining the Advancement of Central Committee Members in China." *American Political Science Review* 106 (2012): 166–87.

Shirk, Susan L. *China: Fragile Superpower.* New York: Oxford University Press, 2007.

Sim, Isabel, Steen Thomsen, and Gerard Yeong. "The State as Shareholder: The Case of Singapore." *Centre for Governance, Institutions & Organisations NUS Business School*, 2014. Accessed June 3, 2015. http://bschool.nus.edu/Portals/0/docs/FinalReport_SOE_1July2014.pdf.

Sina News. "Jiedu: Wang qishan zuixin jianghua toulu chu de jiwei xindongxiang" 解读：王岐山最新讲话透露出的纪委新动向 [New Trend in *jiwei* Revealed in Wang Qishan's Speech]. July 11, 2015. Accessed January 30, 2016. http://news.sina.com.cn/c/2015–07–11/004132095831.shtml.

Sokol, D. Daniel. "Law and Development – The Way Forward or Just Stuck in the Same Place?" *Northwestern University Law Review Colloquy* 104 (2010): 238–50.

Sornarajah, M. *Resistance and Change in the International Law on Foreign Investment.* Cambridge: Cambridge University Press, 2015.

Spalding, Andrew. "The Irony of International Business Law: U.S. Progressivism and China's New Laissez-Faire." *UCLA Law Review* 59 (2011): 354–413.

Spence, Jonathan. *The Search for Modern China.* New York: W. W. Norton, 2013.

State Administration of Taxation. "Shuiwu zuzhi jigou" 税务组织机构 [Organizational Structure of Tax Administration]. Accessed December 29, 2015. www.chinatax.gov.cn/n810351/n810901/n848227/c1161559/content.html.

Stein, Gertrude. *Everybody's Autobiography.* New York: Random House, 1937.

Stern, Rachel E. *Environmental Litigation in China: A Study in Political Ambivalence.* Cambridge: Cambridge University Press, 2014.

Stiglitz, Joseph E. *Globalization and Its Discontents.* New York: W. W. Norton, 2002.

Stiglitz, Joseph E. "Is there a Post–Washington Consensus Consensus?" In *The Washington Consensus Reconsidered*, edited by Joseph E. Stiglitz and Narcis Serra, 41–56. Oxford: Oxford University Press, 2008.

Storper, Michael. *The Regional World: Territorial Development in a Global Economy.* New York: Guilford Press, 1997.

Su, Yang, and Xin He. "Street as Courtroom: State Accommodation of Labor Protest in South China." *Law and Society Review* 44 (2010): 157–84.

Sun, Xiulin 孙秀林 and Feizhou Zhou 周飞舟. "Tudi caizheng yu fenshiuzhi: yige shizheng jieshi" 土地财政与分税制：个实证解释 [Land-Oriented Fiscal Policy and the Tax Sharing System: An Empirical Explanation] *Zhongguo shehui kexue*中国社会科学 (2013): 40–59.

Sun, Yamei, Yonglong Lu, Tieyu Wang, Hua Ma, and Guizhen He. "Pattern of Patent-Based Environmental Technology Innovation in China." *Technological Forecasting & Social Change* 75 (2008): 1032–42.

Sunstein, Cass R. "Incompletely Theorized Agreements." *Harvard Law Review* 108 (1995): 1733–72.

Swanson, Kate E., and Richard G. Kuhn. "Environmental Policy Implementation in Rural China: A Case Study of Yuhang, Zhejiang." *Environmental Management* 27 (2001): 481–91.

Tan, Cheng-Han, Daniel Puchniak, and Umakanth Varottil. "State-Owned Enterprises in Singapore: Historical Insights into a Chosen Model for Reform." *Columbia Journal for Asian Law* 28 (2015): 61–97.

Tan, Lay-Hong, and Wang Jiangyu. "Modelling an Effective Corporate Governance System for China's Listed State-Owned Enterprises." *Journal of Corporate Law Studies* 7 (2007): 143–83.

Tate, C. Neal, and Stacia L. Haynie. "Authoritarianism and the Functions of Courts: A Time Series Analysis of the Philippine Supreme Court 1961–1987." *Law & Society Review* 27 (1993): 707–40.

Temasek Holdings (Private) Limited. "FAQS." Accessed January 23, 2016. www.temasek.com.sg/abouttemasek/faqs.

Temasek Holdings (Private) Limited. *Temasek Review 2014.* Accessed May 21, 2015. www.temasek.com.sg/documents/download/downloads/20140707170404/Temasek-Review-2014-En.pdf.

The Economist. "Mobile Money in Africa – Press 1 for Modernity: One Business Where the Poorest Continent is Miles Ahead." April 28, 2012. www.economist.com/node/21553510.

The Economist. "Planet Plutocrat." March 15, 2014.

The Economist. "Reforming China's State-Owned Firms: From SOE to GLC – China's Rulers Look to Singapore for Tips on Portfolio Management." November 23, 2013. Accessed June 3, 2015. www.economist.com/news/finance-and-economics/21590562-chinas-rulers-look-singapore-tips-portfolio-management-soe-glc.

The Economist. "The New Age of Crony Capitalism." March 15, 2014.

Thompson, Drew. "China's Soft Power in Africa: From the Beijing Consensus to Health Diplomacy." *China Brief* 5 (2005): 1–4.

Tilly, Chris, Rina Agarwala, Pun Ngai, Carlos Salas, and Hina Sheikh. "Informal Worker Organizing as a Strategy for Improving Subcontracted Work in the Textile and Apparel Industries of Brazil, South Africa, India and China." *UCLA Institute for Research on Labor and Employment* (2013): 1–167.

Toharia, Jose J. "Judicial Independence in an Authoritarian Regime: The Case of Contemporary Spain." *Law and Society Review* 9 (1975): 475–96.

Trebilcock, Michael J. *Dealing with Losers: The Political Economy of Policy Transitions.* New York: Oxford University Press, 2014.

Trebilcock, Michael J., and Mariana Mota Prado. *Advanced Introduction to Law and Development.* Cheltenham, UK: Edward Elgar, 2014.

Trebilcock, Michael J., and Mariana Mota Prado. *What Makes Poor Countries Poor? Institutional Determinants of Development.* Cheltenham, UK: Edward Elgar, 2011.

Trebilcock, Michael J., and Ronald Daniels. *Rule of Law Reform and Development: Charting the Fragile Path of Progress.* Cheltenham, UK: Edward Elgar, 2008.

Trivedi, Anjani. "Use of Yuan as Global Payment Currency Fails." *Wall Street Journal,* March 26, 2014. Accessed November 27, 2015. http://online.wsj.com/news/articles/SB10001424052702304688104579462870399966210.

Troyjo, Marcus. "Brasil, Chines de Menos" [Brazil, Too Little (of) China]. *Instituto Millenium*, November 15, 2014. Accessed January 16, 2016. http://imil.org.br/artigos/brasil-chins-de-menos/.

Tung, Chen-yuan, Wang Guo-chen, and Jason Yeh. "Renminbi Internationalization: Progress, Prospect and Comparison." *China and World Economy* 20 (2012): 63–82.

Turnbull, Constance Mary. *A History of Modern Singapore, 1819–2005*. Singapore: NUS Press, 2009.

Tushnet, Mark. "Authoritarian Constitutionalism." *Cornell Law Review* 100 (2015): 391–461.

Upham, Frank. "Demsetz to Deng: Speculations on the Implications of Chinese Growth for Law and Development Theory."*International Law and Politics* 41 (2009): 551–602.

Vadell, Javier, Leonardo Ramos, and Pedro Neves. "The International Implications of the Chinese Model of Development in the Global South." *Revista Brasileira de Politica Internacional* [Brazilian Review of International Politics] 57 (2014): 91–107.

van Rooij, Benjamin. *Regulating Land and Pollution in China: Lawmaking, Compliance, and Enforcement; Theory and Cases*. Leiden, Netherlands: Leiden University Press, 2006.

van Rooij, Benjamin. "The People's Regulation, Citizens and Implementation of Law in China." *Columbia Journal of Asian Law* 25 (2012): 116–79.

Verma, Anil, and Ana Gomes. "Labor Market Flexibility and Trajectories of Development."*Indian Journal of Industrial Relations* 60 (2014): 51–74.

Vogel, Ezra. *Deng Xiaoping and the Transformation of China*. Cambridge, MA: Belknap Press of Harvard University Press, 2013.

Volosovych, Vadym. "Risk Sharing from International Factor Income: Explaining Cross-country Differences." *Applied Economics* 45 (2013): 1435–59.

Volz, Ulrich. "RMB Internationalization and Currency Co-operation in East Asia." Working Paper No. 125, Universität Leipzig Wirtschaftswissenschaftliche Fakultät, 2013.

Wade, Robert. "From 'Miracle' to 'Cronyism': Explaining the Great Asian Slump." *Cambridge Journal of Economics* 22 (1998): 693–706.

Wade, Robert. "Japan, the World Bank, and the Art of Paradigm Maintenance: The East Asian Miracle in Political Perspective." *New Left Review* (1996): 3–36.

Wang, Chuanhui. *The Constitutional Protection of Private Property in China: Historical Evolution and Comparative Research*. Cambridge, MA: Cambridge University Press, 2016.

Wang, Gungwu. *Renewal: The Chinese State and the New Global History*. Hong Kong: The Chinese University Press, 2013.

Wang, Jiangyu. "The Political Logic of Corporate Governance in China's State-Owned Enterprises." *Cornell International Law Journal* 47 (2014): 631–69.

Wang, Shaoguang 王绍光. "Xuexi jizhi yu shiying nengli: Zhongguo nongcun hezuo yiliao tizhi bianqian de qishi" 学习机制与适应能力：中国农村合作医疗体制变迁的启示 [The Learning Mechanism and Adaptive Capacity: Insights from the Transformation of China's Rural Cooperative Healthcare System]. *Zhongguo shehui kexue* 中国社会科学 6 (2008): 111–33.

Wang, Shaoguang, and Angang Hu. *The Chinese Economy in Crisis: State Capacity and Tax Reform*. New York: M. E. Sharpe, 2001.

Wank, D. L. "Producing Property Rights: Strategies, Networks, and Efficiency in Urban China's Nonstate Firms." In *Property Rights and Economic Reform in China*, edited by Jean Oi and Andrew Walder, 248–74. Stanford, CA: Stanford University Press, 1999.

Want China Times. "30 Chinese SOEs to Follow Temasek Model by 2020." May 30, 2014. Accessed June 3, 2015. www.wantchinatimes.com/news-subclass-cnt.aspx?id&20140530000094&cid=1201.

Webster, Tim. "China's Human Rights Footprint in Africa." *Columbia Journal of Transnational Law* 51 (2013): 626–63.

Wei, Shang-Jin. "Gradualism versus Big Bang: Speed and Sustainability of Reforms." *The Canadian Journal of Economics* 30 (1997): 1234–47.

Wei, Xiaohang 魏晓航. "'Yuediaoyan' geshuiqizhengdiantigao" "粤调研"个税起征点提高 [Guangdong Experiments Raising Income Tax Exemption Level]. *Xinxi shibao* 信息时报, December 14, 2004.

Wen, Ren 文人. "Yifa Zhishui Jiaqiang Zhengguan – guojia shuiwu zongju juzhang xie xuren dajizhewen" 依法治税加强征管 – 国家税务总局局长谢旭人答记者问 [Strengthen Tax Administration in Accordance with Law – Director of SAT Answer Journalists' Questions]. *Zibenshichang* 资本市场 (2003): 64–65.

Whitman, James Q. *Harsh Justice: Criminal Punishment and the Widening Divide between American and Europe*. New York: Oxford University Press, 2003.

Williamson, John. "A Brief History of the Washington Consensus." In *The Washington Consensus Reconsidered*, edited by Joseph E. Stiglitz and Narcis Serra, 14–30. Oxford: Oxford University Press, 2008.

Williamson, John. "Beijing Consensus versus Washington Consensus?" Peterson Institute for International Economics, 2010. Accessed June 3, 2015. www.piie.com/publications/interviews/pp20101102williamson.pdf.

Williamson, John. "Did the Washington Consensus Fail?" Peterson Institute for International Economics, 2002. Accessed June 3, 2015. www.iie.com/publications/papers/paper.cfm?ResearchID=488.

Williamson, John. "Is the 'Beijing Consensus' Now Dominant?" *Asia Policy* 13 (2012): 1–16.

Williamson, John. "What Washington Means by Policy Reform." In *Latin American Adjustment: How Much Has Happened?* Edited by John Williamson, chapter 2. Washington, DC: Peterson Institute for International Economics, 1990.

Willis, Graham, and Mariana Mota Prado. "Process and Pattern in Institutional Reforms: A Case Study of the Police Pacifying Units in Brazil." *World Development* 64 (2014): 232–42.

Wilson, Edward O. *Consilience: The Unity of Knowledge.* New York: Alfred A. Knopf, 1998.

Winn, Jane K., and Angela Zhang. "China's Golden Tax Project: A Technological Strategy for Reducing VAT Fraud." *Peking University Journal of Law School* 1 (2013): 1–33.

Winter, Brian and Caroline Stauffer. "China Has Soured on Brazil." *Business Insider*, November 1, 2013.

WongPartnership. "SGX and China Securities Regulatory Commission Establish Direct Listing Framework." Accessed November 27, 2015. www.wongpartnership.com/index.php/files/download/1134.

World Bank. *China 2030: Building a Modern, Harmonious and Creative Society.* Washington, DC: World Bank, 2013.

World Bank. *The Economic Development of Malaya.* Washington, DC: International Bank for Reconstruction and Development, 1955.

World Bank. *World Development Report 1996: From Plan to Market.* New York: Oxford University Press, 1996.

World Federation of Exchanges. "Monthly Reports of December 2014." Accessed April 29, 2015. www.world-exchanges.org/home/index.php/statistics/monthly-reports.

Wu, Lihua吴黎华. "Xiaogang: zhuajin xiuding 'zhengjuanfa'" 肖钢：抓紧修订《证券法》[Xiao Gang: Pay Close Attention to the Amendment of "Security Law"]. *Economic Information*, August 2, 2013. Accessed January 20, 2016. http://jjckb.xinhuanet.com/2013–08/02/content_459153.htm.

Wu, Mark. "The WTO and China's Unique Economic Structure." In *Regulating the Visible Hand? The Institutional Implications of Chinese State Capitalism*, edited by Benjamin Liebman and Curtis J. Milhaupt, 313–52. New York: Oxford University Press, 2016.

Wu, Meihua 吴美华. "Zhongguo gongchandang jicha jigou de lishi yange ji qi zhineng yanbian" 中国共产党纪检机构的历史沿革及其职能演变 [Historical Evolution and Changing Functions of the Chinese Communist Party's Disciplinary Inspection Organs] *Zhongguo gongchandang xinwen wang* 中国共产党新闻网, May 6, 2009. Accessed January 30, 2016. http://dangshi.people.com.cn/GB/138903/138911/9249192.html.

Wu, Qiuyu 吴秋余. "Fanbishui yinian gongxian shuishou 468 yi bushao kuaguo qiye zhuanzhou lirun" 反避税1年贡献税收468亿 不少跨国企业转走利润 [One Year of Anti-Tax Avoidance Enforcement Raises Revenue of 46.8

Billion, Many Multinational Companies Turn Profitable]. *Renmin ribao*人民日报, October 13, 2014.

Xiang, Bo (ed.). "China Expected to Revise Securities Law in 2015." *English.news.cn*, March 10, 2015. Accessed January 20, 2016. http://news.xinhuanet.com/english/2015–03/10/c_134055479.htm.

Xiao, Bing肖宾. *Gu shi feng yun* 股市风云 [Stock Market Storms]. Beijing: China Machine Press, 2010.

Xin, Chunying 信春鹰. "Shenru tuijin kexue lifa minzhu lifa" 深入推进科学立法民主立法 [Xin Chunying: Profoundly Promote Scientific and Democratic Legislation]. *Renminwang* 人民网, October 31, 2014. Accessed July 31, 2015. http://theory.people.com.cn/n/2014/1031/c40531–25944235.html.

Xinhuanet. "'Shengjiban' fantan zhongju jiangcheng zhonggong xin fanfu "liji" "升级版"反贪总局将成中共新反腐利器 [A New Anti-Corruption Authority Will Become a Sharp Weapon of the CCP]. November 4, 2011. http://news.xinhuanet.com/politics/2014–11/04/c_1113115543.htm.

Xinhuanet. "Wang Qishan: Wangji guoqu jiu yiweizhe beipan" 王岐山：忘记过去就意味着背叛 [Wang Qishan: Forgetting the Past Means Betrayal]. November 24, 2013. Accessed January 30, 2016. http://news.xinhuanet.com/politics/2013–11/24/c_118270161.htm.

Xinhuawang 新华社. "Xinhuashe: zhonggong shibajie sizhong quanhui jueding quanwen" 新华社：中共十八届四中全会决定全文 [Xinhua Agency: Decision of the Fourth Plenary Session of the 18th CCP Central Committee]. October 29, 2014. Accessed May 24, 2015. www.cunet.com.cn/gaozhao/HTML/212606.html.

Xinhuawang 新华网. "Jiang Zemin zai zhongguo gongchandang di shiwu ci quanguo daibiao dahui shang de baogao" 江泽民在中国共产党第十五次全国代表大会上的报告[Report of Jiang Zemin at the Fifteenth National Congress of the Communist Party of China]. September 12, 1997. Accessed July 31, 2015. http://news.xinhuanet.com/zhengfu/2004–04/29/content_1447509.htm.

Xinhuawang 新华网. "Lingdao ganbu ganyu sifa huodong, chashou juti anjian chuli de jilu, tongbao he zeren zuijiu guiding yinfa" 领导干部干预司法活动、插手具体案件处理的记录、通报和责任追究规定 印发 [Penalties for Party Officials' Interference in Court Decision Making]. March 30, 2015. Accessed January 30, 2016. http://news.xinhuanet.com/legal/2015–03/30/c_1114812232.htm.

Xinhuawang 新华网. "Xin sanban xinpi jidai guifan: zhaochao wangnian baioshu diji cuowu binxiang" 新三板信披亟待规范：照抄往年表述 低级错误频现 [New Third Board Needs Standardization: Low-Level Errors Are Frequently Seen]. April 12, 2011. Accessed January 26, 2016. http://news.xinhuanet.com/fortune/2011–04/12/c_121294589.htm.

Xinhuawang 新华网. "Zhengjianhui jiu aosaikang shijian chuju jingshihan" 证监会就奥赛康事件出具警示函 [The CSRC Issued a Warning Letter to

Aosaikang]. June 14, 2014. Accessed January 20, 2016. http://news.xinhuanet.com/fortune/2014–06/14/c_126618283.htm.

Xinhuawang 新华网. "Zhongyang zhongyang yinfa 'Guanyu jinyibu jiaqiang he wanshan nongye shenchan zerenzhi de jige wenti'" 中共中央印发"关于进一步加强和完善农业生产责任制的几个问题"的通知 [Central Committee Announces a "Notice on Several Issues Concerning Strengthening and Improving the Agricultural Production Responsibility System"]. September 27, 1980. Accessed January 16, 2016. http://news.xinhuanet.com/ziliao/2005–02/04/content_2547020.htm.

Xinjingbao 新京报."Yusuan fa xiugai yu caishui tizhi gaige 'hepai'" 预算法修改与财税体制改革'合拍' [Amendment of Budget Law Match Fiscal System Reform]. September 2, 2014. Accessed September 2, 2014. http://epaper.bjnews.com.cn/html/2014–09/02/content_532751.htm?div=0.

Xiong, Qiuhong 熊秋红. "Sifa gaige zhong de falun wenti" 司法改革中的方法论问题 [Methodologies in Judicial Reform]. *Fazhi yu shehui fazhan* 法制与社会发展 6 (2014): 23–25.

Xu, Beina. "CFR Backgrounders: China's Environmental Crisis." *Council for Foreign Relations*, April 25, 2014. Accessed January 30, 2016. www.cfr.org/china/chinas-environmental-crisis/p12608.

Xu, Chenggang. "The Fundamental Institutions of China's Reforms and Development." *Journal of Economic Literature* 49 (2011): 1076–151.

Xu, Jian 徐键. "Fenshui zhixia de caiquan jizhong peizhi: guocheng ji qi yingxiang" 分税制下的财权集中配置：过程及其影响 [Concentration of Fiscal Power under the Tax Sharing System: Process and Influence]. *Peking University Law Journal* 24 (2012): 800–14.

Yellen, Janet. "Speech: Vice Chair Janet Yellen at the Society of American Business Editors and Writers." Board of Governors of the Federal Reserve System, April 4, 2013. Accessed November 27, 2015. www.federalreserve.gov/newsevents/speech/yellen20130404a.htm.

Yong, Kang, Lu Shi, and Elizabeth D. Brown. "The Rand Corporation, Chinese Corporate Governance: History and Institutional Framework." Rand Corporation Technical Report Series TR-618-RC, Rand Corporation, 2008. Accessed November 27, 2015. www.rand.org/pubs/technical_reports/TR618.html.

Yoshino, Naoyuki, Sahoko Kaji, and Tamon Asonuma. "Dynamic Transition of Exchange Rate Regime in China." *China and World Economy* 22 (2014): 36–55.

Young, Graham. "Control and Style: Discipline Inspection Commissions since the 11th Congress." *The China Quarterly* 97 (1984): 24–52.

Younis, Musab. "BRICS: Let's Talk about Labour." *Open Democracy*, May 14, 2013. Accessed January 16, 2016. www.opendemocracy.net/musab-younis/brics-let%E2%80%99s-talk-about-labour.

Yu, Jeanny. "Yuan to Trade Directly with UK Pound: Today's Change Replaces System of Referencing the Two Currencies' Rates against US Dollar." *South China Morning Post*, June 19, 2014. Accessed November 27, 2015. www.scmp.com/business/banking-finance/article/1535833/yuan-trade-directly-uk-pound.

Yu, Jianrong. "Rigid Stability: An Explanatory Framework for China's Social Situation." *Contemporary Chinese Thought* 46 (2014): 72–84.

Yu, Verna. "Tales of Torture: Time Spent in Chinese Police Custody Leaves Victims Permanently Scarred." *South China Morning Post*, June 27, 2015.

Yu, Xiaohong. "Judicial Empowerment within/out of the Political-Legal System in China?" Unpublished manuscript, September 2014. On file with the author.

Yu, Yong Ding. "Comment from the Editor-in-Chief." *China and World Economy* 22 (2014): 32.

Zeng, Kanghua, Shan Li, and Qian Li. "The Impact of Economic Growth and Tax Reform on Tax Revenue and Structure: Evidence from China Experience." *Modern Economy* 4 (2013): 839–51.

Zhang, Jun 张军 and Li-An Zhou 周黎安. *Weizengzhang erjingzheng: zhongguo zengzhangde zhengzhijingjixue* 为增长而竞争：中国增长的政治经济学 [Growth from Below: The Political Economy of China's Economic Growth]. Shanghai: Gezhi chubanshe 格致出版社, 2008.

Zhang, Le-Yin. "Chinese Central-Provincial Fiscal Relationships, Budgetary Decline and the Impact of the 1994 Fiscal Reform: An Evaluation." *The China Quarterly* 157 (1999): 115–41.

Zhang, Wenxian 张文显. "Jianshe zhongguo tese shehui zhuyi fazhi tixi" 建设中国特色社会主义法治体系 [Constructing a Socialist Rule of Law System with Special Chinese Characteristics]. *Faxue Yanjiu* 法学研究 1350; 6 (2014): 13–19.

Zhang, Wenxian 张文显 and Gu Zhaomin 谷昭民. "Zhongguo falü waijiao de lilun yu shixian" 中国法律外交的理论与实践 [The Theory and Practice of China's LegalForeign Relations]. Guoji Zhanwang 国际展望 2 (2013): 1–20.

Zhao, Yining 赵忆宁. "Woguo fenshuizhi juece beijing lishi huifang" 我国分税制决策背景历史回放 [Historical Background of the Tax-Sharing Reform]. *Liaowang* 瞭望, August 4, 2008.

Zheng, Lei, Benjamin Liebman, and Curtis J. Milhaupt. "SOEs and State Governance: How State-Owned Enterprises Influence China's Legal System." In *Regulating the Visible Hand? The Institutional Implications of Chinese State Capitalism*, edited by Benjamin Liebman and Curtis J. Milhaupt, 203–24. New York: Oxford University Press, 2016.

Zheng, Ruichen. "A Percepcao Academica Chinesa Sobre o Brasil e a Relacao Bilateral." MA thesis, University of Sao Paulo, 2014.

Zheng, Yongnian. "China: An Emerging Power, Is Exploring Its Own Development Model." *China Economist* 1 (2010): 71–84.

Zhi, Zhenfeng 支振锋. "Fazhi zhuanxing de 'guojia nengli beilun'" 法治转型的"国家能力悖论" [The "Paradox of State Ability" in Rule of Law Transitions]. In "Governing the Nation According to Law and Rule of Law China." *Chinese Academy of Social Sciences* (2014): 92–99.

Zhonghua renmin gongheguo zuigao renmin fayuan 中华人民共和国最高人民法院 [Supreme People's Court of the People's Republic of China]. "China Judgments Online." January 30, 2016. www.court.gov.cn/zgcpwsw/.

Zhou, Li-An 周黎安. *Zhuanxing zhongde difang zhengfu: guanyuanjili yu zhili* 转型中的地方政府:官员激励与治理 [Local Governments in Transition: Official Incentives and Governance] Shanghai: Gezhi Publishing 格致出版社, 2008.

Zhou, Xiaoxiao 周潇枭. "Shuishou zhengguan faxiu zhengan da tiaozheng" 税收征管法修正案大调整 [Major Changes to the Amendment of Tax Administration Law]. *21 Shiji jingji baodao* 21 世纪经济报道, September 22, 2014.

Zhu, Jia-ming 朱嘉明. *Cong zi you dao longduan: zhongguo huobi jingji liangqiannian (shang)* 从自由到垄断：中国货币经济两千年[上] [From Laissez-Faire to Monopoly: The Monetary Economy of China – Past and Present, Vol. 1]. Taipei: Yuan-Liou, 2012.

Zhu, Suli. "'Judicial Politics' as State Building." In *Building Constitutionalism in China*, edited by Stephenie Balme and Michael Dowdle, 23–36. New York: Palgrave Macmillan, 2009.

Zhu Yihong. "Swap Agreements & China's RMB Currency Network, CSIS Asia Program." *CogitAsia*, May 22, 2015. Accessed November 27, 2015. http://cogitasia.com/swap-agreements-chinas-rmb-currency-network/.

II Rules and Legislation

Amendment to Administrative Litigation Law. Effective May 1, 2015. Accessed January 21, 2016. www.npc.gov.cn/npc/xinwen/2014–11/02/content_1884662.htm.

Administrative Procedure Law of the People's Republic of China. Effective October 1, 1990. Accessed December 29, 2015. www.china.org.cn/english/government/207335.htm.

Amendment to the Constitution of PRC (1999). Effective March 15, 1999. Accessed 19 October 2015. www.npc.gov.cn/wxzl/wxzl/2000–12/10/content_7075.htm.

Baojianren jinzhi diaocha gongzuo zhunze 保荐人尽职调查工作准则 [Sponsor Due Diligence Working Guidelines]. Issued by the CSRC on May 29, 2006.

China Communist Party Central Committee. Zhonggong zhongyang guanyu quanmian shenhua gaige ruogan zhongda wenti de jueding 中共中央关于全面深化改革若干重大问题的决定 [Decisions of the China Communist

Party Central Committee Regarding Several Key Issues of Deepening and Expanding Reforms]. Issued by the CCPCC on November 15, 2013.

Constitution of the People's Republic of China. Effective December 4, 1982. Accessed January 20, 2016. www.npc.gov.cn/englishnpc/Constitution/node_2825.htm.

Enterprise Income Tax Law of the People's Republic of China. Effective January 1, 2008. Accessed December 29, 2015. www.fdi.gov.cn/1800000121_39_3339_0_7.html.

Gongkai faxing zhengquan de gongsi xinxi pilu geshi zhunze dishiyihao – shangshi gongsi gongkai faxing zhengquan muji shuomingshu 公开发行证券的公司信息披露与格式准则第十一号 – 上市公司公开发行证券募集说明书 [Information Disclosure Form and Content Requirements No. 11 for Companies Conducting Public Securities Offerings – Listed Companies Public Offering Securities Prospectuses]. Issued by the CSRC on May 8, 2005.

Gongkai faxing zhengquan de gongsi xinxi pilu yu geshi zhunze diyihao – zhaogu shuomingshu 公开发行证券的公司信息披露与格式准则第一号 – 招股说明书 [Information Disclosure Form and Content Requirements No. 1 for Companies Conducting Public Securities Offerings – Prospectuses]. Issued by the CSRC on May 18, 2005.

Gongkai faxing zhengquan de gongsi xinxi pilu yu geshi zhunze dijiuhao – shouci gongkai faxing bing shangshi shenqing wenjian 公开发行证券的公司信息披露与格式准则第九号 – 首次公开发行并上市申请文件 [Information Disclosure Form and Content Requirements No. 9 for Companies Conducting Public Securities Offerings – Initial Public Securities Offering and Listing Application Documents]. Amended by the CSRC on March 19, 2006.

Gongkai faxing zhengquan de gongsi xinxi pilu yu geshi zhunze dierhao – jidu baogao de neirong yugeshi 公开发行证券的公司信息披露与格式准则第二号 – 季度报告的内容与格式 [Information Disclosure Form and Content Requirements No. 13 for Companies Conducting Public Securities Offerings – Quarterly Report Content and Format]. Amended by the CSRC on March 26, 2007.

Gongkai faxing zhengquan de gongsi xinxi pilu yu geshi zhunze dishierhao – gongkai faxing zhengquan de falü yijian shuhe lüshi gongzuo baogao 公开发行证券的公司信息披露与格式准则第十二号 – 公开发行证券的法律意见书和律师工作报告 [Information Disclosure Form and Content Requirements No. 12 for Companies Conducting Public Securities Offerings – Public Securities Offering Legal Opinions and Lawyer Work Report]. Amended by the CSRC on March 26, 2006.

Gongkai faxing zhengquan de gongsi xinxi pilu yu geshi zhunze disanhao – banniandu baogao de neirong yu geshi 公开发行证券的公司信息披露与格式

准则第三号 – 半年度报告的内容与格式 [Information Disclosure Form and Content Requirements No. 3 for Companies Conducting Public Securities Offerings – Semi Annual Report Content and Format]. Amended by the CSRC on June 29, 2007.

Gongkai faxing zhengquan de gongsi xinxi pilu yu geshi zhunze dierhao – niandu baogao de neirong yu geshi公开发行证券的公司信息披露与格式准则第二号 – 年度报告的内容与格式 [Information Disclosure Form and Content Requirements No. 2 for Companies Conducting Public Securities Offerings – Annual Report Content and Format]. Amended by the CSRC on December 17, 2007.

Guanyu xingu dingjia xiangguan wenti de tongzhi 关于新股定价相关问题的通知 [Notice on Issues Related to the Pricing of IPO]. Issued by the CSRC on May 23, 2012.

Guojia shuiwu zongju daqiye shuishou fuwu he guanli guicheng (shixing) 国家税务总局大企业税收服务和管理规程 (试行) [SAT Large Enterprises Tax Service Provision and Administration Rules (Trial)], Guoshuifa No. 71 (2011). Effective date July 13, 2011. www.lawinfochina.com/display.aspx?lib=law&id=11183. Accessed January 21, 2016.

Guowuyuan guanyu zai zhongguo (Shanghai) ziyoumaoyi shiyanqu nei zanshi tiaozheng shishi youguan xingzheng fagui he jing guowuyuan pizhun de bumen guiding de zhunru tebie guanli cuoshi de jueding 国务院关于在中国 (上海)自由贸易试验区内暂时调整实施有关行政法规和经国务院批准的部门规章规定的准入特别管理措施的决定 [The Decision of the State Council on Adjusting Temporarily Administrative Approval Items and Special Administrative Measures for Access Prescribed by Related Administrative Regulations]. Effective September 4, 2014. Accessed January 31, 2016. www.china-shftz.gov.cn/PublicInformation.aspx?GID=c39042c4-eac2–4d94–9766–2443119d7346&CID=953a259a-1544–4d72-be6a-264677089690&MenuType=1&navType=1.

Income Tax Law of the People's Republic of China Enterprises with Foreign Investment and Foreign Enterprises. Effective July 1, 1991. Accessed January 26, 2015. www.china.org.cn/english/14960.htm.

Law of the People's Republic of China on Administrative Supervision. Effective May 9, 1997, amended June 25, 2010. Accessed October 21, 2015. www.npc.gov.cn/englishnpc/Law/2007-12/11/content_1383546.htm.

Law on Administrative Reconsideration. Effective October 1, 1999. Accessed December 29, 2015. www.gov.cn/banshi/2005-08/21/content_25100.htm.

Legislation Law of the People's Republic of China. Effective September 1, 2000. Accessed December 29, 2015. http://english1.english.gov.cn/laws/2005-08/20/content_29724.htm.

Lüshi shiwusuo congshi zhengquan lüyewu guanli ban fa 律师事务所从事证券法律业务管理办法 [The Administration Measures for Law Firms Engaging Securities' Legal Service]. Issued by the CSRC May 7, 2007.

Securities Law of the People's Republic of China. Effective July 1, 1999. Amended January 1, 2006. Accessed January 26, 2016. www.npc.gov.cn/englishnpc/Law/2007-12/11/content_1383569.htm.

Shuiwu xingzheng fuyi guize 税务行政复议规则 [Rules Concerning Tax Administrative Reconsideration]. Guojia shuiwu zongjuling di ershiyi hao 国家税务总局令第21号 [SAT Rule No.21]. Effective April 1, 2010. Accessed December 29, 2015. www.chinatax.gov.cn/n810341/n810765/n812161/n812579/c1086133/content.html.

Supreme People's Court of China 最高人民法院. "Guanyu quanmian shenhua renmin fayuan gaige de yijian" 关于全面深化人民法院改革的意见 [Opinion on Fully Deepening Reforms to the People's Courts]. February 4, 2015. Accessed 19 October 2015. www.chinacourt.org/law/detail/2015/02/id/148096.shtml.

III Cases

The Appeal of Ma Haitao v. Li Yulan in a Property Contractual Dispute (2007). 马海涛与李玉兰房屋买卖合同纠纷上诉案 [Ma haitao yu li yulan fangwu maimai hetong jiufen shangsu an]. Second Intermediate People's Civil Court Final Judgment No. 13692. Beijing Second Intermediate People's Court Civil Judgment, October 20, 2008.

Qi Yuling v. Chen Xiaoqi Case of Infringement of Citizen's Fundamental Rights of Receiving Education Under the Protection of the Constitution by Means of Infringing Right of Name. 5 (2001) Supreme People's Court Gazette 158.

INDEX

Lightning Source UK Ltd.
Milton Keynes UK
UKHW020225151218
334055UK00006B/114/P

9 781316 503034